The Semiotic Field of the Garden

A volume in
Advances in Cultural Psychology: Constructing Human Development
Jaan Valsiner, *Series Editor*

Advances in Cultural Psychology: Constructing Human Development

Jaan Valsiner, *Series Editor*

Home in Transition: The Cultural Construction of Heimat (2023)
    Meike Watzlawik

Drama of Multilingualism: Literature Review and Liberation (2022)
    Gabrijela Aleksić

Deep Loyalties: Values in Military Lives (2022)
    Daniela Schmitz Wortmeyer

From Dream to Action: Imagination and (Im)Possible Futures (2021)
    Tatiana Valério, Ana Clara S. Bastos, and Luca Tateo

Making of Distinctions: Towards a Social Science of Inclusive Oppositions (2021)
    Antony Palackal, Nandita Chaudhary, and Giuseppina Marsico

Culture, Work and Psychology: Invitations to Dialogue (2019)
    Pedro F. Bendassolli

Ornamented Lives (2018)
    Jaan Valsiner

Cultural Psychology of Intervention in the Globalized World (2018)
    Sanna Schliewe, Nandita Chaudhary, and Giuseppina Marsico

Cultures of Care in Aging (2018)
    Thomas Boll, Dieter Ferring, and Jaan Valsiner

Beyond the Mind: Cultural Dynamics of the Psyche (2018)
    Giuseppina Marsico

Internationalizing the Teaching of Psychology (2017)
    Grant J. Rich, Uwe Gielen, and Harold Takooshian

Healthcare and Culture: Subjectivity in Medical Contexts (2017)
    Maria Francesca Freda and Raffaele De Luca Picione

Memory Practices and Learning: Interactional, Institutional and Sociocultural Perspectives (2017)
    Åsa Mäkitalo, Per Linell, and Roger Säljö

The Subjectified and Subjectifying Mind (2017)
    Min Han and Carla Cunha

Making of The Future: The Trajectory Equifinality Approach in Cultural Psychology (2016)
    Tatsuya Sato, Naohisa Mori, and Jaan Valsiner

Cultural Psychology of Musical Experience (2016)
    Sven Hroar Klempe

Amerindian Paths: Guiding Dialogues With Psychology (2016)
    Danilo Silva Guimarães

Psychology in Black and White: The Project of a Theory-Driven Science (2015)
    Sergio Salvatore

Cultural Psychology of Recursive Processes (2015)
    Zachary Beckstead

Temporality: Culture in the Flow of Human Experience (2015)
    Livia Mathias Simão, Danilo Silva Guimarães, and Jaan Valsiner

Making Our Ideas Clear: Pragmatism in Psychoanalysis (2015)
    Philip Rosenbaum

Biographical Ruptures and Their Repair: Cultural Transitions in Development (2014)
    Amrei C. Joerchel and Gerhard Benetka

Culture and Political Psychology: A Societal Perspective (2014)
    Thalia Magioglou

Fooling Around: Creative Learning Pathways (2014)
    Lene Tanggaard

Lives and Relationships: Culture in Transitions Between Social Roles (2013)
    Yasuhiro Omi, Lilian Patricia Rodriguez, and María Claudia Peralta-Gómez

Dialogical Approaches to Trust in Communication (2013)
    Per Linell and Ivana Markova

Crossing Boundaries: Intercontextual Dynamics Between Family and School (2013)
    Giuseppina Marsico, Koji Komatsu, and Antonio Iannaccone

Cross-Cultural Psychology: Why Culture Matters (2013)
    Krum Krumov and Knud S. Larsen

Interplays Between Dialogical Learning and Dialogical Self (2013)
    M. Beatrice Ligorio and Margarida César

Dialogic Formations: Investigations Into the Origins and Development of the Dialogical Self (2013)
    Marie-Cécile Bertau, Miguel M. Gonçalves, and Peter T. F. Raggatt

Cultural Dynamics of Women's Lives (2012)
    Ana Clara S. Bastos, Kristiina Uriko, and Jaan Valsiner

Culture and Social Change: Transforming Society through the Power of Ideas (2012)
    Brady Wagoner, Eric Jensen, and Julian A. Oldmeadow

Cultural Psychology of Human Values (2012)
    Jaan Valsiner and Angela Uchoa Branco

Researcher Race: Social Constructions in the Research Process (2012)
    Lauren Mizock and Debra Harkins

Cultural Psychology and Psychoanalysis: Pathways to Synthesis (2011)
    Sergio Salvatore and Tania Zittoun

Apprentice in a Changing Trade (2011)
    Jean-François Perret, Anne-Nelly Perret-Clermont, Danièle Golay Schilter, Claude Kaiser, and Luc-Olivier Pochon

Constructing Patriotism: Teaching History and Memories in Global Worlds (2011)
    Mario Carretero

Methodological Thinking in Psychology: 60 Years Gone Astray? (2010)
    Aaro Toomela and Jaan Valsiner

Living in Poverty: Developmental Poetics of Cultural Realities (2010)
    Ana Clara S. Bastos and Elaine P. Rabinovich

Relating to Environments: A New Look at Umwelt (2009)
    Rosemarie Sokol Chang

Rethinking Language, Mind, and World Dialogically (2009)
    Per Linell

Innovating Genesis: Microgenesis and the Constructive Mind in Action (2008)
    Emily Abbey and Rainer Diriwächter

Trust and Distrust: Sociocultural Perspectives (2007)
    Ivana Markova and Alex Gillespie

Discovering Cultural Psychology: A Profile and Selected Readings of Ernest E. Boesch (2007)
    Walter J. Lonner and Susanna A. Hayes

Semiotic Rotations: Modes of Meanings in Cultural Worlds (2007)
    SunHee Kim Gertz, Jaan Valsiner, and Jean-Paul Breaux

Otherness in Question: Development of the Self (2007)
    Livia Mathias Simão and Jaan Valsiner

Becoming Other: From Social Interaction to Self-Reflection (2006)
    Alex Gillespie

Transitions: Symbolic Resources in Development (2006)
    Tania Zittoun

The Semiotic Field of the Garden

Personal Culture and Collective Culture

edited by

Teppei Tsuchimoto
Chukyo University

INFORMATION AGE PUBLISHING, INC.
Charlotte, NC • www.infoagepub.com

Library of Congress Cataloging-in-Publication Data

A CIP record for this book is available from the Library of Congress
http://www.loc.gov

ISBN: 979-8-88730-634-6 (Paperback)
       979-8-88730-635-3 (Hardcover)
       979-8-88730-636-0 (E-Book)

Copyright © 2024 Information Age Publishing Inc.

All rights reserved. No part of this publication may be reproduced, stored in a retrieval system, or transmitted, in any form or by any means, electronic, mechanical, photocopying, microfilming, recording or otherwise, without written permission from the publisher.

Printed in the United States of America

CONTENTS

Series Editors Preface—Cultivating Gardens:
Dialogues Within the Self xv
Jaan Valsiner

Editorial Introduction—Expanding the Concept of the Garden:
From Japanese Zen Gardens to Human Development xx
Teppei Tsuchimoto

PART I

GARDENS WITH HUMAN LIFE

1. The Garden as a Symbolic Space: Trajectories of Affective-Semiotic Cultivation 5
   Daniela Schmitz Wortmeyer

2. Garden as a Sign of Happiness 35
   Ramon Cerqueira Gomes

3. Mirrors of a Garden: Understanding Ecological Units Over Time 47
   Enno Freiherr von Fircks and Marc Antoine Campill

4. "I Need a Garden," a Survivor Said: A Garden as a Place Where Survivors Become Relational Beings for Disaster Recovery 71
   Ryohei Miyamae

5 Radioactive Waste Publicly Placed in a Space That Used to be a Yard as a Private Place: Time and Sign in the Designated Evacuation Areas After Fukushima Nuclear Power Plant Accident 89
Tomoo Hidaka and Hideaki Kasuga

Commentary Part IA—Multilayered and Complex Issue of Garden 111
Eemeli Hakoköngäs

Commentary Part IB—Commentary to the Garden: A Place to Cultivate in Pain and Comfort 119
Marc Antoine Campill

PART II

GARDEN METAPHOR: EXPLORING PERSONAL <> COLLECTIVE CULTURE

6 From God's Garden to Garden of Memories: Personal and Collective Cultures in a Northern Finland Cemetery 127
Eemeli Hakoköngäs

7 The Humanistic Garden of the Renaissance: Where Human, Society, and Cosmos Meet: An Introduction to Machiavelli's Political Ideas 149
Line Joranger

8 Constant Fear of Ostracism 167
Miho Zlazli

9 Djinns and Radioactive Materials: An Abductive Autoethnography on a Garden of Invisible Entities 195
Yusuke Katsura

10 The Transition of a Beginning Nursery Teacher's Interaction With Children From a "Garden" Perspective 213
Kiyoshi Hamana

Commentary Part IIA—Garden as an Expression of Human Life 233
Ramon Cerqueira Gomes

Commentary Part IIB—Enriching the Semiotic Field of the Garden Through Metaphors 241
Enno von Fircks

PART III

MOVING THROUGH GARDENS: A JOURNEY TO SELF-CULTIVATION

11 Cultivation in Self and Environment: When a Voice Echoes From One Garden to Another 259
    Marc Antoine Campill

12 Moving Through Racial Gardens: Personal and Collective Dimensions of Racial Becoming: A Transcultural Autoethnographic Account 279
    Márcio de Abreu

13 Life in a Different Soil: My Existential Mobility as an Immigrant 295
    Rennan Okawa

14 Chinese-Born Korean People's Experience and Present-Day Japan: Using TEA 311
    Akiko Ichikawa

15 "Qualia" of Transgender Experiences: What Visual Images Tells Us 335
    Naoto Machida

    Commentary Part IIIA—Self-Cultivation: The Process of Finding Space for Oneself and Others 343
    Line Joranger

    Commentary Part IIIB—The Garden as a Metaphor for Cultivation of the Self and the Other 349
    Daniela Schmitz Wortmeyer

PART IV

THE "GARDEN PROJECT"

16 The "Garden Project": Initiating International Cultural Exchange Through Gardens 363
    Teppei Tsuchimoto, Yuki Saito, Misato Furuse, and Tatsuya Sato

17 The Inner Sanctum as a "Garden of Buddha" and the People Who "Take Care" of It: How the Priest's Eldest Son Discovered the "Garden" 377
    Gishin Tsukuba

| 18 | Analysis of Personal Culture Appearing in the Japanese Garden 389
Megumi Nishikawa |
|---|---|
| 19 | Personal Feeling Toward Three Gardens in My Life: Example of the Yu Garden 397
Xiaoxue Chen |
| 20 | Garden as Infinity... 405
Fumiyuki Taka |

Commentary Part IV—Reflecting on Oneself and Garden: Projecting Happy Memories Into the Future 421
Tatsuya Sato

Epilogue—Living With Gardening, Living as Gardening 429
Teppei Tsuchimoto

SERIES EDITORS PREFACE

CULTIVATING GARDENS
Dialogues Within the Self

Jaan Valsiner
Aalborg University

Gardens are liminal spaces between their makers and the Nature. As such they unite the maker and maintainer of that space with nature at large. Gardens are borders that unify—even as they create distance from the Self to the Nature. As Teppei Tsuchimoto succinctly states in his Epilogue,

> As we cultivate the garden, we become the garden.

The crucial feature here is the affective "bridge" that unites the person with the Nature. The meta-theoretical basis for it is the notion of *Einfühlung*—feeling into the world—the concept that Theodor Lipps (1851–1914) brought into Occidental psychology (Lipps, 1903) on the basis of German aesthetics of the 19th century (Ianelli, 2024). As the reader of this volume can find out, the introduction parallels the basic premises of the Zen philosophy (Chapter 1). Zen *teaches* nothing—but includes the maximum richness of *experiencing* that its practitioners explore. This—along the theme of

---

The Semiotic Field of the Garden, pages xv–xix
Copyright © 2024 by Information Age Publishing
www.infoagepub.com
All rights of reproduction in any form reserved.

this book—East and West meet each other in the garden. Taking care of the garden is an important part of caring for one's own Self. Likewise—the subjective internal infinity of a person meets the aesthetic canons of one's society in the act of taking care of one's personal garden—big or small, visible or invisible.

What is of fundamental relevance for psychology in this unity of Einfühlung is the developmental dynamics involved—we *feel into* our environment and turn it into a personally meaningful form (*Umwelt*) *through* which we develop further in our lives in irreversible life courses. This feel-forward process is the basis for all development that takes place in the form of *persistent imitation* (a concept introduced by James Mark Baldwin in the 1890s)—trying and trying again, beyond the previous models provided (Valsiner, 2009). Semiosis—creation and use of signs based on affective apperception—is thus the basis for all human higher psychological processes.

The unique general feature of this book is its focus on the dynamic relationships of internalization and externalization. Gardens are a result of externalization of the subjective needs of a person—while feeding forward to further internalization. Study of that dynamic relationship needs new scientific tools—which are powerfully present in this book. Cultural psychology becomes increasingly focused on the role of human imagination as the basis for creating the psychological realities in the course of human life. The synthesis of two time-honored (even if often distrusted) methods of *introspection* in psychology and *ethnography* in cultural anthropology gives us the synthesis of autoethnography. The primacy of the personal self-observation, inevitably mixed with affective self-relating, becomes recognized in autoethnography. As a result, research in cultural psychology eliminates the artificial barrier set up to eliminate the use of fictional characters of novels as legitimate data sources for psychology (Moghaddam, 2004). Fiction writers are researchers in their own right—often by far more insightful in making up their imaginary characters in ways that lure us to re-read novels of Dostoyevski or Hemingway being fully aware of the complete non-reality of the described characters full of life, suffering, and happiness. Novel writers have the luxury of creating complex characters (Brinkmann, 2009)—without any need to subject them to censorship by one or another "institutional review board." Shakespeare's Hamlet is probably the most investigated person in the history of psychology. Or at least the most challenging one (Zittoun & Stenner, 2021). The challenges start from what we could consider "Hamlet's Garden"—the liminal space where his father's ghost appears and all the court intrigues around him lead his soul-searching about being and non-being. The latter resonates with ordinary human beings all over the World[1]—even if Hamlet's personality was never tested by any method of the "Big Five" variety. Scientific psychology in its measurement practices here loses out to the needs of ordinary human beings to answer existential questions in their gardens.

Gardens are cultivated. They are liminal spaces—set up on the nobody's imaginary land between my Self and the Others. Borders unite—while making distinctions. Gardens are such borders—yet often with fuzzy edges. The border zone—the garden—is itself bordered— by efforts to close it off, or by the effort to extend it to include far-off landscapes. The Japanese notion of *shakkei* the reader encounters in this book is an example of such extension. Shakkei has been developing as a boundary operation tool to extend the boundaries of the small space of the garden and to bring distant visions into one's garden. Here is the dialogue of the person with the horizon—striving towards it, while recognizing that it can never be reached. Behind a horizon is another, further extended, horizon. A graveyard may be a garden which the living cultivate and the dead inhabit. Shakkei here involves inclusion of the infinity of imaginary living beyond death. Yet there exists the opposite move—maybe it can be called *counter-Shakkei*—where undesirable objects end up invading the gardens. The arrival of radioactive materials in the yards of local inhabitants after a nuclear plant disaster triggers sophisticated psychological adaptations to such invasions. The reader of this book will have a good opportunity to contemplate this negative scenario based on the descriptions of such adaptations.

Opening one's garden to the view towards infinity gives direction to the person in one's life course. At the same time—the care of the garden in the liminal zone provides us with a view of the cultivation of the Self. Thus it is a location where observation of concrete acts of caring for one's beloved objects—trees, insects, flowers, pets, or any special object in the garden—is the alley of externalization of the Self that can tell us about the inner infinity of the Self. And understanding of that inner infinity is towards which cultural psychology strives.

—Jaan Valsiner

NOTE

1. Albeit in various versions of interpretation—see Bohannan, 1979.

REFERENCES

Bohannan, L. (1979). Miching mallecho, that means witchcraft. In J. Middleton (Ed.), *Magic, witchcraft and curing* (pp. 43–54). University of Texas Press.

Brinkmann, S. (2009). Literature as qualitative inquiry: The novelist as researcher. *Qualitative Inquiry, 15*(8), 1376–1394.

Iannelli, F. (2024). Robert Vischer and the aesthetic foundation of *Einfühlung*. In C. Cornejo & C. H. Maturana (Eds.), *Forgotten streams in the history of 19th century German psychology*. Springer.

Lipps, T. (1903). Einfühlung, innere Nachahmung und Organempfindungen [Empathy, inner imitation and organ sensations]. *Archiv für die gesamte Psychologie, 1*, 185–204.

Moghaddam, F. (2004). From "psychology in literature" to "psychology is literature." *Theory & Psychology, 14*(4), 505–525.

Valsiner, J. (2009). Baldwin's quest: A universal logic of development. In J. W. Clegg (Ed.), *The observation of human systems: Lessons from the history of anti-reductionistic empirical psychology* (pp. 45–82). Transaction Publishers.

Zittoun, T., & Stenner, P. (2021). Vygotsky's tragedy: Hamlet and the psychology of art. *Review of General Psychology, 25*(3) 223–238. https://doi.org/10.1177/10892680211013293

A garden representing the introduction of Buddhism.
Left: India, Center: China, right: Japan.
(Reigenin sub-temple of Kennin-ji Temple, Kyoto Japan)

EDITORIAL INTRODUCTION

EXPANDING THE CONCEPT OF THE GARDEN

From Japanese Zen Gardens to Human Development

Teppei Tsuchimoto
Chukyo University

PERSONAL AND COLLECTIVE CULTURE IN THE GARDEN

How do people make meanings of gardens? How has the meaning of a certain garden changed? How do they transact with nature that resists culture—against one's intentions, a tulip seed may not sprout, or a flower may not bloom—in their daily lives? We rarely look at these questions, but they are important for understanding the culture that is closest to our lives. This is because culture grows from the relationship between the person and nature, mediating the *personal<>collective* relationship. This chapter presents several examples of analysis and methodological possibilities for dealing with the cultural nature of the garden as an object of cultural psychology, taking the Japanese garden as a starting point. First, I will ethnographically examine several Japanese gardens to understand the relationship between personal<>collective culture.

The "garden" is a very interesting topic from the perspective of cultural psychology. All of us are constructing subjective *Umwelt* (Chang, 2009)—briefly, the subjective environment—in our mind, and that relationship often manifests itself in a handmade nature that the person has developed (or with others), such as a "favorite garden" or a "garden of memories." It may be one's grandfather's garden or the small plants in one's balcony. Also, gardening is a process by which humans transact with or cultivate nature, while integrating the duality of personal and collective culture. Nature as an object stands against its modification (*Gegenstand*; Valsiner, 2014). Here, we can observe the opposition between culture<>nature. This opposition is rooted in Vygotsky (1934/1962). The duality and integrative moment of culture<>nature was fundamental to his developmental theory and his perspective on this mutual relationship remains operative despite criticisms from the Soviet era (Kamiya, 2005).

Gardens function as an important part of a person's life—either for healing or peace of mind. For instance, there is a tool made of bamboo called *Shishi-odoshi* (鹿威し) or *Sozu* (僧都, 添水) in the traditional Japanese garden (Figure I.1). This tool makes a sound when filled with water. It was originally a farming tool used to drive wild animals away with its sound. Therefore, this cultural tool is a product generated as a result of human

Figure I.1   Shishi-odoshi in the Shisen-do Temple (Kyoto, Japan).

negotiation with the nature of animals. Jozan Ishiyama (石山丈山), who built Shisen-do (詩仙堂), was the first to introduce this tool to the garden, and loved the sound of it in the silence, which gave him comfort during his retired life (Shisen-do, n.d.). Nowadays, we find the sound of Shishi-odoshi soothing and use it to create the ambience of a Japanese garden rather than for the agricultural purpose it was initially intended for. When this sound is internalized via various forms in our everyday activities, such as commercials, animations, and historical dramas, it mediates the aesthetic feelings of Japanese gardens.

Furthermore, gardens have constructed collective cultures by being considered symbols of power and by having religious and mythological significance. Jagger (2015) examines the symbolic nature of the garden and how power and privilege have been represented in it. The structure of the gardens such as Plato's Academy and the Epicurean Garden, Medieval Monastic Gardens, Renaissance gardens, and the gardens of Versailles are represented. Thus, "an increasing control of the natural world and through garden design and maintenance celebrates human's ability, and perhaps inclination, to assert power over the other-than-human world" (Jagger, 2015, p. 641). Another remarkable example of the dynamism of power in the garden can be found in Rome. In the 16th century, anyone was free to enter a private garden in Rome according to the idea of the "law of the garden" (Lex Hortorum), which stated that the wealthy had to give a portion of their wealth back to society (Kuwakino, 2019). The exhibition of rich artworks in the garden functioned as a patronage achievement of the Pope's love of ancient art, the garden owner's discernment, and a demonstration of the financial strength of the *Holy See* that made the collection possible. Thus, the garden served as a space for collections of art and sculpture and the transmission of powerful political messages (Kuwakino, 2019).

○△□ GARDEN: THE UNIVERSE OF MIND AND ITS CONTINUITY

What is important to note here is that a garden can be both personal and collective. One person makes meanings of a particular garden, but those meanings differ from others'. On the other hand, similar (but not the same) meanings may be given to a particular garden, or to the sign of the garden, interpersonally. Such *collective<>personal culture relationships* are crucial for our understanding of both continuity and discontinuity in the human *psyche* (Valsiner, 2014; Valsiner et al., 2023).

If so, how does the relationship between personal and collective culture relationships appear in the garden? The garden in the Kennin-ji Temple (Kyoto, Japan) is a notable example that shows how a person (in this case,

xxiv ▪ Expanding the Concept of the Garden

the temple president, the creator of the garden) expresses the collective culture of Zen (禅) in the garden. At the Kennin-ji Temple (建仁寺), there is a Zen garden called "○△□ Garden." The Kennin-ji Temple is the oldest Zen Buddhist temple in Kyoto, the former capital of Japan. It was founded by Eisai (栄西) in 1202. After studying in China (Southern Song Dynasty) twice, Eisai returned to Japan and became well known for introducing and spreading the philosophy of Zen and the practice of drinking tea. This garden is deeply related to Zen philosophy. From the Muromachi period (1336–1573), many gardens were constructed for Zen practice. The gardens were a place for practicing Zen, and creating the garden itself was also a practice of Zen. I start with a brief explanation of Zen. The question, "What is Zen?" is quite difficult to answer, but it can be described in the following words:

> There may be an intellectual element in Zen, for Zen is the whole mind, and in it we find a great many things; but the mind is not a composite thing that is to be divided into so many faculties, leaving nothing behind when the dissection is over. Zen has nothing to teach us in the way of intellectual analysis; nor has it any set doctrines which are imposed on its followers for acceptance. In this respect Zen is quite chaotic if you choose to say so. Probably Zen followers may have sets of doctrines, but they have them on their own account, and for their own benefit; they do not owe the fact to Zen. Therefore, there are in Zen no sacred books or dogmatic tenets, nor are there any symbolic formulae through which an access might be gained into the signification of Zen. If I am asked, then, what Zen teaches, I would answer, Zen teaches nothing. Whatever teachings there are in Zen, they come out of one's own mind. We teach ourselves; Zen merely points the way. Unless this pointing is teaching, there is certainly nothing in Zen purposely set up as its cardinal doctrines or as its fundamental philosophy. (Suzuki, 1964, p. 38)

The answer to "What is Zen?" lies in each person. Therefore, Zen is not to be taught by someone, but to be grasped by oneself. Zen practitioners explore the mind. Eisai, the founder of Kennin-ji, wrote in the beginning of his text on the essentials of Zen, saying: "What a vast thing is the mind!" (大哉心乎). Zen indicates the universe in our mind, which is also part of our daily lives. Zen is "the ocean, Zen is the air, Zen is the mountain, Zen is thunder and lightning, the spring flower, summer heat, and winter snow; nay, more than that, Zen is the man" (Suzuki, 1964, p. 45).

According to Zen, the universe or the vast mind comprises four primordial elements: earth(土), water(水), fire(火), and wind(風; Kennin-ji, n.d.). These ideas are represented in the "○△□ Garden" as a square (earth), circle (water), and triangle (fire) (Kennin-ji, n.d., Figure I.2 & Figure I.3). Thus, the symbols of ○△□ represent the mind (universe) that Zen seeks

Expanding the Concept of the Garden ▪ **xxv**

Figure I.2 ○△□ Garden at the Kennin-ji Temple.

to explore. The presence of these symbols in the courtyard of a Zen Temple with an 800 year-old history has a deep meaning.

The circle is found in the moss at the base of the tree (Figure I.2). The square is represented by the well placed at the far end of the picture. The triangle is the raised sand in the front portion of the picture. This design is based on the famous ○△□ calligraphic work by Gibon Sengai (仙厓義梵: Kennin-ji, n.d.). A room in the Kennin-ji Temple has a calligraphic rendition of ○△□ created by Taigan Kobori (小堀泰巖), the current president

Figure I.3 A guide to the ○△□ Garden.

of the Kennin-ji Temple (Figure I.4). One may think that "wind" does not exist here, but according to a monk at the Kennin-ji Temple, "The 'wind' is there itself, even if it is not expressed. You can't see 'emptiness' (空, Śūnyatā), but it is floating in the air. When 'emptiness' moves, it becomes 'wind,' so there is no need to express it."

The symbol ○△□ was also used to mark graves. The Gorinto stupa (五輪塔) is an old grave that comprises these symbols (Figure I.5). Although this type of a tomb is rarely seen in Japan these days, it was used as a memorial tower or grave marker for the dead in the middle of the Heian period (Heian period: around 794 to 1192) (Encyclopedia Nipponica, 1984–1994). According to a monk at the Kennin-ji Temple, the Chinese

Expanding the Concept of the Garden • **xxvii**

Figure I.4 Calligraphic rendition of ○△□ by Taigan Kobori.

Figure I.5 Gorinto stupa in the Reigen-in temple garden (Part of the Kennin-ji Temple).

character "life" (命) can also be seen as ○△□. These simple symbols express the profundity of Zen in that they also appear as graves that actually indicate the end of a person's life.

In this chapter, I present examples of gardens with the ○△□ symbol, and since ancient times in Japan, deep emotions have been integrated into gardens. Other examples include mythological motifs like cranes, turtles, and Mt. Horai (蓬莱山: a legendary place where hermits live), under the influence of Taoism. The Byodoin Phoenix Hall (平等院鳳凰堂) was created in the Heian period. Its garden was influenced by the Latter Day of the Law (the belief that Buddhism will decline), and people created gardens to represent paradise.

Personal subjective feelings are inseparable from culture. The garden thus inevitably implies reflecting on the relationship between personal and collective cultures. It is important to note "the contrast between sign-mediated negotiations in the person's immediate *Umwelt*—the arena of collective culture—and within the intra-personal 'infinity' of the personal culture" (Valsiner, 2014). If we look at a small object at the edge of the garden, we may encounter a vast universe.

Thus far we have explored the symbolically constructed aspects of the garden. Although this chapter focuses on Japanese gardens, the discussion of "gardens" here is somehow linked to gardens worldwide. For example, as a result of religious bonds, we see similarities in Iranian and Japanese gardens. Persian gardens are known for their "four gardens" (Chahar Bagh) style, consisting of four sections, symbolizing "Paradise" (Garden of Eden; UNESCO, n.d.). Although one example is provided in this chapter, several Persian gardens have also taken on this style. The first Persian garden on record is Pasargadae, built in approximately 600 BC by the Achaemenid emperor Cyrus, which is based on the Zoroastrian division of the universe in four parts, four seasons or four elements: water, wind, earth, and fire (Faghih & Sadeghy, 2012). The ○△□ Zen Garden, mentioned above, developed uniquely in Japan, but with the historical flow of religious ideas from Persian gardens, these deep feelings are connected through gardens worldwide.

AUTOETHNOGRAPHY AND GARDENS

This section deals with how a person's autobiographical memory is connected to the garden. This leads to the presentation of the more daily and personal aspects of the garden. The connections between gardens can be found in various fields: garden cemeteries, parks, temples, meadows, gardens of emperors, lords and royalty, and home gardens. Thus, the search for the meaning of the garden is not a comparison of "national cultures." Instead, it is a way of life that has been historically woven through gardening.

The garden also functions to encounter and dialogue with the self, and it is important to understand this aspect of it. As Maran (2004) exemplifies, "The changes in the appearance of home gardens, for instance, the growth of trees, are slow enough to provide important landmarks in one's biography" (p. 124). In other words, it has been pointed out that gardens have an important role in the embodiment of memories (the process of autocommunication, which involves carrying and evoking memories; Maran, 2004). Lindström (2010) introduced that Yuri Lotman (1990) illustrated the Zen Garden in Japan as an example of autocommunication. To deepen our understanding of autocommunication in the garden, I would like to introduce the example of the Shinji-ike Pond (心字池), which is said to represent the Chinese character "heart" (心). According to Kawahara (2009), Shinji-ike Pond is not always in the form of the character for "mind," but is a method of enjoying complex changes in the shoreline. Many of the Shinji-ike ponds are included in Soseki Muso's (夢窓疎石) garden, which is considered deeply related to the Zen philosophy as discussed earlier. He was a famous garden designer in the Muromachi period. His gardens exuded a deep insight into nature and a powerful artistic desire often cultivated by placing the Japanese Zen philosophy and garden design at the same level (Amagasaki, 2014b). There are many Shinji-ike Ponds all over Japan. However, it is very difficult to see these ponds as the character for "heart," even if we see it from the sky.

Here I would like to introduce a narrative that I encountered during my research on the Shinji-ike Pond. Tenryu-ji Temple (天龍寺) has a garden called Sogenchi (曹源池: Figure I.6), and the author initially thought that

Figure I.6 Sougenchi Pond in Tenryu-ji (Kyoto, Japan).

this pond might be one of the Shinji-ike Ponds. However, when the author asked Ogawa Shusei, who is the general secretary of Tenryu-ji Temple, he said that the important point was not whether this pond itself could be seen as the Chinese character for heart but whether the heart can feel "beautiful" when looking at this garden. He also remarked on how significant this pond is as a place for Zen practice. This pond is a garden that Soseki created and left for his and his disciples' practice. One practice is not to leave a single speck of dust around this pond to polish one's heart. Additionally, every evening at nine o'clock, *Unsui* (雲水; ascetic monks), who practice in Tenryu-ji's specialized training hall, come out of the Zen hall (禅堂) with only a *Zabuton* (座布団; a Japanese cushion), and sit on this *Engawa* (縁側; veranda; Figure I.6), looking at the garden, for about 2 hours of *Zazen* (座禅). This is called *Yaza* (夜坐).

As Zen has ultimately sought to explore the mind, expressing it in the pond may have itself been a Zen practice. Thus, this pond—and the garden—is maintained to date and functions as an important place of autocommunication for Zen.

To summarize, we can deepen the dialogue within the self through the mediating object of the garden. As externalizations of personal culture, objects are the way for human beings to guide their development (Valsiner, 2014). An autoethnographic approach (or auto-TEM; Tsuchimoto, 2022) is suitable to access this very human component of the garden. It is an approach that enables deepening of our understanding of how such autocommunication is performed in terms of the connection between personal and collective culture, from a "turtle's view" (first-person perspective) and a "bird's view" (third-person perspective; Tsuchimoto, 2021; Figure I.7).

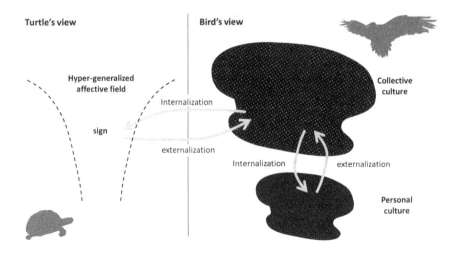

Figure I.7 The "turtle's" and the "bird's" view.

Expanding the Concept of the Garden ▪ **xxxi**

GARDEN BORDER: A POETIC AUTOETHNOGRAPHY

The garden border
From the bottoms of my feet, where I arrived
Through the straight lines of stones
From the ground, through my body, and up into my throat
"Nostalgia" is a past memory?
When we live relating with another,
The thing as they should be and fun
like water splashing in the ocean
BLENDING in the swell of the sewage

庭への境目で
たどりついた足の裏から、
まっすぐに並んだ、石の筋をとおして
地面からからだを通って、のどの中に込みあがってくる
なつかしさは、昔の記憶なのだろうか?
人をたよりに生きていれば
しかたのないこと　楽しいことが
海に水が跳ねるように
下水道のうねりの中で混ぜくられていく

This autoethnographic poem talks about my feelings around stepping over the boundary to enter the garden at my grandfather's house, which I used to visit every year when I was young. This poem shows that the boundary of the garden has intra-personal "infinity" (Valsiner, 2014). "I arrived at my grandfather's house after a two-hour drive" (Figure I.8). "The boundary of

Figure I.8 My grandfather's garden.

Figure I.9   The border of the garden.

my grandfather's house is 'there,' where the ground switches from straight stones to smooth concrete" (Figure I.9). "However, this boundary extends infinitely. Memories of falling into the sewer and injuring myself while trying to save my little nephew, the warm smiles of my grandfather and grandmother, our dog Marron, the small field where I harvested radishes, and the nearby park—all of these are within that border of the 'garden.'" The feeling I experience when I arrive at my grandfather's garden can be described as "nostalgia," but there is more. This feeling of nostalgia is hyper-generalized and is not a "memory of the past" in the sense of the dictionary definition. For me, the garden is everywhere, like an endless seashore, and the feeling is too complex to put into words. From a subjective perspective, the boundary as *Gegenstand* is constantly moving dynamically (Campill & Tsuchimoto, 2022).

The garden is an affectively generalized (hyper-generalized) sign field. According to Valsiner (2006), the sign has two forms of generalization

Expanding the Concept of the Garden ▪ **xxxiii**

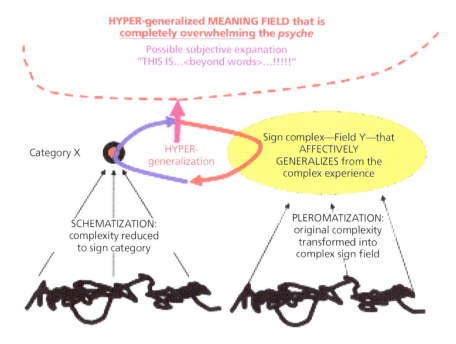

Figure I.10 The processes of affective generalization and hyper-generalization (Valsiner, 2006).

(Figure I.10). "Schematization" simply categorizes experiences (left), and "pleromatization" generalizes while maintaining the richness of experiences (right). Hyper-generalization is a process of affective synthesis of these signs, where a vague meaning field that overwhelms the human psyche emerges. The garden is a deeply significant place in most people's minds, and exists as a hyper-generalized field.

Pleromatization and hyper-generalization are key concepts in Jaan Valsiner et al.'s (2023) *cultural psychology of dynamic semiotics*, and are described as follows:

> The process of pleromatization involves abstraction of the general meaning from already complex affective experience (e.g., dropping a precious vase that breaks into pieces) to field-like generalization ("I am always so clumsy such losses happen all the time") and finally to generalized sign field of the generalized feeling of loss. The original object—the event of the broken vase—is replaced by the general field of feeling a loss. At the same time, on the side of schematization, the cognitive understanding of the value of the broken object can be rationally contemplated. The affective field-like generalization—pleromatic generalization—is primary with the cognitive (schematic) counterpart. (p. 581)

xxxiv ▪ Expanding the Concept of the Garden

The poem at the beginning is interesting as it is concerned with "liminality." Being liminal indicates a state in which time and space are in motion at the boundary to the proximal future on the edge of the 'here and now' sphere of experience. In other words, it refers to an 'in-between' state that is neither inside nor outside the garden. For instance, the Estonian-Russian border zones (spatial) involve all things such as the boundary of the self, history, religion, and law (Tateo et al., 2018). The point of bifurcation where developmental possibilities are opened in the life trajectory (Sato, 2017; Sato et al., 2016) is also temporal liminality. We move from the present moment (space) to the next, toward the future, in a contingent time that is neither coincidental nor inevitable. In the developmental sense, a person is always operating at the liminal tension between "as-is" and "as if" and being on the boundary (Valsiner, 2007).

Such manipulation of the boundary can also be seen in a traditional Japanese garden construction technique called *Shakkei* (借景). Shakkei is "a method to organically connect the external landscape and the garden space by setting a specific viewpoint as well as selecting an object to borrow" (Amagasaki, 2014a, pp. 80–81). In the Sengan-en Garden (仙巌園, Kagoshima, Japan), the garden and the volcano (Mt. Sakurajima) across the sea are fused together to create a single scenery (Figure I.11 & Figure I.12).

The structure of the garden intentionally eliminates the boundary between the garden and the background. Shakkei has been developed as a

Figure I.11 A view of Sengan-en from the sky.

Expanding the Concept of the Garden ▪ **xxxv**

Figure I.12   Fusion of landscapes by Shakkei in Sengan-en.

boundary operation tool to extend the boundaries of the small space of the garden and to bring distant things "into" one's own garden. The idea that the boundary disappears through the perspective from the garden is suggestive of cultural psychology. The border that surrounds us is not a given but typically something that we have constructed. If we attempt to "borrow" a distant volcano from nature for our home garden, we will encounter resistance, such as the need to cut down the trees in that part of the garden. Gardens are objects that stand against the pressure applied to them when we act to modify their boundaries (*Gegenstand*).

TOWARD THE CONSTRUCTION OF A NEW GARDEN FOR CULTURAL PSYCHOLOGY

The inquiry into the meaning of garden for one offers profound insights on the relationship between personal and collective culture. The process of constructing a garden makes nature the object, in which various liminal, aesthetic, and symbolic activities take place directly. The term *garden* includes a multitude of meanings. It is a place for recreation and is a symbol of power. For the gardener, it is a place of work. Alternatively, the feeling of the garden is deeply rooted in people's hearts and has an aesthetic meaning.

However, the relationship between the "personal" and "collective" is very central to cultural psychology, and I would like to consider this with a wider range of topics. It will also lead to the depiction of infinite possibilities that extend from the garden. Therefore, in this book, we take the garden as our starting point for the following discussions:

Part I   Gardens with Human Life
Part II   Garden Metaphor: Exploring Personal <> Collective Culture
Part III   Moving Through Gardens: A Journey to Self-Cultivation
Part IV   The "Garden Project"

As mentioned earlier, this book is not only a direct study of gardens, but also aims to deepen our understanding of the relationship between personal and collective culture, an important component of cultural psychology (no doubt, the garden is an attractive field for such exploration). Putting human and garden considerations at the same level has a sort of metaphorical function. Readers can use their experiences to deepen their understanding of personal and collective culture in the context of a familiar garden—such as their home garden, neighborhood park, cemetery, or schoolyard. I hope the unique diversity in the perspectives provided in this book will encourage us to open up new "gardens" in cultural psychology.

REFERENCES

Amagasaki, H. (2014a). Traditional spatial perception of Japanese gardens. In T. Nomura (Ed.), *What is the fuugetsu, moon, garden, and fragrance?* (pp. 73–81). Geijutsu Gakusha. (Original in Japanese)

Amagasaki, H. (2014b). Abstraction of garden designs. In T Nomura (Ed.), *What is the fuugetsu, moon, garden, and fragrance?* (pp. 73–81). Geijutsu Gakusha. (Original in Japanese)

Campill, M. A., & Tsuchimoto, T. (2022). Moving up the stream beyond resistance to counter move. *Culture & Psychology, 29*(4). https://doi.org/10.1177/1354067X221111452

Chang, R. S. (Ed.). (2009). *Relating to environments: A new look at umwelt*. Information Age Publishing.
Encyclopedia Nipponica. (1984–1994). *Gorinto* (五輪塔). Shogakukan [Digital ed.]. https://kotobank.jp/word/%E4%BA%94%E8%BC%AA%E5%A1%94-66586 (Original in Japanese)
Faghih, N., & Sadeghy, A. (2012). Persian gardens and landscapes. *Architectural Design*, *82*(3), 38–51.
Jagger S. (2015). What does your garden show? Explorations of the semiotics of the garden. In P. Trifonas (Eds.), *International handbook of semiotics* (pp. 629–645). Springer. https://doi.org/10.1007/978-94-017-9404-6_29
Kamiya, E. (2005). Development of Vygotskian theory and its periodisation (Part I). *Journal of the Faculty of Social Welfare*, 1, 81–98. (Original in Japanese)
Kawahara, T. (2009). Ike(池). In *Heibonsha's world encyclopedia* (2nd ed.) [Digital ed.]. Heibonsha. Retrieved June, 2021 from https://kotobank.jp/word/%E5%BF%83%E5%AD%97%E6%B1%A0-537610
Kennin-ji. (n.d.). *The oldest Zen Temple in Kyoto Kennin-ji* (local leaflet). Retrieved from June, 2021 from https://www.kenninji.jp/ebook/leaflet/#
Kuwakino, K. (2019). *A spiritual history of Renaissance Gardens: Media spaces of power, knowledge, and beauty* [Kindle ed.]. Hakusuisha. (Original in Japanese).
Lindström, K. (2010). Autocommunication and perceptual markers in landscape: Japanese examples. *Biosemiotics*, *3*(3), 359–373. https://doi.org/10.1007/s12304-010-9082-0
Lotman, Y. M. (1990). *Universe of the mind: A semiotic theory of culture* (A. Shukman, Trans.). Indiana University Press.
Maran, T. (2004). Gardens and gardening: An ecosemiotic view. *Semiotica*, *150*(1999), 119–133. https://doi.org/10.1515/semi.2004.039
Sato, T. (2017). *Collected papers on trajectory equifinality approach*. Chitose Press. (Original in Japanese)
Sato, T., Mori, N., & Valsiner, J. (2016). *Making of the future: The trajectory equifinality approach in cultural psychology*. Information Age Publishing.
Shisen-do. (n.d.). *Shisen-do: Jozan-ji* (Local leaflet). (Original in Japanese)
Suzuki, D. T. (1964). *An introduction to Zen Buddhism*. Grove Press, inc.
Tateo, L., Español, A., Kullasepp, K., Marsico, G., & Palang, H. (2018). Five gazes on the border: A collective auto-ethnographic writing. *Human Arenas*, *1*(2), 113–133. https://doi.org/10.1007/s42087-018-0010-1
Tsuchimoto, T. (2021). Transfer of specific moment to general knowledge: Suggestions from cultural developmental autoethnography and autoethnographic trajectory equifinality modeling. *Human Arenas*, *4*, 302–210. https://doi.org/10.1007/s42087-021-00220-3
Tsuchimoto, T. (2022). *Autoethnography of career support in transition*. Nakanishiya.
UNESCO (n.d.). *The Persian Garden*. https://whc.unesco.org/en/list/1372/
Valsiner, J. (2006, June 12). The overwhelming world: Functions of pleromatization in creating diversity in cultural and natural constructions [Keynote lecture]. *International Summer School of Semiotic and Structural Studies*, Imatra, Finland.
Valsiner, J. (2007). *Culture in minds and societies: Foundations of cultural psychology*. SAGE Publications.
Valsiner, J. (2014). *An invitation to cultural psychology*. SAGE Publishing.

Valsiner, J., Tsuchimoto, T., Ozawa, I., Chen, X., & Horie, K. (2021). The Intermodal pre-construction method (IMPreC): Exploring hyper-generalization. *Human Arenas—An Interdisciplinary Jouranl of Psychology, Culture, and Meaning, 6*(3), 580–598. https://doi.org/10.1007/s42087-021-00237-8

Vygotsky, L. (1962). *Thought and language*. MIT Press. (Original work published 1934)

PART I

GARDENS WITH HUMAN LIFE

Eixão Sul do Lazer (oil on canvas by Otoniel Fernandes Neto)

CHAPTER 1

THE GARDEN AS A SYMBOLIC SPACE

Trajectories of Affective-Semiotic Cultivation

Daniela Schmitz Wortmeyer
Independent Researcher

> I'm not even sure how it all started. The midday sun, the heat and the desire to arrive soon and rest, plus the anxiety for the new, amid a profusion of colors and smells. I looked around and didn't seem to believe what I saw: an ecstatic garden, filled with multiple species of varying sizes. Fruits, flowers, grasses... I didn't know where to look first. When I realized, I was voraciously savoring the sweet, succulent fruits of a blackberry tree with huge thorns. The occasional jabs in the fingers made that moment even more gratifying, with a childhood feel, and with a mischievous air I looked around, wondering if there would be any spectators for my prank. But there wasn't. I was free to be a kid again, feeling an unexpected euphoria at the start of a vacation.
>
> —Wortmeyer, 2015, para. 1

This is the beginning of a text I wrote a few years ago, after being immersed in a very special garden. There, the myriad of sensations provoked

---

The Semiotic Field of the Garden, pages 5–32
Copyright © 2024 by Information Age Publishing
www.infoagepub.com
All rights of reproduction in any form reserved.

by colors, smells, flavors, sounds, and tactile surfaces took me beyond the here-and-now, triggering "memories of enchantment and joy, difficult to locate in time and space," as I registered ahead in the same text. The feeling of childhood, of being in a "fairy-tale garden," was evoked by the particular configuration of that environment, and this initial affective atmosphere was extended to reflections on the gardener's work and how it can be seen as a metaphor for life in a broader sense. Thus, the desire to share this meaningful experience with others was channeled into the writing of the mentioned text, as well as into the cultivation of a garden in an urban public space, close to my place of residence. The latter was also a way to bring something related to that special environment with me, making the deep feelings evoked during that vacation period more accessible in my daily life.

This personal story can be a good start to reflect on how our experiences related to natural elements and landscapes are filled with affects and meanings derived from our individual life trajectories, which necessarily stem from and feed back into a socio-cultural context, in a process of mutual development of the person and the environment, as pointed out by Tsuchimoto in the "Editorial Introduction" of this volume.

As human beings, we are sensitive to what reaches our sensory organs, and this immediately provokes an affective tone, entailing meaning-making processes. "The reply of the human subjectivity to physiological sensations triggered is affective—the sensation becomes filled with sense" (Valsiner, 2019, p. 9). The physical and social environment that surrounds us acts then as a promoter of different levels of affective meaning-making, sometimes reaching increasing generalization, towards wide feelings and interpretations that involve us as a whole, and which words are never enough to fully describe (Valsiner, 2012, 2014).

These very personal and deep experiences, derived from the internalization of the external environment, also feedback this environment through different forms of externalization by the subject: Telling about it to others, writing a text, composing a poem or a painting, cultivating a garden, or even in more indirect and subtle ways. By these actions, we configure our life environments in meaningful ways, creating a particular *Umwelt*[1] that implicitly carries messages of values and worldviews. These *Umwelten* constitute an affective-semiotic frame for the subjective experiences of those who circulate in them, channeling their sensitivity in certain directions and provoking a particular *Einfühlung*[2] ("feeling-in") in relation to that environment (Valsiner, 2014, 2019).

Thus, we are constantly affected and psychologically transformed by our environments, as well as we do transform these surroundings in meaningful ways, potentially affecting other beings through such actions, in a continuous dynamic of internalization and externalization (Valsiner, 2012, 2014). It is important to stress that, in all these processes, we make use of semiotic mediation, the proper human psychological resource for finding stability and orienting ourselves in our relations with the world, towards the unknown future moment. By using signs, which may be words, images, sounds, gestures, or material objects that evoke some idea, feeling, or object beyond themselves, we associate immediate body sensations to other experiences and meanings, reaching high levels of generalization and abstraction. This can reach the post-verbal level of hypergeneralization, in which personal values, life philosophies, aesthetic feelings, and experiences of transcendence are found (Valsiner, 2012, 2014; Vygotsky, 1988, 2001; Wortmeyer, 2022; Wortmeyer & Branco, 2016).

Therefore, human experiences are always intertwined in a web of affects and meanings that go far beyond the here-and-now, which were woven throughout our life trajectories and continue to be in the present, with the always open possibility of being enriched and transformed by new experiences. The development of such capacity of affective-semiotic regulation occurs through significant social interactions in a culturally organized environment, in which the symbols, values, practices, and objects that constitute the collective culture of a particular social group in a specific historical time are presented to us and mediate our relations with the world. Notwithstanding, each person draws a singular trajectory and actively internalizes these social suggestions, constructing his or her idiosyncratic inner reality and externalizing it in unique ways, which represents one's own personal culture (Valsiner, 2012, 2014; Wortmeyer, 2017; Zittoun et al., 2013).

After briefly introducing some theoretical underpinnings that will guide this chapter, I aim to focus on how these affective-semiotic processes permeate our encounters with what we usually call "nature," particularly considering human cultivated natural environments as private and public gardens. Although we are "natural" beings due to our biological connections, I intend to explore how relationships with the natural environment inevitably have a symbolic character for human beings, acquiring meaning in light of specific interpretations and feelings about the material world. I argue that the relationships of human beings with nature are imbricated in specific collective cultural configurations (Eckerdal, 2017), at the same time that they acquire unique symbolic meanings in the webs woven into individual life trajectories.

This discussion will be based on two case studies, which were conducted following an idiographic research approach (Valsiner, 2014; Zittoun & Valsiner, 2016). A semi-structured interview was carried out with each research participant, in order to promote their narratives on personal experiences related to the topic (Jovchelovitch & Bauer, 2002; Schütze, 2011). Interviews were recorded and verbatim transcribed by me. The research information constructed underwent a qualitative analysis, which was benefited by some recommendations by Charmaz (2009) and fundamentally guided by the perspective of cultural psychology of semiotic dynamics that underlies this work (Branco & Valsiner, 1997, 1999; Valsiner, 2012, 2014).

In the first case, I went back to the special garden that I referred to in the opening of this chapter and invited the gardener, a son of Japanese immigrants, to narrate in more detail the story of that garden, exploring the meanings of gardening in his life and how it emerged in his personal trajectory, with a specific cultural background. In the second case, an artist who painted the landscapes of Brasília, the Brazilian capital, approached his aesthetic experiences related to nature and how this urban environment promoted a particular Einfühlung, inspiring a collection of paintings in which the natural elements are in the foreground.

In both cases, the hypergeneralized affects and meanings emerging in the subjects' relations with nature will be analyzed, including the canalization of such experiences to artistic forms of expression. The case studies will support the more general discussion about how collective and personal cultures are constantly intertwined, being mutually affected and transformed, in a continuous symbolic activity that encompasses psychological and material dimensions.

AFFECTIVE-SEMIOTIC CULTIVATION OF A GARDEN

Yoshiharu Endo[3] is a 71 year-old man who owns a beautiful inn situated in a region involved by natural preservation areas in Central Brazil. His place stands out for the garden that surrounds the apartments and chalets, combining native and exotic species of flowers and trees, some of which produce fruits that attract wild birds such as macaws, parrots, and parakeets. Mr. Endo works personally in gardening, as well as overseeing the garden-related work of inn staff. He also writes poems that reflect his feelings about nature.

On the morning of January 13, 2021, sitting in a pleasant place in a dining room, listening to the singing of many birds, we conducted a semi-structured interview lasting about an hour. Next, I will analyze the participant's trajectory, considering the affective-semiotic dimensions of his relationship with nature, and then discuss how personal and collective culture are externalized by him in the cultivation of the garden.

Childhood Memories

> Happy Childhood[4]
>
> I miss my childhood,
> barefoot, shirtless,
> and naked baths in the small dam.

I still miss baseball in the meadow and
the balconies of our little house up there.

There were the Izumi family sheds there,
Umekawa's silkworms,
Tanaka's hotel banks,
clear water well of Mrs. Momose and
comic book "manga" by Mr. Goto.

I also remember the Yuba's farms,
the Maeda's cotton plantations,
the old Yoda's tractor trailer,
the Morita's cattle breeding and
the coffee groves in the Tanabe's uphill.

I loved the Ikuta's tangerines,
the Kato's giant watermelons,
the Morita's Coração de Boi[5] mangos,
the Fujissawa's Bahia[6] oranges and
the Horie's chocolate persimmons.

At the end of July it was the Japanese party of the place,
with its Nodo Jiman[7] chants,
Undo-kai[8] and colony games,
in addition to the typical foods at Obento[9] and
open-air cinemas as the main attraction.

From everything, however, I will never forget
that last journey of moving
in Mr. Maruyama's yellow bus
bound for Mirandópolis,
never to return
to that happy childhood.

(In honor of my parents Morimi and Kiyoko Endo, Japanese immigrants, who settled in the Japanese colony of Três Alianças, in the city of Mirandópolis, São Paulo, Brazil.)

Mr. Endo was born in a rural Japanese colony in the southeastern part of Brazil. His parents emigrated from Japan before the Second World War; they settled down, married, and raised a family in Brazil. As expressed in the poem previously quoted, Endo's childhood was lived in a rural community characterized by Japanese culture, where the immigrants cultivated their small properties in a cooperative system. He attributes his current pleasure in working with plants to these earlier experiences, as reported:

My father was a farmer, a silkworm breeder, right? But, in addition to the silkworm, he cultivated things, right: rice, vegetables... We had a very humble life, but we never went hungry. Thank God right? So this side of my childhood, which I lived in the countryside, with the plants, my parents cultivating, I think that was impregnated in me.

Endo mentioned the stories told by his father about the difficulties in his first times in the new land. He highlighted the initial sufferings of coming across a "virgin forest," having to "start life braving the forest." He expressed the perception of the wildness of that environment as follows: "It's like a family thrown in the middle of the Amazon forest."

In these accounts, the contrast of affective-semiotic constructions related to nature, which I labeled "wild nature" versus "cultivated nature," is remarkable. Wilderness needed to be overcome, channeled, and transformed through work to build human community—as also analyzed by Campill, who considered the act of cultivation as a continuous effort to prevent the potential "junglification" of the own field (see Chapter 11, "Cultivation in Self and Environment"). At the same time, nature remained fundamental to the survival of the community—therefore, it could not simply be destroyed.

When asked about how he perceived the relationship with nature of his parents and other adults in the colony, Endo explained that it was more associated with "survival" and "utility," as they cultivated vegetables and fruits predominantly for food. However, he stressed that there was also a "preservation side," since Japanese immigrants used to maintain a native forest preservation area on their land. In this way, it is possible to identify a kind of complementarity and balance between the wild and cultivated dimensions of nature in that collective culture.

Further, the affective memories related to freedom, community, and happiness in the colony's natural environment were contrasted by opposite feelings, when Endo narrated the family's moving to the "big city" in search of better living conditions. This event is also addressed in the last part of the quoted poem, which expresses the feeling of loss of "that happy childhood."

Leaving and Returning to Paradise

Moving from a close Japanese community in a rural colony ("We didn't even have electricity") to the metropolis of São Paulo was defined by Endo as a "radical change" in his life. He compared, "It was almost an immigration from Japan..."

In São Paulo, at the age of 13, Endo began his professional life facing the tough relationships in a big city. When talking about these first experiences, the interviewee non-verbal expressions, such as the look and intonation of the voice, denoted deep affective impacts. He summed up, "Imagine the trauma..."

Even so, he overcame the challenges of the new environment and continued working during the day and studying at night. Then, at the beginning of higher education, at age 23, he passed a public examination and moved to another city. This time, he went alone to Brasília, the capital of Brazil, where he made a career in a bank and raised his own family.

Several years passed and he traveled to a small location in Central Brazil to treat health issues. Endo was about to retire and became enchanted by the nature and climate there. He then bought a piece of land in that place ("an open field, a pasture, there was absolutely nothing") and began to build what would be his "retirement house."

About this project, he expressed, "That retiree's dream...settling down, having a country house with that thing about gardening, fruit trees, cultivating something, and...living close to nature." And at this point, 21 years ago, began the story of the garden that inspired the present investigation.

When I asked how he started to cultivate the garden, Endo told me:

> So, it was a curious thing. I went to head one of the boards of a public bank, right, and...there was a habit for managers, every time they came to talk to the director, to bring a little gift. I have a very ethical education, right, that my parents gave me, I said, "Let's end this play." Then I made the mistake of saying the following: "The only thing I willingly accept is seedlings of exotic plants." Look, how curious, right?

The week after this, to his surprise, Endo began to receive several seedlings as a donation, coming from different places. The solution found for these unexpected gifts was to plant them in his new land, where the house was under construction.

Later the interview, when I asked what was on his mind when he said that, he replied:

> Because...Well, first because of my connection with nature, right? I *love* it...[emphasis] I think that human beings have this contact with nature, right? I do not know. It suddenly came to my head, because the gifts that came sounded like a...a kind of "bribe," in quotes, to eventually a manager, right, yeah...please me to get some return, right? This...is not part of my education, right? And then...And the seedling sounded like something to me, it's a kind of symbolic thing, so I didn't see a problem with...But it came out, like that, all of a sudden. [contained laugh]

In fact, the seedlings ended up having "symbolic" meanings, as in this example:

> And one of the seedlings, it's curious, it's... A manager from Bauru, he gave me a cherry tree from Japan. A curious thing, because a cherry tree is a snow tree, it's from the cold, right? And this gentleman got a... I think he was a botanist, he got a variety that suits that hot region of Bauru. And he gave me this seedling. So there it is, one of the seedlings is still there today, right... And last year it bloomed as beautiful as in Japan.

However, despite his dedication to cultivating the garden, as Endo said, "life turns around..." After retirement, he received an offer to go back to work in São Paulo and accepted it. The house was then transformed into an inn and, initially, was managed by his sister and brother-in-law, who had just returned from Japan. To this day, the participant maintains an office in São Paulo, but he comes to take care of the inn's garden at least twice a month.

Affective Meanings in the Garden

> But, as I have this special affection... I could even sell the inn, undo it... But that side was kept... so much... I would say sentimental with the place, right... I feel welcome here. It's not because of the financial side, but of the side like: "Hey, I planted that tree, look how beautiful it is." This thing attracts me; you know? And then, when, in this pandemic, I had more time, I said, "I'm going to dedicate it to the garden." Because at the same time I exercise, sunbathe, right, I try to give a gardening orientation... pruning at the right time, fertilizing at the right time... And... I always had that dream of transforming the inn into a place so wonderful in terms of garden. Then, at the time of the pandemic, I managed to make some beds with roses... I planted them, right? I came here in March, I planted, it's already showing results... I think, like, that's... the plant responding, I get like this... I like it, understand? Then that's it.

When telling about the meaning of gardening in his life, Endo usually refers to an intense feeling of "love for nature," which he believes became "impregnated" in him from childhood experiences. He considers the contact with nature as a necessity for human beings, as expressed in the following quote:

> So, I think it's more of a need for you to be together with the plants. I think that human beings are part of Nature as a whole, right. So if you cut that umbilical cord, let's say it like this, you don't feel good. At least I don't feel good.

Endo explained that, by cultivating the garden of the current inn, he had more opportunities to be with nature. However, even when living in urban environments, this need was still present for him. Thus, he usually keeps many plants in his office, as well as in his apartment in the city:

So, it [the Nature] was there because, because... when I bought a place to live and build a family, I always wanted a balcony... [Smiles] My priority was to have a balcony with some plants... Until today, where I have an apartment in São Paulo, there's a huge balcony with lots of plants, right... Even with vegetables. In this pandemic, I have vegetables there, organic, there on the balcony.

Among the various affective meanings that permeate the relationships of Endo with nature, it is possible to identify two different categories, which are expressed in the configuration of his garden.

The first category is related to "utility" and is expressed, for example, when he reports cultivating fruit trees whose crops can be used by the inn and its employees ("things that give benefits"). This category was evoked by the respondent when I asked him what was in his garden, which reminded him of the environment of the Japanese colony in which he lived his childhood:

> **Endo:** Ah, I remember... that my father was a silkworm breeder, right? And what fed the silkworms was the mulberry trees.
> **Researcher:** Yes...
> **E:** So, one thing that reminds me is the mulberry trees, right? I have a great memory of the mulberry trees. And the... my father also had a fruit crop, right? Fruit tree... I have memories of mandarins, tangerines, all those fruits... I have great memories. It was never lacking, there, in the countryside.
> **R:** U-hum.
> **E:** And then I tried to keep it here. You can come here in March and there will be a lot of mandarins.

The second category is related to "beauty." It emerged when I asked him what was in his garden that was different from the environment of his original colony: "So, this part of gardening is different, right. I think maybe for lack of time, he [his father] had practically no garden. And I like the garden."

Endo explained that he cultivates many flowers just because of their "beautiful visual" and that he "always appreciated the beautiful." He argues, "The beauty, I think is natural to everyone, I think, right? Some more, others less... Hard for a person to contemplate a rose and not see a beauty, right?" In line with this, the participant's hobby is taking pictures of flowers, which he shares with his friends: "Then as it blooms, I take pictures and share it with my contacts... [smiles]."

Thus, both categories, utility and beauty, flow in the search to share with others. Endo explained that his purpose is to share with the inn guests all these benefits of being close to nature:

I think that the human being, he naturally likes nature, right? But sometimes you don't have this opportunity, right? So, I think my purpose is to offer this differential where the person is comfortably installed and at the same time is in a pleasant place close to nature. That's my purpose. That's my purpose, which I would like to share with everyone.

As already mentioned, integration with nature is perceived by Endo as fundamental for human beings. Throughout our interview, he emphasized his enthusiasm in collaborating with natural development, as in this excerpt:

When you see a healthy plant, right, bearing fruit, flowering, you feel, feel good, let's put it that way. Not only to enjoy, you know, but you feel good because you helped to take care of that plant... When the opposite happens, a termite spoils, right, you don't feel good... It doesn't feel good, because you... it is part of you, of your feeling with nature.

His deep feelings regarding nature, usually labeled by him as "love," "need," and "being part of a whole," are often canalized into poems. This desire for integration is movingly expressed in this poem about his "last wish":

For my daughters[10]

When I die, I ask you
let my ashes be thrown
in the front Jabuticaba[11] tree,
a handful for the Buritis[12] and
pink flowers cherry trees.

Don't forget the azaleas,
hydrangeas, white roses,
old tree of saint john,
red calliandras and
sweet atemoyas.

The remainder to the mill stream
follow my last trip,
and finally when the lady of the night[13] cries and
the northwest wind blows, let me float
to the green hills of the plateau... goodbye.

Case Discussion

Through this brief analytical reconstruction of Endo's life trajectory, it was possible to identify how the meaningful social interactions along his childhood in a Japanese colony in Brazil promoted the construction of deep affective meanings about the relationship with nature.

Many practices, symbols, and values of the Japanese collective culture were clearly present in the participant's childhood environment. In our interview, when asked to what extent he believes that his view of nature is related to Japanese culture, he answered:

> I think it's very related, because I had the opportunity to go to Japan, and... Of course, each people has a good side, a bad side, right? It has the strengths and... But the strength of the Japanese, I think this love for nature is very strong. I went at that time of the cherry blossoms. Most beautiful thing, right? They have a habit of living with this wonderful event, right... I think it is related, yes. But I think societies are changing, right? I don't know the new generations have this same... this love for nature.

Moreover, his perception of human beings as part of nature as a whole, as well as the expression of desire and necessity of integration to this wholeness, converges with the "holistic harmonious perspective with a focus on humans as part of the world," analyzed by Eckerdal (2017, p. 288) in relation to Japanese view of nature. This deep relationship is repeatedly represented by the participant through a hypergeneralized sign—a sign with infinite borders (Valsiner, 2014, 2019): "love."

The strong attachment of people to their childhood gardens, often related to a sense of freedom and wildness, was also verified by Francis (1995). In his studies, it was found that these early experiences are currently reflected in people's ideal images of gardens, in ways that they try to recreate some of the qualities and images from early experiences of gardens in their present environments.

In the same vein, Li et al. (2010) found that gardening provides an important sense of identity to migrants, allowing them to reflect values and meanings related to their cultural heritages: "Through the physical act of gardening, people reshape a physical space, turning it into a place that reflects the efforts, desires, history and biography of gardeners" (p. 787). Through gardening, people reflect memories of childhood and other previous biographical experiences. For example, by growing seeds from the immigrants' countries of origin—and then possibly introducing and sharing the cultivated vegetables with their new neighbors. At the same time, they integrate elements of both old and new cultural landscapes, configuring a "transnational space": "These gardens lie between the here and there, the then and now, desire and realization, and physical and the imagined geographies" (p. 794).

In our case, Endo's garden is full of species that reflect his collective cultural background and childhood memories: The cherry trees symbolically associated with Japan, the mulberry trees that resemble his father's silkworm breeding, the fruit trees of various native and exotic species, whose production he shares with the guests and workers of the inn. Further, the collective culture of his original community is perceived in the affective-semiotic field of utility that mediates his relationship with nature, expressed in his concern and satisfaction in making the garden productive for food consumption.[14]

Curiously, the participant started to cultivate the garden from seedlings received during a professional activity that he carried out in an urban environment. As he reported, these gifts were related to a moral positioning in his new role, representing commitment to his original family values. They formed a bridge with his retirement dream of living close to nature, and seemingly provided consistency and continuity to his trajectory.

Besides that, Endo also innovated in relation to his family trajectory, by adding elements that are singular of his personal culture. He cultivates flowers only for their "beautiful visual," with no utilitarian purposes. The affective-semiotic field of beauty guides his meaning making on contemplation, which includes the act of taking pictures of flowers and sharing them with friends.

In line with Li et al.'s (2010) findings, it is remarkable that Endo cultivates the garden as a place for one's self, reflecting meaningful memories of his life trajectory and experiencing a sense of identity and integration with nature. As the authors beautifully expressed, "The roots of a garden spread out through time and space providing grafts between the past, present and future" (p. 789). The deep and hypergeneralized character of these experiences is mirrored in the poems composed by the participant—as was also the case with Tsuchimoto, who expressed through poetry and drawing the nostalgia that he felt on the border of his grandfather's garden (see Editorial Introduction).

On the other hand, the garden constitutes a link with others (Freeman et al., 2012; Li et al., 2010), as it mediates sharing objects and values with guests and workers. The cultivated natural environment is an expression of the hypergeneralized value of love for nature, which Endo intends to spread by creating an environment that fosters a particular Einfühlung (feeling-in) to those who enter his inn. By doing this, he feeds forward the collective culture, promoting potentially transformative experiences in the social context.

In the next section, I will expand this discussion based on a case that begins with the Einfühlung in a particular cultivated natural environment: the city of Brasília.

AFFECTIVE CANALIZATION BY AN URBAN NATURAL LANDSCAPE

Brasília is at an altitude of one thousand meters, with large plains, in the middle of the Cerrado,[15] under a transparent sky, with lots of trees and flowers, like a large and

> *spacious garden. It is a colorful, illuminated city-park, with large green areas that will always be worshiped and with ingenious urban design and architecture.*
>
> —Introduction of the exhibition *Brasília 60 Anos, Um Atelier ao Ar Livre* [Brasília 60 Years, An Outdoor Studio] (Memorial TJDF, 2020, para. 2)

Otoniel Fernandes Neto is a 57-year-old artist who was born in Fortaleza, Ceará, in northeastern Brazil, but soon moved with his family to Brasília, where he was educated and lived for four decades. Along his career, he made several artistic expeditions to different regions of Brazil, portraying their natural landscapes and people, and the collections of paintings produced were compiled into 15 books. Nowadays, he lives in the same region of central Brazil as our previous interviewee.

After this experience of distancing himself from the city, he returned to Brasília to paint its landscapes. The result was a collection of 60 works, in which he honors the city's 60 years with a painting for each year of existence. In this collection, the city's natural landscapes and elements are highlighted, with architectural constructions usually in the background.

In order to explore Otoniel's relationships with the city's natural environments, we conducted a semi-structured interview on April 14, 2021 by videoconference, which lasted about an hour and a half. Next, I will outline the main aspects that emerged regarding the meaning of nature in his life, the experience within Brasília environments, the affective-semiotic aspects behind his works and the ways to communicate them to others through art. Then, I will discuss some general implications of his trajectory for understanding the internalization and externalization dynamics in cultural processes.

Vocation for Nature

When analyzing the artistic trajectory of Otoniel Fernandes, the presence of nature in his works stands out, which portray various ecosystems in the regions of Brazil, sometimes alongside aspects of the culture of local populations. When I asked him what nature means to him, how the attraction to nature emerged in his trajectory, he reported:

> I always had this interest in the woods. I was interested. If anyone talked about going to the forest, "Let's go." And I was going to paint. Friends said, "Oh, are we going to fish in the Araguaia?" "Let's go." But I never took... What I took was: the canvas, the easel, and while the group was fishing, I was on the boat painting. And I was able to paint a lot in Araguaia, in São Francisco, in Tocantins[16] River... So, nature always awakened me a lot, I always wanted to paint nature. And then, what attracts in nature: the colors, the flowers, the natural garden... You can explore this from the plastic point of view, of putting an extremely colorful and warm foreground, and a very distant

second and third plan, in infinity, everything is grayed out...And to give this effect, right, so that the person has this desire to enter the painting, to enter, walk through the painting...And explore these resources, which are the resources that the painting technique thus offers: the effect of light, color, three-dimensionality...This ends up causing the viewer, both the most demanding viewer, or even the viewer who is not demanding, need not have studied, direct communication.

In Otoniel's narratives, the look at the plasticity of nature and the desire to provoke aesthetic pleasure in spectators are highlighted. This is also revealed in the following quote:

It's really not easy to explain, but like...I have an interest, a very great vocation really for nature, right, I really love the Caatinga, I love the Cerrado, the Atlantic Forest,[17] the sea...So, all this, in addition to the taste, even, particular, personal, is what I like to paint. I like to paint a beautiful beach, a beautiful field, a path, a beautiful waterfall...It's kind of like showing it like this: "Look, as this is beautiful, this cannot go unnoticed." This one has to be sung, this one has to be photographed, this one has to be painted, right, this one has to be...shown, awakened to your friend, to your family, to the world. Like this: "Look how beautiful it is here, this one, let's say, this Cambuí tree or this pink Ipê...[18] Look how beautiful the spaces in Brasília are..." So, I always *liked* it [emphasis]...There it is a personal thing: I always liked nature.

The interviewee's deep feelings for nature and the desire to share this experience of beauty with other people were for a long time led to remote natural landscapes, difficult to access and with few traces of human presence. However, when he decided to live far from the urban environment of Brasília, it became possible to see the city from another perspective and appreciate the beauty of the space cultivated by human beings (Figure 1.1), as he expressed:

For a long time, I was painting natural landscapes, the less human action within that landscape...the more it attracted me, I found it more interesting to paint. And Brasília showed me the opposite: That with human action, we have all the resources, like all the plastic, all the beauty there, to present...And we have a lot of nature in the spaces of Brasília, right? So, as you observed, I always preferred to highlight even a Flamboyant, a yellow Ipê, or a Cambuí, or even the waters of the lake, and put the urban landscape in the background. Even if this one, that architectural monument, in this case, the Cathedral, for example, or the National Congress, which are symbols, right, of the architecture of Brasília, but even so I always put: the lawn, the trees, the birds...Then Brasília there, inserted, in that nature. And it turned out that this exhibition of Brasília really shows a lot of green, a lot of space, like that, natural, but with man's planting, with the gardens that man has put up, because all these plants, some are from the Cerrado, others are not even from

Figure 1.1 *Domingo na Esplanada com Joões-de-Barro* (oil on canvas—50 × 150 cm).

the Cerrado, there are some that are more from the Amazon, or even from the Atlantic Forest, but the trees are here... And man planted them in abundance, right? And I tried to show it.

Einfühlung in the City Landscapes

Otoniel moved to Brasília as a child and reported that, although he has always noticed the interest aroused by various artists in the city's landscapes, he initially felt a certain nostalgia for the Northeast, were he was born, so he started working with themes related to the northeastern hinterland and coast. Nevertheless, the participant pointed out that he always had in mind that one day he would devote himself to painting Brasília, and he believes that this has occurred at a time when he is already artistically mature to portray the diversity of elements in the city's landscape. He argues that:

Because Brasília has these elements that will, like this, always attract an impressionist painter, which is my style, right, because I look for light and color. Brasília has these spaces, we can notice, they are plains, right, we have that vision of infinity and there is the presence of flowers, right, the natural gardens, which man has done, right... Brasília has so much flowering: the yellow Ipês, then the pink Ipês, when the rains start the Flamboyants, the Flamboyants are already exotic species, right... Then come the Cambuís, those yellow tufts... Brasília is always showing a lot of color, right? So I think Brasília is a complete inspiration for a painter, I think for all artists. Brasília is really a very inspiring city, it has this unique architecture, an ingenious planning, by Lúcio Costa, and this also ingenious architecture by Niemeyer, and now man can fill Brasília, with all its spaces, with so many trees, so many gardens, these trees are blooming, so many birds... And we have these wonderful places in Brasília. Mainly in this central area, this area that is protected, right.

The participant reflects that, even if the beauty of the city's landscapes is not at the center of people's attention on a daily basis, it ends up being noticed, mainly by the exuberance of nature that stands out in certain seasons (Figure 1.2):

> It's true that in the hustle and bustle of everyday life, in that coming and going, we end up not realizing it. But placing the easel in the spaces of Brasília, on the lawns, in front of the architectural monuments... and any other spaces in Brasília, then you start to notice better. And all this with lots of light and lots of color, right. Brasília really is very inspiring. And sometimes, at first sight, an unnoticed look, right, we can pass through Brasília and not even feel it. But who is indifferent when it's that intense flowering of Flamboyants? A tree that isn't even Brazilian, right? Or in the intense flowering of yellow Ipê trees? So, there's no way, I think there's no way to remain indifferent.

In his particular case, Otoniel explained that he was able to see Brasilia better after leaving it. Returning to the city with the goal of painting it, he spent a year doing his work in the field, placing his easel among the landscapes. In this way, he managed to look more carefully at the city, with a specific intention. When I asked him about what he considered to have changed in his view of Brasília, he replied:

> Maybe because I looked for it. When I left Brasília and when I wanted to dedicate myself to Brasília, maybe because I was looking for just this beautiful side... And I really found it in abundance, right? So, it was a year of painting, right, of painting in the field. So, we can follow the seasons, the flowering, the

Figure 1.2 *No Ipê da Rodoviária* (oil on canvas—60 × 120 cm).

> extremely green lawn, then the dry lawn, the extremely transparent sky, then the sky itself with fog and traces of smoke and everything else... So, like that, I think that the distance made me see Brasilia better, but I also searched, my search was already sort of directed, right? My look at Brasília was really with this tendency... to really look for the *beautiful* side [emphasis]. The picturesque side and the challenging side for a landscape painter.

Thus, as he was no longer positioned as one of the city's inhabitants, oriented in that environment by the goals of everyday life, Otoniel no longer perceived the beauty of natural landscapes only in an episodic and peripheral way—although relevant to configure a way of feeling-in that environment. By taking a certain distance and then returning to the city with a specific objective, he began to perceive Brasília's environment as a wholeness, through a filter that constitutes the purpose of his work: The search for beauty.

Beauty as Purpose

> My purpose in painting is to show the *beautiful* [emphasis] of nature. Because, for me, beauty *matters* [emphasis]. The beauty, I think it's a purpose... Unique, it will never be. But, it is a purpose, thus, *crucial* [emphasis], fundamental of art. Art without beauty, it is already losing a little in front of the others. I could... Just to give you an example, like, Rembrandt himself painted the ox, there, butchered, anatomy lessons, right... It is... But he managed to print beauty, even in a scene, like, a lot specific as an anatomy lesson, right... When you see a very strong painting by Iberê Camargo, but he manages, in some denouncements, to be beautiful, to have a fantastic plastic, colorful, like that, masterful... So, by more than his art wants to make an impact, wants to denounce, or even to attack, but there's a beauty there... Thus, the beauty, this feeling, this esthesia, that's what I think is fundamental for any art.

As has been shown throughout the quotes of Otoniel's interview, the experience of beauty constitutes a central aspect of his being-into-the-world, configuring a hypergeneralized affective-semiotic field, which filters his perception of reality and guides the purpose of his work as an artist (Figure 1.3). His relationship with nature is also strongly driven by this hypergeneralized value, as expressed below:

> But I always looked: I'm going to paint the river, I'm going to look for the most beautiful angle of the river. I'm going to paint a beach scene, I'm going to put the best colors... This the masters have already taught us: Everything is there for us to do. Gauguin himself, the great colorist, the great impressionist who later went to symbolism, said, "When you paint a coconut tree, when you paint nature, choose the best colors you have in your palette." If you're going

Figure 1.3 *O Flamboyant do TJDFT* (oil on canvas—70 × 130 cm).

to put land, you have to do your best, you have to do that thing with exuberance, you can't spare efforts to try to imprint the beauty that the land has.

When asked about what is the function of beauty in human life, for instance, in an urban environment, the participant answered:

Wow... that's wonderful: what is the function of beauty, right? It's... I think the same... Beauty, we need it every day, I think it's a human need, for beauty.... It's like breathing pure air, drinking pure, crystalline water, having a good bath in the river, a bath in the sea... The beauty, in my opinion, is very necessary for our soul, for our spirit. If we don't have beauty with us, life will be very sterile and very suffocating. We have to have. The function of beauty is a vital function, I think, of balance, right, spiritual... Without beauty, we are lost. Without good music, without painting or a good film, without good literature... I think this need for beauty is very important.

Then, after considering that there are different perceptions of what is beautiful among people, Otoniel argued that some things are unanimous. And these universals lead, notably, to nature:

How are you going to see a beautiful flower, a beautiful tree, a beautiful jaguar, I don't know, a beautiful... rattlesnake... that will catch your attention, right? A beautiful sunset... Right? Imagine if everything was dark... All right, a clear, starry night, a rising moon... And I put it, I also looked for those obvious things and commonplaces, really. I wanted to catch the rising moon, the setting moon, the setting sun, the rising sun... I really wanted to explore in this way what is already kind of a convention... People are moved by a beautiful sunset, or by a dawn. Certain things... you can't escape. How are you going to be indifferent when you see a yellow Ipê contrasted with an indigo blue? That gives you a pleasure, like, aesthetic, a visual pleasure, right... And we need it. Beauty is part of the food the soul needs. The beautiful, for me, is a nutrient for the soul, thus, very important. It's like water for the soul: Without beauty, then... I think it gets complicated.

It is interesting to note that Otoniel not only intimately experiences his deep feelings related to nature, which flow into experiences of beauty and transcendence, but also feels the need to communicate them to others, for example, through his paintings. Next, we will focus on how this externalization process takes place.

Affective Communication

Otoniel works with oil painting technique. Thus, due to the time required for drying the paint on the various planes of painting, he never finishes his work in the field. Generally, he takes a day painting in the field, more around 2 days painting in his studio to finish the work. Sometimes he will complete a painting years after starting it. He explains how this process takes place:

I go back to those landscapes... and that makes me come back, like this. Because when I'm painting that landscape that I was 2, 3 years ago, when I return to that canvas, I have the same sensations, right, that I had when I was with the easel there, in the heat, in the shade of a tree, or after diving in the water, so... this experience with nature, I think, for me, is crucial and... I don't know, like, at least people say: "Oh, I like it, because I feel the emotion when I see...."—at least some people tell me, right—"When I appreciate a painting by you..." I attribute it to the experience, even, right, of that landscape, that I was there, and we end up transmitting this, whether by the color, the heat, the light that we try to print, right, by the elements that also fascinated us on that crossing... Because I have the freedom, too, to put one or another flower, one or another Canela-de-Ema[19] wherever I want, or a bird and such, right? Since it is from the region... So, people end up, at least what we hear, that people like it, right? They feel good, enjoying a landscape.

As described in this last quotation, through an exercise of reconstructive imagination (Zittoun et al., 2013), the artist remembers in his studio the sensations he experienced in nature, and tries to channel these affective impressions into painting. In so doing, he represents the original landscape in a transformed way, using different resources to promote a corresponding emotional impact on viewers. He can even add some element that wasn't really in place, but *could* be, in order to maximize the viewer's imaginary immersion in that particular landscape. With the aim to trigger aesthetic pleasure, he also makes use of various painting techniques, as he exemplified in the following quote:

> My desire is always to provoke *beauty* [emphasis]. So, bring about that aesthetic pleasure. And in this we have to be careful. For example: like this picture that is there, back here [reproduced in Figure 1.4], which is even a landscape of Brasília, right, we know that we also have to be careful so that it doesn't get, kind of, exaggerated, so... So it doesn't get too much, let's say, sugary... So, it's all a matter of dosing... In my case, I look for other resources so that the person doesn't feel, like, get a shock, like this, in pink, right... because of the flowering Ipê trees. But then I'll show the viewer that there are other things out there: the luminosity itself, the chiaroscuro of the rose, to show that this rose in the foreground is much more intense than that rose in the line of horizon, right... Because, I'm talking here now about plan conventions in painting... I put precisely in the top third, which would be the convention of the third plane, I show that the tree is here in the foreground, and if I even throw a little bird in front of all this, where is it that I'll be able to illude the viewer and give this feeling of three-dimensionality... Both in perspective, because of the size, proportions, and the intensity of light and color.

Therefore, the painting does not correspond to a mere reproduction of reality, but to its intentional recreation from the artist's perspective, with

Figure 1.4   *Atelier ao Ar Livre na Esplanada* (oil on canvas—100 × 120 cm).

a view to provoking certain emotional reactions in the spectator. By doing this through specific techniques, Otoniel evokes the feelings, memories, and fantasies of those who appreciate his work. As he reported:

> But how many times do people get emotional, too: "Oh, I've been in this waterfall," "Oh, I saw this landscape," "Wow, that's cool, you painted the sunset, I'm remembering when I went there at sunset…" So, like, there's this complicity later…And this, when…If we consider, too…Recently, I sent a painting, like, a photo of a painting to a friend, he said, "Wow, my homeland, I was moved…" and such, from the backlands of Bahia. So, like this, this complicity remains, too. Many people want to see, or review what they already know…Or, to know for the first time, right, to be able to make painting or photography a way, too, to travel, to a new place, and everything else.

In this way, the painter builds a channel of communication with the viewer, enabling an effective encounter around meaningful experiences that Otoniel called "complicity." In the following quote, he addressed the communication power of art that goes beyond words in their literal sense:

> The arts, in general, end up transmitting and communicating a little more than the purely spoken word, right? A word said in a poetic tone, I think it has a lot more capacity, like in music…In cinema, photography, in all the arts…In sculpture, right? So, in fact, many people arrive, look at the painting, some don't say anything, some get really emotional…Many times, many times, people have already come with their eyes, like, teasing, to talk about a painting they appreciated, right? Because then people travel, right, they travel…They remember childhood things and everything else…Art, in fact, has this wonderful power, right, of communication and of really touching feelings, in joy, in memories and everything else.

Case Discussion

Brasília is a city ornamented with nature. Its original urban design includes many landscaped areas and parks, in addition to architectural monuments, and currently constitutes a collective cultural heritage. It's a human-made Umwelt that presents nature through a specific lens. This environment frames city dwellers daily experiences, promoting a particular Einfühlung, through affective-semiotic suggestions implicitly encoded in landscape configurations (Valsiner, 2014, 2019). Even if generally peripheral in the perceptual system of passersby, the city's natural ornamentation creates an "unavoidable" reality, catalyzing specific feelings and worldviews. As stated by Valsiner (2019), "Human history is that of parallel development of actions upon the environments and projecting into the environments meanings that are assumed to act upon the persons themselves" (p. 97).

Otoniel's case presents a path of immersion in such an environment that constitutes a collective cultural artifact. From the position of a city dweller experiencing its landscapes episodically, in search of adventures and beautiful nature in remote places, he became a more distant observer who returned with the objective of a "disinterested" contemplation, guided by the search for beauty. As evidenced in various interview quotes along this section, beauty constitutes a hypergeneralized value (Valsiner, 2012, 2014) that is central for the participant, mediating his relationships with nature and guiding the purpose of his work as an artist.

As Otoniel reported, for painting the collection in honor of the city's 60 years, he came to Brasília to experience and show "its beautiful side," and it was not difficult for him:

> Finding beauty in Brasília didn't give me any trouble. It was all very natural: because any monument I wanted to paint, and it was really in the background, I had a tree in front of it that gave me shade and a studio. And that also gave me all the visual resources, all the color I needed. So, I had no difficulty, like, to propose, to present a beautiful Brasília. It showed up naturally.

Therefore, from this frame of experience, the artist was impacted by the urban landscapes with its varied planes, shapes, textures, colors and lights throughout the seasons, which promoted an Einfühlung of particular affective-semiotic kind, represented by the hypergeneralized sign—a sign with infinite borders (Valsiner, 2014, 2019)—of beauty.

Although landscape paintings appear at first sight to be iconic signs, they actually constitute signs of a symbolic type, as they are constructed by the artist from his own Einfühlung in real or imagined landscapes, with the deliberate intention of causing an affective impact on the viewer. As observed by Valsiner (2019), "The painting is different from the objects depicted on it—it guides us to the formation of an affective *Gestalt* within our psyche" (p. 103).

Thus, from his own internalization of Brasília's landscapes, based on the perspective made possible by his unique life trajectory and personal culture, Otoniel sought to translate these deep feelings and meanings through the language of painting. As described in this section, he made use of various semiotic resources in the composition of his canvases, with a view to achieving an effective, non-verbal communication with the viewer.

> By painting a landscape an artist is creating a self-portrait—without the iconic depiction of the self. It is an indexical self-portrait that begins to communicate—without the need of words—with the equally deep and nonverbal feelings into the world, on the side of the viewers. (Valsiner, 2019, p. 105)

Figure 1.5 Me, my mother Marlene, and my brother Leo at the exhibition Brasília, Um Atelier ao Ar Livre (2022).

By externalizing his personal experiences through paintings, Otoniel feeds back into collective culture, creating new cultural artifacts that will potentially mediate people's perception of the urban landscapes. By triggering aesthetic experiences related to nature cultivated in the city—as through the exhibition *Brasília, Um Atelier ao Ar Livre* [Brasília, An Outdoor Studio][20] (see Figure 1.5)—he guides affective generalization processes by others, promoting transformations in the social context, in particular, with regard to the development of meanings and values.

CONCLUDING REMARKS

In this chapter, I have sought to address the affective and semiotic dimensions that mediate people's relationships with nature, especially with regard to human-cultivated environments such as private and public gardens, based on two case studies.

In analyzing the experiences of our research subjects, the centrality of affects in the interactions of human beings with the environment was highlighted, whose initial sensory impacts are immediately loaded with meanings (Innis, 2016; Valsiner, 2012, 2014, 2019). In both cases, the relationships with nature were based primarily on physical interaction with the natural elements in their material properties, and were gradually intertwined by affective-semiotic processes of increasing generalization, reaching hypergeneralized experiences related, for instance, to love, integration, beauty, and transcendence.

It was remarkable how the semiotic function acts in the mediation of human relationships with natural environments. Thus, there is no mutually exclusive opposition between nature and culture, but a co-agentic interaction (Glăveanu, 2015; Wortmeyer, 2022), which is inevitably overlapped by human interpretation. Even though we are dealing with wild nature, the human condition gives rise to the saturation of this relationship by culturally based affects and meanings that reach beyond the here-and-now, acquiring a symbolic character.

As emphasized by Li et al. (2010), "Gardens are culturally loaded spaces that are textured by human movement and action, identities and relationships" (p. 794). Throughout this chapter, it was evidenced that human beings project into their relationships with nature the meanings and values they have internalized throughout their developmental trajectories, which are nurtured by the collective culture of specific social contexts. At the same time, each person actively reconstructs these experiences, developing a unique perspective on the world and building a personal culture. In this way, human beings also promote innovations and changes in the collective culture, which will affect them later, in a feedback process that involves a continuous dynamic of internalization and externalization (Valsiner, 2012, 2014).

Evidently, the present study constitutes an initial exploratory effort on the subject. The investigation in relation to the affective-semiotic processes and values that guide the being-into-the-world of our research participants could be deepened and expanded in a more comprehensive research design. On the other hand, the multiple possibilities of constructing affects and meanings in experiences linked to nature constitute an open avenue for exploration from the perspective of cultural psychology of semiotic dynamics. It is a precious opportunity to better understand how our psychological lives are affected by our surrounding worlds, while significantly shaping our Umwelten (Valsiner, 2019).

Still, I believe this work could shed light on how natural environments impact people's intuitive perceptions, framing their experiences in the world and triggering complex affective-semiotic processes that cannot be fully translated into words. Due to their hypergeneralized character, as illustrated in this study, these deep experiences often find a more appropriate channel of expression in the symbolic languages of the arts.

NOTES

1. *Umwelt* ("environment," in literal translation from German) is a concept developed by Alex von Uexküll (1829–1891) to describe the "holistic subpart of the environment that carries meaning in the context of the organism's relating with it" (Valsiner, 2019, p. 131).
2. *Einfühlung* ("feeling-in") is the German expression (first introduced by Robert Vischer) used by Theodor Lipps (1851–1914) to refer to the psychological attachment to certain experiences, places, people, or material objects, which often mobilize meanings beyond words, evoking generalized affective tones (Valsiner, 2019).
3. The two interviewees mentioned in this chapter gave their informed consent to participate in the project, with the option of having their names and personal data disclosed or not. I decided to offer them this option, rather than adopting a standard procedure of anonymity, as I felt that we were not dealing with particularly sensitive information and identification could be a good way for valuing and recognizing their trajectories. In the end, both happily agreed to be identified in the text.
4. Original text in Portuguese: "Infância Feliz–Tenho saudades da minha infância,/dos pés descalços, sem camisa,/e banhos pelados na represinha./Sinto falta ainda do beisebol no pasto e/das varandas de nossa casinha lá no alto./Ali tinha os galpões da família Izumi,/bichos da seda dos Umekawa,/bancos de hotel dos Tanaka,/poço de águas límpidas da Sra. Momose e/revista em quadrinhos "manga" do Sr. Goto./Lembro-me também das granjas dos Yuba,/das plantações de algodão dos Maeda,/do velho trator com carreta dos Yoda,/da criação de gado dos Morita e/dos cafezais no subidão dos Tanabe./Adorava as mexericas dos Ikuta,/melancias gigantes dos Kato,/mangas coração de boi dos Morita,/laranjas bahia dos Fujissawa e/caquis chocolate dos Horie./No final de julho era a festa japonesa do lugar,/com seus cantos de "nodô-di-mam",/Undo-kai e brincadeiras da colônia,/além das comidas típicas no "obentô" e/cinemas ao ar livre como atração principal./De tudo, contudo, jamais esquecerei/aquela última viagem de mudança/na jardineira amarela do Sr. Maruyama/com destino a Mirandópolis,/para nunca mais retornar/àquela infância feliz."
5. Coração de Boi ("literally, oxheart") is the name of a species of mango cultivated in Brazil.
6. Bahia orange is a well-known variety of orange produced in Brazil.
7. Nodo Jiman is a popular Japanese variety show in which ordinary people compete with each other to see who can do the best Karaoke.
8. Undokai is a sports day in Japan.
9. Obento is a single-portion takeout or home-packed meal common in Japanese cuisine.
10. Original in Portuguese: "Para minhas filhas–Quando eu morrer, peço-lhes/que joguem minhas cinzas/na jabuticabeira da frente,/um punhado para os buritis e/cerejeiras flores rosa./Não se esqueçam das azaléias,/hortências, rosas brancas,/velha árvore de são joão,/caliandras vermelhas e/doces

atemóias do conde./O restante para o córrego do moinho/acompanhar a minha última viagem,/e, finalmente, quando a dama da noite chorar e/o vento noroeste soprar, deixem-me flutuar/até os montes verdes da chapada.... adeus."
11. Jabuticaba is a Brazilian fruit.
12. Buriti is the name of a palm tree typical of the Brazilian Cerrado.
13. "Lady of the night" is a night blooming Brazilian flower, which is called *Dama da Noite* in Portuguese.
14. Such meaning making processes related to utilitarian purposes and productivity were also verified in previous studies, as an important source of satisfaction to gardeners (Freeman et al., 2012; Li et al., 2010).
15. The Cerrado, also known as the Brazilian savanna, is the second largest biome in Brazil and South America.
16. Araguaia, São Francisco, and Tocantins are names of Brazilian rivers.
17. Caatinga, Cerrado, and Atlantic Forest are Brazilian ecosystems.
18. Cambuí and Ipê are tree species from Brazil.
19. Canela-de-Ema is a flower typical of the Brazilian Cerrado.
20. Due to the restrictions of the COVID-19 pandemic, the first in-person exhibition of the collection by Otoniel Fernandes mentioned in this chapter was *Brasília: Um Atelier ao Ar Livre* [Brasília, An Outdoor Studio], which took place in the Federal District Legislative Chamber, Brasília-DF, from April to June 2022.

REFERENCES

Branco, A. U., & Valsiner, J. (1997). Changing methodologies: A co-constructivist study of goal orientations in social interactions. *Psychology and Developing Societies*, *9*(1), 35–64.

Branco, A. U., & Valsiner, J. (1999). A questão do método na psicologia do desenvolvimento: Uma perspectiva co-construtivista [The question of method in developmental psychology: A co-constructivist perspective]. In M. G. T. Paz & A. Tamayo (Eds.), *Escola, saúde e trabalho: Estudos psicológicos* [School, health and work: Psychological studies] (pp. 23–39). Editora da Universidade de Brasília.

Charmaz, K. (2009). *A construção da teoria fundamentada: Guia prático para análise qualitativa* [The construction of grounded theory: Practical guide for qualitative analysis]. Artmed.

Eckerdal, R. M. (2017). Feeling oneself into nature: Reflections on picking flowers in Japan and Denmark. In B. Wagoner, I. Brescó de Luna, & S. H. Awad (Eds.), *The psychology of imagination: History, theory, and new research horizons* (pp. 283–293). Information Age Publishing.

Francis, M. (1995). Childhood's garden: Memory and meaning of gardens. *Children's Environments*, *12*(2), 1–16.

Freeman, C., Dickinson, K. J. M., Porter, S., & van Heezik, Y. (2012). "My garden is an expression of me": Exploring householders' relationships with their gardens. *Journal of Environmental Psychology, 32*(2012), 135–143.

Glăveanu, V. P. (2015). From individual agency to co-agency. In C. W. Gruber, M. G. Clark, S. H. Klempe, & J. Valsiner (Eds.), *Constraints of agency: Explorations of theory in everyday life* (pp. 245–265). Springer.

Innis, R. (2016). Affective semiosis: Philosophical links to cultural psychology. In J. Valsiner, G. Marsico, N. Chaudhary, T. Sato, & V. Dazzani (Eds.), *Psychology as the science of human being: The Yokohama Manifesto* (pp. 87–104). Springer.

Jovchelovitch, S., & Bauer, M. (2002). Entrevista narrativa [Narrative interview]. In M. Bauer & G. Gaskell (Eds.), *Pesquisa qualitativa com texto, imagem e som: Um manual prático* [Qualitative research with text, images and sounds: A practical manual] (pp. 90–113). Vozes.

Li, W. W., Hodgetts, D., & Ho, E. (2010). Gardens, transitions and identity reconstruction among older Chinese immigrants to New Zealand. *Journal of Health Psychology, 15*(5), 786–796.

Memorial TJDFT. (2020). *Otoniel Fernandes: Brasília 60 anos, um atelier ao ar livre* [Otoniel Fernandes: Brasília 60 years, an outdoor studio]. https://www.exposicoesvirtuais-tjdft.online/bras%C3%ADlia-60-anos-um-atelier-ao-ar-l

Schütze, F. (2011). Pesquisa biográfica e entrevista narrativa [Biographical research and narrative interview]. In W. Weller & N. Pfaff (Eds.), *Metodologias da pesquisa qualitativa em educação: Teoria e prática* [Qualitative research methodologies in education: Theory and practice] (2nd ed., pp. 210–222). Vozes.

Valsiner, J. (2012). *Fundamentos da psicologia cultural: Mundos da mente, mundos da vida* [Fundamentals of cultural psychology: Worlds of the mind, worlds of life]. Artmed.

Valsiner, J. (2014). *An invitation to cultural psychology.* SAGE Publications.

Valsiner, J. (2019). *Ornamented lives.* Information Age Publishing.

Vygotsky, L. S. (1988). *Thought and language.* Cambridge University Press.

Vygotsky, L. S. (2001). *A construção do pensamento e da linguagem* [The construction of thought and language]. Martins Fontes.

Wortmeyer, D. S. (2015). *Um mestre jardineiro* [A master gardener]. O Vaga-Lume. https://www.graal.org.br/blogs/o-vaga-lume/um-mestre-jardineiro

Wortmeyer, D. S. (2017). *O desenvolvimento de valores morais na socialização militar: Entre a liberdade subjetiva e o controle institucional* [The development of moral values in military socialization: Between subjective freedom and institutional control] (Unpublished doctoral dissertation). Universidade de Brasília.

Wortmeyer, D. S. (2022). *Deep loyalties: Values in military lives.* Information Age Publishing.

Wortmeyer, D. S., & Branco, A. U. (2016). Institutional guidance of affective bonding: Moral values development in Brazilian military education. *Integrative Psychological and Behavioral Science, 50*(3), 447–469.

Zittoun, T., & Valsiner, J. (2016). Imagining the past and remembering the future: How the unreal defines the real. In T. Sato, N. Mori, & J. Valsiner (Eds.),

Making of the future: The trajectory equifinality approach in cultural psychology (pp. 3–19). Information Age Publishing.

Zittoun, T., Valsiner, J., Vedeler, D., Salgado, J., Gonçalves, M., & Ferring, D. (2013). *Human development in the life course: Melodies of living*. Cambridge University Press.

Botanic Garden in Curitiba-PR-Brazil
Source: Author (2014)

CHAPTER 2

GARDEN AS A SIGN OF HAPPINESS

Ramon Cerqueira Gomes
Federal Institute Bahian of Education, Science, and Technology

PREAMBLE

Gardens are a cultural artifact full of signs shared among people that somehow run through their everyday lives, even though they have never actually stepped in one. In architectural projects, in the available corners of earth or in our backyards, in a potted plant, in a dream of an enchanting place or even in the spiritual destiny of benefactors in so many religions, in the lyrics of songs and in poets' verses the image of the garden transcends all immediate space-time, by pointing to the potentially saving place of our earthly pains. There, in the garden, concrete or of our dreams, we are/we will be fuller and more joyful.

In this chapter, we'll discuss the notion of gardens as a sign used by the people around the world to find a better place/state of living his/her life. It is not our objective to fulfill every possibility of semiotic use of gardens. In spite of it, here we'll have the chance of reflect about by: (a) identifying some scientific conclusions about gardens and its impacts on well-being in the people; (b) understanding the relationship between the semiotic cultural psychology and the garden as a sign; and (c) elaborating a view of gardens as a sign shared among human beings related to happiness.

GARDEN AS A NATURAL/SYMBOLIC RESOURCE FOR PROMOTING WELL-BEING

Many people search to find a house with some kind of garden, visiting new places where they are built, or to see paradise gardens in other spiritual dimensions in so many religions. Even historic places in remote times point out to the interesting and cultural power of gardens in many places or still in stories not very known, such as the Hanging Gardens of Babylon, but are so widespread in our imaginations. We find these examples today in several important touristic gardens around the world with these examples pointed out by Marubayashi (2020): Ornamental Garden of the Bahai Temple in Haifa, Israel; Versailles Garden in France; Keukenhof Park—Lisse in Holland; Koishikawa Korakuen Gardens in Japan; Schloss Mirabell in Áustria; and Botanic Garden in Rio de Janeiro, Brazil.[1]

The relationship between gardens and health is well-known, and *salutogenic landscapes* are places with certain combinations of characteristics which support our general physical and mental health and well-being and can include a range of natural and man-made places. Different frameworks can be used in evaluating health supportive environments (Maikov, 2016). Several of the concepts related to garden environments in health care settings are relevant to the notions of salutogenesis and pathogenesis (Bengtsson & Grahn, 2014).

While the salutogenic orientation has been proposed as providing a direction and focus to concern with the entire spectrum of health ease/disease and on salutary rather than risk factors, and always to see the entire person (or collective) rather than the disease (or disease rate), the pathogenic orientation which suffuses all western medical thinking conceives the human organism as a splendid system, a marvel of mechanical organization, which is now and then attacked by a pathogen and damaged, acutely or chronically or fatally without considering multiple causation theory and the biopsychosocial model (Antonovsky, 1996).

Cooper Marcus and Barnes (1999, as cited by Bengtsson & Grahn, 2014) outlined three aspects of the healing process that help clarify how garden environments can have therapeutic benefits: (a) relief from physical symptoms, (b) stress reduction, and (c) improvement of the overall sense of well-being. These three aspects correspond to pathogenic as well as salutogenic strategies. As can be seen, according to these authors, gardens are places in which people can experience some kind of subjective changes to prevent or treat diseases and be more healthy.

As well as using existing or planning new landscapes such as forests and parks for health-promoting possibilities, there are also specially designed types of spaces. Healing gardens are designed to offer a specific health supporting function. The healing garden concept became popular in both research and practice following the 1995 publication, *Gardens in Healthcare Facilities,* by Clare Cooper Marcus and Marni Barnes, and it refers to places where people obtain generally passive experiences of (cultivated) nature (Maikov, 2016).

Another important notion related in studies with gardens and human beings is "restoration," or "restorativeness" which refers to the personal psychological restoration following demands to one's attention and faculties. An environment is restorative if it enables psychological or physiological restoration from depleted attention and faculties. The perception of green space has a positive effect on perceived stress and psychological restoration (Hipp et al., 2016).

Nearby access to natural landscapes or a garden can enhance people's ability to deal with stress and thus potentially improve health outcomes even if these people are spending long stressing hours in a hospital. In past centuries, green nature, sunlight, and fresh air were seen as essential components of healing in settings ranging from medieval monastic infirmaries; to large municipal hospitals of the 17th and 18th centuries; to pavilion-style hospitals, asylums, and sanitoria of the 19th and early 20th centuries inspired by the work of public health reformer, Florence Nightingale (Marcus, 2007).

In their study, Cervinkaa, Schwaba, Schönbauera, Hämmerlec, Pirgiea, and Sudkampa (2016) aimed at exploring perceived restorativeness of private gardens and its predictors. Altogether, 856 respondents rated the perceived restorativeness of private gardens, attached outdoor green spaces, and living rooms with green elements. Private gardens appeared the most restorative private green space compared to attached outdoor green spaces and green indoor spaces. To make full use of a garden's restorative potential, it seems therefore indispensable to develop and maintain an intensive positive relationship with the garden.

Hipp et al. (2016) developed the following questions in their study: "Can green campus spaces provide restorative potential to university students?" and "Do students perceive the greenness and restorative benefits?" They evaluated students at three universities (convenience sample) and were surveyed with items on perceived greenness of campus, perceived restorativeness of campus, and the World Health Organization Quality-of-Life Scale. The findings in this study indicated that availability of green campus space enhances the quality of life by enhancing the perception of greenness and impacting opportunities for restoration. Hence, this study made a specific conceptual contribution by considering the university campus environment as a health resource for its students.

In another example, McAllister et al. (2017) examined the effects of virtual contact with nature on positive and negative affect, and investigated the psychological process of perceived restorativeness as a mediator of this relationship. Participants were adults randomly allocated to one of the three experimental conditions experienced through video presentations: (a) "wild" nature, (b) "urban" nature, and (c) non-nature control. The results of the present study indicated that exposure to virtual nature for 2–3 minutes can produce significant improvements in affective states. Their results add further evidence to the known beneficial effects of nature experience in improving mood. This finding has practical implications, as viewing short virtual nature videos could provide easily accessible and low-cost intervention to improve mood and mental health.

In Japan, "Shinrin-yoku," which can be defined as "taking in the forest atmosphere or forest bathing" is currently receiving increasing attention for its capacity to provide relaxation and reduce stress. Shinrin-yoku is considered to be one of the most accessible ways to get in touch with the natural world and to lower excessive stress to levels that are commensurate with what our bodies are "expected" to cope with. In western societies, this approach has been incorporated into the lives of individuals since the 19th century. The best known example of this may be Kneipp therapy in Germany (Tsunetsugu et al., 2010).

Although we can find several researches where people in direct contact with natural spaces like gardens show a positive change of mood and well-being, it is interesting to realize the power of the garden as a sign in our minds. Several therapeutic methods use, for example, thinking in an environment, such as a garden, as a strategic way of improving quality of life of people. Even if people are only thinking about gardens they can be feeling better. It points out the role of gardens in people's minds that change their subjective states. So, it is interesting to analyze the gardens as signs that affect many people's minds.

THE SEMIOTIC EXPERIENCE OF GARDENS

Self is culturally guided and personally enacted. Whereas culture provides the semiotic resources to model the experience and the expression of the "Self," that is the term commonly used to indicate the uniqueness of my psychological experience and my agentic role in the world (Marsico et al., 2019).

A sign is "that which, in a certain aspect or way, represents something to someone [...] in order for something to be a sign, that something must 'represent', as we say, something, called its object" (Peirce, 1977, p. 46–47).

For example, suppose two friends are standing in a square and looking at the horizon; the first says he is seeing a hurricane forming, the second says he is seeing only a localized fire beginning. In this case, although the concrete object is unknown to us, both friends used different signs to represent it, which, in turn, necessarily defines for each one the distinction of the personal use of the sign, as well as its object referent.

Every experience happens within ourselves by means of signs and generalization happens at every moment in our sign use. Its results—categories or abstract depictions—make psychologically distanced reflection upon the world possible. Such reflection transcends irreversible time, creating sign fields that can be considered to be beyond the generalized categories—hyper generalized sign fields. These fields "capture" the whole of the person—in devotion, or in fear, or in passion (Valsiner, 2014).

The person re-positions himself/herself by way of relating a present experience to that of the past—and the past is brought into the present. It results in the establishment of a hyper-generalized sign. The process of signification—meaning-making—works in the direction of generalization. We need signs—indexes, icons, and words—to "break away" from the concrete realities of our lives, so as to return to these in a different, affectively flavored context. The collective action of such a breakaway leads to the emergence of a semiosphere around our bodies-in-action in the here and-now contexts (Valsiner, 2014).

A sign can be related to its object by resembling, or sharing a defining quality or pattern of relations with its object. For example, images of all sort, diagrams, and, on Peirce's reckoning, metaphors, with their pictorial envelops, even mathematical equations, belong to a class that Peirce calls "icons," exemplifying and realizing the semiotic modality of iconicity (Innis, 2016).

Meanwhile, ways of behaving connected with occupations, blushes, scars, all physical traces, personal pronouns, and so forth are instances of "indices," exemplifying the semiotic modality of indexicality. And, as the last ultimate category, a sign can be related to its object purely by convention or effective mutual agreement, with no reliance upon resemblance or real connection. Such are "symbols," the principal semiotic modality operative in human language, which, however, has incorporated the two other semiotic modalities into its own condition of symbol. Iconicity and indexicality, however, are not foreign to the symbolic dimension of meaning-making (Innis, 2016). For example: Imagine a garden has a big cloud-shaped pruned tree with white leaves. Below, it has a plate with this expression: "Come on heaven." In this situation, it has a icon (cloud-shaped), an index (white leaves as natural clouds in sunny days), and a symbol (Come on Heaven—high abstraction). The last can exist here because icon and index participate on symbol construction.

Self can be conceived in terms of a dynamic multiplicity of relatively autonomous "I" positions in an imaginary landscape. In its most concise form this conception can be formulated as follows. The I has the possibility to move, as in a space, from one position to the other in accordance with changes in situation and time. The I fluctuates among different and even opposed positions. The I has the capacity to imaginatively endow each position with a voice so that dialogical relations between positions can be established (Hermans et al., 1992, p. 28). These voices/positionings are constituted by different signs that allow us to somehow express our experiences in life. For instance, "I am feeling good"/"It is awful"/"I feel scared of it"/"Here, I am happy." Every report brings signs that are affecting a person's mind and his/her subjective state.

These positionings, therefore, are clusters of self-related meanings that converge into specific "positionings" within the system, and they are supported by hyper generalized affective-semiotic field-like signs highly invested with affect. These signs or affective-semiotic fields (ASF), on their turn, play a significant role in mobilizing the dialogical self-system (DSS) throughout the individual's life. Such fields (ASF) are also characterized by a continuous tension and ambiguity (Branco, 2016).

For instance, a religious person can say, "It is hard to explain how good I feel when I imagine myself in a paradise as a very beautiful garden in my future spiritual life." This affective-semiotic field is a value and has the power to guide several attitudes and actions forward to ensure the most of possible the person will be there. For that, this person will follow rules and repress wishes so that he/she can follow seeing him/her in the future there, in a paradise garden. This person will produce an ambiguous field of meanings—"garden versus no-garden"—and another field as "I can go there versus No, I can go there."

The crucial feature of sign mediation of the human psyche is not merely presentation of the world via signs (that stand for something else), which is the prevailing static view present in semiotics, but in the dynamic movement from one structure of signs to another. Affective tensions emerge—and find their resolution—in such a movement. Some of these transformations of signs are rapid and directed towards the complete takeover of the person's psyche. I call such rapidly expanding/constricting signs with infinite borders (SWIBs; Valsiner, 2014).

The SWIBs are dynamic hyper-generalized signs of field-like nature. Their borders are indeterminate as it expands and constricts precisely on the moving border (PRESENT) between PAST and FUTURE. Its borders, which are rapidly moving and indeterminate, are the locations for tension between the opposites of EXPAND<>non-EXPAND {maintain, constrict, diminish, or demolish all sign hierarchy}. Human beings make signs, use signs, abandon signs, and go on making more signs. Some of these signs emerge slowly; others in an instant. The latter are SWIBs; Valsiner, 2014).

The role of SWIBs in the making (and un-making) of crowd feelings and group atmospheres is crucial in the field of social actions—hence the efforts by social institutions either to escalate the coordinated actions of affect-driven mobs (create an act of demonstration, attack, or revolution), or to calm them down by rules of social control (Valsiner, 2014). When a person is in front of a beautiful garden, he/she can be in a contemplation state and be full of hyper-generalized meanings like, "I feel something over me, a complex sensation but it makes me feel very well."

Gardens indicated to be SWIB's, field-like signs within the hyper generalized affective-semiotic fields have their power in so many different human beings. They appear as a value, a pleasurable and peaceful place, where people are happier: a garden is a field-like sign as a "place where I am fuller and happier." It is enrolled of so many meanings depending on the contexts people are living. Hence, gardens promote interpretation, meaning making, and expectations for the future in daily life of so many people.

GARDENS AND OUR SEARCH FOR HAPPINESS

Think with me, all mental or organic diseases are an embarrassment to live in fullness. Gardens are environments where we are invited to live with all of the opportunities of being in a state near the plenitude of sensations. Sounds, smells, colors, water, trees, fruits take us to experience all of body senses. It is where life is celebrated in everything it was created to be: a zone of rich and dynamic sensations.

It is obvious in our life we have to feel uncomfortable sensations and they are important in several moments. Anxiety and fear can be very protective and keep us away from problems and painful situations. Sometimes, nevertheless, they can be wrong. Decontextualized feelings arise from thoughts or signs/positions we cultivate in our minds without concrete relationship with current events. In this way, a person encloses himself/herself and blocks the circulation of his/her other sensations or feelings. Thus, anxiety and fear can dominate his/her mind and body so that he/she cannot see nor live in a garden—openness of sensations, that is, state of contemplation and interaction based on safety and environmental comfort.

Since a person cannot yet be in his/her state of living openness of sensations fullnessly, he/she can expect to find this. Gardens are powerful not only spaces concrete to walk and be. They can be important resources for creating new possibilities for life's sensations horizons. In several alternative therapies the people are taken to imagine an environment similar to gardens where they can find several kinds of elements of nature such as clean air, sounds of kind animals, and so on. Afterwards, these people express calm and peace, commonly, despite any situations they may be facing in their life.

Gardens are very important places where human beings experience a mix of hyper-generalized feelings in so many different civilizations. It's common for people to express sensations of well-being during and after visiting planned gardens. A person believes he/she will be in after dying in a very beautiful garden has a hyper generalized affective-semiotic field-like signs highly invested with affect, this is "Garden as a blessing, a salvation, a place of pleasures and security." These signs or affective-semiotic fields, on their turn, play a significant role in mobilizing on his/her self changing his/her experience when he/she is inside some garden. For this person, gardens have a special value and a specific experience can be produced within these places.

Our human lives are full of signs we use every day in our minds. But apparently some signs can be as a lighthouse we can reactivate in moments of deep tensions. In these cases, each one will search his/her signs to remind his/her gardens (environments) to meet his/her life purpose: reconnect him/herself with the body in its openness of sensations in circulation.

Generally, gardens bring a series of meanings with direct and positive effects on our bodies and minds. In gardens, we could live a closer way to a fuller life. Gardens will be experienced by people in unique ways inside their cultural orientations, especially those related to spiritual, social, and artistic values. And in many situations they can be SWIB's, hyper generalized affective-semiotic field-like signs, that is, values related to dominant meanings belong to one's life.

FINAL THOUGHTS

As we can see, gardens are being used to improve health and prevent diseases in people in many contexts like hospitals, schools, and cities. According to Valsiner (2014), the SWIB is a dynamic hyper-generalized sign of field-like nature and its borders expand and constrict precisely on the moving border (PRESENT) between PAST and FUTURE. Gardens point us to signs that in our species are related to survival, comfort, and safety (smells, visions of colors, air breezes, mild noises from docile animals, plants or waters, and maybe even fruits from trees) in irreversible time.

Gardens incite the production of SWIBs whereas, according to Valsiner the SWIBs signs are rapid and directed towards the complete takeover of the person's *psyche* (Valsiner, 2014). It is exactly what happens when so many people have virtual or concrete contact with gardens and they report good sensations and a generalized state of well being. Gardens are not only beautiful planned places to be a part of time. It has a powerful effect in our lives because in these spaces with a lot of possibilities of sensations produced by so many signs (flowers, trees, animals, colors, sounds, and so on) we can feel ourselves fuller and more alive.

Gardens are inviting environments to find our most inner sensations of life, an invitation to feel several kinds of sensory pleasures. In these spaces our minds and bodies enjoy their senses in relative harmony. Living healthily presupposes a state of dynamic flexibility of feelings that let us be here and now, even with the psychological dimension of the past and the future. Gardens promote us to live openness of sensations in the present. It is a very powerful way to connect the human being with his/her capacity of existing in fullness and well-being.

NOTE

1. Accessed from https://viagemeturismo.abril.com.br/materias/os-15-mais-belos-jardins-do-mundo/, in July, 31th, 2021.

REFERENCES

Antonovsky, A., (1996). The salutogenic model as a theory to guide health promotion. *Health Promotion International, 11*(1), 11–18.

Bengtsson, A., & Grahn, P. (2014). Outdoor environments in healthcare settings: A quality evaluation tool for use in designing healthcare gardens. *Urban Forestry & Urban Greening, 13*(2014), 878–891.

Branco, A. U. (2016). Values and their ways in guiding the psyche. In J. Valsiner, G. Marsico, N. Chaudhary, T. Sato, & V. Dazzani (Eds.), *Psychology as the science of human being: The Yokohama Manifesto* (pp. 225–244). Springer.

Cervinka, R., Schwab, M., Schönbauer, R., Hämmerle, I., Pirgie, L., & Sudkamp, J. (2016). My garden—my mate? Perceived restorativeness of private gardens and its predictors. *Urban Forestry & Urban Greening, 16*, 182–187.

Cooper Marcus, M., & Barnes, M. (1999). Introduction: Historic and cultural overview. In M. Cooper Marcus & M. Barnes (Eds.), *Healing gardens: Therapeutic benefits and design recommendations* (pp. 1–26). John Wiley & Sons.

Hermans, H. J. M., Kempen, H. J. G., & van Loon, R. J. P. (1992). The dialogical self: Beyond individualism and rationalism. *American Psychologist, 47*(1), 23–33. https://doi.org/10.1037/0003-066X.47.1.23

Hipp, J. A., Betrabet Gulwadi, G., Alves, S., & Sequeira, S. (2016). The relationship between perceived greenness and perceived restorativeness of university campuses and student-reported quality of life. *Environment and Behavior, 48*(10), 1292–1308. https://doi.org/10.1177/0013916515598200

Innis, R. E. (2016). Affective semiosis: Philosophical links to cultural psychology. In J. Valsiner, G. Marsico, N. Chaudhary, T. Sato, & V. Dazzani (Eds.), *Psychology as the science of human being: The Yokohama manifesto* (pp. 87–104). Springer.

Maikov, K. (2016). Exploring the salutogenic properties of the landscape: From garden to forest. *Thesis*, Estonian University of Life Sciences. https://dspace.emu.ee/xmlui/bitstream/handle/10492/3024/Kadri_Maikov_2016DO.pdf?sequence=1&isAllowed=y

Marcus, C. C. (2007). Healing gardens in hospitals. *Interdisciplinary Design and Research e-Journal, 1*(1), 1–27.

Marsico, G., Tateo, L., Gomes, R. C., & Dazzani, V. (2019). Educational processes and dialogical construction of self. In N. Mercer, R. Wegerif, & L. Major (Ed.), *The Routledge international handbook of research on dialogic education* (pp. 50–61). Routledge.

Marubayashi, E. (2020, June 1). *Os 15 mais belos jardins do mundo* [The 15 the most beautiful gardens of the world]. https://viagemeturismo.abril.com.br/materias/os-15-mais-belos-jardins-do-mundo/

McAllister, E., Bhullar, N., & Schutte, N. S. (2017). Into the woods or a stroll in the park: How virtual contact with nature impacts positive and negative affect. *International Journal of Environmental Research and Public Health, 14*(7), 786. https://doi.org/10.3390/ijerph14070786

Peirce, C. S. (1977) *Semiótica*. Tradução J. Teixeira Coelho Netto. Perspectiva. Collected Papers of Charles Sanders Peirce. 1931–1958.

Tsunetsugu, Y., Park, B. J., & Miyazaki, Y. (2010). Trends in research related to "Shinrin-yoku" (taking in the forest atmosphere or forest bathing) in Japan. *Environmental Health and Preventive Medicine, 15*(1), 27–37.

Valsiner, J. (2014). *An invitation to cultural psychology*. SAGE Publications. https://www.doi.org/10.4135/9781473905986

Culture and Nature in Interaction

CHAPTER 3

MIRRORS OF A GARDEN

Understanding Ecological Units Over Time

Enno Freiherr von Fircks
Sigmund Freud University, Vienna

Marc Antoine Campill
University of Salerno

THE GARDEN AS CULTURAL AND PERSONAL ARENA OF HUMAN LIVING

We want to take the reader with us on a journey where we jointly discover the garden of the first author's family. Here, we rely on axioms of active research that help us as researchers to do research that does yield into concrete findings with concrete implications for the readers. This particular kind of research is grounded mostly upon personal involvement, social interaction, and dynamic processes that help us as researchers to unravel deeper levels of human wishing and willing (May, 1969/2007) realized into semiotic material. Like on a journey, we make different propositions hoping that the reader might stop, maybe stumble on them, pause, wonder, and look for their application within his/her (garden) setting. In the end, we think this is the goal of cultural psychology that we might better understand ourselves and others within the environments we live in, which we create, construct and deconstruct, and use for our own way of living. A journey towards such a place seems reasonable.

The Garden as Arena for Play

When I project myself back into my childhood, I remember especially one thing.[1] My garden. When I look back at old photos of my family, I often come across moments I spent in the garden. However, most of the time it was not me alone who played in the garden, but I was accompanied by friends or family.

But me and my friends/family did not find ourselves in the garden simply by coincidence. Mostly, we were bound by our intention to do something in the garden. The garden is inherently social as others might have emphasized in this volume, before. But what interests us secondly are the conditions for the genesis of the garden's social function. Most of the time, me and my friends/family were finding ourselves in the garden because we wanted to play something. Often, our motivation was to play soccer. Here, we did not care about the season or weather. We wanted to play soccer independent from unfortunate conditions. Playing and losing ourselves in the moment, imagining being a particular soccer player and laughing about our skills when we did fail was more decisive than getting wet or our clothes dirty. No particular kind of resistance could stop us, and often we played until the sunset in the summer.

What we did, seems simple. One person was the goalkeeper, the other tried to mark a goal. We used a tree and sometimes a bottle or a branch as goalposts and the hedge was imagined to be the crossbar to evaluate if the ball was in or outside the goal (see Figure 3.1). Therefore, we used the garden's parts as tools for our soccer play. A tree, branches, and the hedge become semiotic tools to set the stage for the soccer hours.[2] These parts were sufficient for me and my friends to spend hours and hours in the garden without getting bored in the meantime. Therefore, *the garden bears a certain meaning potential*. Certain parts of the garden are not simply given but unfold specific consequences based on the meaning the implied persons decide to attribute to the objects. Play is a key factor to initiate such meaning making processes between persons that are bound together by similar intentions. *Play transforms the garden.*

What is central is that the meaning attributed to the garden's parts is not fixed but flexible. The tree used by two persons as a goalpost can also become a hiding place for children playing hide and seek. The garden is therefore a

Figure 3.1 Tree and hedge as goalposts.

source of creativity/inspiration for children structuring their play. The transformation of objects within the garden is based on goals that are pursued intentionally, and different parts of the garden become differentially signified. Here, we are in line with Alfred Lang who provided us with an important definition of a sign as it not only stands for something for someone based on Peirce's triadic notion but *unfolds clear effects within our environment,* or as Lang would say in our ecological units (Lang, 1992, 1993).

Lang and his research group elaborated his ideas about semiosis in an interesting investigation about a couple changing their former basket for dirty clothes with a new, bigger chest. Before purchasing the new chest, the woman was mostly doing the laundry as she was disturbed watching the basket get over-filled. As the couple changed the basket with the chest, the woman suddenly stopped doing the laundry as regularly as before because the chest had more storage space. However, her partner was running out of clothes more rapidly and decided therefore to do the laundry more usually as before. Here, Lang tried to overcome simple monistic ideologies in science as he accounted for the dynamics of the relationship (subject) as well as the dynamics of the ecological givens (object). Analyzing these ecological units which—unfold clear effects—are crucial for Lang to create tangible knowledge. Applying that to the garden story, we see how the dynamic of the garden (its ever changing nature) is used in meaningful ways as it is used to structure the action field according to personal goals. The garden therefore becomes a cultural gift as it is transformed by concrete agents and their concrete action fields (see also Boesch, 1991, 1998, 2002). The natural environment is hence appropriated and becomes a cultural environment (Toomela, 2021). This cultural environment will be the focus for our manuscript.

The Garden as Developmental Arena

However, we want to come back to the activity. Playing in the garden no matter how rainy or windy it was, had significant consequences for us as children. Often, we were only allowed by our parents to play as extensively as we did if we took old trousers and shirts for our soccer units and if we thought about a bag of extra clothes. Playing soccer in the garden became therefore more than simply exercising a particular activity in a particular setting. I, for example, had to pay attention which trousers I took for the play because my parents objected that I already destroyed too many. Therefore, we needed to plan our activity in the garden such as preparing an extra bag with extra clothes, a football, a ball pump, and so forth. *Playing soccer in the garden was consequently more than just chasing or kicking a ball.* We as children needed to anticipate potential problems as well as parental objections. We needed to communicate who takes the ball, the pump, and so forth. We needed to deal with resistances. It is noteworthy that we did not think about all these crucial conditions for the successful play, right away, but that we did learn to respect these conditions by the virtue of finding ourselves in the garden with dirty clothes, a ball that was running out of air, and so forth.

The Role of Trajectory Equifinality Model for Play in the Garden

To underline the developmental processes implied in the construction of a successful play in the garden, we want to rely on the trajectory equifinality model (TEM) by Tatsuya Sato (Sato et al., 2009; Sato & Tanimura, 2016). We can define as the central equifinality point the wish/intention to play soccer in the garden. Here, we can imagine multiple trajectories that make it possible to reach that wish/goal as well as trajectories that prevent the actors implied in the play to reach their goal.

To understand TEM within developmental processes, we would like to use one of the first author's paper (von Fircks, 2020): The example stems from applying TEM to basic leadership interventions (see Figure 3.2).

If my goal is to stimulate the influx of creative ideas but my leading conduct is mostly based on explaining (Trajectory A) rather than creating a

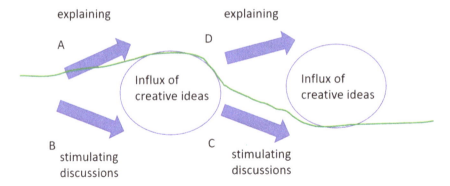

Figure 3.2 Understanding TEM.

working climate where each and everybody wants to contribute with his/her own ideas (Trajectory B), I am not reaching that goal. Here, the leader learns fast that the chosen decision to lead rather than to stimulate does not flow into the aimed goal but into the opposite. Therefore, he adjusts his leadership conduct (Trajectory C) by approaching the followers and encouraging them to share their creativity rather than to refrain from it (Trajectory D). Essentially, the leader needed to learn that Trajectory A did not lead into the aimed goal which resulted into a re-actualization of the leadership conduct better aimed at the goal. The advantage of TEM (Zittoun & Valsiner, 2016) is the *genetic focus that operates between past, present, and future.* The try-and-try-again strategy is crucial for TEM as the leader needs to learn from the unfolding past to actualize the unfolding present into an unfolding, anticipated future.

Drawing on the first author's experience, the first trajectories implied in the soccer example could look like the following (see Figure 3.3). Like in the leadership example, the actualized trajectory—here being prepared to potential problems and parental objections—only comes into being by experiencing that doing the opposite such as wanting to go to your friend and playing soccer without any preparation does not lead into the wishful outcome but only while respecting the conditions that make it possible within a given social system. The TEM example shows something crucial implied for the play in the garden:

Children learn within play to bear responsibility under which their play can unfold sustainably (ball pump) as well as without damaging or destroying valuable goods (clothes) guided by parental demands (signs). Here, playing soccer is therefore not only kicking or chasing a ball but assuming personal responsibilities on the side of the children that make play possible. As the latin root educo suggests, playing in the garden grows out primary responsibilities that the children implied need to respect if they want to play soccer

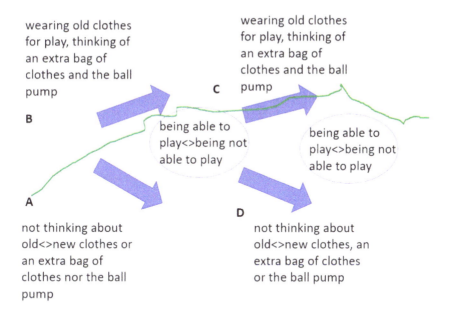

Figure 3.3 Learning to anticipate problems during play.

without permanent ruptures/objections, for example, from their parents. Therefore, we can find educational traces that are inherently interwoven within the play in the garden. This leads us to the conclusion that the garden is deeply existential as it helps children to get familiar with human ontology because taking decisions, assuming responsibility, learning from the consequences, adjusting the next moves, and getting ahead of problems and difficulties is a fundamental part of becoming a human being. *The garden is therefore not solely a cultural environment but also a developmental and existential one.*

The Garden and Ontological Transparency

Speaking with the voice of the cultural psychologist Ernst. E. Boesch (1991, 1998, 2002), playing in the garden leads to higher degrees of transparency, first on a motoric and kinesthetic level but secondly on higher psychological ones when the children learn to make decisions and deal with their consequences. *Transparency* is a term that is inherently interwoven with Boesch's concept of action potential. As the child grows older, his action potential grows, too. However, the action potential needs to rely on transparency, the process of getting familiar with unknown places, objects, persons, and their interpretation. Books for example are important instruments for children to attain high levels of transparency. Here, the children

Mirrors of a Garden • 53

deal with new words and new worlds. They might encounter activities happening in the book that they want to try out, too. They might like a certain character/protagonist of the book because of action XY which helps him/her to get familiar with primary processes of valuation. Here, they discover lived lives never seen before which enhance their action potential in the unknown future. These developmental processes leading into higher degrees of transparency unfold direct consequences for the actions the child might want to take in the unknown future such as playing soccer because it seemed fun in the book and so forth. In relation to Boesch we want to call what is described in Figure 3.4a *ontological transparency*.[3] As we have described above, playing in the garden shows implicitly an ontological sphere of transparency (see Figure 3.4a) preparing children to become human beings within a certain group. Imagine for example a mother forbidding her child to play with another child. Often, the mother/parent does not fear the concrete activity, but the ontological sphere encountered in the pauses of the play such as the conversation between the children about infrequent or taboo topics or the encounter of the family's personal culture such as weapons as wall decoration.

It is essential to connect the ontological sphere to its phenomenological habitat, the generated meaning.[4] This connection allows us to go deeper into the phenomenon which is rooting in our everyday occurrence and that flows into a distinct understanding of the meaning behind situation X, here playing in the garden. The stagnating nature of the ontological sphere needs therefore to be connected to a certain type of time dimension. This allows us to become aware of the repeating, but never similar, behavior in our everyday life (Campill & Valsiner, 2021). In our specified example of playing in the garden, we can conclude that over a period Y the environment and Self are changing by making new experiences which results therefore in a new meaning behind the act of playing:

> As for example we can say that a child is playing soccer in the garden and imagines how he/she is making the necessary goal to win the world cup. The

Figure 3.4a Ontological sphere of garden play.

next day after soccer training in his club, the child plays soccer again, but now not anymore in the same manner as the day before. Now slightly better trained and with a new interpretation of how an amazing goal should look like. Five years later we can see the boy playing soccer in the garden, again. From outside it looks identical to us as before: A child playing in the garden. Of course, this observation is correct, but the motivation changed completely. By taking a closer look we can observe a change in behavior, speed, and power, but much more important the own motivation changed as well. The playing child is not anymore copying his favorite player, he/she is focusing now on how the passing/shots could be improved so that s/he can higher the chances to win in the next training.

Playing in the garden is after time Y still connected with a similar ontological sphere, whereby it is now not only rooting within the experience of the past situation (see Figure 3.4b), but roots now within new made experiences, *a new now*. The meaning behind the playing of our observed individual changed by further experiences embedded in a social chain of actions. This means that playing in the garden not only shows the implicit ontological sphere of transparency, but also underlines the importance of re-defining the newly observed behavior in the garden along a temporal axis. Essentially, this is in line with Boesch (1991) who emphasized that an ecological type of psychology must be always interested in understanding

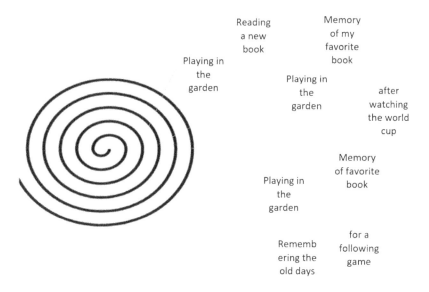

Figure 3.4b   Playing in the garden as spiraling-live-construction.

actions embedded in bigger and smaller social action chains. The garden setting is especially illustrative for that.

The Garden and Its Role for Motoric Transparency

However, playing soccer in the garden is also important for the motoric transparency of the child. We highly prefer the use of transparency rather than development in this context because of the relation between transparency and the action potential of the child which explicates better the past, present, future axes and their relation to the child's development, in general. I myself have tried out tricks and skills within the garden setting that I implemented later in the official soccer training of my village.[5] Without probing and getting used to them, I would not have had the courage to try them out later in the official training. Here, playing in *the garden is an opportunity* to intensify motoric transparency of the soccer skills. I not only became better within basic soccer skills, but my former trainer observed my development and made me a central part of the team. Consequently, I was almost always seeded in the team. Being seeded, getting the trust of the trainer, making an important contribution against an adversary team helps to gain playing practice and to get even better, thus to reach even higher kinesthetic or motoric transparency. We do not wish to call that self-fulfilling prophecy. In contrast, it reminds us more of the deviation-amplifying theory of Maruyama (1963, 1974). Maruyama uses highly illustrative examples to explain his scientific approach. In one of his papers (Maruyama, 1974) he describes what happens if a farmer decides to buy farmland in a structurally weak region by explaining that time after time other farmers might see the potential of the region and decide to settle there, too. Suddenly, there are a bunch of families present at that land: kindergartens, schools, churches, and so forth might develop as an answer to organize life which allows the development of new jobs as well as pulls new people to the former structurally weak region. When one first reads Maruyama as well as his examples of the deviation-amplifying theory the picture of a person throwing a stone into water creating circles over circles that grow constantly in their radius can come into the mind of the readers. Something similar happened with me playing soccer in the garden. The increasing motoric transparency that I gained during my soccer sessions in my garden, allowed me to develop certain soccer skills that I could try out in the official soccer training of my village. These skills have been acknowledged by my former trainer, increasing his trust in my soccer skills as well as his wish to rely on these during match time. Allowing me to implement the skills during soccer matches increased my self-confidence in my skills which made me better right away and allowed me to get seeded in the team (Figure 3.5a).

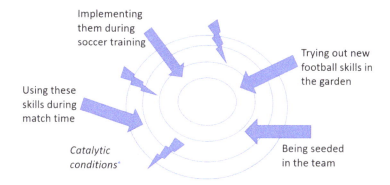

Figure 3.5a The garden as deviation-amplifying ground for motoric transparency.

These circles are not to be understood in a simple causal way. It depends on their interrelated conditions, if they become bigger in their radius or not. *A garden does not lead causally into a better soccer player*. This is simply impossible. But the garden can be the starting point of a journey where one can enhance his motoric skills which are a crucial condition to become a better soccer player. The garden is here just one condition among many others. The jump from the inner circles to the outer ones happen therefore under catalytic conditions (see flashes).[6] Catalytic conditions and its influence on a phenomenon have been first raised by Lewin (1927) who explained that we cannot say/see whether a person is working voluntarily or under obligation, phenomenologically. Here, it depends upon the personological factors (Valsiner, 2014). If the person for example explains himself that he works only to feed his family and that without it, he would be studying rather than working, the condition of family<>non-family helps to explain why this person works under feelings of obligation. However, we cannot say that feeding your family causes natural feelings of obligation when working. There might be persons who have a family, who try to feed them while studying and working part time. The person might answer the question, "Do you feel obliged or free when working?" with a statement like, "I feel free because I can choose where I want to work as well as how I want to feed my family in the future. Hence, I do not feel obliged but free." Here, it depends upon the stance the person takes towards the condition of family and feeding. Similarly, a person does not become a better soccer player because s/he plays soccer in the garden but because s/he creates the multiple conditions at hand under which s/he can structure his/her play (goalposts, ball, ball pump, the seize of the garden). These conditions and the particular stance towards them (I do not want to get interrupted because my ball is running out of air, therefore I buy a ball pump) allow a child to structure his/her play in the garden sustainably.

Similarly, the trainer in my village also provided us young players with the opportunity to try out several skills in his training, fostering an ambiance of bringing courageously new knowledge into his soccer sessions. The acknowledgment of these skills was also a crucial condition for further development during match time as well as during numerous trainings. If successfully implemented, the trainer needed to see that these skills did make an important contribution during match time which is one condition for being seeded in the team. Again, the trainer could only facilitate conditionally that we as players wanted to try out new skills in the training. He could only encourage us to do so but he was not able to pull those out of us: On the contrary, it was the willful decision of us as players if we trusted the trainer and his words. The trainer could only flood the periphery of our perceptual focus with multiple signs that he is serious and trustable—comparable to an offer—with his intervention but he could not cause it. Simultaneously, we as players could not cause being seeded for the next match. In a similar vein, we could make the trainer an offer. In the end, it was him, who decided if trying out new skills is an important condition to win the next match. This surely is not always the case in soccer as tactics vary with the adversary's team, so that professional trainers almost never promise a player to have a regular place in his/her team.

The analogy shows that the environmental challenges of our lives are too dynamic that we can anticipate those with a fixed, always pre-planned meaning structure. There are for example famous soccer players who learned to play as aesthetically and as technically talented by playing with table tennis balls. Here, we can say that these players did not learn soccer as the majority of their friends/colleagues but differently (deviation). Essentially, their skills were amplified by their environment which recognized the particular excellence of this technique. Such as in the farmer analogy of Maruyama (1974), these players cultivated a technique on a spot that was not yet discovered (playing with table tennis balls) and which were promoted in the right moment and catalyzed therefore their development in soccer. What we learn from Maruyama (1963) is that we must account for the analysis of potential feedback networks when analyzing human phenomena. Soccer skills are not primarily developed in official training sessions; the feedback networks might be too static if the trainer does not want to see that a player loses the ball too much because he is trying out new skills. Playing in an unofficial setting like the garden is one among many (deviation)—for example, together with a close friend who not only supports your courage of being creative but tries to do the same—is such a feedback network for the cultivation of higher levels of motoric transparency. What we want to show with our writings is that we should not only analyze primary ecological units (networks) like playing soccer in a garden but multiple networks (ecological units) which are interrelated. *The question of causality is not of practical help but the determination of some of the multiple networks that are in relation one to the other as well as their conditional intertwining.* Like a good engineer, we must see the complex whole of different networks being in relation to each other and analyze which oil (conditions) lets them work faster and faster. The garden, the official soccer training, amateur soccer fields—which are found in every smaller city—streets, beaches among many things have to be analyzed within this multiple-network perspective and in conjunction.

The argument is the following when it comes to the motoric transparency and its relation to the garden:

> The garden is an important opportunity for the motoric development of the child which can under several conditions unfold in a deviation-amplifying manner into different favorable horizons of higher transparency.

Spirality of Time

Returning now to the spirality of time. It is now crucial to observe the evolution of the garden's meaning, while following the "I-as a player in the Garden" during the process of helping the individual growing over period Y.

By remembering the example of a child playing in the garden we can anticipate the changes of the garden's meaning, while some fragments of such meaning are preserved. As it is visible in Figure 3.5b, the new book becomes the favorite book, where not the actual sentences of the book are preserved but rather fragments of the favorite parts. This process can also be found in the change of the garden's meaning, in Figure 3.5b. The meaning we had before, the one we remember, the meaning we are connected to in the here and now are both impacting our understanding of the

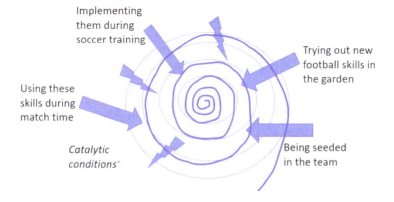

Figure 3.5b Meaning horizon over time.

Mirrors of a Garden • 59

world because self and environment are in a constant dialogue over time (Campill & Valsiner, 2021).

Complexity arises because of the social action chain that is always impacting the meaning-making process of playing in the garden. The phenomenon of playing in the garden is ever-growing (Campill & Valsiner, 2021), while we are confronted with a polysemic multivoice, a complex *whole of different social networks being in relation to each other* that might influence our meaning making. This can be the trainer that provides the players with exercises to be executed in the garden. This can be an interview of a favorite soccer player. It can be a video footage of creative skills probed out elsewhere than in training. It can be a book about a trainer and his recommendations to become a better player and so forth. This interaction of forces is implemented in the generation of our meaning making that can but does not necessarily need to become central for a person X over a period of time Y at a location Z such as the garden.

This means in conclusion that our experiences made, and the experience we acquire are creating a field in which we as human beings can grow/change, whereby we change not only in our construction of who we want to be (e.g., I as soccer player) but also in the construction of what meaning lies behind that. The garden is for sure a starting point for the motoric development of the child, but also the place where we realize our fantasy, our meanings of who we want to be over time. *We are historical beings in historical environments (cultures). And as such beings our personal meaning changes over time with the alteration of cultural meanings.* These alterations of meanings embedded in a social chain of action can be found within the setting of our garden by the dynamic use of signs. This leads us directly into the next paragraph.

SEMIOTIC MARKERS AND THEIR GUIDING ROLE FOR ATTENTIONAL PROCESSES

As visible in the above-mentioned paragraphs, soccer is an essential part of my garden. Here, it is no wonder that soccer has left its traces there. While I was wandering around in the garden for the present study, I encountered many balls and clearly visible in Figure 3.6a a flagpole with the favorite soccer team of my family which is the 1. FC Cologne. Cologne, as a city and sign, still plays an important role in my family's life as my mother was born and raised there. For her, the flag often becomes a sign (symbol) for her home (Heimat).

The flag is not only a sign (symbol) for my mother's Heimat[7] as well as her relation towards it, but it also operates as a semiotic marker for other persons encountering it. Essentially, the flag is social as guests interested in soccer

Figure 3.6a Flagpole with my family's favorite soccer team.

often thematize the last match or the general condition of the soccer team while entering the dining room of the house from which you can see the flag immediately (Figure 3.6b). Regularly, the sign allows for a kind of loose small talk between guests and house owners to get familiar with each other. *It bears expressive and appellative functions.* These conversations can be described as small talk, but we do not want to underestimate its central function. Soccer plays for many persons a central role in life as they become part of fan clubs, decorate every room in their houses with ornaments of the particular soccer club, or overflood their gardens with such symbols. Acknowledging the other in central positions as soccer is one among many, is to acknowledge him/her in his/her being and the related externalization/cultivation processes—as

Mirrors of a Garden • **61**

Figure 3.6b Flagpole from the perspective of the entrance and dining room.

the flag is for example one. Here, the sign, for example, the flag can be used as a semiotic marker to not only bridge the time until dinner—when invited—but essentially to enhance the meeting potential between two persons. From our own personal experience, we can report that meeting another person, getting familiar, sympathizing with him/her is much facilitated if one can discover rapidly common ground of experience. *The flag as semiotic marker plays a key role for intensifying the eventual meeting potential.* The present paragraph leads us to the following conclusion:

> The central semiotic markers in the garden are inherently interwoven with the (personological) existence of the person. If positioned centrally, the personological objects can become social signs with a certain appeal function for other persons to feel into them as well as to thematize the context that surrounds the sign. The social nature of these signs—their appellative and expressive function—makes it possible for people to find common ground of experience which enhances their meeting potential, thus the quality spent together.

The Garden as Arena for Societal Cleavages

Yet there is another dimension which goes beyond the individual one that we want to address: While going around in the garden, I came across different tools that are important for our garden work. These tools were highly different in their technological advancement and mirror therefore the cleavage of our modern times between a highly technologized new and an old analogue world. On the one hand, I found an ax and a block of wood to divide bigger pieces of wood for the tiled stove in the house as well as an old wheelbarrow used for all imaginary purposes. Again, *the transformation of the garden, its cultivation, is based on the person's action field* structured by goals such as making fire for the tiled stove. But there is more complexity within that process: On the other hand, I found an old lawnmower used with gasoline as well as a new automatic lawn mower that operates on his own (Figure 3.7). Essentially, the new automatic lawn mower cannot do all the work we could do with the old one. Here, the old one allows it to go deeper into the corners as well as under bigger hedges where the new one would only get stuck. In the same breath, we use the old one after winter to cut the grass that is at this time too high to be cut with the automatic one.

Essentially, the technology analogy shows two important things. First, it underlines the *historicity of our action field* and secondly the technological cleavage between new highly automatized tools for the garden work and old ones. The automatized garden tools are not yet able to substitute the old ones which mirrors the technological cleavage beyond the garden work because it is applicable to other domains in our lives such as teleworking and working in the office, phoning, facetiming with our friends or meeting them personally, writing with our computers and office programs, or creating documents and letters by our own handwriting and so forth. As visible in the garden story, the new technologies do not do justice to the complexity of the garden's work and cannot fully substitute the old ones which are for several purposes more precise than the new ones. Here, it depends on the agent's goals. Again, I needed to learn first that we were not able to cut the grass as precisely as we did in the past with the new lawnmower choosing voluntarily in the next present moment the old lawnmower to correct for the imprecisions the new one left us with. This brings us back to TEM, the necessary lections we need to learn from the unfolding past to adjust our actions in the present moment to guarantee our goal attainment in the unfolding future (see Figure 3.8).

Figure 3.7 Carport for the Automatized Lawnmower vs. Petrol Powered Lawnmower.

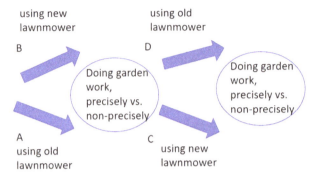

Figure 3.8 Learning to unit the different garden tools (TEM).

Speaking with Simmel (1910) the garden tools are part of different sign manifolds, products of their time with possibilities and limitations. Learning to use the advantages of both sign-manifolds while reducing their negative impact is necessary to deal with the conflicts of the liminal world or the liminal state of being between two ages. *The garden is a liminal world.*

Here the TEM is in close relation to similar experiences in my past experiences such as writing a letter by hand or by computer while comparing the effects the different letters unfolded for the targeted person I was writing for. Most central the TEM shows for the garden work and beyond that we still live in an age where we cannot rely fully on automatized tools for our goals because these do not do justice to the goals we are aiming at. We do not wish to generalize this finding onto different parts in the world, for example, on Asian gardens among many others, but we wish to capture the following:

The garden can function as a minimal mirror for basic conflicts in society as well as for potential circumvention strategies to deal with those. Here, we can find similar solutions. As the garden analogy showed, me and my family used a hybrid strategy for cutting the gras. Similarly, in the entrepreneurial domain, CEOs and management boards do not rely fully on telework or home office but also implement hybrid strategies trying to use the advantages of both strategies as well as to minimize the negative outcomes of both at the same time. *If we analyze present cleavages within society, we argue we can find most of them within the minimal setting of our gardens.*

THE GARDEN AS MULTIDIMENSIONAL MIRROR

We want to highlight the central axes of the present manuscript:

> The garden becomes an arena of different kinds of signs based on active agents and their action fields structured by goals such as playing in the garden

embedded in a larger cultural setting. The garden as a natural environment is appropriated and transformed into a cultural environment given with multiple opportunities for the children involved in play.

Playing in the garden is for children a central source to enhance their motoric transparency. The intensification of this kinesthetic transparency does not lead causally into better abilities in sportive activities. However, this particular intensification works under the premise of the deviation-amplifying theory of Maruyama. Under favorable circumstances, the enhanced motoric transparency can unfold into other settings in the unknown future which—if acknowledged—create new conditional circles that unfold specific effects in particular settings. Moreover, it is not enough to only look at the garden: We have to spot its interrelatedness with other ecological units (networks) and how they do work one with the other in a feedback-like manner. The garden can be the starting point, but our research journey should not end there. *A garden does not make a proper soccer player, but the networks in their intensifying interconnectedness can account for that.*

Learning to play in the garden does not only involve the enhancement of motoric transparency but also the process of getting familiar with the process of becoming a human being. Preparing for play, anticipating potential problems during play as well as parental objections and negotiating the details of play, help the children to make decisions and to bear responsibilities. We call that ontological transparency because the children learn to stand up for themselves as well as for their choices quite early on. And the garden is its arena.

Moreover, the garden is inherently interwoven with our existence. We leave traces in our gardens because we create them based on our goals and needs. We propose that we need to understand such traces as daseins semiotic[8] markers that have not only a social function but reveal the unfolding being of persons cultivating their garden. In certain moments, these daseins semiotic markers can enhance the meeting potential between persons if placed centrally within the house<>garden setting which we tried to outline with the photo of the flagpole and its perceptual access from the house.

Lastly, the garden operates as a minimal mirror for political cleavages that are found on the societal level. Here, we see in the tradition of Erich Stern (1920) that political/societal problems occur first within the minimal setting of concrete persons that find through canalizing catalysts their way up to the societal level. The cleavage between highly advanced technological garden tools and old, more analogous ones is one of central interest and validates the cleavage in other domains of living. That the more analogous tools are still used for precise work and the technological ones for the rough surface reveals much about the general conflict of human beings living in an age between an old not-yet-abandoned and a not-yet established all automatized world and their circumvention strategies.

The Garden and Its Role for Theory of Science

Last, we want to use the opportunity to express ourselves about the theory of science. In the tradition of Smedslund (2012, 2016), Toomela (2007, 2021), and Valsiner (2014, 2017) we are making a plea for active research. Here, we are proposing four corners of vivid research (see Figure 3.9) that are an antidote to mainstream psychology and its quantitative imperative leading into small effect sizes/correlations in strange survey settings. These do not help us to make adequate predictions about human behavior because they do not take into account the personological, situational and environmental factors.

These more qualitative factors, if we have access to them, are sufficient to anticipate human behavior in specific environmental settings (Smedslund & Ross, 2014). Gaining access to them is however only possible if we as researchers are practically involved in our research foci such as in the present manuscript with a specific garden setting. It is the personal involvement that makes it possible for us as researchers to explore goals, wishing and willing of the persons implied in our research that cannot be assessed via abbreviated pre-given statements like items in strange surveys. The social function of the garden is a central example that underlines the need for personal involvement within research that unravels deeper layers of our action fields. Through this particular kind of access, we can analyze the role of semiotic markers that are inherently interwoven with our existence and mediate our social interaction with the social other. Again, we can call these kinds of signs daseins semiotic markers (von Fircks, 2021) because by their revelation we can get a glimpse into the unfolding being and its construction of existence as we tried to show with the flagpole in the garden that

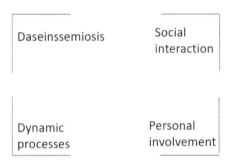

Figure 3.9 Four corners of vivid research.

is not only central for small talk but an essential cultural product of home that guides our attention processes and those of others. These semiotic markers unfold their effects in dynamic processes such as social interaction. Only by acknowledging the dynamic character of our psychological processes can we do justice to the meaning potential of our environment.

The garden is therefore an interesting social good that is a mirror for us. Essentially, it shows how dynamic knowledge is created in a dynamic environment with dynamic agents. In the end, a glimpse into our garden is a glimpse into ourselves. A journey towards such a place seems more than reasonable.

NOTES

1. Here, the first author describes his experience while playing in the garden. Therefore, he switches to the first person singular. When making systemic generalizations about the garden and its role for cultural psychology, we switch to the first-person plural. We wish to emphasize the personal connotation of the paper which we consider important when writing papers in cultural psychology.
2. We follow here Peirce triadic definition of sign constituting of the object, the subject and the sign which are all bound together simultaneously. Essentially, we also make the plea of understanding the sign-making process against the background of a persons' action field that is structured by overreaching goals and their valences (Boesch, 1991, 2002). Importantly the person in his/her action field is in a liminal state between a not-yet reached but reachable goal.
3. During the review process important questions were raised concerning Figure 3.4a: What is the relation between the inner and outer sphere of the circle? What is the boundary? We will explain ourselves: The inner circle represents the very core of the action field and its goals (playing soccer in the garden), yet in order to reach that goal and to cross the boundary, one has first of all to acknowledge the (parental) definition of playing appropriately as well as the conditions that make up for sustainable play. Play only comes into being if the child complies with the constraints of the play or in other words if the child ensures himself/herself to not violate the interdependence of his action field with the ones of his parents (if I destroy my trousers, my mother needs to buy me another pair of trousers).
4. The efforts of linking the ontological sphere to a temporal axis as visible in the following two figures goes back to the second author who tries to show in his writings that ecological development needs to be studied always over a certain period of time. Interested readers might want to look at Campill and Valsiner (2021).
5. We want to specify that playing in the garden is just one among many possibilities to enhance the motoric transparency. As almost equally important, I would describe books/novels about soccer which I read at that time, extensively and which I think motivated me to go again and again in the garden.

6. The jump from the outer to the inner circles only comes into being if the different action fields are positively interdependent (and hence interlocked one with the other) and catalyze symbiotically their mutual growth. Playing in the garden and learning new tricks does only unfold effects if the trainer acknowledges the benefits of such play. Equally, such benefits can not come into being if there are people not having a garden. What we want to say is that A does not cause B, but A and B are impacting each other within positive feedback loops, and which might lead into the catalyzation of a new structure. The successful jump from the outer to the inner circle only comes into existence if concrete feedback-loop networks are at place.
7. Still when listening to Colognian songs, she gets highly emotional as she appreciates the openness, the warm-heartedness of the people, the opportunities to play in the central park of Cologne, the opportunities of going out and having fun among many other things. Most essentially her parents were able to settle in Cologne offering their children a good childhood which was for them as war-generation a deep underlying wish.
8. We cannot get tired of repeating that we as psychologists must understand the creation of signs against the background of an I that is thrown into his action field. Here, a person tries to get ahead of goals that are not yet reached but potentially reachable. The I develops (entwerfen) concrete plans, life-trajectories to get ahead of that state in order to reach his goals. Here, the sign always shows traces of that initial thrownness and the existential answer of that particular I.

REFERENCES

Boesch, E. E. (1991). *Symbolic action theory and cultural psychology*. Springer New York.

Boesch, E. E. (1998). *Sehnsucht: Von der Suche nach Glück und Sinn* [Longing: On the search of joy and meaning] (1st ed.). Huber.

Boesch, E. E. (2002). Genese der subjektiven Kultur [Genesis of subjective culture]. In M. Hildebrand-Nilshon, C.-H. Kim, & D. Papadopoulos (Eds.), *Kultur (in) der Psychologie: Über das Abenteuer des Kulturbegriffs in der psychologischen Theorienbildung* [Culture (in) psychology: About the adventure of the concept of culture in psychological theory formation] (pp. 67–95). Asanger.

Campill, M. A., & Valsiner, J. (2021). Spiral and helical models for psychology: Leaving linearity behind. *Human Arenas: An Interdisciplinary Journal of Psychology, Culture, and Meaning, 6*(2), 1–21. https://doi.org/10.1007/s42087-021-00194-2

Lang, A. (1992). On the knowledge in things and places. In M. von Cranach, W. Doise, & G. Mugny (Eds.), *Social representations and the social basis of knowledge* (pp. 76–83). Hans Huber.

Lang, A. (1993). Non-cartesian artefacts in dwelling activities: Step towards a semiotic ecology. *Schweizerische Zeitschrift Für Psychologie, 52*(2), 138–147. http://www.langpapers.org/pap2/1993-01noncartesartefact.htm

Lewin, K. (1927). Gesetz und experiment in der psychologie [law and experiment in psychology]. *Symposion*, 375–421.

Maruyama, M. (1963). The second cybernetics: Deviation-amplifying mutual causal processes. *American scientist, 51*(2), 164–179.

Maruyama, M. (1974). Hierarchists, individualists and mutualists. *Futures, 6*(2), 103–113. https://doi.org/10.1016/0016-3287(74)90017-2

May, R. (2007). *Love and will.* W. W. Norton. (Original work published 1969).

Sato, T., & Tanimura, H. (2016). The trajectory equifinality model (TEM) as a general tool for understanding human life course within irreversible time. In T. Sato, N. Mori, & J. Valsiner (Eds.), *Making of the future: The trajectory equifinality approach in cultural psychology* (pp. 21–43). Information Age Publishing.

Sato, T., Hidaka, T., & Fukuda, M. (2009). Depicting the dynamics of living the life: The trajectory equifinality model. In J. Valsiner, N. Chaudhary, M. C. D. P. Lyra, & P. C. M. Molenaar (Eds.), *Dynamic process methodology in the social and developmental sciences* (pp. 217–240). Springer.

Simmel, G. (1910, February 6). Vom Wesen der Philosophie [About the essence of philosophy]. *Frankfurter Zeitung und Handelsblatt, Nr. 36, 54.* http://socio.ch/sim/verschiedenes/1910/philosophie.htm

Smedslund, J. (2012). The *bricoleur* model of psychological practice. *Theory & Psychology, 22*(5), 643–657. https://doi.org/10.1177/0959354312441277

Smedslund, J. (2016). Why psychology cannot be an empirical science. *Integrative Psychological & Behavioral Science, 50*(2), 185–195. https://doi.org/10.1007/s12124-015-9339-x

Smedslund, J., & Ross, L. (2014). Research-based knowledge in psychology: What, if anything, is its incremental value to the practitioner? *Integrative Psychological & Behavioral Science, 48*(4), 365–383. https://doi.org/10.1007/s12124-014-9275-1

Stern, E. (1920). Probleme der Kulturpsychologie [problems of cultural psychology] *Zeitschrift für die gesamte Staatswissenschaft/Journal of Institutional and Theoretical Economics,* (H. 3), 267–301.

Toomela, A. (2007). Culture of science: Strange history of the methodological thinking in psychology. *Integrative Psychological & Behavioral Science, 41*(1), 6–20. https://doi.org/10.1007/s12124-007-9004-0

Toomela, A. (2021). *Culture, Speech, and MySelf.* Porcos ante Margaritas.

Valsiner, J. (2014). *An invitation to cultural psychology.* SAGE Publications.

Valsiner, J. (2017). *From methodology to methods in human psychology.* Springer.

von Fircks, E. F. (2020). Existential humanistic leadership (EHL) as a dialogical process: Equality of the non-equality in organizations. *Integrative Psychological and Behavioral Science, 54,* 4, 1–23. https://doi.org/10.1007/s12124-020-09560-1

von Fircks, E. F. (2021). Daseinssemiosis: A new look at the phenomenology of Theodor Lipps. *Human Arenas, 5,* 592–608. https://doi.org/10.1007/s42087-020-00159-x

Zittoun, T., & Valsiner, J. (2016). Imagining the past and remembering the future: How the unreal defines the real. In T. Sato, N. Mori, & J. Valsiner (Eds.), *Making of the future: The trajectory equifinality approach in cultural psychology* (pp. 3–21). Information Age Publishing.

Fourteen-meter-high embankments, protecting villages and keeping the sea away from villages. (*Source*: author)

CHAPTER 4

"I NEED A GARDEN," A SURVIVOR SAID

A Garden as a Place Where Survivors Become Relational Beings for Disaster Recovery

Ryohei Miyamae
Fukuyama City University

"I NEED A GARDEN," A SURVIVOR SAID

What is a disaster? What is the recovery from a disaster? In this section, I define disaster as something that takes away the foundations of a survivor's life. A disaster takes away many things from the survivors. It can take away the home in which they live, the family photos that capture their precious memories, the furniture they are used to, and sometimes even the friends and family who are an integral part of their lives. Thus, to put it more abstractly, a disaster removes all kinds of connections. I will focus on disconnection from the past and the loss of the community. I will try to make sense of the "garden" as a place where survivors can restore their connections.

The Semiotic Field of the Garden, pages 71–86
Copyright © 2024 by Information Age Publishing
www.infoagepub.com
All rights of reproduction in any form reserved.

Before starting the discussion, I would like to share my personal experiences. The following description could be autoethnographic (Adams et al., 2015). Auto-ethnography is an ethnography that is primarily but not exclusively self-descriptive. The world is depicted from the author's point of view, and new aspects of others and the environment are discovered. Let us leave the preliminaries aside and move on to a description of my experience.

I was 19 years old and in my first year of undergraduate studies when the Great East Japan Earthquake and Tsunami occurred, leaving around 20,000 people dead or missing. At the moment of the disaster, a friend who lived in the same dormitory called me in panic and urged me to watch TV as soon as possible. I did not have a TV at home, so I rode my bike to the nearest appliance store and tried to get some information from the TVs on display. All I could see were houses burning and being swept away by the tsunami and cars speeding away from the tsunami. That sent my spine chills down. I could not leave until I realized that the same images were repeated. This was close to the closing time.

I would have been applauded if I had immediately gone to Tohoku to volunteer, but in reality, I did not. Like many Japanese university students, I was busy with club activities and part-time jobs. However, I still wanted to go to the disaster areas of Tohoku one day.

When I decided to attend graduate school, I wanted to research volunteerism. I chose to study volunteerism because it would allow me to visit the disaster-affected areas of Tohoku for a good reason: to write my master's thesis. This is how I ended up specialising in disaster volunteerism. It was in 2014, 3 years after the disaster.

My first visit to the affected areas in Tohoku occurred in February 2014. I remember the freezing weather of that day. I went to the small village of Noda in Iwate Prefecture, located in the northern part of the tsunami-affected area (Figure 4.1). At the time, in Noda village, some people moved from temporary housing to public housing for disaster survivors (Figures 4.2–4.6). Nevertheless, it was difficult for them to move out independently because many of them were older people living alone and did not have relatives who helped them. I visited Noda to help them move.

While helping people move, I heard many things from one survivor: She told me that the walls of her temporary housing were so thin that she could hear everything from her neighbor's house. She also said that it was fine if she could hear the noise of her neighbors, but she was worried that the noises she made were too loud and disturbed her neighbor, so she tried not to make any noise whenever she stayed in temporary housing. She was happy to say that her new house was smaller but detached and that she would have more privacy.

When we went to her new home, a public disaster housing complex, the sofas and dining table had already been brought in, and a small but comfortable space had been set up. When I told her that it looked nice and comfortable to live in, she said she felt as if she were finally returning to her

"I Need a Garden," a Survivor Said ▪ **73**

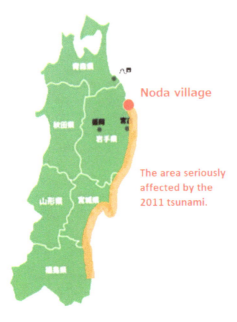

Figure 4.1 The 2011 tsunami-damaged area (Miyamae & Atsumi, 2017).

Figure 4.2 Empty temporary housing (photo by the author).

life before the disaster. She continued, "But I also feel a bit lonely now that I live alone." She added, "When I was in temporary housing, we were like one big family, including the neighbors." She looked lonely.

Figure 4.3 A station of the local train in Nodamura village; a gateway and an exit to the city (photo by the author).

Figure 4.4 Ocean; gifts and tsunamis came from here (photo by the author).

"I Need a Garden," a Survivor Said • 75

Figure 4.5 Fourteen-metre-high embankments, protecting villages and keeping the sea away from villages (photo by the author).

Figure 4.6 Community destroyed by the tsunami (retrieved from KNF Disaster Archive).

Her face brightened when she showed me the small garden of her new house. She said, "I need a garden," adding, "I need something to grow." It seemed to me that the little garden she was now showing me would be a nexus between her and her new community.

Over the next 7 years, I went to Noda about 50 times. Throughout my visits, my perspective on recovery underwent many changes. In the first year or so, the more I went, the more I felt I was getting to know the people in Noda, and the more I thought we were becoming friends who shared the reality of recovery.

"I COULD NEVER BE A SURVIVOR," AN EXTERNAL SUPPORTER SAID

The more I went to the tsunami-stricken area, the more I felt like I had become a *Tojisha*, as the Japanese say. The word Tojisha is one of the most difficult Japanese words to translate. If you look at a Japanese–English dictionary, you will find such translations of Tojisha as "person concerned" or "interested party." However, the word Tojisha has a different and multi-layered nuance. For example, a person with a disability is sometimes referred to as a tojisha with a disability. This implies that they are not just disabled people but that their disability is deeply rooted in their identity and that they live with it. When we refer to people who have been affected by a disaster as "Tojisha affected by the disaster," this implies that they are people who have experienced a tragedy. In other words, when we say "Tojisha" in Japanese, there is the nuance of having a direct experience of an event as the basis of identity, without which the person would not exist.

However, I became aware that I would not be a Tojisha of the disaster. There seemed to be a big gap between me, who had not experienced the disaster, and those who had. I did not experience the disaster first-hand. Therefore, unless I can go back in time, I cannot be the Tojisha of the disaster. I also live in Osaka, which was not affected by the disaster. Therefore, I am not living in the middle of a catastrophe like the people living in the Great East Japan Earthquake and Tsunami. Unlike survivors, I can live my life with total ignorance of the disaster. Disaster is not an integral part of my life. It is as if I am a majority male who can live with total disregard for issues of misogyny.

This phenomenon is called a "sudden drop" when the level of involvement with a Tojisha exceeds a certain threshold, "the Tojisha dilemma" (see Figure 4.7). As a concrete example, I quote the narrative of a female volunteer in Fukushima. She now works for a general incorporated association to engage in recovery assistance in Fukushima. She has often participated in her university's volunteer program in Fukushima. She subsequently exchanged letters with an older woman living in a temporary house and

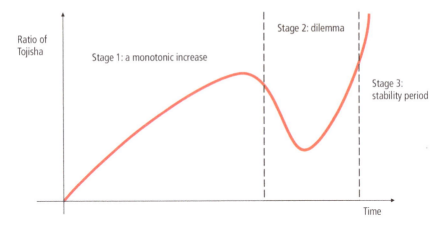

Figure 4.7 Tojisha dilemma.

became friendly with her elderly pen pals. A year and a half after her first visit, as a university student, she started a 1-year temporary work assignment at the association in Fukushima. Four days after the interview, she married a local man who had worked at a town office. The following is about her changing relationship with survivors in Fukushima.

She first experienced a monotonous increase in her identification with a Tojisha. In other words, as she continued to visit the areas affected by the Great East Japan Earthquake and Tsunami and became closer to the survivors she met, she felt that she was becoming a Tojisha of the disaster. It was as if she had become a child or grandchild of the survivors:

> I visited Fukushima four or five times a year as a volunteer, and I wanted to see survivors in Fukushima not as a volunteer but as a friend or a grandchild for them.

She then corresponded with the Fukushima survivors by sending letters after returning to Kyoto, where she lived. Eventually, she wanted to know more about the disaster area and started thinking about moving to Fukushima:

> The letter from an older woman whom we made friends with when visiting a temporary house in Fukushima also said difficult things to ask when we met in person. While writing a letter in Kyoto, I thought Fukushima was a bit far away. Then, I realized I was eager to live there!

What is essential here is that she felt a comparatively heightened level of involvement. Several years had passed since the Great East Japan Earthquake and Tsunami. In Kyoto, far from the disaster area, opportunities to remember the disaster rapidly disappeared. In the midst of everything, she continued to go to disaster areas and corresponded with survivors in Fukushima. In other words, we can assume that she was more involved in the disaster than her friends in Kyoto, who were losing interest in it.

She then took a year off from her university to work as a temporary worker in one of Fukushima's affected areas, which is still heavily influenced by radioactive contamination. She began to experience the psychological dilemma of Tojisha. She described this dilemma in simple terms as follows: "The closer I get to them, the more distant I feel from them." Why did she feel distant from the survivors even though she lived in the affected area? She said the following:

> I thought I was a stranger even though I had lived there for one year. I thought it was vital to determine whether I was in Fukushima when the disaster had happened. I could never be "a survivor" despite how much I empathize with them.

The more involved she became, the more she was confronted with the fact that she could not be a Tojisha. As she could not be a Tojisha, all she could do was empathize and speak for survivors. These are fundamental aspects of support. However, her deep insights, based on long-term support for survivors, led her to question whether genuine empathy and representation were possible. In other words, she was confronted with anguish that the empathy she felt was a selfish assumption and that the representation she felt was depriving the survivors of their stories. This anguish was a question that could never be resolved for her, as she could not take the position of a person who had directly experienced the disaster.

Here, we can see the pitfalls of what Gergen (2009) calls "individualism." In his book, he asks a fascinating question that goes to the heart of existence. He asks what it is that separates the self from others. A simple answer is that the skin separates us from us. Humans are bound by beings. When children draw a picture of a human being, they begin by outlining a person with a crayon. However, this idea is based on fundamental separation. He observed the following.

> My private world is unavailable to you. What is essential to me is "in here," a private space that neither you nor anyone else can enter. (p. 6)

In this way, we fall into an isolated view that "I'm the only one who knows me." Indeed, the psychological dilemma of Tojisha is born by the assumption that Tojisha and non-Tojisha are separated and cannot share their minds. The above interviewee was in anguish over the dichotomy between the survivor and the volunteer.

In Chapter 6, Hakoköngäs discusses the relationship between the dead and the living using the garden concept. He addressed the semantic transition of cemeteries in Finland and gave an interesting statement; namely, that "cemeteries are at the same time places for the dead and the living," encompassing opposing actors: the dead and the living. Moreover, they even reconcile conflicting concepts such as the sacred-secular, and the equal-hierarchical. To summarize his argument from my perspective, the grave is a public space that encompasses contradictions.

Here, I am tempted to extend his discussion of the tomb to the disaster area as I believe it makes sense to construe the disaster area as an extended grave. To draw on the discussion in this chapter, the real Tojisha in both the cemetery and the disaster area is the dead. The Tojisha dilemma discussed earlier may stem from a disconnection in which we can never reach the dead—the true Tojisha—unless we are dead.

FORGETFULNESS OF FORGETTING

Now, I would like to discuss the role of the garden in overcoming these divisions, but before I do so, I wish to point out that such divisions riddle disaster recovery. I hope to highlight two points that I consider particularly important.

The first is disconnection from the past. Disasters cause a disconnection between the pre- and post-disaster periods. For example, when researchers ask disaster survivors to talk about a disaster, they tend to tell only post-disaster stories (Yamori & Sugiyama, 2015). It is as if their lives before the disaster were entirely forgotten. This disconnection is not limited to disasters. For example, Hiroshima has now been treated *a priori* as an A-bombed city. We cannot imagine what Hiroshima was like before the bombing event. This has led to the publication of a highly acclaimed manga (Kono, 2011) depicting Hiroshima before it became a bombed city and the people who lived there.

The contradiction in the following sentence typifies disconnection: "The Jews should have fled before the Holocaust happened." At first glance, this seems reasonable. However, the narrative "Jews should have fled before the Holocaust" could never have been told before. Before the Holocaust, there was no Holocaust in the world.

Disconnection from the past comes in the form of forgetting it. One solution to this problem is to remember the past. We can find stone monuments that tell us of the arrival of the tsunami: "Do not build your house below here." Furthermore, a memorial of the atomic bombing set in Hiroshima Peace Memorial Park told us, "Let all the souls here rest in peace, for we shall not repeat the evil." These appear to be robust solutions to our disconnection from the past. However, while they allowed us to remember the events of the tsunami and the A-bomb, they did not remind us of what the city was like before.

Therefore, photographs captured before a disaster are a valuable medium for recalling what it was like before the disaster. When you visit the 9/11 Memorial and Museum in New York, you can see an exhibition with a photograph of the World Trade Center building on September 10, 2001. This photograph reminds us that there had been buildings previously.

Similarly, in areas affected by the Great East Japan Earthquake, family photos stored in homes were washed away by the tsunami. The tsunami damaged more than one million photos across the region, most of which were collected and cleaned by volunteers, Self-Defense Forces personnel, and the survivors themselves (Hatton, 2021).

I have also volunteered to help find the owners of photographs damaged by the tsunami (Figures 4.8–4.9). One day, a woman in her 80s came to the photo return gathering. She told us that she had come to look for a portrait of her deceased mother: Members of her family were killed in the tsunami, but she said she had already had a funeral. When she moved to her new house after the reconstruction, she realized that she had lost a photo of her deceased mother. However, once she noticed the absence of her mother's remains, she became curious about them, and her mother began to appear in her dreams.

Her story made me think about losing the remains and made me realize that there were two kinds of forgetting (Miyamae & Atsumi, 2017). The

Figure 4.8 Survivors finding their photos (photo by the author).

Figure 4.9 Survivors observing bridal photos (photo by the author).

first is forgetting in the sense of everyday language, which means that they have forgotten memories; however, they can remember them if reminded (e.g., damaged photographs). The second is the amnesia she is facing now that she has lost her remains—what we might call the "forgetfulness of forgetting." This means they lose reminders; therefore, they will forget what they remember, and they will forget that they have forgotten their memories. Thus, when she loses her reminders, she loses the ability to remember her mother. Likewise, if the unclaimed photos washed away by the tsunami are not returned to their owners, an increasing number of survivors will fall into forgetfulness of forgetting.

In other words, disconnection means forgetting the days before the disaster and losing the reminders of the days before the disaster, thus losing the opportunity to recall. Therefore, to prevent forgetfulness, it is necessary to keep as many objects as possible to remember our memories, such as family photos taken before a disaster. Simultaneously, it is necessary for someone to have a chat. Reminiscence is more effective when conducted with more than one person. It is also essential that people who do not know the area before the disaster can ask survivors about the area's history. Ideally, in this way, a place of remembrance can be created in which both Tojisha and non-Tojisha can get together.

COLLECTIVE TRAUMA

The second fragmentation in disaster recovery is the loss of community. Disasters divide communities. Often, we can see houses damaged by the tsunami and houses entirely intact side-by-side across the street. Owners of damaged homes do not always build their houses in the same place after a disaster. Survivors often live in temporary housing after a disaster, but those living next to temporary housing are not always the families they know. In addition, temporary housing is occupied by people planning to move out within a few years, which makes it difficult for community activities to occur there. It is common for people to leave their temporary accommodation without knowing who their neighbors are.

In the aftermath of the Great East Japan Earthquake and Tsunami, which also caused a nuclear accident, residents of surrounding areas were displaced from the regions where they were born and raised. This forced relocation resulted in the survivors not fitting well with their new communities and in numerous problems of mindless discrimination and bullying.

One of the tragic consequences of community loss is solitary death. Lonely death means that a person lives alone and dies without being attended to. People often do not even know that a person has died in a room. Moreover, only after the smell of decay has leaked out do neighbors realize that something is wrong. It is well known that lonely deaths are more common in temporary and reconstruction housing. In three prefectures affected by the Great East Japan Earthquake and Tsunami (Iwate, Miyagi, & Fukushima), 614 people died alone over a period of 10 years (Asahi Newspaper, 2021). People die, are isolated from their communities, and are found dead in loneliness, suggesting a community breakdown.

The loss of the community can be psychologically traumatizing to those affected. The American sociologist Kai Erikson (1976) theorized this as "collective trauma" (p. 186), based on his research in Buffalo Creek, West Virginia, which had been damaged by a flood caused by collapsed dams in 1972. Erikson defined collective trauma as "a blow to the basic tissues of social life that damages the bonds attaching people together and impairs the prevailing sense of commonality" (p. 154). Erikson quotes one survivor as follows:

> My lonely feelings is my most difficult problem. I feel as if we were living in a different place, even though we are still in our own home. Nothing seems the same. (p. 211)

The survivor feels the loss of their community, even though they had lived in it for many years before the disaster. In some cases, this may be stronger than the sense of loss they feel when they are forced out of their community.

Erikson suggested that collective trauma intensifies during recovery. Buffalo Creek survivors believed that those displaced in the immediate aftermath of the disaster would return once the town recovered. However, this was not the case. Once they left, they never returned, and the reconstruction left them nowhere to return. Temporary housing, which was intended for temporary living, turned out to be permanent residences. Disaster reconstruction has perpetuated a temporary breakdown of the community in the immediate aftermath of a disaster.

The fable "double-layered town" (Seo, 2021) is an excellent example of the perpetuation of loss through reconstruction. The story is set in the year 2031 in a disaster-stricken area of Tohoku. A young boy born after the disaster realizes that underneath the ground where he is standing is the town where his father grew up. When his father takes him down to the city underneath, he walks where he used to live and tells his young child that this is where the house used to be. It is as if the house is still there, and his father can see it. The boy prays to people who may still be in the town below and those who died in the disaster.

This tale reflects the situation in the affected areas after the disaster. For example, Rikuzentakata City, severely damaged by the tsunami, was raised to an average height of 10 m above sea level after the disaster. It is as if another town had been built on the ground and swept away by the tsunami in a double layer. This means that the pre-tsunami town would never have been restored. A community that once lived there would never be the same. The tsunami removed the community, but it perpetuated the loss of the community due to the recovery.

THE GARDEN AS A TOOL FOR DISASTER RECOVERY

The disconnection I described—the disconnection between Tojisha and non-Tojisha, the disconnection with the past, and the loss of community—can be understood in terms of individualism. The disconnection between Tojisha and non-Tojisha is a bounded being that creates the alienation of not understanding each other's true feelings. Disconnection with the past stems from the difficulty of recovering personal memories, something that only the individual has. The loss of community implies that reconstruction will peel away the skin of the community and that we will have to live as individuals. If so, we need a place to break through individualism and create new connections. Gardens have great potential to play this role.

First, the garden is distinct in that it is both inside and outside the house. The garden is inside because it is within the territory of the house. However, it is also outside the walls and is surrounded by open space. This contrasts with temporary housing, where the victims lived for several years after the disaster until they rebuilt their houses. First, there was no inside temporary housing. Owing to their construction limitations, they are connected to their neighbors' houses, and the walls are so thin that the noise of their lives can be transmitted to their neighbors' homes. There was also no temporary housing outside. There are no porches or verandas (*Engawa* in Japanese) that are open to others.

Moreover, the survivors only rented land from the city for a limited period. In contrast, for survivors who have moved from temporary housing to reconstruction housing, the garden is a precious space within their land where they can enjoy their private time, greet their neighbors and passersby, and make small talk. The place between intimate and social spheres is crucial for restoring connections between people.

Second, the garden transforms disaster survivors cared for by supporters into gardeners. Disaster survivors have been cared for since the disaster. In evacuation centers, they are recipients of aid supplies and food, while in temporary housing, they are recipients of support. They have always been the object of protection whenever help arrives from outside. Support for survivors is essential; however, it has the disadvantage of rendering them powerless. I knew a survivor who seemed to lose energy by receiving more help from outside. She said, "I am sorry that I am always receiving. I feel so bad that I cannot give anything back to them." However, the garden transformed survivors into caring subjects. Planting flowers in the garden means watering them daily, applying fertilizer appropriately, and worrying whether the roots will rot during heavy rains. A small plant becomes the object of care, and the survivor becomes the subject of care. If they plant vegetables, such as tomatoes, they can invite their neighbors to enjoy a home-cooked meal when they harvest. This balance between living as an object of care and as a subject of care is an opportunity to restore human ties.

In Chapter 17, Tsukuba describes the care of the inner sanctum of a Buddhist temple based on his experience as the eldest son of a Buddhist temple priest. He focuses on the laborious process nature of cleaning and decorating, and the fact that it is laborious separates "pure land" from this world. Pure land does not require human care; however, the world in which we live is made up of care. This is precisely because the process is laborious for our world to have meaning. Thus, his point overlaps with my discussion on the subjectification of care in a disaster area.

Chapter 2, Gomes focuses on the curative effects of gardens. According to his systematic review, gardens cure illnesses, reduce stress, and improve the overall sense of well-being. Gardens are also referred to as "healing gardens," and it has been suggested that they should be embedded in healthcare facilities. Why do gardens have healing effects? He focuses on the interaction between gardens and people: Gardens not only provide passive experiences of nature, but they also enable active interaction with people and natural elements. His point of view matches the case of disaster-affected areas.

As relationships are restored in this way, survivors become independent. When we hear the word "independence," we often think of someone doing everything independently. However, independence is not about doing everything independently but being connected to various dependents. The synonym for independence is isolation rather than dependence. We live in a network of dependences on all kinds of people and things. Sometimes, we are helped; sometimes, we help others in the community. However, disasters disrupt our dependence networks and isolate us from ordinary relationships. Lonely deaths in temporary housing occurred because there was no one close to whom they could depend. Dependency on a person is neither a problem nor abnormal; independence is, in effect, about having a viable set of dispersed dependencies (Easton-Calabria & Herson, 2020). The idea of dispersing dependency is vital to rebuilding communities that disasters have destroyed.

GETTING TOJISHA AND NON-TOJISHA TOGETHER

Finally, we would like to give you (supporters, non-Tojisha) some hints on spending time in the garden with survivors. So far, we have discussed the garden's function, but how we spend time with others in the garden is an important aspect. I wrote a paper (Miyamae & Atsumi, 2020) on the importance of spending time together:

> In psychological interviews, the most important element is for the researcher to build a rapport with the interviewee. However, the researcher–interviewee rapport is essentially a calculated relationship, one designed to produce a good interview. In the same way, a doctor may form a relationship with a patient solely for medical purposes. In contrast, human relationships that are not calculated in this way can allow for friendships between people who spend time with each other. In other words, setting a goal to make a human connection may be incongruous with actually making one. (p. 99)

In other words, setting a goal to make a human connection may not be incongruous with actually making one connection. Therefore, simply spending time sitting on a bench in the garden, enjoying the warmth of the sunshine, and carrying on an aimless conversation can restore the human connection. It is not about relationships with a purpose, such as support or research, but simply about being there for the person. Gardens have great potential as places to spend this kind of time.

The community is already there when we notice it. Kai Erikson pointed out,

> In places like Buffalo Creek, where attachments between people are seen as a part of the natural scheme of things—inherited by birth or acquired by proximity—the very idea of 'forming' friendships or 'building' relationships seems a little odd. Attachments like those that are not engineered; they just happen when the communal tone is right. (Erikson, 1976, p. 226)

It is imperative to rebuild a community in disaster recovery where diverse people mix and spend time together. A garden is one of the stages of recovering a community.

REFERENCES

Adams, T. E., Jones, S. H., & Ellis, C. (2015). *Autoethnography*. Oxford University Press.

Asahi Newspaper. (2021, June 25). *614 'lonely deaths' in temporary and reconstruction housing over ten years in three prefectures* (in Japanese). https://www.asahi.com/articles/ASP3762H2P35UTIL0BR.html (2021-6-25)

Easton-Calabria, E., & Maurice, H. (2020). In praise of dependencies: Dispersed dependencies and displacement. *Disasters, 44*(1), 44–62.

Erikson, K. T. (1976). *Everything in its path*. Simon & Schuster.

Gergen, K. J. (2009). *Relational being: Beyond self and community*. Oxford University Press.

Hatton, C. (2021, March). *The memory hunters*. BBC News. https://bbc.co.uk/news/extra/uoo2d6sp5o/japan-photos-tsunami

Kono, F. (2011). *In this corner of the world* [in Japanese]. Futabasha.

Miyamae, R., & Atsumi, T. (2017). Fostering the recovery process of disaster victims from "second loss" through the volunteer "photo restoration gathering" movement [in Japanese]. *The Japanese Journal of Experimental Social Psychology, 56*(2), 122–136.

Miyamae, R., & Atsumi, T. (2020). The picturesque movement: Restoring photographs following the 2011 Tsunami in Japan. *Disasters, 44*(1), 85–102.

Seo, N. (2021). *Double layered town/making a song to replace our positions* [in Japanese]. Shoshikankanbou.

Yamori, K., & Sugiyama, T. (2015). Theoretical consideration of "days-before" narratives [in Japanese]. *Japanese Journal of Qualitative Psychology, 14*, 110–127.

Flexible containers placed in front of private houses, photographed by the first author at municipality X in April 16th, 2015.

The black bags at the bottom of the photo are flexible containers filled with radioactive waste generated by radiation decontamination work. The roofed building on the right side of the photo is a part of a private house, indicating that countless flexible containers are placed very close to the houses where the residents live. Note that the structure of the building at the top of the photo has been blurred out for privacy concerns.

CHAPTER 5

RADIOACTIVE WASTE PUBLICLY PLACED IN A SPACE THAT USED TO BE A YARD AS A PRIVATE PLACE

Time and Sign in the Designated Evacuation Areas After Fukushima Nuclear Power Plant Accident

Tomoo Hidaka
Fukushima Medical University

Hideaki Kasuga
Fukushima Medical University

The effects of the placement of undesirable facilities on residents' immediate environments have been studied in environmental psychology. Such facilities are referred to as locally unwanted land use (LULU) facilities that threaten their surroundings by inflicting or promising to inflict negative

---

The Semiotic Field of the Garden, pages 89–109
Copyright © 2024 by Information Age Publishing
www.infoagepub.com
All rights of reproduction in any form reserved.

externalities on the surrounding environment (Popper, 1985). Among LULU facilities nuclear-related facilities, such as radioactive waste disposal facilities and nuclear power plants, are regarded as highly involuntary, unknown, delayed, new, uncontrollable, fatal, and catastrophic (Fischhoff et al., 1978; Slovic, 1987); thus, these LULU facilities are perceived as most dangerous and as having a high risk for nearby residents. The burden of the presence of LULU facilities on residents can take many forms, including economic loss, reduction of health and quality of life, degradation of the physical environment, and damage to the landscape (Gregory et al., 1991; Haggett, 2011; Schively, 2007). As Armour (1991) suggested, the benefits of LULU facilities are often broadly distributed, whereas the costs tend to be localized to residents.

As a result of the radiation decontamination work started after the Fukushima nuclear power plant (FNP) accident, countless numbers of temporary storage areas for the package called *flexible containers* filled with radioactive waste produced by radiation decontamination work have been placed in the yards of residents in Fukushima Prefecture, which can be considered as LULU facilities. The Great East Japan Earthquake of March 2011 and the subsequent FNP accident contaminated broad areas with radiation. Since the half-lives of radionuclides emitted by nuclear power plants are long (2 years and 30.2 years for cesium-134 and cesium-137, respectively), environmental and health problems have become issues of concern (Hidaka et al., 2016). Full-scale radiation decontamination work was launched in 2012 with the initiative of the Japanese government, and radiation levels in the affected area were reduced to habitable levels by such radiation decontamination work; however, the flexible containers had to be stored somewhere, at least until a final disposal site could be found. Figure 5.1 shows flexible containers, the black-colored bag, on the ground in an area where all residents were evacuated due to high radiation doses. It is important to note that even after decontamination work has reduced the radiation dose and the areas become habitable, the flexible containers will remain in place unless a final disposal site is decided. Considering past studies that revealed that residents consider nuclear-related facilities as high risk (Slovic, 1987; Fischhoff et al., 1978), the placement of flexible containers is assumed to be a threat to residents.

Although there seems to be no doubt that the installation of flexible containers causes discomfort to nearby residents, the reason for this is not apparent. In general, place attachment can explain why the presence of LULU facilities, or changes in the environment of a place due to such installation, can harm people. Place attachment is the emotional connection between people and place (Low & Altman, 1992), and defined as "a bond between an individual or group and a place that can vary in terms of spatial

Figure 5.1 Flexible containers placed in front of private houses, photographed by the first author at municipality X on April 16, 2015.[1]

level, degree of specificity, and social or physical features of the place, and is manifested through affective, cognitive, and behavioral psychological processes" (Scannell & Gifford, 2010, p. 5). Place attachment contributes to emotional and physical health (Swenson, 1998) and establishes community and neighborhood bonds (Long & Perkins, 2007). However, the loss of loved places or damage to the landscape due to the installation of LULU facilities, or a disaster, invokes severe psychological distress (Fried, 2000) and aggressive and denial feelings toward the responsible stakeholders, such as the government (Anton & Lawrence, 2014; Devine-Wright, 2013). Individuals who face such threats to place attachment seek a solution to the situation by actions ranging from an administrative lawsuit for withdrawal of a plan to violence directed toward the stakeholder (Gladwin, 1980), or more mild options than those that engage in the recovery process to restore stability in life, such as joining a self-help group (Zheng et al., 2019).

Importantly, Devine-Wright (2009), in his discussion of place attachment and place identity, pointed out that physical changes in a place are not necessarily required for psychological changes. This view leads us to the idea that people psychologically construct a place, or more precisely, people experience their psychologically constructed places. As place attachment has been described by Smaldone et al. (2008) as "the more emotional or symbolic meanings that people give to places" (p. 480), the meanings attached to places must be explored to understand the experience of place attachment and the threats to place attachment. In this regard, the theoretical perspective of cultural psychology provides clues for a more in-depth understanding. Murrani (2020) differentiated the term "space," which is characterized by multidimensionality and edgelessness, from "place," which is tangible, geographical, and grounded. In Murrani (2020), the reality of the physical field is no longer assumed; instead, a dynamic perspective is adopted in which both space and place are psychologically constructed.

Considering previous studies, the experience of flexible containers being placed in the yard seems to be explained by a sense of injustice (Lind & Tyler, 1988; Smith & Tyler, 1996; Tyler & Lind, 1992) that our land, rather than someone else's, has been unfairly targeted. However, we believe that it is difficult to inquire about the experience of installing flexible containers only using the concept of justice/injustice. While research on sense of justice/injustice over LULU facilities focuses on a subset of human experiences, the entire picture of that experience may be much larger; the questions from micro-genetic perspective should be asked as to why or how experiences, including inequities, arise. To inquire about this, it would be helpful to explore what changed before and after the installation of the flexible containers, and we suspect that the transformation of meaning in the same physical space, which can be used as a garden/yard or temporary storage for flexible containers, is responsible for the difference in the way it is experienced. Research from such a perspective also needs to be explored through narratives to understand the place and its transformation in the life course, as Bailey et al. showed (Bailey et al., 2016). We believe this study may provide fundamental and theoretical insights into the relationship between people and place and provide clues to practical assistance by clarifying the reasons for the suffering of the local landowners who offered their land as a temporary storage site for flexible containers.

This study aims to describe the experience of having a flexible container placed in an individual's yard and discuss it from the theoretical perspectives of cultural psychology and semiotics.

METHODS

This study was conducted as part of our research project in municipality X, Fukushima, Japan. Note that some parts of the methods section's descriptions are common to our previous study (e.g., Hidaka et al., 2021).

Study Location and Situation

The study location, municipality X, had three designated evacuation areas from 2011 to 2017 within its land. These three evacuation areas were made based on the severity of radioactive pollution: the "difficult-to-return zones," with 50 mSv/year or more; the "restricted residence zones," between 20 and 50 mSv/year; and the evacuation order cancellation preparation zones, with 20 mSv/year or less (Ministry of Health, Labour & Welfare, n.d.). The difficult-to-return zones were off-limits areas where nobody could stay due to its severe radioactive pollution, while the other two zones were on-limits areas where individuals could temporarily enter for decontamination work, home maintenance, and business. Although the evacuation orders in restricted residence zones and evacuation order cancellation preparation zones were lifted in April 2017 after the completion of radiation decontamination work, these three evacuation areas were still functioning at the time this study was conducted.

Municipality X was located about 40 km from the FNP, and all residents of the municipality had to evacuate due to the spread of radioactive materials caused by the FNP accident in March 2011. However, since the decontamination work started in 2012, many residents have continued to engage in decontamination work in their municipality to rebuild their hometowns with their own hands. Residents were aware of the official timeline for lifting evacuation orders for the restricted residence zones and evacuation order cancellation preparation zones in April 2017, when this study was conducted. Therefore, the residents, including informants, actively collected information on the recovery situation in municipality X to decide whether to return to their hometown. Inevitably, this situation highlighted the gap between the ideal state of "recovery" for the residents themselves and the actual state of the recovery, thus creating conditions suitable for information collection for the purpose of this study.

Theoretical Background of Inquiry

We employed the trajectory equifinality approach (TEA; Sato, 2016), one of the approaches in cultural psychology to gauge individuals' experiences through qualitative research. As Sato (2016) explained, TEA describes the meaning processes of how individuals live their lives with social, historical, and semiotic conditions, considering that people are active, goal-oriented agents. In this study, we inductively explored how the transformation occurred from "my yard" to "public garbage site" regarding the private land even though the land itself was physically the same and how informants, the landowners, engaged in the meaning-making regarding the transformation situation. The TEA is considered effective in elucidating these processes of transformation around the land, or garden, and is also suitable for depicting the conflicts between collective and individual cultures, and thus employed in this study.

Data Collection

Interviewee Recruitment: Historical Structured Inviting

The interviews were held with the employee of a company operating the radiation decontamination work in municipality X, Fukushima Prefecture, since 2012. Most of the workers employed by the company comprised individuals from municipality X. The interviewees were selected based on the notion of historical structured inviting (HSI). In HSI, the informant, who has a psychological state or life event on which the researcher's interest is focused, is invited to participate in the research, and then his/her actual or possible life event experiences are investigated (Sato, 2016).

Interviewee

The interviewees were 14 employees of the said company; note, they are described with symbols "A" to "N" throughout this manuscript for anonymity. The first author was involved in the company for monthly occupational health support since 2013. Thus, although the author and employees, including interviewees, knew each other before this study, the relationship was that of supporter and support recipients. Through daily conversations with employees, the following facts were discovered: many employees deeply concerned about whether they should return to their hometown after the lifting of the evacuation order had views and opinions about the ideal form of reconstruction and had offered their land to the government as a temporary storage site for nuclear waste. Fourteen potential interviewees had these characteristics in common and thus had experienced the transformation from my yard to public garbage site regarding the land. Thus, we considered that they were suitable informants for study purposes and invited/recruited them to participate in this study.

Interview Procedure

The first author conducted data collection longitudinally in time between interviewees' tasks using an ethnographic interview method (Spradley, 1979). An ethnographic interview is a method used to gather information in a naturalistic setting through informal interviews, investigating the context of the informant's daily activities (Spradley, 1979). An ethnographic interview method was employed because interviewees had no time to be interviewed other than during business hours because of their busy private schedules. The following two questions were used in the interviews: "What conditions do you think are necessary for recovery from the Great East Japan Earthquake and FNP accident?" and "What kind of state do you need to feel that recovery is completed?" These questions were designed to highlight how the interviewees perceived the gap between the ideal state of recovery and the current state and investigate the inhibiting factors contributing to that gap. In addition to these core questions, information, such as fundamental attributes like age, attachment to municipality X, and his relationship with family and other residents, were collected in the interviews. The form of questions and interview locations changed and remained flexible depending on the interviewee's preferences. Interviews were recorded with notes and, if possible, by an IC recorder and then produced as a transcript.

Study Period, Interview Times, and Lengths

This study was conducted from 2014 to 2017. As shown in Table 5.1, the time and length of the interviews varied from interviewee to interviewee,

TABLE 5.1   Interview Details

Interviewee's Name (symbol)	Basic Attribution	Date	Time
A	40s male	April 24th in 2014; March 24th and April 16th in 2015; April 11th, June 10th and December 14th in 2016.	6
B	50s male	March 9th in 2015.	1
C	60s male	April 16th and December 14th in 2015; February 17th in 2016.	3
D	30s male	November 24th in 2015; July 21st in 2016.	2
E	50s male	November 24th in 2015	1
F	50s female	February 17th in 2016.	1
G	40s female	February 17th, December 14th in 2016; March 23rd in 2017.	3
H	40s male	July 7th in 2016; March 15th in 2017.	2
I	30s male	August 3rd in 2016,	1
J	50s male	September 14th in 2016; January 25th in 2017.	2
K	60s male	September 14th in 2016.	1
L	50s male	September 29th in 2016.	1
M	60s male	October 25th in 2016.	1
N	60s male	January 25th in 2017.	1

Note: Interviewees were sorted by, and their age class was the initial interview date. Although not all the interviewees' episodes described here were presented in the text, the models we organized using Vygotsky's notion of sign and longitudinally as a minimum TEM are based on all interviewees' narratives.

depending on their work schedules. Although the interview lengths were inconsistent, the average interview length was 51 min, and the total length was 612 minutes.

Analysis

The transcripts were coded using open coding (Holton, 2007). The first and second authors confirmed 50 responses to the questions using fieldnotes; more accurate data were obtained from the corresponding IC recorder audio recordings, if possible. Then, those responses were coded, and the interviewees' style of narrating the ideal recovery and its impediments were identified by repeatedly reviewing the fieldnotes and transcripts. The interviewees' narratives had the following three characteristics: First, the interviewees ideally wanted the situation back before the disaster, but realistically recognized that such ideal reconstruction on their land was not possible. The following excerpt provides an example:

> For me, the ideal situation is one in which the landscape is recovered, regardless of the dose in my land. It would be nice if there were no more decontamination wastes and decontamination workers. The best solution is the restoration of the land to its pre-disaster state. However, I know it is idealistic. (Interviewee G)

Second, the obstruction toward such ideal land status tended to be attributed to the presence of "flexible containers," a black package of radioactive waste from radiation decontamination work placed across municipality X, including in the yard of interviewees' homes (see Figure 5.1). This characteristic was exemplified by the following response:

> I, as well as other residents, are becoming more comfortable with flexible containers. However, if you take a step back and think about it, the current situation is generally abnormal. Who would want to live in a place where radioactive waste is in plain sight? (Interviewee H)

Third, the interviewees seemed to skillfully use the words "place" and space interchangeably: the word space was preferred when interviewees referred to physical aspects of their yard, whereas the word "place" was often used to refer to relationships, such as family and self, memories of the past, and expectations of the future. Although Murrani (2020) distinguished between the terms "place" and space from an academic perspective, we focused on inductively examining the possible meanings of such word usage as indicated by the interviewees regardless of Murrani's differentiation, since such word usage may be expected to have cultural meaning among interviewees, landowners. These three characteristics were important because they reflect the typical narrative storyline of the interviewees; thus, they were selected as a unit for further analysis.

This unit of analysis was theoretically reorganized as a structure consisting of the following three items: the interviewee(s) as subject; ideal recovery of the land, a perceived meaning in their backyard, as an object/goal; the situation before/after the placement of flexible containers as a sign. This structure seems to be consistent with Vygotsky's sign theory (Wertsch, 1985), thus, this theoretical model was applied to the structure. Because seemingly the meaning of "yard," which should be physically identical, was psychologically transformed before and after the placement of the flexible containers, the events before and after the placement of the containers were featured based on the narratives. The mediative function was inductively found for how interviewees perceived their "yard" and how they psychologically assessed their yard. The following response suggests the presence of such mediation both before/after the installation of flexible containers:

> It is absolutely disappointing to see the containers. I lose my motivation to return to my home every time I see them. I feel as if it was not my yard, where my children used to play tree climbing. I am sure that I have offered my land to the government as a temporary storage place for the flexible containers. So I knew this would happen. However, it is unacceptable that my yard is now in miserable sight, a public garbage dump for radioactive waste. (Interviewee G)

Here, the Interviewee G felt as if his yard was not his own, and this strange feeling of transformation of meaning from my yard to public garbage site has seemed to be mediated and perceived by the flexible containers, or more precisely, the semiotic mediation by sign originated from such containers. In addition, we investigated what signs worked before the placement of the containers to clarify the transformation.

To provide a theoretical discussion on such relationships between interviewees, containers, and meaning on their yard in detail, the *trajectory equifinality modeling* (TEM; Sato, 2016) was employed. TEM is a model included in TEA for depicting the moments when changes occur in the human life trajectory, exploring the social factors that affect those changes within chronological and experience-based periods. We used the following three analytical tools for TEM. *Equifinality point* (EFP) is the point at which diverse trajectories converge, and the *polarized equifinality point* (P-EFP) is the notion of a complementary set of EFP to relativize the EFP. *Bifurcation point* (BFP) is the point at which more than two trajectories diverge and where sign works. In this study, BFP had a vital role in explaining the transformation of meaning on the yard before/after the placement of flexible containers. Importantly, it seemed that interviewees' meaning regarding land corresponds with EFP, whereas the placement of flexible containers works as a sign at BFP. In this study, we did not firmly emphasize the entire picture of human life trajectory; instead, we pursued the experience of psychological transformation regarding the lands before/after the placement of radioactive waste, the flexible containers. Therefore, the interviewee's experience was depicted by only using the concepts of BFP and EFP/P-EFP in addition to the notion of sign to organize the minimum model.

RESULTS AND DISCUSSION

The transformation of the meaning of the land from yard to public garbage site before and after the placement of flexible containers was depicted as models from Vygotsky's notion of sign and longitudinally as a minimum TEM, as shown in Figure 5.2, 5.3, and 5.4.

Although the individual episodes differed from interviewee to interviewee, these abstract models seemed to be common to all. In the following descriptions, we will explain trajectories regarding the transformation of meaning from my yard to public garbage site using TEM (Figure 5.2), and its related signs work at the BFPs of whether the physically same space is perceived as a my yard or a public garbage site are focused and explained (Figure 5.3–5.4). The reasons why the interviewees felt that transformation was painful were discussed from the perspective of the conflict between collective and individual cultures over the psychological meaning of a place in the evacuation areas. For readability, the episode/narrative is placed in quotation marks on the interview date.

As shown in Figure 5.2, the process had the start point "space next to my home," the first BFP of whether such place would become my yard or not, and then the second BFP to EFP/P-EFP of "Keep becoming as my yard" and "Becoming public garbage site." The following three characteristics need to be emphasized. First, a place must be given more meaning than mere space, or such a space cannot be perceived as a place. The following narrative will illustrate that an interviewee felt the lack of such meaning in the start point "space next to my home" and that the physical space came to be perceived as a psychological place by being filled with meaning:

> Our ancestors and we have been gradually clearing mountains and cultivating fields to incorporate into our land for generations. This land is like our backyard, where we used to gather mushrooms. Our land can be used as the place for our life when we live there and take care of it, but once people are gone, the land will return to undeveloped space, nothing but bushes. (Interviewee A, December 14, 2016)

In this narrative, the interviewee told his recognition that the undeveloped spaces became their land, even backyard, through the continuous efforts of him and his ancestor, and that the place will be lost in the form of

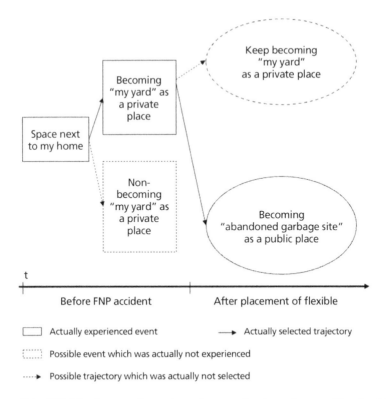

Figure 5.2 TEM for the transformation of perception from "my yard" to "public garbage site" among landowners/interviewees in evacuation areas.[2]

a return to undeveloped space if continuous efforts are not made. To feel that a specific space is "my (back)yard," it seems that the act of continuing to become is necessary.

This perspective of "become (becoming)" has important cultural psychological implications. The second feature is that the interviewee's experience does not begin with the conflict between my yard and the public garbage site, but that such conflict occurs after the experience of "becoming" my yard, instead of "being" my yard. The concept of becoming and being should be distinguished because of their nature. In cultural psychology, the process of "becoming" is treated as a creative adaptation that goes beyond the immediate needs of the environment (Valsiner, 2007b, p. 197); this concept is necessarily accompanied by irreversible time and the goal-oriented nature of humans (Valsiner, 2017b). The concept of becoming has often been employed in research on developmental psychological topics related to transformation and adaptation, for example, a study of motherhood (e.g., Cabell et al., 2015). This concept can be applied to the interpretation of psychological places as exemplified above by Interviewee A, according to the notion that places belong to people, but not vice versa, in cultural psychology (Sato et al., 2012).

The details of the psychological event at this start point and the first BFP are depicted as a sign-mediated becoming process, as shown in Figure 5.3. Interview A's experience may be understood as a sign mediated becoming process in which this space next to my home became my yard as a private place due to the presence of temporal connections between past ancestors, present self, and future yet unseen descendants working as a sign, which is perceived through the developed field. Since Interviewee A emphasized his connection to past generations by using words such as "for generations" and "ancestor," and he is also concerned about the future by mentioning the possibility of abandoning the land, it is rational to highlight the process of how this land had become. This "process of how this land had become" seems to be well explained by employing the concept of becoming. According to Valsiner (2017a), the social sciences habitually turn the phenomenon of becoming into those of being, which treats what has emerged "as it now is," whereas not "as it came to be"; therefore, the concept of becoming is suitable for interpretation of his narrative.

Notably, as shown in Figure 5.3, the whole process of this becoming may be represented as the establishment of an individual culture of creating my yard. Here, we can see the emergence of a culture of carving out fields and mountains and turning the land into a private place for residents' lives. Note that there is generality in how a sign works, whereas there is diversity in what works as a sign. What kind of meaning we find from a matter differs from individual to individual; therefore, a human may select a sign from multiple signs on his or her initiative. This "the principle of redundant control" (Valsiner, 2007a, p. 57) makes it possible to explain the balance of

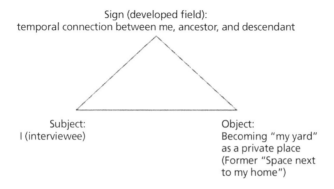

Figure 5.3 Sign mediated becoming process from space next to my home to "my yard" as private place before FNP accident.[3]

the diversity in what works as a sign for "becoming my yard" and generality in how sign works for transforming space next to his/her home into a private place. The following narrative represents the presence of a similar privatizing process of space by a different sign from the previous example:

> I cannot even hear the children's voices in municipality X. No community can be sustainable with only older people or adults. For me, a hometown is a place where everyone, young and old, men, and women, can be found. The grandchildren's shrieks of laughter used to give me the feeling of living in my own home and yard as a safe place, but that feeling has been lost. (Interviewee C, December 14, 2015)

Though the tone of loss is more robust than in the previous example, this narrative emphasizes the importance of intergenerational connections between the younger generation, such as grandchildren, the elderly, and himself as an intermediate generation between them. The "grandchildren's shrieks of laughter" seemingly serves as a sign, and space seems to be privatized by this sign; what works as a sign varies from person to person, but how the sign works is similar.

Related to these episodes regarding the experiences of "becoming my yard," the third characteristic is that the placement of flexible containers on interviewees' land is the experience of "forced overwriting" of my yard once filled with personal meanings by the public's will. The "Keep becoming my yard as a private place" is juxtaposed with the "Becoming abandoned public garbage site as a public place" as shown in the EFP/P-EFP and the second BFP in Figure 5.2. The installation of flexible containers seemed to damage the landscape, and indeed there were narratives in line with it; however, the interviewees emphasized more about the nuance of "abandonment" than the damage to the landscape. The episodes related to damage to the landscape are as follows:

> There is a lot of flexible containers around my house. I do not want to go back to those places. A vast number of them are piling up in the fields and rice paddies. I am disappointed to see them. (Interviewee J, September 14, 2016)

> Black bags, I do not like the color. Municipality X has been economically poor, but it has richly endowed nature, with flowers in all seasons and crops. (Interviewee A, April 16, 2015)

In the first Interviewee J's case, he described the accumulation of flexible containers in the fields and rice paddies, which symbolized agriculture as the primary industry of municipality X. He felt disappointed that such containers damaged familiar landscapes. In the following case by Interviewee A, he expressed flexible containers as "black bags" and contrasted their unnatural "blackness" with the richness of natural flowers and crops to show how the flexible containers damaged municipality X, including his land.

However, as mentioned earlier, the sense of abandonment seems to be more critical than superficial blows to the landscape:

> The Ministry of the Environment said that the flexible containers would be removed entirely in 5 years, but this is probably impossible due to the vast amount of waste, and it may take 10 to 20 years. We provided our lands for the temporary storage of the flexible containers on the assumption that they will be moved to other suitable sites soon. However, the containers may be reclaimed in the X municipality since there is not enough space available to relocate the flexible containers outside of municipality X. It is like we have drawn the shortest straw. (Interviewee A, January 25, 2017)

> The severely contaminated areas in municipality X are possibly no longer inhabitable even after decontamination, so there is an option to use those areas as landfill sites for decontamination wastes, flexible containers. However, the mere fact that a flexible container is buried in this part of the village makes me sick. Some hope that other municipalities would take over the project, but that did not happen actually. (Interviewee G, December 14, 2016)

These narratives vividly illustrate the isolation of the residents of municipality X caused by the fact that the decision to use the space of municipality X as a storage site for flexible containers was initiated publicly and supported as part of a national policy. The interviewees felt that their lands were forced into a disadvantageous role and were publicly abandoned due to the imposition of temporary storage and final disposal sites for flexible containers. Ideally, the storage of the flexible containers resulting from the FNP accident, which was one of the most significant accidents in history that shook the entire country, should have been taken by the responsibility of other prefectures or municipalities in Japan, not just Fukushima Prefecture or X municipality. The Japanese government claims that the final disposal of the waste will be done outside of Fukushima Prefecture by 2045 (Okutsu & Hanafusa, 2021), but this schedule is too long-term to be accepted by the residents with any sense of reality. Many residents suspect that the final disposal will occur in Fukushima Prefecture, even though the storage in Fukushima Prefecture was supposed to be temporary (Saito, 2015). This situation, which could be interpreted as the agreement, in a possibly reluctant manner, of the entire population outside Fukushima Prefecture to store radioactive waste in X municipality, caused a deep sense of disappointment among the interviewees, the landowners. A sense of injustice may be behind interviewees' sense of abandonment, as indicated by Interviewee A's statement above that he was "drawn the short straw"; given that injustice in environmental discourse is strongly associated with feelings of anger, deprivation, and discrimination (Tyler, 2000; Taylor, 2000), it is rational that the

Radioactive Waste Publicly Placed in a Space That Used to be a Yard • 103

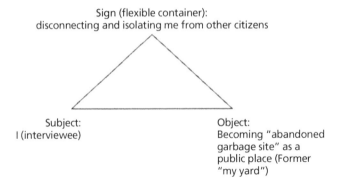

Figure 5.4 Sign mediated transformation from space next to my home to "public garbage site" as a public place after the placement of flexible containers.[4]

placement of flexible containers with an uncertain future is experienced as psychological rather than spatial.

A detailed depiction of this scenario is shown in Figure 5.4. A sign "disconnecting and isolating me from other citizens" worked, and thus the object, originally the my yard, became an "abandoned garbage site" as a public place that is difficult to pass on to children and descendants. This may contrast favorably with the situation shown in Figure 5.3, where the temporal connection between generations functioned as a sign. Although such temporal connections used to work as a sign and thus interviewees could perceive their space as my yard in the past, the disconnecting and isolating sign after the placement of flexible containers threatened such temporal connection, and then the place turned into an abandoned garbage site.

This interpretation may be supported by the following narrative, which shows that there is no practical vision or model for the future. Therefore, it has become difficult to pass on my yard to the next generation:

> After the decontamination, it is important to take over the work and human resources for the reconstruction. Even after the decontamination is finished, there are various issues, such as how to return the farmland to landowners who evacuated to other areas than municipality X. By the way, who will come back? Sure, the older adults may come back, but they do not have much time left in their life, so it is not easy to expect their contribution to municipality X's reconstruction. Young people and children have evacuated to other areas, and they must have felt that those areas are their hometowns. No reasons found for younger generations' return to municipality X. (Interviewee A, March 24, 2015)

> The government says that they will remove the flexible containers in 5 years. It is impossible. It will take at least 10 to 20 years. How can we wait that long? Rather, there is a possibility that they will just landfill such containers. They

will probably make excuses that the radiation level has dropped; it is no longer radioactive waste and, therefore, can be buried. Naturally, young people will not come back because they are concerned about radiation's health risks and hazards. So, who maintains our lands? (Interviewee N, January 25, 2017)

GENERAL DISCUSSION

Our cultural psychological reflections emphasize that individuals can construct a psychological reality in which individuals feel my yard, even though space is only a "space next to my home" through the work of signs. Therefore, the change of sign leads us to the transformative experience where individuals access, at least psychologically. The space next to my home can be experienced as my yard, where individual culture is established, or it also can become a decontaminated waste dump in general, where collective culture is dominant.

The experience of transforming the one and only my yard into a general storage area for flexible containers is important because such experience suggests that the transformation of individual culture into collective culture may have psychological impacts. A "stable, meaningful, and valuable" experience in a place of residence contributes to the development of an individual's positive sense of self (Nowell et al., 2006); for interviewees, the experience of meaning a space next to their home as my yard and of having used the place for generations seems to be consistent with the Nowell et al.'s concept of stable, meaningful, and valuable experience. In other words, the installation of the flexible container is the experience of the loss of my yard, an irreplaceable place, and thus may be perceived as a threat to positive self and identity, as well as an invasion of an individual's life, including that of ancestors and descendants. Previous studies have indicated that such threats and invasions are associated with psychological distress in the context of place attachment (Fried, 2000; Pickover & Slowik, 2013), and it is also known that high levels of place attachment and inequity predict low receptivity to land-use change (Devine-Wright & Howes, 2010; Devine-Wright, 2013; Vorkinn & Riese, 2001). Considering these previous studies and the fact that interviewees mentioned the land-use change from my yard to garbage site, the interviewees' strong perceptions of distress, dissatisfaction, and inequity would not be surprising; in light of the notion that the garden is inherently interwoven with our existence (see Chapter 3), such land-use change may be experienced as a threat to their existence. What is important here is that, unlike these previous studies, our study assumes a psychological construction of place, which may allow for a deeper interpretation of the relationship between cultural transformation and place in mind. We posit that people may feel psychological distress over the dwarfing of an important private place into a public place, in short, the transformation into a collective culture.

A more practical question about coping with such invasive cultural transformation is as follows: How can the uniqueness of my yard be recovered/revitalized? As we exemplified by Interviewee G in the analysis sub-section, there is no doubt that the best solution is restoring the land to its pre-disaster state, if possible. However, a human being is in an irreversible time and thus cannot take such an option; a disaster harms time perspectives and community and thus may lead to the loss of human relationships in the past and possible future (see Chapter 6, this volume). Considering the data in this study, the temporal connection with ancestors and descendants makes it possible to construct a unique my yard. Previous studies have suggested that dialogs with ancestors and descendants that we have never seen are based on an extremely high level of intelligence that humans have acquired evolutionarily (Bering, 2006), and such dialogs have the function to construct/reconstruct time, encompassing imagination and dreams (Amoureux & Reddy, 2021; Whyte, 2018), and enable individuals to understand their existence in relation to specific places and practices (Rua et al., 2017). Given these suggestions, the meaning of place may become comprehensive through dialog with ancestors and descendants, and such meaning-making may contribute to the recovery of a feeling of uniqueness of the place, my yard.

Importantly, if the yard can be psychologically constructed, it may be possible to maintain a sense of home and (re)create one's own yard/garden as a private place physically elsewhere, even if a person leaves the X municipality; this is a practical application of the idea that the place belongs to the person (Sato et al., 2012). Here, we find the relevant connection with an argument suggested by cultural anthropologists and deconstructionists that the concept of "home" should be de-territorialized and no longer perceived as bound to fixed places (Kokot, 2006; Gupta & Ferguson, 1992). As Brah (1996) had employed the concept of "homing desire" instead of "desire for a homeland" in his discussion of diaspora, to understand a place dynamically; just as nostalgia can be described as a home-making practice, the interest in a garden can be established and explained as a yard-making/garden-making practice, which is the result of work of signs (Murrani, 2020). This dynamic is explained by the agency of the human being in the loss of place; because this agency is not fixed but plastic (Murrani, 2020); it will lead the individual to a "variable future" and a "place that belongs to the person." Although these discussions have provided insights into the relationship between place, human, and psychology, its detailed processes and social directions/guidance have not yet been explored. We are convinced that these explorations will provide fundamental and theoretical contributions to psychology and, therefore, knowledge on which to base support for evacuees who are still suffering ten years after the FNP accident.

NOTE

1. The black bags at the bottom of the photo are flexible containers filled with radioactive waste generated by radiation decontamination work. The roofed building on the right side of the photo is a part of a private house, indicating that countless flexible containers are placed very close to the houses where the residents live. Note that the architecture structure at the top of the photo has been blurred out for privacy concerns.
2. The space associated with his/her home became the yard at the bifurcation point before the FNP accident, whereas they perceived the same space as a place for garbage dump after the placement of flexible containers. Note that signs are at work at each bifurcation point, as shown in detail in Figures 5.3 and 5.4, and that the place is psychologically constructed.
3. The interviewees seemed to have transformed and accessed the space physically next to their home into a psychologically private place, my yard, by a sign that allowed them to feel a temporal connection with themselves, their ancestors, and their descendants. This triangular structure, in which physical space is transformed into a psychological place, indicates the establishment of the garden as an individual culture.
4. The interviewees seemed to have transformed and accessed the space physically next to their home into a psychologically public place, an abandoned garbage site, by a sign of disconnection and isolation that made them feel that their land had been abandoned by the people they were supposed to share their pain with. This triangular structure exemplifies that the place belongs to a collective culture.

ACKNOWLEDGMENT

We thank all the interviewees for their cooperation in this study. This work was supported by JSPS KAKENHI Grant Number JP16K17338 and the 2015 Japanese Psychological Association Research Grant for Disaster Recovery.

REFERENCES

Amoureux, J., & Reddy, V. (2021). Multiple anthropocenes: Pluralizing space-time as a response to 'the Anthropocene.' *Globalizations, 18*(6). https://doi.org/10.1080/14747731.2020.1864178

Anton, C. E., & Lawrence, C. (2014). Home is where the heart is: The effect of place of residence on place attachment and community participation. *Journal of Environmental Psychology, 40*, 451–461.

Armour, A. M. (1991). The siting of locally unwanted land uses: Towards a cooperative approach. *Progress in Planning, 35*, 1–74.

Bailey, E., Devine-Wright, P., & Batel, S. (2016). Using a narrative approach to understand place attachments and responses to power line proposals: The

importance of life-place trajectories. *Journal of Environmental Psychology, 48,* 200–211.
Bering, J. M. (2006). The folk psychology of souls. *Behavioral and Brain sciences, 29,* 453–498.
Brah, A. (1996). *Cartographies of diaspora: Contesting identities.* Routledge.
Cabell, K. R., Marsico, G., Cornejo, C., & Valsiner, J. (2015). *Making meaning, making motherhood.* Information Age Publishing.
Devine-Wright, P. (2009). Rethinking NIMBYism: The role of place attachment and place identity in explaining place-protective action. *Journal of Community & Applied Social Psychology, 19,* 426–441.
Devine-Wright, P. (2013). Explaining "NIMBY" objections to a power line: the role of personal, place attachment and project-related factors. *Environment and Behavior, 45,* 761–781.
Devine-Wright, P., & Howes, Y. (2010). Disruption to place attachment and the protection of restorative environments: A wind energy case study. *Journal of Environmental Psychology, 30,* 271–280.
Fischhoff, B., Slovic, P., Lichtenstein, S., Read, S., & Combs, B. (1978). How safe is safe enough? A psychometric study of attitudes towards technological risks and benefits. *Policy Sciences, 9,* 127–152.
Fried, M. (2000). Continuities and discontinuities of place. *Journal of Environmental Psychology, 20,* 193–205.
Gladwin, T. N. (1980). Patterns of environmental conflict over industrial facilities in the United States, 1970–78. *Natural Resource Journal, 20,* 243–274.
Gregory, R., Kunreuther, H., Easterling, D., & Richards, K. (1991). Incentives policies to site hazardous waste facilities. *Risk Analysis, 11,* 667–675.
Gupta, A., & Ferguson, J. (1992). Beyond "culture": Space, identity, and the politics of difference. *Cultural Anthropology, 7,* 6–23.
Haggett, C. (2011). Understanding public responses to offshore wind power. *Energy Policy, 39,* 503–510.
Hidaka, T., Kakamu, T., Hayakawa, T., Kumagai, T., Jinnouchi, T., Sato, S., Tsuji, M., Nakano, S., Koyama, K., & Fukushima, T. (2016). Effect of age and social connection on perceived anxiety over radiation exposure among decontamination workers in Fukushima Prefecture, Japan. *Journal of Occupational Health, 58,* 186–195.
Hidaka, T., Kasuga, H., Kakamu, T., & Fukushima, T. (2021). Discovery and revitalization of "Feeling of Hometown" from a disaster site inhabitant's continuous engagement in reconstruction work: Ethnographic interviews with a radiation decontamination worker over 5 years following the Fukushima Nuclear Power Plant Accident. *Japanese Psychological Research.* https://doi.org/10.1111/jpr.12369
Holton, J. A. (2007). The coding process and its challenges. In A. Bryant & K. Charmaz (Eds.), *The SAGE handbook of grounded theory: Part III* (pp. 265–289). SAGE.
Kokot, W. (2006). Culture and space: Anthropological approaches. *Ethnoscripts, 9,* 10–23.
Lind, E. A., & Tyler, T. R. (1988). *The social psychology of social justice.* Plenum.

Long, D. A., & Perkins, D. D. (2007). Community social and place predictors of sense of community: A multilevel and longitudinal analysis. *Journal of Community Psychology, 35*, 563–581.

Low, S. M., & Altman, I. (1992). Place attachment: A conceptual inquiry. In I. Altman & S. M. Low (Eds.), *Place attachment* (pp. 1–12). Plenum.

Ministry of Health, Labour, and Welfare. (n.d.). *Guidance on the prevention of radiation hazards during works under a designated dose rate.* Retrieved June 24, 2019 from http://www.mhlw.go.jp/english/topics/2011eq/workers/dr/dr/pr_120615_a08.pdf

Murrani, S. (2020). Contingency and plasticity: The dialectical re-construction of the concept of home in forced displacement. *Culture & Psychology, 26*, 173–186.

Nowell, B. L., Berkowitz, S. L., Deacon, Z., & Foster-Fishman, P. (2006). Revealing the cues within community places: Stories of identity, history, and possibility. *American Journal of Community Psychology, 37*, 29–46.

Okutsu, A., & Hanafusa R. (2021, March 10). *Fukushima 10 years on: Toxic problem, few solutions—Why Japan's nuclear power dilemma has only worsened with time.* Nikkei Asia. https://asia.nikkei.com/Spotlight/The-Big-Story/Fukushima-10-years-on-toxic-problem-few-solutions

Pickover, S., & Slowik, L. H. (2013). Repercussions of mortgage foreclosure: Loss of place attachment, adult roles, and trust. *Adultspan Journal, 12*, 113–123.

Popper, F. J. (1985). The environmentalist and the LULU. *Environment: Science and Policy for Sustainable Development, 27*, 7–40.

Rua, M., Hodgetts, D., & Stolte, O. E. E. (2017). Māori men: An indigenous psychological perspective on the interconnected self. *New Zealand Journal of Psychology, 46*, 55–63.

Saito, M. (2015, March 9). *Fukushima residents torn over nuclear waste storage plan.* Reuters. https://jp.reuters.com/article/us-japan-tsunami-widerimage/fukushima-residents-torn-over-nuclear-waste-storage-plan-idINKBN0M50HS20150309

Sato, T. (2016). From TEM to TEA: The making of a new approach. In T. Sato, N. Mori, & J. Valsiner (Eds.), *Making of the future: The trajectory equifinality approach in cultural psychology* (pp. 7–12). Information Age Publishing.

Sato, T., Fukuda, M., Hidaka, T., Kido, A., Nishida, M., & Akasaka, M. (2012). The authentic culture of living well: Pathways to psychological well-being. In J. Valsiner (Ed.), *The Oxford handbook of culture and psychology* (pp. 1078–1091). Oxford University Press.

Scannell, L., & Gifford, R. (2010). Defining place attachment: A tripartite organizing framework. *Journal of Environmental Psychology, 30*, 1–10.

Schively, C. (2007). Understanding the NIMBY and LULU phenomena: Reassessing our knowledge base and informing future research. *Journal of Planning Literature, 21*, 255–266.

Slovic, P. (1987). Perception of risk. *Science, 236*, 280–285.

Smaldone, D., Harris, C., & Sanyal, N. (2008). The role of time in developing place meanings. *Journal of Leisure Research, 40*, 479–504.

Smith, H. J., & Tyler, T. R. (1996). Justice and power: When will justice concerns encourage the advantaged to support policies which redistribute economic resources and the disadvantaged to willingly obey the law? *European Journal of Social Psychology, 26*, 171–200.

Spradley, J. P. (1979). *The ethnographic interview*. Holt, Rinehart and Winston.

Swenson, M. M. (1998). The meaning of home to five elderly women. *Health Care for Women International, 19*, 381–393.

Taylor, D. E. (2000). The rise of the Environmental Justice paradigm: Injustice framing and the social construction of environmental discourses. *American Behavioral Scientist, 43*, 508–580.

Tyler, T. R. (2000). Social justice: Outcome and procedure. *International Journal of Psychology*, 35, 117–125.

Tyler, T. R., & Lind, E. A. (1992). A relational model of authority in groups. In M. Zanna (Ed.), *Advances in experimental social psychology* (pp. 115–191). Academic Press.

Valsiner, J. (2007a). *Culture in minds and societies*. Sage.

Valsiner, J. (2007b). Developmental epistemology and implications for methodology. In R. M. Lerner (Ed), *Handbook of child psychology* (6th ed.; pp.166–209). John Wiley & Sons.

Valsiner, J. (2017a). Culture, development, and methodology in psychology: Beyond alienation through data. In M. Raudsepp (Ed.), *Between self and societies: Creating psychology in a new key* (pp. 121–139). TLU Press.

Valsiner, J. (2017b). General epistemology of open systems. In J. Valsiner (Ed), *From methodology to methods in human psychology* (pp. 13–24). Springer International Publishing.

Vorkinn, M., & Riese, H. (2001). Environmental concern in a local context: The significance of place attachment. *Environment and Behavior, 33*, 249–263.

Wertsch, J. (1985). *Vygotsky and the social formation of mind*. Harvard University Press.

Whyte, K. P. (2018). Food sovereignty, justice, and indigenous peoples: An essay on settler colonialism and collective continuance. In A. Barnhill, M. Budolfson, & T. Doggett (Eds.), *The Oxford handbook of food ethics*. Oxford University Press.

Zheng, C., Zhang, J., Guo, Y., Zhang, Y., & Qian, L. (2019). Disruption and reestablishment of place attachment after large-scale disasters: The role of perceived risk, negative emotions, and coping. *International Journal of Disaster Risk Reduction, 40*, 101273. https://doi.org/10.1016/j.ijdrr.2019.101273

"Garden." *Source:* Photograph: Samuli Paulaharju 1934. Finnish National Board of Antiquities. CC BY 4.0.

COMMENTARY PART IA

MULTILAYERED AND COMPLEX ISSUE OF GARDEN

Eemeli Hakoköngäs
University of Helsinki

The first part, "Gardens With Human Life," presents five inspiring chapters addressing personal and collective cultures in the context of a "garden." Those who have read Teppei Tsuchimoto's introduction to the book may already expect the authors not to narrowly reduce the concept of garden to a cultivated outdoor environment producing food or facilitating aesthetic pleasure. Although this idea may well be the social representation of the garden, the authors, in line with the general aims of the book, offer a broad picture of what garden can mean and how such meanings may be studied by employing both more and less traditional methodical approaches.

Maybe the most important overall contribution by the chapters is that, by drawing from various cultural and social contexts, they show that it is possible to bridge the gap between individual and social (cultural). To this end, the authors build on Professor Jaan Valsiner's pioneering research on cultural psychology. Valsiner has been striving to highlight that observation of the individual's unique development need not rule out the role of culture as some psychologists might think. At the same time, he has illustrated that considering the role of the cultural, social, and natural environment surrounding the studied phenomenon does not make it necessary to turn a blind eye to the uniqueness of the individual, a preconceived idea which some social psychologists might have.

Although taking the connections between these two levels into account would appear reasonable, reducing the tension between individual-centered and cultural-centered approaches is a challenging task as the division is deeply rooted in principles of many disciplines. That is where the articles of the present part serve to illustrate theoretical—and sometimes admittedly difficult—concepts of cultural psychology through empirical analysis. Besides demonstrating how the processes of internalization and externalization occur in human life, several chapters provide illustrative examples of use of the trajectory equifinality approach (TEA) in research. TEA, developed in particular by Jaan Valsiner, Tatsuya Sato, and Yuko Yasuda, is an approach in cultural psychology which focuses on the meaning-making process in a social and historical context. The approach does not reduce humans to mere beings controlled deterministically by the rules set by the environment, but considers people as active and goal-oriented actors. According to this view, TEA is consistent with the principles of new social cognition research, which arose as a critique of the individual-centered and mechanistic image of human nature in developmental and cognition psychology.

AN OVERVIEW OF THE CHAPTERS OF PART I

In Chapter 1—"The Garden as a Symbolic Space"—Daniela Schmitz Wortmeyer turns the reader's attention to individual life trajectories and the way in which humans fill natural elements with their personal meanings, and also how those meanings stem from a sociocultural context. Schmitz Wortmeyer illustrates her analysis of affective-semiotic cultivation of a garden through two fascinating life stories. The first describes the life trajectory of a son of Japanese immigrants in Brazil. This story of a second-generation immigrant in a country that differs culturally and environmentally from the protagonist's country of origin is a fruitful starting point to observe the intersections of individual and cultural meaning-making processes. Schmitz Wortmeyer shows how the main character's garden includes elements of both old and new cultural landscapes, constituting a "transnational space." The other life trajectory presented in the chapter tells the story of a Brazilian artist committed to portraying local natural landscapes and people in his art. While the first trajectory convincingly shows how the process of externalizing personal and collective cultures can happen simultaneously through gardening, the second life trajectory sheds light on the interesting question of the role of collective and personal culture in artistic work. The latter case provides an interesting pathway for future research by addressing semiotic processes in artistic and other creative work. Together, the trajectories provide a demonstrative example of an affective-semiotic framework of subjective experiences. Schmitz Wortmeyer argues that sensory stimulus—in natural environments all the senses are involved—leads to affective meaning-making.

In Chapter 2—"Garden as a Sign of Happiness"—Ramon Cerqueira Gomes addresses the topical issue of the relationship between gardens and holistic well-being. In everyday life we still often neglect the health benefits of nature and, for example, in urban planning tend to prefer human-built landscapes instead of salutogenic landscapes featuring natural elements. From previous health research we nevertheless know that natural environments have a number of positive effects on our physical and mental health and overall well-being. Research has shown that even a passive link to nature or the indirect perception of wildlife through photographs enhances psychological restoration. Happiness, as an outcome of general well-being, has become a topic of great interest to social scientists in recent years, even though operationalizing and measuring happiness in research has proven to be a challenge. Cerqueira Gomes makes a novel contribution to the above-mentioned discussions by approaching gardens and happiness from the perspective of cultural psychology. The chapter draws our attention to an aspect that is often overlooked in studies seeking the causal relationship between the natural environment and positive outcomes in our bodies and minds. The author strives to explain salutogenic characteristics of gardens from the fundamental process of human meaning-making. From this viewpoint, the explanation for the health effects of gardens cannot be reduced to any particular objective, physical element in the landscape, but rather lies in the generalized series of positive meanings that can be activated even by just imagining a garden.

Chapter 3—"Mirrors of a Garden: Understanding Ecological Units Over Time" by Enno Freiherr von Fircks and Marc A. Campill—presents an analysis of an individual's life trajectory with a special focus on the social function of a garden. The garden of the first author's family constitutes the general context in which the authors analyze the general role of a garden as a cultural and developmental environment. This specific garden is something that could be appropriately described as "ordinary" with a mowed lawn, planted bushes and a wooden fence. However, due to the personal history of the researcher, it is also much more: a place of childhood memories and growth as a person. The chapter presents a tangible example of applying the TEA in developmental research. In childhood, playing is an obvious starting point in the individual and social meaning-making process. There are always multiple trajectories that can either guide us towards reaching certain goals or prevent us from reaching them. The parts of the garden that seem uninteresting to an adult may become an environment of collective imagining and adventure for children. The trajectories may have significant symbolic value. These memorable experiences follow us and change us over the course of our lives. The authors argue that the garden can function as a mirror for societal conflicts and the strategies for solving them. In cultures of material abundance, it is easy to think that, in order to develop, children need a pedagogically designed and carefully implemented environment with the finest accessories. Freiherr von Fircks and Campill importantly note that even a modest backyard can be just as valuable and interesting in the light of developmental studies.

While the above-mentioned authors focus on the developmental and recuperative characteristics of gardens, Ryohei Miyamae approaches the topic from a quite different perspective by addressing the aftermath of the Great East Japan Earthquake and the Tsunami in 2011. Chapter 4—"'I Need a Garden,' a Survivor Said: A Garden as a Place Where Survivors Become Relational Beings for Disaster Recovery"—turns the analytical gaze to the possibilities of gardens and gardening in respect of overcoming traumatic events. The natural disaster and subsequent nuclear accident led to forced relocation for many people. For a number of them, the relocation became a long-term or even permanent life change and meant disconnection from their past lives and the loss of community. As always occurs when the acute phase of the crisis is over, various social processes took place, including discrimination and bullying of the evacuees. Negative treatment by the ingroup makes living as an internal evacuee difficult as it calls into question the notion of belonging to an ingroup. On the other hand, catastrophes also create a desire to help. The author draws from personal experience and researches the role of volunteerism in creating new relationships and breaking with forced individualism. Gardens appeared to be environments that facilitated recovery by changing those subjects of care into caring subjects. The contribution of the chapter is not limited to describing the consequences of one earthquake in Japan. Being forced to leave home and settle in a new place touches people in different parts of the world. The article creates the hope that restorative practices and experiences can be encountered following relocation, for example, by establishing a garden.

Tomoo Hidaka and Hideaki Kasuga continue addressing the aftermath of natural disasters. The authors answer the question of how a familiar and comfortable environment can become something threatening and obnoxious. The title of the chapter provides all the essential information about the context of the study: "Radioactive Waste Publicly Placed in a Space That Used To Be a Yard as a Private Place: Time and Sign in the Designated Evacuation Areas After the Fukushima Nuclear Power Plant Accident." The Great East Japan Earthquake happened in March 2011 and the resulting nuclear disaster meant that vast areas were contaminated by radiation. As part of the cleaning and protection measures, contaminated soil was stored in flexible containers in individuals' yards and gardens. Even though the storage was meant to be temporary, storing hazardous waste in a person's backyard is a shocking and conflictive experience for people. By employing an ethnographic interview method, the authors analyze how places of individual culture become objects of coercion of collective culture. It is obvious that radioactive waste changes the meanings of familiar places, but as the authors importantly note, the forced implementation of collective culture may also question positive identity and the temporal connections to ancestors as well as to descendants. The article draws attention to natural pollution and environmental disasters that happen all over the world on different scales. Aside from the physiological consequences on human health, changes in the environment also have a psychological dimension, as this chapter notes.

FUTURE RESEARCH INTO GARDENS WITH HUMAN LIFE

The title of the "Gardens With Human Life" part offers endless perspectives on the theme of the present book. The five chapters described above provide inspiration for future research by offering examples of how to approach the multilayered and complex issue of a garden in different contexts. What is common among these chapters is that they all emphasize the fundamentality of the relationship between humans and nature. The relationship exists and affects our everyday life even if the "nature" in the living world is not consciously recognized or is replaced by human-made artefacts and constructions.

Jaan Valsiner's ideas form the starting point for several of the chapters. His thinking is characterized by interdisciplinarity, the ability to draw from different disciplines. In the present part, the authors bring conceptual tools introduced by Valsiner into dialogue with the texts of their own disciplines. Readers who wish to expand their knowledge are also recommended to read reference lists to the chapters as these references can open up new paths for developing ideas.

The individual chapters employ various methodical and theoretical approaches to address gardens with human life in different cultural contexts. Employed theoretical frameworks, such as the TEA, remind readers and future researchers that understanding meaning making requires taking into account besides social and cultural, also temporal dimensions in the analysis. Even though focusing on a certain point in time may be the easiest and thus most attractive solution in research, it does not give full value to the richness and complexity of human life.

Together, the texts provide a solid basis to better understand how personal culture, each person's unique perspective on the world, and the meanings nurtured by the collective culture are connected. As Valsiner has aptly pointed out, the connection is reciprocal. It seems that for practical reasons in developmental research, the process of internalization, adopting collective culture, is more accessible. However, it is suggested through the process of externalization that individuals also contribute to collective culture.

Externalization gives rise to innovation and changes, as well as conflicts and debates. The chapters of the present part provide examples and ideas of externalization, but also evoke the notion that externalization is a process that future researchers should look at more closely. Employing creative approaches, analysis of life trajectories, autobiographies, autoethnographies, and interviews, as well as combinations of the foregoing, could provide tools to illustrate the bidirectional relationship between internalization and externalization, taking into account personological, situational, and environmental factors.

Photograph: Created by the artist Joshua Marx (shared for the purpose of the volume). The poem has been written by the author as a reflection of the commentary and the photograph.

"Falling"

Garden remembers the disappeared,

What human life has been,

Remembered in the burgeoning green.

COMMENTARY PART IB

COMMENTARY TO THE GARDEN

A Place to Cultivate in Pain and Comfort

Marc Antoine Campill
Free Researcher, Luxembourg

Life has many nuances of *how* it can be "done/managed." All of them connected while staying unique on their own. Central is the awareness that not only living but also dying is implied in the construct called "life." It is in our life as a human where we experience, generate, and cultivate meaning (Campill, in press). A process that underlines that also our self-expression and general communication abilities are bonded to our experience of life and so leads to the phenomenon that gardens can represent these nuances of existence—representing human life, while also being a place to return to.

What should be seen as a central take-home message is definitely that gardens are more than just a space of green in the possession of an individual—they are overloaded spaces of meaning, meaning that has been cultivated by its inhabitants and by its environment. Chapter 1 underlined the relationship to our surroundings, and so, especially to our gardens, which

The Semiotic Field of the Garden, pages 119–123
Copyright © 2024 by Information Age Publishing
www.infoagepub.com
All rights of reproduction in any form reserved.

inhabit personal meanings and values that have been cultivated throughout the encounter of developmental trajectories. A field that is also nurtured and/or poisoned by the collective culture of specific social contexts and individual culture, the self is currently representing.

Ironically, it has to be underlined here that each person is not simply reconstructing the experiences made but is cultivating a unique perspective of the experienced phenomenon and meanwhile on the world/environments and social-cultural meaning. Personal cultures and collective cultures are constructs that are influencing each other constantly in the same form as the caretaker and the garden are influencing each other's life, making it strictly impossible to speak about one unit without considering the other one. It is precisely this symbiotic coexistence that offers innovations and changes, when it is seen as the continuous dynamic it always has been—in between internalization and externalization lies the experiencing of naturality.

Maybe it is impossible to fully understand how environments, especially in an organic context, are impacting people's intuitive perceptions but it is crucial to try such investigations as it allows a clearer understanding of the affective-semiotic processes and values that are guiding us through our life. The garden as metaphor allows specifically to explore the multi-complex context in which meaning is cultivated while it underlines the needed awareness of its temporal units—the garden is always changing through the irreversible stream of time. We should use such a precious opportunity of using metaphors, for the sake of a better understanding of how we are interacting with our surrounding worlds, and vice versa.

DIVING DEEPER: INTO THE HUMAN GARDEN DIALOGUE

To say that the garden is a practical example of the human–environment dialogue, means also that the emotional connectivity between the green field and the human being needs to be taken into consideration. A garden is not simply a natural domain. The garden is much more as it exists in millions of ways and allows us to move in as many ways through it. Every—accessible—human sense is activated when entering the garden. A simple collection of examples may be that we smell the fresh green after a rainy day, we feel how our shoes are sinking into the muddy ground, we hear the sound of the shoes escaping the mud and invading it "Smack," we see how the flowers create a colorful contrast from the dark green and we taste the bittersweetness of the raspberries hidden in a corner of the garden. Gardens can offer an experience far beyond our homes as they remind us of the organic diversity that exists—by pushing us actively to encounter them (Chapter 2). Signs that remind us that not only we but also our environment is alive.

Gardens are fields with complex meaning links that cannot be sufficiently explored when the hypergeneralized nuances are not taken into consideration. The garden represents a sign of the power of individuality and diversity symbiosis. This leads us to the central understanding that gardens are not only experienced by our senses but also in our emotional sense-making. A pleasurable and peaceful or toxic and sorrowful place, maybe also a little bit of both. For example, as a child, we loved to play in the gardens, as grown-ups we may start to sadly remember what we cannot experience anymore, and as elderly individuals, we may enjoy the sorrowful beauty of remembering the good old days (Chapter 2, 3).

It appears to be a valuable place, where people report their awareness of the existence and so their awareness of being contradictory/paradoxical/ambivalent beings. In other words, the nature of the garden of signs inhabits different essences once it represents a relation toward happiness (Chapter 2), while also representing our journey to a better understanding of ourselves and toward our environmental setting (Chapter 3), or our losses and our emotional damage we had to experience—by losing our beloved environment to toxic waste (Chapter 5).

WHEN THE HUMAN BEING IS CONFRONTED WITH THE LOST: A POISONED GARDEN

Gardens are often possible spaces to encounter happiness, meanwhile, they also gain the risk of tremendous pain—remembering what we could have or remembering what we have lost. As Chapter 5 elaborated the disaster of the Fukushima nuclear power plant (FNP) accident, is a horrific and précised example of such loss. It is here, where the garden is expropriated from its meaning of a happy place and is transformed into so-called temporary storage areas for flexible containers filled with radioactive waste. As in the case of Chapter 5, 14 residents shared their experiences of having their land transformed into temporary storage summarizing the distress triggered when it comes to such a disappearance of a sign of happiness, as with their garden. A space that has been part of their home—a place of self-realization and a place of connectivity between the possessor and their ancestors, and descendants—shifts into a "public garbage dumpster"—a place contaminated by the mistakes of others and so represents the influences of collectivity. In other words, it represents the experience of personal disaster (Chapter 4) that traumatizes the cultivator and its connectivity to its environment. A disaster that takes away honored and cultivated connections.

Nevertheless, it does not need to stay a ruin of pain and loss, as it is not simply a sign that can disappear through time but that can also restore its past meaning (Chapter 4). I would like for this particular sequence to quote two sentences of this volume's Part I: "Garden With Human life":

"A journey towards such a place seems reasonable." (Chapter 3, p. 48)

"In the gardens, our minds and bodies are invited to be here and now: We called to feel happier." (Chapter 2)

To entangle the past losses, it is needed to focus on disconnecting oneself—the thoughts—from the past and from the context that has triggered the emotional damage—often by the community. A process in which the process sounds at first repetitive: An untangling and reconnecting loop, which can lead to reproducing the positivity of meaning into the garden. That can lead to the return of the "garden," and so to the restoration of the survivors' precious bonds. Even though the process of losing those connections has resulted from a powerful multitude of factors that overwhelmed its victims, the process of restoration can be found in simplicity. The restoration of the beloved memories can result simply through mindful stagnation in a beloved environment. In other words, spending time in the garden—even simply sitting—and enjoying the harmony of the cultivated nature in its environmental setting can restore the disconnected meaning of happiness (Chapter 4).

"The garden is one of the stages for recovering a community." (Chapter 4, p. 86)

Even though some gardens can never be returned, there is always a path to approaching the feeling of having been there. As we know no garden stays the same, and so also every garden can become a door to the remembered past—even when it will never be the same. No radioactive wasted garden can be touched (in same manners as in the past) by the same generation, but with every new home the family will cultivate a new space that allows the emergence of memories of the past homes and so also to our gardens we have lived in.

THE GARDEN OF HUMAN LIFE

In conclusion, the garden is the space for the human to cultivate, while the human is also garden-like, and so cultivated by the garden as caretaker. This implies that certain interactions happen automatically even when we simply rest in the garden, we interact with it and so certain bonds in life are made—through intense dialogues that we passively encounter. Better living conditions can be found by Endo through a long journey (Chapter 1) or the simple vegetation in their garden (Chapter 4), whereas the meaning-making is in both cases traveling beside time and space—creating the sense toward our chosen path of cultivation.

Every emotion and every phenomenon accrued in everyday life can be retraced in the fenced green field. Whereas the ability to gain awareness of the existence and stream of forces seems to become clearer and more bearable for the human being. It is happiness and sadness that we can find in our gardens, but what we choose to see depends on our perspective. It is the human as well who becomes part of the garden, and so results in being perfectly representable by the organic green: Making the world the playground of its perceiver or in other words transforms the complex meaning of psychological phenomena into the barrable context: describable as a "garden of human life.

REFERENCE

Campill, M. A. (in press). Cultivation of humanity: How we can stagnate within the eternal flow. *Culture & Psychology*.

PART II

GARDEN METAPHOR:
EXPLORING PERSONAL <> COLLECTIVE CULTURE

Wooded cemetery in Hailuoto in an island in the
Northern Baltic Sea. Photograph: Samuli Paulaharju 1913.
Finnish National Board of Antiquities. CC BY 4.0

CHAPTER 6

FROM GOD'S GARDEN TO GARDEN OF MEMORIES

Personal and Collective Cultures in a Northern Finland Cemetery

Eemeli Hakoköngäs
University of Helsinki, Finland

A cemetery is an area for both individuals and communities to remember the deceased, but a garden cemetery also carries a variety of other meanings, providing a standpoint from which to analyze the relation between *personal<>collective*. The idea of garden-like cemetery landscape is nowadays widely shared in Finland, and the maintenance of graveyards, burial plots, and monuments, as well as (in)appropriate behavior in cemeteries, is defined by law. However, only a hundred years ago a Finnish cemetery was typically flowerless and treeless. Monuments were rare and the sacristan's sheep and cattle grazed among the graves. The description "very little longed-for, soon forgotten" was used to describe the way in which individuals and collectives took care of the final resting place of the deceased.

Garden—a cultivated landscape serving a variety of purposes, such as evoking aesthetic and emotional experiences, producing pleasure or facilitating interaction is an arena of "various social functions in parallel" (Valsiner, 2014, p. 182, "Introduction"). Drawing from the history of a small rural cemetery in Northern Finland, I show how the negotiation of these functions has taken place over hundreds of years. By analyzing historical documents, I demonstrate how opposite notions such as *we<>others, sacred<>secular* and *equal<>hierarchical* have been negotiated at local level and how the garden cemetery, "God's garden," idea has evolved into a "garden of memories." Previous research on Finnish cemeteries is limited, and the present article paves the way for future cultural psychological inspections of commemorative culture in Finland.

PERSONAL AND COLLECTIVE CULTURES IN CEMETERIES

Human encounters construct meanings of places (Valsiner, 2014, p. 174) and, if we look more closely, a landscape that at first glance seems insignificant may appear to be charged with multiple signs corresponding to our inner landscapes (Jørgensen, 1998, "Introduction"). In the present article, I employ Jaan Valsiner's (2014) conceptualization of personal and collective culture in the analysis of the construction of meanings in Finnish garden cemeteries.

The individuals are always intertwined with the collective by sharing socially constructed conceptions (Moscovici, 1984). The norms, meanings, and practices constituting collective cultures are adopted through constructive *internalization* in communication and interaction with the other group members. The collective culture restricts the construction of personal cultures and guides the ways culture is *externalized* in everyday practices. However, individuals are thinking, feeling, and creative beings. They modify, interpret, and criticize the given elements of collective culture. Externalization is thus also a constructive act, as it participates in the ongoing dialogue on shared meanings (Valsiner, 2014, p. 214). The negotiation may lead to differing opinions and this leads to there being not just one collective culture but various cultures, some of which may be in a hegemonic position in relation to the others (e.g., Moscovici, 1984).

Places are often approached from the perspective of archaeology or geography emphasizing the *structure* of externalized culture. The cultural psychological approach complements the investigation by taking into account the (social) psychological processes within, and functions of, places (Valsiner, 2014, pp. 178–179). Wagoner et al. (2019) have noted that public memorials constitute *mnemonic environments* concentrating symbolic meanings and mediating memories. Drawing from their example I argue that a cemetery as a whole is a mnemonic environment where personal meanings and memories intersect with social meanings and stories (e.g., Buckham, 2003) providing a fruitful context to approach the intersection of personal and collective cultures.

Cemeteries are at the same time places for the dead and for the living, and Valsiner (2014, p. 189) emphasizes their specific nature as liminal places in human-created landscapes. In the midst of everyday life a cemetery constitutes a demarcated area where different customs and even laws and statutes apply. There is unseen guidance, as in many cultures burial places are considered to be sacred and to require respectful behavior. Besides being a normative environment, a cemetery is also a physical place where paths, gates, walls and seats as material objects direct and restrict our action. Normative and material guidance demonstrates a process of *behavior setting* (Valsiner, 2014, p. 177), guiding the encounter with a place in a particular direction. The meanings in these encounters arise through the mediation between the place and the observer (relative, visitor, tourist; Jørgensen, 1998).

Commemorative practices in cemeteries are related both to the expression of the personal relationship with the deceased and the connection to social groups (Buckham, 2003). In a cemetery, "the individualized person continued to have a social identity past the point of their death" (Tarlow, 2000, p. 234). Cemeteries are often characterized by hierarchical landscapes reflecting the social distinction of the living (e.g., Laqueur, 1993) and, according to Talve (1988, p. 3), graveyards show the social structure of the local community in miniature. Selecting burial plots, acquiring memorials, taking care of the plots and visiting them are parts of encounters and means to participate in the collective ritual of giving meaning to a place.

Meaning making is a continuous process, as new generations re-interpret the old signs and evaluate their significance from their own perspective. A tourist or an occasional visitor to a cemetery is likely to construct different meanings than the locals. Koskinen-Koivisto (2016) have shown how visiting gravesites serves multiple purposes for people: It may deepen their experience of understanding history, but the experience may also include more sensual and spiritual (not necessarily religious) dimensions evoking, for example, a reflection of one's own mortality.

THE EMERGENCE OF THE IDEA OF A GARDEN CEMETERY

In many countries closed cemeteries were transformed into public gardens and parks, especially in the late 19th century, to promote fire safety, public comfort, and health in the cities (Mytum, 1989; Schalin, 2005). In contrast, a *garden cemetery* represents a specific type of public place that is still used for cemetery purposes, but which shares certain features of an "ordinary" garden. Tarlow (2000) names, for example, a naturalistic style, an emphasis on living plants as well as a semi-rural or suburban location as characteristics of garden cemeteries in England.

The idea of the garden cemetery originates from the writings of a German philosopher and garden theorist C. C. L. Hirschfeld (1742–1792), whose concept of a *sensitive landscape* draws from moral enlightenment philosophy and also paves the way for romanticism in the next century. In brief, Hirschfeld's idea was that landscapes should evoke sensitive feelings such as compassion to promote human moral growth. He particularly advocated planting trees to create an awe-inspiring atmosphere in the gardens (Knapas, 2005).

Hirschfeld's ideas were applied in the design of cemeteries, especially in France, England, and the United States in the 19th century. The Père-Lachaise cemetery in Paris, which opened in 1804, became the most famous reference point for cemetery planning for example in England and the United States (Tarlow, 2000)—as well as much later in Finland. According to Etlin (1984), the holistic design implemented in garden cemeteries altered public attitudes towards death, remembrance, and commemoration. Cemeteries were no longer frightening places to be avoided but provided an inviting and inspiring environment to visit and to develop oneself spiritually. Tarlow (2000) has called the new cemetery type "an aesthetic and sentimental landscape of remembering" (p. 218).

THE FINNISH GARDEN CEMETERY

In the Middle Ages, horticulture and gardening were practiced in a few monasteries in Finland and, according to Erkamo (1979), it is possible that the custom of planting trees and other plants in churchyards originated from that point in history. Finland was part of Sweden, and as a result of the Swedish Reformation in the late 1500s, the Protestant King Gustav I made the church the property of the state and ordered the stone walls of churchyards to be demolished to prevent them from becoming defensive forts for the Catholics. The church lost its power and, as a side effect, the public's respect towards churchyards was replaced by fear (Erkamo, 1979).

For centuries there was no need to cultivate cemeteries, as the social elite bought their burial plots inside the church. The status of the buried was shown by the location and decoration of tombs. However, the space in the churches was limited and practical problems such as the smell in summer hindered worship. The priests called to end the practice, and in 1783 the Swedish King Gustav III prohibited burials inside churches. In the Northern periphery the new practice was adopted slowly, and church burials ended 40 years later in 1823 by order of the Tsar when the country was already part of the Russian Empire (e.g., Gardberg, 2003).

The final abolition of church burials in the 1820s gave impetus to the cultivation of Finnish cemetery landscapes. When it was not possible to show social status inside the church, it was shown to churchgoers in the churchyard. Cemeteries were first divided into two kinds of areas: cheap line graves (row burials) where the deceased were buried side by side in the order in which they died, and private family graves into which several generations could be buried. Later, four categories, the first-, second-, and third-class areas, priced in the same order, and a free-of-charge "poor man's mold," were established, reflecting the structure of the class society (Talve, 1988, pp. 6–7).

The social elite first adopted new means of commemoration such as showy iron and stone monuments, and the lower classes imitated them by erecting self-made wooden or stone memorials. The roots of the garden-like cemetery in Finland date back from the late 19th and early 20th centuries (Erkamo, 1979). Ilmari Wirkkala (1890–1973), a Finnish cemetery architect, was the main spokesman for importing the garden cemetery idea to Finnish churchyards in the 1920s and the 1930s. In a newly independent (1917) and post-Civil War (1918) Finland, Wirkkala represented the hegemonic political ideology and saw the potential of cemeteries to support the construction of a strong nation. Wirkkala's thinking was inspired by the cemeteries in Sweden and Germany, particularly the latter, where the ideal was to achieve an aesthetic environment through strict order (Lempiäinen, 1990, p. 16).

Wirkkala's friend, the author Maila Talvio, edited an extensive volume entitled *God's Gardens* (in Finnish: Jumalan puistot; Talvio, 1927) in the 1920s, presenting hundreds of photographs depicting cemeteries and tombstones in different parts of Finland. In line with European ideals of the garden cemetery notion, Talvio emphasized the role of cemeteries as places of *contemplation*. In the foreword, she underlined how all people buried in the same cemetery, regardless of their social status, together represent the homeland (Talvio, 1927, n.p.).

Personal and collective cultures were united in Wirkkala's and Talvio's ideology, where taking care of a burial plot was presented as a sign of love and reverence towards the deceased and, as practiced collectively, towards the Finnish nation. In his small handbook, *Nurturing a Grave and a Graveyard* (Haudan ja hautausmaan hoito), Wirkkala (1930) argued that respect towards graves and cemeteries should also elevate people morally:

> Are we not, as Christians, far behind in honoring the memory of our ancestors of those we call Gentiles in China and whom we seek to convert to Christianity (...) our own graves are consecrated as God's land and our cemeteries as God's Gardens, into which, when we are buried, all that is unruly and raw in us shall be left outside the gates. And as we step in the midst of these mounds,

let us step carefully, speak quietly and think beautiful thoughts, for those who rest below our feet are closer to God than we are. (Wirkkala, 1930, p. 6)

As the highest ideal of the Finnish cemetery, Wirkkala (1930, 1945) identified "the forest cemetery," in which naturalness would replace the unnecessary desire to show. In different countries, the garden cemetery notion takes on different forms, reflecting the local cultural and religious features. For example, in Protestant England virtues such as simplicity and naturalness were emphasized over the spectacle (e.g., Tarlow, 2000). Similarly, in Finland Wirkkala advocated humility by claiming that the modest memorials correspond better with Luther's idea of a cemetery as "the field of the God" than a place decorated with pompous stones (Wirkkala 1945, p. 54).

CONTEXT: TERVOLA CEMETERY IN NORTHERN FINLAND

Jørgensen (1998) argues in favor of the usefulness of the case study approach when analyzing the construction of meanings in a landscape. Case studies provide a detailed context which allows for the interpretation of signs and meanings that would be challenging to notice in a broader view. The case in the present study is the Tervola parish cemetery. Tervola is a municipality in Northern Finland (66° 5′ 20″ N, 24° 48′ 40″ E) close to the Arctic Circle (66.5° N). With its 2,900 inhabitants (in 2020), it is a small town even on a Finnish scale. Its northern location has shaped the local way of living—for example, the land is covered with snow for several months (from December to April) and the growing season is short (from June to August) making summer an intensive gardening time.

Both historically and in the present day, the Tervola municipality could be described as a *nodal area* between two *central areas*. The municipality is located halfway between two cities (Rovaniemi in the north and Kemi in the south), and the areas are historically connected by river and currently by railway and an arterial road. Permanent settlement in the area started from the 16th century onward. The Lutheran (Protestant) chapel in Tervola was established in 1673 and the wooden church, which exists to this day, was built in 1687–1689. On the basis of population growth estimates in the 19th century, a new wooden church was built in 1861–1864 in front of the old church. The cemetery is located in the immediate vicinity of the two churches. In the 2010s, over 80% of the population of the municipality were members of the Lutheran church. Besides Lutherans, there are two notable religious minorities in the municipality, namely, Jehovah's Witnesses and Greek Catholics (Hakoköngäs, 2014).

As a result of the Protestant reformation cemeteries and church were subsequently separated from each other in many countries (Valsiner, 2014, pp. 189–190) and urbanization, population growth, and religious liberty acts in the 19th century diversified the management of burial sites. For example, in Britain specific cemetery companies were established to sell and manage graves (e.g., Tarlow, 2000). Reflecting the relatively homogeneous population and shared norms (collective culture) in Finland, cemeteries are still mainly owned by the Lutheran church. Private cemeteries and cemeteries owned by minority religious groups are rare. In this sense, Tervola cemetery represents a typical Finnish cemetery.

Valsiner (2014) argues that human-created places provide fruitful material for the analysis of different meaning-making processes as they are relatively stable. On the other hand, places change constantly, as signs are replaced by other signs in the process of symbolic insertion and removal (Valsiner, 2014, pp. 175–177). I understand human-made places and landscapes as the result of externalization of social knowledge that is simultaneously changing and resisting change (see Moscovici, 1984). In the present study, the recorded history of the place subject to analysis extends back more than 300 years in written documents, and even further in oral folklore. Although the use of this kind of historical material entails several challenges—for example, fragmentation of the data and the possible limits of understanding human meaning making in the distant past—I argue that the historical approach allows us to perceive the evolution of meanings of places and provides a richer image of personal and collective culture than the analysis of a particular point in time would provide (for the historical approach, see Chapter 7).

The present research material is composed of historical documents mainly from the Tervola parish archive and the Finnish National Archive. For the sake of concision, references are made to the history of the Tervola parish (Hakoköngäs, 2014), where more detailed information on archive units can be found. In addition, local folklore collections are used as a source of oral history and the history of customs. Furthermore, the analysis of recent history is supported by personal experience of working as an assistant gardener in the cemetery for three summers in the 2010s, and the analysis in this sense has an ethnographic background (see Chapter 9, Chapter 10). Working in the cemetery allowed insight to be gained into the subsurface structures of the place and enabled the customs of people visiting the cemetery to be observed.

RESULTS: PERSONAL AND COLLECTIVE CULTURES AT TERVOLA CEMETERY

The analysis of historical documents, local folklore, and observations at Tervola cemetery shows how the cemetery landscape contains and conveys

134 • E. HAKOKÖNGÄS

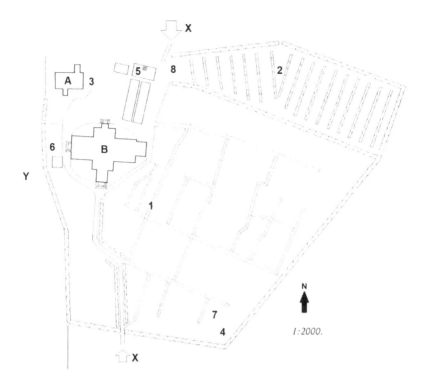

Figure 6.1 A map of Tervola cemetery. *Key:* A Old Church (1680s); B New Church (1860s); X The main entrances to the area; Y Kemi River; **1** Old cemetery (1890s); **2** New cemetery (1960s); **3** Military grave (Civil War, Whites); **4** Military grave (Civil War, Reds); **5** Military grave (WWII); **6** Graves of priests and gentry; **7** Graves of the members of other religious groups; **8** Memorial for those buried elsewhere.

multiple meanings relating, for example, to religion, politics, and social distinction. The central physical features constructing the cemetery are presented in a map in Figure 6.1.

Next, I will explain the historical development of the meanings of the elements of the map in detail. I will proceed in chronological order starting from the establishment of the cemetery. After that, I will present the phases of application of the garden cemetery idea in Tervola. I will then conclude by evaluating recent history in the evolution of meanings in the cemetery.

A Place of Neglect and Fear (Until the 1880s)

Tervola cemetery has been located in the same place since at least the 1680s, when the "old church" (A), which still stands today, was built. The cemetery area was expanded when the "new church" (B) was built in the 1860s. The different names for cemetery in Finland represent the shift from pre-Christianity to the Christian religion in the Middle Ages: The terms of Eastern origin referring to death (kalma), such as *kalmisto*, were replaced by terms of Western origin emphasizing the role of the church, such as *kirkkomaa* (compare: churchyard in English, kyrkogård in Swedish). The term was sometimes literally replaced as the Christian churches were built in the previous location of pre-Christian graveyards (Talve, 1988, p. 5). According to oral tradition, this also happened in Tervola where the churchyard is located in the Lapinniemi (Lapps' cape), referring to indigenous nomadic people who inhabited the Finnish inland before the settlers arrived. The oral tradition recounts that the stones of their place of worship were used as the stairs and stone base of the Christian Old Church (A) (Calamnius 1868, pp. 200–201), symbolically subjugating the old beliefs. The location of the church still carries, 300 years on, the tension between *settlers<>natives* and *Christians<>non-Christians*.

The map shows how the burial plots (1–5) are located to the east and south of the churches. This is partially because of geography: In the west, the area is bordered by a river (Y). The more important reason is, however, cultural: in folk beliefs, the north was considered as demonic and only the non-baptized and criminals were buried on the northern side of the church (e.g., Gardberg, 2003; Wirkkala, 1945). Although the practice is not based on the Christian religion and is barely consciously remembered, the division of *sacred<>secular* and the related *behavior setting* have affected the entire current landscape of the cemetery. A living practice of avoiding the north setting demonstrates how beliefs shared in collective culture may live on over generations even if individuals are not aware of them.

The distinction between *sacred<>secular* was also applied within the cemetery borders, albeit on a smaller scale. In the Roman Catholic era, pilgrimages to the graves of saints were believed to cure ailments and help the souls of the deceased. The relics were often stored near the altar, which made this the most prestigious location for in-church graves (Gardberg, 2003, p. 30). In the north, where the graves of the saints, as well as their relics, were rare, a position close to the church was traditionally the most favorable (i.e., most sacred) place for the deceased. The rain flowing from the church roof was thought to be consecrated and to cool those suffering in purgatory (Lempiäinen, 1990, pp. 7–8). Although Protestantism does not give value to the worship of saints or faith in purgatory, in Tervola these beliefs were externalized, as the burial plots next to the church were still given to priests and local gentry (6) and war heroes (3) in the 20th century.

After the Reformation, public respect for cemeteries declined and cemeteries were neglected. One reason for abandoning them was the fear of death (kalma). Many beliefs were put into practice to avoid misfortune:

For example, it was not acceptable to walk barefoot or without a hat in a cemetery (Gardberg, 2003, p. 79). Since the 18th century, the pursuit of certain hygiene practices led to the reorganization of cities with geometric plans, straight streets and open squares to ensure free air flow. In cemeteries, treeless landscapes were seen as important in order to sweep away the dangerous "bad air," miasma (Etlin, 1984; Mytum, 1989). Miasma theory was widely known in Europe, and in Tervola "bad air" was accused of deadly epidemics in the late 18th century (Hakoköngäs, 2014, pp. 44–45). Tervola cemetery was virtually an empty field: In 1751, when the population of the chapel was around 500, there were only 10 graves in the churchyard. On several occasions, the authorities had to order the parishioners to maintain the graves and the cemetery fence to prevent wildlife from entering the place (Pettersson, 1987, pp. 39–40). The new church (B) was built partially on the site of the old cemetery and possible graves were destroyed (Riska, 1987, p. 42).

Valsiner (2014, pp. 189–190) has noted that the location of burial places after the Protestant Reformation indicates a pattern of distancing. A distance from the immediate proximity of the living and from churches also characterized 19th century garden cemeteries in France and in England (Etlin, 1984; Tarlow, 2000). In Tervola, there was also an attempt to move the cemetery outside the settlement. For hygiene reasons, the old cemetery was thought to be located too close to people and a new cemetery was founded outside the village in the 1880s. However, in 1892 the parish priest already applied for permission to use the old family grave in the closed cemetery. In this case, the personal culture—the priest's will to maintain a connection to his deceased family members—affected the collective culture, as others soon preferred the old site, and in 1897 the closed cemetery was opened again. Some graves were even moved from the distant cemetery to the churchyard (Hakoköngäs, 2014, pp. 83–84).

The Change in Personal and Collective Cultures (From the 1890s to the 1930s)

Although private gardens were already typical among Finnish bourgeoise families at the beginning of the 19th century, and public parks were also established in the cities, cemeteries remained woodless and flowerless with few exceptions until the end of the century. The European ideas of a garden cemetery as a sentimental landscape reached the north only at the turn of the century. People in Tervola did not show much interest in cultivating the cemetery even in the early 20th century, although the locals' desire to preserve their family graves in the 1890s indicated the change in the collective culture.

The pressure for internalization of the new customs was set by the church authority bishop Koskimies, who visited the parish in 1903 and accused the locals of taking poor care of the graves. According to him, the inscription: "Very little longed-for, soon forgotten" (Hakoköngäs, 2014, p. 122) could have been added to most of the memorials. The bishop employed the dichotomy between *decent<>unworthy* people by arguing that caring for a grave shows respect towards the deceased and therefore indicates the decency of the living. Even though some individuals followed the bishop's call and paid more attention to their family graves, collectively, the change was slow. Figure 6.2 shows how the landscape was still virtually deserted a decade later (the 1910s), and how, 10 years after that (in the 1920s), little progress had been made in the cultivation of the area. The photograph on the left shows that trees were planted at the cemetery in the 1910s after the bishop's visit, but memorials, not to mention flowers, were rare. In the image on the right the trees have grown and grass has covered the empty sand area. However, there are only a few new monuments and the landscape looks wild and unmanaged rather than being a planned garden.

Two events in the social context brought forward the change towards the garden cemetery notion in local culture. Firstly, in 1918 the Civil War tore the recently independent nation into two groups. In many countries, cemeteries have been politicized by placing religious memorials in the service of nation (Brescó & Martínez-Guerrero, 2019) and in Finland, the winners of the war, the Whites, also strengthened their position in power by setting up a memorial culture in which cemeteries played a central role in supporting the patriotic atmosphere (e.g., Sirola, 2017). In Tervola, a memorial to fallen Whites was erected in 1926 (3). The positioning of the monument is symbolic as it stands next to the old church altar wall, reflecting the historical distinction between *sacred<>secular*, in which the closeness of the church was seen as the most advantageous location (Lempiäinen, 1990; Gardberg, 2003).

Figure 6.2 *Left:* A view of Tervola cemetery in approximately 1913. *Right:* A view of the cemetery from the church tower in the 1920s. Photographs from a private collection.

The inscription on the Whites memorial states: "Free land, / worship your Lord / and honor your heroes / who once fell for you" (Hakoköngäs, 2014, p. 123). The text suggests that the nation should remember both the heavenly ruler and the earthly winners to ensure its freedom. The main garden cemetery ideologist in Finland, Ilmari Wirkkala, had a clear nationalist aim in his message: "The history of the homeland is buried in the cemetery, and people who do not learn to love this history do not learn either to know and love the whole great Fatherland, the soil in which our whole past rests" (Wirkkala, 1930, p. 8).

The inscription on the memorial as well as Wirkkala's view reflect the basic distinction constituting the social identity: *we<>others* (*Whites<>Reds; heroes<>traitors*) and the moral distinction between *decent<>unworthy*. In Tervola, the new culture was adopted simultaneously at the personal and collective levels: The relatives of the fallen Whites brought flowers to the monument, and organizations such as the Civil Guard organized public memorials in the churchyard to elevate patriotic feeling. The practice of commemorating and showing commemoration by nurturing graves was considered *decent* and soon also became common with respect to private graves (Wirkkala, 1945, p. 55; Erkamo, 1979, p. 99).

The second issue that affected the collective culture was caused by the 1923 Act of Religious Freedom. Following the Act, the Lutheran church remained the main owner and manager of cemeteries but, on a local level, burying "non-believers" conflicted with the collective culture. A distinction between *believers<>non-believers* basically reflected the nationalist distinction between *we<>others*. In Tervola, Jehovah's Witnesses formed an active religious and pacifist minority outside the hegemonic and nationalist Protestantism of the time. The parish did not allow Jehovah's Witnesses to bury their deceased in the churchyard but instructed them to use the once discarded cemetery outside the village. At least one body was excavated and forcibly transferred before the court ordered the parish to allow the burials in the main cemetery (Hakoköngäs, 2014, p. 101). When it was not possible to shut "the others" outside the place, their grave plots were designated to the farthest corner of the cemetery (7) following the old distinction between *sacred<>secular*. The area had already been perceived earlier as inappropriate for *decent* people, as the fallen and executed Red soldiers in 1918 were buried there, though no monument was allowed to be erected on their graves. Later, other non-Protestants, such as after the Second World War, Greek Catholic evacuees, were also buried in the same corner together with the other "different" people.

The effects of the Civil War and the Act of Religious Freedom intensified the different statuses between the various parts of the churchyard. There was a greater need for *behavior setting*, as the cemetery had areas that were to be emphasized, such as the Whites memorial (3), and parts that were to

Figure 6.3 An aerial view of Tervola cemetery in the late 1930s, from South to North. Photograph from a private collection.

be hidden and silenced, such as the graves of the Reds and non-Lutherans (4, 7). The reorganization of the landscape took place when the garden cemetery principles were put into practice in the 1930s. A garden plan was ordered from the Finnish Garden Association (Kotipuutarhaliitto) and two gardeners were hired to take care of the plants. The parish received a private donation to cultivate the churchyard, and an initiative to build a well for watering flowers and to incorporate chairs to make the cemetery "a cozy place for evening walks" was implemented. To cherish local history, as suggested by Wirkkala (1930), old gravestones of priests and local gentry were renovated (Hakoköngäs, 2014, p. 122). At the end of the 1930s, the cemetery followed a clear plan with sandy roads separating green lawn areas, as shown in Figure 6.3.

Democratization of the Cemetery (From the 1940s to the 1980s)

In Finland in the earlier centuries, the burial site was seen as a more practical body repository site. It was common for graves in churches and churchyards to be regularly emptied and reused (Gardberg, 2003, p. 53). Mytum (1989) connects the birth of the modern cemetery with (relatively) permanent plots to the development of private property and increasing individualism in Europe in the 19th century, when the idea of private ownership was expanded to include the individual's body in its final resting place. In Tervola, the connection between private property and the birth of the modern cemetery is clearly articulated on one gravestone, where the inscription states: "Since for me there was no land the width of my palm when I lived/I bought two burial sites so I would one day have land"—The person whose name is mentioned on the memorial is not even buried in the cemetery but in the other burial plot he acquired while still alive (Hakoköngäs, 2014, p. 122).

Previously, only priests and gentry had permanent monuments in Tervola cemetery. Between the World Wars ordinary people also started to acquire factory-made memorials, as shown in the comparison between Images 1 and 2. This was partially possible due to economic reasons, as surplus funds permitted (and the collective culture's idea of decency so required) more fashionable memorials, but erecting a stone or an iron monument in the burial plot also helped to maintain the grave over generations, unlike the previously-used decaying wooden markers. Competition for the central burial sites led to increasing hierarchy in the landscape (Laqueur, 1993). In Tervola, teachers, merchants, and more prosperous peasants bought family graves in locations close to the established passageways where churchgoers would see the graves and the people visiting them, demonstrating Tarlow's (2000) observation that "the grave was a place to look *from* as well as a site to look *at*" (p. 234; emphasis in original).

The increasing hierarchy in Finnish cemeteries came to an abrupt end as a result of the Second World War. During the war, instead of establishing massive military cemeteries, the fallen were transported and buried in their hometowns. In Tervola, just like after the Civil War, "the graves of heroes" were located close to the churches (5) (Hakoköngäs, 2014, p. 112). In an effort to unite the divided nation and emphasize the shared goal, all those buried, irrespective of their military rank, received the same stone or cross (Gardberg, 2003, p. 129). Unlike in the case of the Civil War monuments, all manner of belligerence was avoided and collective loss was emphasized. Wirkkala (1930) had previously stated that "the vitality and greenery of the whole nature of the cemetery is the best counterbalance to the sorrows hidden beneath, and a consolation to the survivors" (p. 49). In Tervola, the statue erected after the war shows a grieving man and woman, and the name of the monument, "Consolation" (Lohdutus), makes direct allusion to the intended emotional atmosphere (Hakoköngäs, 2014, p. 113).

The collective pursuit of unification was also demonstrated by the fact that the Reds buried in 1918 in the farthest corner of the cemetery received their memorial during the Second World War (4). The stone was erected by two individuals, but it was, without objection, collectively allowed to stay in the churchyard. The renegotiation of the dichotomy between *Whites<>Reds* and *heroes<>traitors* is explained in the inscription of the monument, which states: "They fell and were cursed/But the new morning created new Finland/They were again blessed" (Hakoköngäs, 2014, p. 125).

After the Second World War, the democracy practiced in respect of military graves was extended to the entire Finnish cemetery landscape. In the 1950s, the church committee published a handbook entitled, *God's Gardens Beautiful* (Jumalan puistot kauniiksi, 1955), underlining how making a social distinction in cemeteries should be avoided as much as possible (Jumalan puistot kauniiksi, 1955, p. 21). Firstly, the collective line graves were discontinued and the social difference between the buried dispelled. The different price categories of graves were to be based on length of possession time instead of location in the cemetery. Before that, the free line graves were the most typical burial method in Western Finland (accounting for approximately 80% of burials; Lempiäinen, 1990, pp. 12, 18).

Equality was considered to come about when the collective took responsibility over individuals:

> To establish order, it is necessary for the individual member of the parish who obtained a private grave to take one step back and for the parish to take one step forward. This means that the parish prescribes the memorials as well as the mounds. (Jumalan puistot kauniiksi, 1955, p. 66)

Although ideals of garden cemeteries preferred a varied, natural landscape, the social equality requirement led to centralized control over the cemetery and strict rules to guide the size and appearance of individual memorials.

In the 1930s, Wirkkala (1930) was already calling for the concealment of social differences to thus create a harmonic landscape: "Every grave that strives for proud specialty and isolates itself from the environment breaks the atmosphere of the cemetery... Modesty is a virtue to be followed even at the gates of death" (p. 22). According to Wirkkala's ideology, it was important to make a distinction between *good taste<>bad taste*, a dichotomy which fundamentally reflected the distinction between *sacred<>secular* (e.g., Wirkkala, 1945, p. 68). In line with the fact that in the 1950s the previous monuments were officially criticized as "testimonies of bad taste and a desire to show" ("Jumalan puistot kauniiksi," 1955, pp. 73–74), the aim of cultivating public taste was a goal of garden theorists in the early 19th century, and the ideal of simplicity also characterized early Protestant garden cemeteries (Tarlow, 2000).

In Tervola, a new area for burial plots (2) in the churchyard was opened in the 1960s (Riska, 1987, p. 43). The design of the area followed democratic landscape principles by placing the graves in strict lines. The size of the stones was harmonized, as only horizontal rectangles and square-shaped stones, known as "suitcase stones," were allowed. Avoiding vertical memorials prevented the distinction of one individual reaching towards the sky over the others, but also led to a loss in the variety typical of the old part of the cemetery, as shown in Figure 6.4.

Figure 6.4 *Left:* The varied landscape of the pre-WWII area in Tervola cemetery. *Right:* Democratized post-WWII area in Tervola cemetery. Photographs from a private collection.

In the post-war cemetery design, the negotiation regarding social identity, *we<>others*, was no longer based on political orientation (*Whites<>Reds*) as it was after the Civil War, or on religion (*believers<>non-believers*) as it was following the Act of Freedom of Religion, but rather on the simpler distinction between *similar<>different* and *conformity<>distinction*, whereby accepting uniformity in individual graves was considered *decent* in a democratic welfare society. The pursuit of individuality and personality in the graves was considered as a sign of pre-war unequal class society.

From God's Garden to Garden of Memories? (From the 1990s to the Present)

By the 1980s, many ideals of welfare society had proven difficult to implement in practice. Individualization came about as a result of the dissolution of a relatively homogeneous agrarian society. In the process, the forced uniformity in the cemeteries started to arouse resentment. Art historian Brita Nickels (1990) stated in the 1990s that "the similarity, anonymity, and collectivity of the deceased are totally realized in the memorials. The deceased are left without a history that would elevate the human experience of the past" (p. 21). Wirkkala had already advocated the role of the cemetery as a lesson in local and national history back in the 1930s. In the 1990s, Nickels no longer spoke about the possibility of learning about collectivity and fastening the social bonds, but saw the cemetery as a possible lesson in human diversity.

The sculptor Häiväoja and Nickels (1990) went on to state that

> the monotony of cemeteries has been defended by democracy, by the equality of citizens in death. However, equality is not similarity, so individuality and the variety of life and death could also be seen in the cemeteries and in the monuments. (p. 42)

The writer's argument questioned whether the dichotomies between *similar<>different* and *conformity<>distinction* would go against Finnish values and claimed that the possibility of presenting differences in the cemeteries would appreciate the unique personality of individuals. The arguments in the 1990s draw from the elementary distinction between *personal<>collective*, preferring, in line with the spirit of the time, liberating individuality over restrictive collectivity.

In Tervola, individual members of the community started to push the limits of collective culture by first adding personal symbols to the uniformly-shaped stones. Small images—for example, boats, animals, trees, and flowers, as well as attributes of different professions—can be seen in the cemetery, as shown in Figure 6.5.

The images convey personal meanings impossible to interpret by the outsider, but at the same time they make the deceased more personal than a uniform stone does. The forced standards surrounding the appearance of stones were soon relaxed as people started to apply for permission for unique, non-strictly geometric stones, often shaped by nature. The gravestone industry also noted the market opportunity and started to offer various ways in which to customize and personalize factory-made memorials.

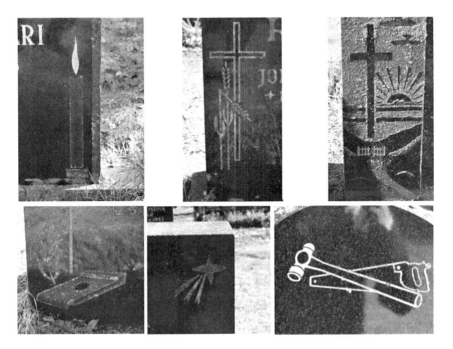

Figure 6.5 Personalization of uniform gravestones in Tervola cemetery. Photograph from a private collection.

Within a decade, the pursuit of individuals to emphasize their uniqueness became a collective culture.

Migration to cities since the 1960s and the increased mobility of people has also affected the cemetery landscape. As relatives living far away cannot personally take care of their family graves, the outsourcing of planting and watering flowers and mowing the lawn at the grave has become common. According to the garden cemetery ideals, the cultivation of graves was thought to raise people morally to learn from history and to think about mortality (e.g., Knapas, 2005; Wirkkala, 1930). In the 2000s, the practice of outsourcing grave visits corresponded with the trend of shutting death out of everyday life and containing it within nursing homes and hospitals, and of avoiding thinking of the limitations of one's own life.

However, it would be too early to say whether the commemoration would also be outsourced or would lose its value. To overcome the challenges caused by the mobility of people, special memorials for the deceased buried elsewhere have begun to be erected, such as in Tervola in the early 2000s (8). The newest monument seems to once again pull together personal and collective cultures in remembering, as the individuals commemorate their close ones by bringing candles and flowers to the memorial at special times (e.g., on the deceased's birthday), but the memorial also provides a place for collective commemoration (e.g., at Christmas, on Mother's / Father's Day). Knapas (2005, p. 83) has aptly described the present-day Finnish cemetery as "a garden of memories" for individuals and the community. This definition casts a new light on the old distinctions of *believers<>non-believers* and *sacred<>secular* as it emphasizes commemoration over religion in a cemetery.

CONCLUSIONS

In the present chapter, I have presented the historical evolution of the cemetery and the implementation of garden cemetery ideals in Finland. Based on the case of a Northern Finnish churchyard, Tervola cemetery, I have shown how individuals have, over time, internalized the collective norms, values, and practices regarding the cemetery and commemoration, and also how individuals have shaped the collective culture and led it in a new direction through externalization. An analysis of the events at micro level revealed how there is a delay in conveying the different elements of collective cultures from central areas to a nodal area, and how the cultures are modified to fit into local natural, social, and economic conditions.

The historical perspective showed how the weight and balance of fundamental distinctions, such as *believers<>non-believers*, *we<>others* and *decent<>unworthy*, have changed over time and how they have guided peoples' encounters with the place. The analysis also demonstrated how some representations, such as *sacred<>non-sacred*, have staunchly resisted change and remained over generations. Even in the current all-diversifying societies, cemeteries constitute a type of liminal space in the human-created landscape around us (Valsiner, 2014).

General secularization and the changing relationship with the institution of the church are affecting individuals' relationships with cemeteries. For many, the term God's garden sounds old-fashioned. For some, a cemetery may be a place of devotion or for maintaining social identity bonds, while for others, cemeteries may reflect the control and power of religious institutions. However, previous research (e.g., Koskinen-Koivisto, 2016; Wagoner et al., 2019) and personal observations at Tervola cemetery have shown that people are interested in cemeteries albeit for different individual reasons. More research is needed in order to understand the various meanings that individuals give to cemeteries in their personal cultures, how those meanings are positioned in relation to collective cultures, and how they are externalized in encounters to construct mnemonic environments.

REFERENCES

Brescó, I., & Martínez-Guerrero, L. (2019). New wine into old wineskins. Examining nationalism as a secular religion. In S. Brown & L. Tateo (Eds.), *The method of Imagination* (pp. 39– 53). Information Age Publishers.

Buckham, S. (2003). Commemoration as an expression of personal relationships and group identities: a case study of York Cemetery. *Mortality,* 8, 160–175.

Calamnius, J. W. (1868). *Muinais-tiedustuksia Pohjanperiltä* [Ancient inquiries from Northern Finland]. SKS.

Erkamo, V. (1979). Suomen hautausmaiden historiasta ja niiden ensimmäisistä koristekasveista [About the history of Finnish cemeteries and their first ornamental plants]. In *Suomen Kirkkohistoriallisen Seuran Vuosikirja 1978–1979* [Yearbook of the Finnish Church Historical Society 1978–1979] (pp. 86–100). SKHS.

Etlin, R. A. (1984). Père Lachaise and the garden cemetery [Père Lachaise and the garden cemetery]. *The Journal of Garden History,* 4, 211–222.

Gardberg, C. J. (2003). *Maan poveen. Suomen luterilaiset hautausmaat, kirkkomaat ja haudat* [To the bosom of the earth: Finnish Lutheran cemeteries, churchyards and graves]. Schildts.

Hakoköngäs, E. (2014). *Arkea ja pyhää. Tervolan seurakunnan historia* [Everyday and sacred: The history of Tervola parish]. Tervolan seurakunta.

Häiväoja, H., & Nickels, B. (1990). *Hautamuistomerkkien hankkiminen* [Acquiring grave markers]. In P. Lempiäinen & B. Nickels (Eds.), *Viimeiset leposijamme: Hautausmaat ja hautamuistomerkit* [Our last resting places: Cemeteries and memorials] (pp. 40–45). SLEY kirjat.

Jørgensen, K. (1998). Semiotics in landscape design. *Landscape review,* 4, 39–47.

Jumalan puistot kauniiksi: Hautausmaiden opas [God's Parks Made Beautiful: A Guide to Cemeteries]. (1955). Suomen Kirkon Sisälähetysseura.

Koskinen-Koivisto, E. (2016). Reminder of lapland's dark heritage—Experiences of Finnish Cemetery tourists of visiting the Norvajärvi German Cemetery. *Thanatos, 5*, 23–41.

Knapas, M. T. (2005). Vanhat hautausmaat—monien muistojen puistot [Old cemeteries—Parks of many memories]. In A.-M. Halme (Ed.), *Puistot ja puutarhat* [Parks and gardens] (pp. 76–83). Suomen Kotiseutuliitto.

Laqueur, T. (1993). Cemeteries, religion and the culture of capitalism. In J. Garnett & C. Matthew (Eds.), *Revival and religion since* 1700 (pp. 183–200). Hambleton Press.

Lempiäinen, P. (1990). Hautausmaaperinteen rikkaus [Richness of cemetery tradition]. In P. Lempiäinen & B. Nickels (Eds.), *Viimeiset leposijamme: Hautausmaat ja hautamuistomerkit* [Our last resting places: Cemeteries and memorials] (pp. 6–20). SLEY kirjat.

Moscovici, S. (1984). The phenomenon of social representations. In S. Moscovici & R. Farr (Eds.), *Social representations* (pp. 3–55). Cambridge University Press.

Mytum, H. (1989). Public health and private sentiment: The development of cemetery architecture and funerary monuments from the eighteenth century onwards. *World Archeology, 21*, 283–297.

Nickels, B. (1990). Uurnahautausmaa [Urn burial ground]. In P. Lempiäinen & B. Nickels (Eds.), *Viimeiset leposijamme: Hautausmaat ja hautamuistomerkit* [Our last resting places: Cemeteries and memorials] (pp. 21–26). Helsinki: SLEY kirjat.

Pettersson, L. (1987). Kirkkotarha [The churchyard]. In T. Riska (Ed.), *Tervolan ja Simon kirkot* [Tervola and Simo churches] (pp. 38–40). Museovirasto.

Riska, T. (1987). Nykyinen kirkkotarha [The current churchyard]. In T. Riska (Ed.), *Tervolan ja Simon kirkot* [Tervola and Simo churches] (pp. 41–43). Museovirasto.

Schalin, M. (2005). Puutarha, puistokadut ja istutukset: Suomalaisen kaupunkipuiston vaiheita [Garden, park streets and plantings: Phases of a Finnish urban park]. In A.-M. Halme (Ed.), *Puistot ja puutarhat* [Parks and gardens] (pp. 12–17). Suomen Kotiseutuliitto.

Sirola, A. (2017). *Puhukoon paatinen pylväs. Vuoden 1918 vapaussodan sankarihautojen muistomerkit ja vapaudenpatsaat* [Let the stone pillar speak: Memorials and statues of freedom of the 1918 War of Independence hero graves]. Väyläkirjat.

Talve, I. (1988). *Kalmisto–hautausmaa–kirkkotarha: Kulttuurihistoriaa Suomen hautausmailla* [Kalmisto–cemetery–churchyard: Cultural history in Finnish cemeteries]. Turun yliopisto.

Talvio, M. (1927). *Jumalan puistot: leposijoja ja hautausmaita* [God's Gardens: last resting places and cemetaries]. WSOY.

Tarlow, S. (2000). Landscapes of memory: The nineteenth-century garden cemetery. *European Journal of Archaeology, 3*, 217–239.

Valsiner, J. (2014). *An invitation to cultural psychology*. SAGE Publications.

Wagoner, B., Brescó, I., & Awad, S. H. (2019). *Remembering as a cultural process*. Springer.

Wirkkala, I. (1930). *Haudan ja hautausmaan hoito* [Nurturing a grave and a graveyard]. Otava.

Wirkkala, I. (1945). *Suomen hautausmaiden historia* [History of Finnish cemeteries]. WSOY.

Lunette of Villa di Castello as it appeared in 1599, painted by Giusto Utens. *Source:* Public domain.

CHAPTER 7

THE HUMANISTIC GARDEN OF THE RENAISSANCE

Where Human, Society, and Cosmos Meet: An Introduction to Machiavelli's Political Ideas

Line Joranger
University of South-Eastern Norway

AN INTRODUCTION TO THE SEMIOTIC FIELD OF THE RENAISSANCE GARDEN

The Renaissance epoch started with the discovery that people in the pre-Christian antiquity had a completely different view of human beings and nature than in the "anti-humanist" Christian Middle Ages, which goal was salvation and saving one's soul through God's will and work. After century when the church had taught mankind to renounce worldly goods for the sake of eternity, the renaissance human showed an insatiable curiosity of the materiality of the here and now, a Faustian itch to explore, know, and

The Semiotic Field of the Garden, pages 149–164
Copyright © 2024 by Information Age Publishing
www.infoagepub.com
All rights of reproduction in any form reserved.

possess every nook and cranny of creation (Joranger, 2011; Porter, 1999; Siraisi, 2000).

The Renaissance is a term used to describe a period in European history marking the transition from the Middle Ages to modernity and covering the 15th and 16th centuries. It occurred after the end of the godly Middle Ages and is associated with great social change in worldview, art, and medicine. In addition to the standard periodization, proponents of a "long Renaissance" may put its beginning in the 14th century and its end in the 17th century. "Historians of different kinds will often make some choice between a long Renaissance (say, 1300–1600), a short one (1453–1527), or somewhere in between (the 15th and 16th centuries, as is commonly adopted in music histories)" (Butt & Carter, 2005, p. 4).

The fact that the humanists and artists of this age saw themselves called to bring the glories of antiquity back to life has given the period its name; the French word "Renaissance" means "rebirth" of ancient political, medical, and philosophical ideas. According to John Jeffries Martin (2003, p. 5), the humanists spoke more often of a renovation, or a renewal, than of a rebirth: a re-naissance; and it was they who first used the term *medium aecum* "the Middle Ages," to describe the long stretch of time that reached from the world of ancient Greece and Rome down to their own day.

The Italian humanists, gardeners, and artist, as early as the 14th century, were self conscious about their endeavour to recover and even bring back to life the world of antiquity (Martin, 2003). The Italian Renaissance poet Francesco Petrarca's inquiring mind and love of classical authors led him to travel, visiting men of learning and searching monastic libraries for classical manuscripts. Petrarca was regarded as the greatest scholar of his age. Together with other learned humanists, such as Marsilio Ficino (1433–1499), an astrologer and a reviver of Neoplatonism as well, Petrarch represents the contemporary scholars who translated many of the ancient great works (Joranger, 2011; Siraisi, 1990).

Thanks to the discovery of the ancient world and worldview, Europe's cultural and intellectual life underwent a mighty rebirth. First in the bustling commercial cities of Italy and later in transalpine courts, the arts and humanities were being restored to a brilliance unknown for centuries. Glory would be achieved and enthusiasts proclaimed, by burying the immediate past and emulating the ancients. New inventions changed not only the intellectual culture but also the material culture: gunpowder, the compass, and not to mention Gutenberg's printing press. For the first time on a relatively large scale, books multiplied, and were cheered on by propagandists and educators. Admiration for all things Greek was in the air: Plato, Aristotle, the poets, sculptures, and orators. These ideas are obviously applicable to medicine and astrology, which included human motions such as, humors, motives, desires, dreams, politics, appetites as well as natural and occult motions that operate in nature and in the cosmos and visualized in the architecture of the renaissance garden.

The Italian renaissance garden, like renaissance art, philosophy, and architecture, emerged from the rediscovery by renaissance scholars of classical Roman models. The classical Italian renaissance garden was a new style of garden which emerged in the late 15th century at villas in Rome and Florence, inspired by classical ideals of order and beauty, and intended for the pleasure of the view of the garden and the landscape beyond, for contemplation, and for the enjoyment of the sights, sounds, and smells of the garden itself. They were inspired by the descriptions of ancient Roman gardens given by Ovid in his *Metamorphoses*, and by the letters of Pliny the Younger, among others, both which gave detailed and lyrical description of the gardens of Roman villas (Attlee, 2006, p. 10, "Introduction"). Pliny the Younger described his life at his villa at Laurentum:

> A good life and a genuine one, which is happy and honourable, more rewarding than any "business" can be. You should take the first opportunity to leave the din, the futile bustle and useless occupations of the city and devote yourself to literature or to leisure. (Attlee, 2006, p. 13)

As highlighted in the Introduction, "personal subjective feelings are inseparable from culture. The garden thus inevitably implies reflecting on the relationship between personal and collective cultures." The purpose of a garden, according to Pliny, was "otium," which could be translated as seclusion, serenity, or relaxation, which was the opposite of the idea of "negotium" that often classified busy urban life (Attlee, 2006, p. 13). Like the Japanese garden (Introduction), the renaissance garden was a place to think, relax, remember, and escape (see also Chapter 6). A place with shaded paths bordered with hedges, ornamental parterres, fountains, and trees and bushes trimmed to geometric or fantastic shapes, all features which would become part of the future renaissance garden.

In the late Renaissance, the gardens became larger, grander, and more symmetrical, and were filled with fountains, statues, grottoes, water organs, and other features designed to delight their owners and amuse and impress visitors (see Figure 7.1). The style was imitated throughout Europe, influencing the gardens of the French Renaissance, the English knot garden, and the French formal garden style developed in the 17th century.

While the early Italian Renaissance gardens were designed for contemplation and pleasure with tunnels of greenery, trees for shade, an enclosed *giardino segreto* (secret garden), and fields for games and amusements, the Medici, the ruling dynasty of Florence, used gardens to demonstrate their own power and magnificence.

Figure 7.1 *Pleasure Garden With a Maze* c. 1579–1584, painted by Lodewick Toeput. *Source:* Wikimedia Commons.

> During the first half of the sixteenth century, magnificence came to be perceived as a princely virtue, and all over the Italian peninsula architects, sculptors, painters, poets, historians and humanist scholars were commissioned to concoct a magnificent image for their powerful patrons. (Attlee, 2006, p. 28)

As Tsuchimoto states in the Introduction:

> The term "garden" includes a multitude of meanings. It is a place for recreation and is a symbol of power. For the gardener, it is a place of work. Alternatively, the feeling of the garden is deeply rooted in people's hearts and has an aesthetic meaning.

The central fountain at Villa di Castello featured a statue of Hercules defeating Antaeus, alluding to the triumph of the garden's builder, Cosimo de' Medici. over a faction of Florentine nobles who had tried to overthrow him (Ballerini, 2011; see Figure 7.2). The garden symbolizes a form of political theater, presenting the power, wisdom, order, beauty, and glory that the Medici had brought to Florence.

Figure 7.2 *Lunette of Villa di Castello as it appeared in 1599*, painted by Giusto Utens. *Source:* License: Public domain. Usage terms: Public domain.

MIND, BODY, AND SOCIETY—HOW THINGS IN THE WORLD ARE GOVERNED

Born into the Renaissance's holistic humanistic worldview and into the power and guidance of the Medici family, the Florentine humanist writer and Diplomat Niccolò Machiavelli changed into the clothes of a courtier to study the art and theater of politic and human nature thought historical examples from the Roman empire and from direct observations from the field.

Machiavelli's most famous work is his political treatise *The Prince* (Il Principe), written about 1513, to the Medici family, as a guidebook in warfare and political strategies. However, in his less famous work, *The Discourses on the First Ten Books of Titus Livius* (Discorsi sopra la prima deca di Tito Livio [Machiavelli, 2000]), written around 1517, published in 1531, often referred to simply as *The Discorsi* or *The Discourses of Livy*, Machiavelli presents in three books, in much larger scale than in *The Prince*, a series of lessons on how a republican city state should be established, structured, and kept alive by balancing the individual mind with the collective mind, the human body with the body of the community and cosmos (Joranger, 2007b, 2011).

The title identifies the work's subject as the first ten books of the Roman historian Titus Livius (64 or 59 BC), who wrote a monumental history of Rome and the Roman people, titled *Ab Urbe Condita* (From the Founding of the City), covering the period from the earliest legends of Rome before the traditional foundation in 753 BC through the reign of Augustus in Livy's own lifetime. Machiavelli saw history in general as a way to learn useful lessons from the past for the present, and also as a type of analysis which could be built upon, as long as each generation did not forget the works of the past. Like Zlazli (Chapter 9), Machiavelli underlines the importance of having an awareness of one's own roots and knowledge system, recognizing the historical context or power relations that we are involved in. Knowing power relations will reduce fear for unknown threats.

Machiavelli frequently describes Romans and other ancient peoples as superior models for his contemporaries, but he also describes political greatness as something which comes and goes amongst peoples, in cycles. In Machiavelli's text as well as in the Greek and renaissance worldview, the human mind not only had a bodily expression. The human mind had also an expression of the nature and soul power of the state. Like the gardeners and like other learned humanists of the time, Machiavelli was influenced by ancient time and by Roman history. According to Machiavelli (2000), if we are to find out what may come, we must carefully study what have been:

> Anyone who studies present and ancient affairs will easily see how in all cities and all people there still exist, and have always existed, the same desires and passions. Thus it is an easy matter for him who carefully examines past event to foresee future events in a republic and to apply the remedies employed by the ancients, or if old remedies cannot be found, to devise new ones based upon the similarity of the events. (p. 90)

"Prudent men often say, neither casually nor groundlessly that anyone wishing to see what is to come should examine what has been, for all the affairs of the world in every age have had their counterpart in ancient times" (Machiavelli, 2000, p. 435). In Livius' writings and in the ancients' texts, Machiavelli finds great examples of governing a state so as to preserve the balance between nature and nurture, human character and environment.

Machiavelli is concerned with how "things of the world" (*cose del mondo*) and "human things" (*cose umane*) are governed (Joranger, 2006, 2007a, 2007b, 2011). In a letter written to his nephew Giovan Battista Soderini or to his patron and superior Piero Soderini, Machiavelli (1979) describes the relationship between nature and nurture, human character and environment, clearly:

> I believe that as Nature has given every man a different face, so she also has given each a different character and imagination. From this it follows that each man governs himself according to his particular character and imagination. And because, on the other hand times change and the order of things always shifts, the fortunate man, the one whose wishes are completely fulfilled, is he who fits his plan of action to the times; to the contrary, the unhappy man

is he who fails to match his actions to the times and to the order of things. Thus, it can easily occur that two men, acting in different ways, can archive the same result, since each of them can fit themselves to the circumstances, for patterns of events are as many as the number of provinces or states. But because the times and affairs are often transformed, both in general and in particulars, and men do not change their imaginations nor their methods, it happens that one man has in one instance good fortune and in another bad. And, truly, anyone so wise as to understand the times and the order of things and be able to accommodate himself to them would always have good fortune, or at least he would avoid the bad, and then the truth would emerge; that the wise man can command the stars and the Fates. (pp. 63–64)

Like another medical Hippocrates who wants to create an ABC for sick human bodies, Machiavelli creates through his studies of historical political affairs, an ABC for sick state bodies. A state body with a soul and a mind, that is, a personality that also showed itself in the renaissance gardens and in the citizens' mind and body. Logically, Machiavelli takes the worldview that he finds in the historical text as an analytical tool. To Machiavelli, diagnosis, prognosis, and treatment of the state body, as well as the state soul, are self-written tasks for a state leader who aims to preserve his state whether it is free or not (Joranger, 2006, 2007a, 2007b, 2011). Like Plato and ancient physicians, he believed that the soul not only had a bodily expression, it was also an expression of the nature and soul power of the state. The foremost task of politics was to establish itself as an overriding political soul force that could create order and conditions for survival in an anarchist chaos. Machiavelli shows great creativity when he transfers concepts from the medicine and anatomy of antiquity to what we can call the free natural body of society, which for Machiavelli was the Republic. In Chapter 30 of Book 2 in the *Discorsi*, he writes:

> When it comes to the body, the heart and the vital limbs must be armed and defended, not the limbs farthest out, because without a heart the body cannot live, and if you damage it, the body will die. Yet states like these ensure that the heart is unarmed, while the hands and feet have weapons. What has caused the disorder in Florence can be seen every day and everywhere. An army that crosses the border can go straight to the heart of the country without meeting resistance, and without having any effective cure. (Machiavelli, 1979, p. 217)

As in several chapters in *The Discorsi* (Machiavelli, 2000), the analogy between human bodies and corporate bodies is invoked to make the point that heaven causes plagues, famines, and floods as means of effective popular control and balance in society. Just as the human body maintains itself in good health through regular purgations, so also the human species maintains itself by periodic demography purges. Such purges are caused by heaven. As to the causes that come from heaven, they are those a part of the world, either through plagues or through famine or through a flood. That such natural calamities occur is not to be doubted, Machiavelli states, since histories are full of accounts of them. Besides, it stands to reason that this should be so, given the analogy between human body and mixed body. In the fifth chapter of Book 2 in *The Discorsi*, Machiavelli (2000) writes:

> Just as in the instance of simple bodies when a great deal of superfluous matter is brought together in them, nature many times moves of herself and makes a purgation of the health of those bodies, the same process appears in this mixed body of the human race. When all the lands are full of inhabitants, so that men cannot live where they are and cannot go elsewhere, since all places are settled and filled full, and when human craft and malice have gone as far as they can go, of necessity the world is humble, men can live more comfortable and grow better. (pp. 149–150)

The renaissance garden and the renaissance worldview of resemblance and signs mirror itself in Machiavelli's work and thinking. It explains how one in the renaissance worldview understands the way persons, cultures, and natures make each other up. A person's mind and body are indissociably embedded in the meanings and resonances that are both its product and its components. To explain health and disorder in the human body (microcosm) in the Renaissance, its relationship to nature and macrocosm was investigated and vice versa. In large health and disorder invokes the foursome of heaven, earth, humans, and society.

The renaissance human used humoral theory and medicine, such as they found it written by the Ancient Greece Hippocrates physicians, and later by Galen, to explain balance and dissonance between personal mind and cultural mind. Signs of dissonance in a human being were signs of dissonance in society. In the renaissance world, physical and psychic well being depends on the preservation of beauty and harmony within the body and beauty and harmony between the body, the environment (such as the garden), and the large order of things. They talked through the other through visible signs, such as balance, harmony, happiness, and peace, as well as fever, hunger, plague, and natural disasters. Healing was a question of knowing how harmony could be restored; and the task of the physician was as much philosophical as technical. The human body was seen as the counterpart of the state and vice versa (Joranger, 2006, 2007a, 2007b, 2011).

The love for human nature, its body and mind, and its connection to the wider cosmos, that is, the mind and body of the outer world, was not only visualized in the renaissance gardens, but also in texts, talks, and paintings, such as the renaissance painter Leonardo da Vinci's *Vitruvian Man* (1490; see Figure 7.3).

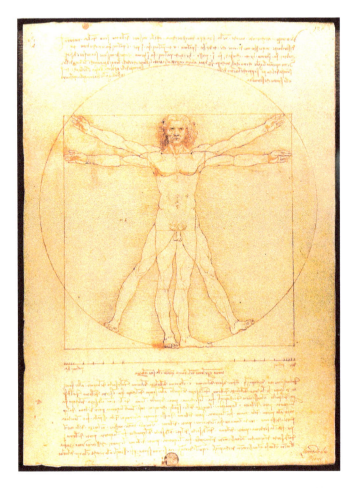

Figure 7.3 Leonardo da Vinci's *Vitruvian Man,* c.1490. *Location:* Gallerie dell'Accademia, Venice Taken from the free Wikipedia.

Like the renaissance garden, The *Vitruvian Man* (1490) has become the central and tutelary figure of renaissance humanism, depicting the classical ideas of symmetry, proportion, harmony, and balance between the inner and outer world (Kemp, 2019). Like the renaissance garden, the human world was seen as the miniature reduplication of the macrocosmic order:

> It was taken as axiomatic in the Middle Ages that the human body and its shaping soul were God's supreme creations, but in the 16th century, this idea was translated into a systematic search for bodily structures and mechanisms. A major factor was the rediscovery of the anatomical writings of Galen, the Roman physician and philosopher who emphasised the detailed mechanical perfection of all the components of the body in the context of the four ele-

ments of earth, water, air, and fire, and the four humours: sanguine, phlegmatic, choleric, and melancholic. The body was a microcosm that manifested in itself the basic properties of the wider cosmos. In this context, anatomy became the science that revealed the divine architecture and engineering of the human body. (Kemp, 2019, p. 1404)

In medicine, astrology, politic, gardens, art, paintings, philosophy, and poetry, the beauty of the human form and the nobility of the human spirit was highlighted, using the emblem of Vitruvian man (1490), in which the idealized naked male human forms was superimposed upon the cosmos at large.

RESEMBLANCE, SIGNS, AND SIGNATURE

To achieve knowledge and to understand the time and the order of things in the outer and inner world there was in the renaissance worldview a certain mark hidden in the circumstances that the fortunate human being could look for or be aware of. In the same way that we today know that vaccines will cure diseases, such as COVID-19, the renaissance human knew that ground walnut mixed with spirits of wine could ease a headache, because of some signs and marks that made them aware of this connection, otherwise, the secret would remain indefinitely hidden. The renaissance human would hardly know that there was a relation of twinship or rivalry between humans and their planet if there were so sign upon their body or amongst the wrinkles on their face that they were an emulator of Mars or akin to Saturn. That is, there are no resemblances without signatures, therefore, the world of similarity could only be a world of signs and signatures.

In *The Order of Things: An Archaeology of the Human Sciences* (Foucault, 1994) (*Les mots et les choses une archeologie des sciences humaines* [Foucault, 1966]), the French intellectual historian Michel Foucault, highlights that the knowledge of similitudes between a person's way of thinking and acting and the environment, in the renaissance worldview is founded upon the unearthing and decipherment of signs and signatures. Exploration of the human mind, and of one's own mind, depended on thinking through the ideas and practices of other people and their cultures. In Chapter 8, 9, and 10, you find several auto ethnographically examples of how one's own mind depends on thinking through the ideas and practices of other people and their cultures. In the renaissance worldview it was useless to go no further than the skin or bark of plants if one wished to know their nature; one had to go straight to their marks. The system of signatures reverses the relation of the visible to the invisible. To Foucault, the face of the renaissance world is covered with blazons, with characters, with symbols and obscure words. The place inhabited by immediate resemblances becomes like a vast open book, bristles with written signs. Every page was seen to be filled with strange figures that intertwined and, in some places, repeated themselves.

> The form making a sign and the form being signalized are resemblances, but they do not overlap. And it is in this respect that resemblance in the sixteenth-century knowledge is without doubt the most universal thing there is: at det same time that which is most clearly visible, yet something that one must nevertheless search for, since it is also the most hidden; what determines the form of knowledge (for knowledge can only follow the paths of similitude), and what guarantees its wealth of content (for the moment one lifts aside the signs and looks at what they indicate, one allows Resemblance itself to emerge into the light of day and shine with its own inner light). (Foucault, 1994, p. 29)

Foucault (1994, p. 29) calls the totality of learning and skills that enable one to make the signs speak and to discover their meaning in the renaissance worldview, "hermeneutics," and the learning and skills that enable one to distinguish the location of the signs, to define what constitutes them as signs, and to know how and by what lays they are linked, "semiology": "the sixteenth century superimposed hermeneutics and semiology in the form of similitude." To search for meaning and the nature for things was in this epistemic context to bring to light a resemblance. To search for the lay governing signs was to discover the things that were alike. The grammar of beings was an exegesis of these things, and what the language they spoke simply told what the syntax was that tied them together. However, resemblance in the knowledge system of the renaissance never remained stable within itself; it could be fixed only if it referred to another similitude, which then in turn, referred to others. Each resemblance, therefore, had value only from the accumulation of all the others, and the whole world had to be explored if even the slightest of analogies was to be justified and finally take on the appearance of certainty. We are speaking of a knowledge where the person, the cultures, and the nature, makes each other up.

In an episteme in which signs, and similitudes is wrapped around one another in an endless spiral, it is essential that the relation of microcosm and macrocosm, a single human being and the world around, should be conceived as both the guarantee of that knowledge and the limit of its expansion. It is the same necessity that obliges knowledge to accept magic and erudition on the same level. To a modern gaze, it may seem that the renaissance learning was made up of an unstable mixture of rational empirical knowledge, notions derived from magical practices, and a whole cultural heritage whose power and authority has been vastly increased by the rediscovery of Greek and Roman authors.

WAYS OF THINKING ABOUT TRUTH AND ABOUT WORLDVIEW

To Foucault (1994), a historical period, such as the Renaissance and the Modernity, is characterized by epistemes, ways of thinking about truth and about worldview, which are common to the fields of knowledge, and determine what ideas it is possible to conceptualize and what ideas it is acceptable to affirm as true. That the acceptable ideas change and develop in the course of time, manifested as paradigm shifts of intellectualism, for instance between the periods of Classical antiquity and Modernity, is support for the thesis that every historical period has underlying epistemic assumptions, ways of thinking that determined what is truth and what is acceptable.

In *The Order of Things*, Foucault (1994) analyses three epistemes: (a) the episteme of the Renaissance, characterized by resemblance and similitude; (b) the episteme of the classical era, characterized by representation and ordering, identity and difference, as categorization and taxonomy; and (c) the episteme of the Modern era, the character of which is the subject of the book. In the classical-era episteme, that is, in the Roman times and the antiquity, the concept of "human" or the distinction between personal culture and collective culture, was not yet defined but spoken of. The understanding of a "person" was not subject to a distinct epistemological awareness, as it is in the modern human sciences. The things in the world were seen as connected, not separated, reduced, and categorized, as in today's scientific universe where the human sciences are separated from astrology and natural sciences, and so on. Up to the end of the 16th century, resemblance played a constructive role in the knowledge of Western culture:

> It was resemblance that largely guided exegesis and the interpretation of texts; it was resemblance that organized the play of symbols, made possible knowledge of things visible and invisible, and controlled the art of representing them. The universe was folded in upon itself; the earth echoing the sky, faces seeing themselves reflected in the stars, and plants holding within their stems the secrets that were of use to man. Painting imitated space. And representation—whether in the service of pleasure or of knowledge—was posited the claim made by all language, its manner of declaring its existence and of formulating its right of speech. (Foucault, 1994, p. 17)

It was from this resemblance epistemic universe that the renaissance gardens were constructed, and Machiavelli related his worldview and his political theories. We are talking of a resemblance that tell us how the world must fold in upon itself, duplicate itself, reflect itself, or form a chain with itself so that things can resemble one another. We are talking of a resemblance that tell us what the paths of similitude are and the direction they take; but not where it is, how one sees it, or by what mark it may be recognized. Every human is different and must therefore act according to one's nature. This is shown in one the Machiavelli (1979) quote:

> Because, on the other hand times change and the order of things always shifts, the fortunate man, the one whose wishes are completely fulfilled, is he who fits his plan of action to the times; to the contrary, the unhappy man is he who fails to match his actions to the times and to the order of things. Thus, it can easily occur that two men, acting in different ways, can archive the same result, since each of them can fit themselves to the circumstances, for patterns of events are as many as the number of provinces or states. (p. 63)

In this quote the personal culture is acting upon the outer world of time and circumstances in order to accommodate to them and in some circumstances in order to command them:

> And, truly, anyone so wise as to understand the times and the order of things and be able to accommodate himself to them would always have good fortune, or at least he would avoid the bad, and then the truth would emerge; that the wise man can command the stars and the Fates. (Machiavelli, 1979, p. 64)

In the renaissance knowledge system, real language was not a totality of independent signs, a uniform and unbroken entity in which things could be reflected one by one, as in a mirror, and to express their truth. Rather it was an opaque mysterious thing closed in upon itself, a fragmented mass. Its enigma renews in every internal which combines here and there with the forms of the world and becomes interwoven with them so much so that all elements, taken together, form a network of marks in which each of them may play in relation to all the others. Unlike modern language, the renaissance language was not an arbitrary system. Words offered themselves to humans as things to be deciphered. Knowledge consisted in resemblance, that is, relating one form of language to another form of language, in restoring the great, unbroken plain of words and things, in making everything speak.

THE MODERN CONSTRUCTION OF A HUMAN BEING

The Order of Things (Foucault, 1994) is about the cognitive status of the modern human sciences in the production of knowledge, the ways of seeing that researchers apply to a subject under examination. To explain the starting point of the modern episteme that order things in the world in isolated and separated categories arbitrary to each other, Foucault points to Descartes' dualism and Bacon's empiricism, among others. Bacon's empiricism and Descartes' dualism fall together with the Copernican Revolution and other scientific discoveries of the 17th century. Together they reinforced the belief that deductions, observations, and experiments, was the only way to knowledge. Bodies were seen as biological organisms to be studied in their constituent parts (materialism) by means of anatomy, physiology, biochemistry, and physics (reductionism). A thinking that fostered the idea of an independent autonomous human being who could be studied empirically and deductively as an object, isolated from culture and the outer world. In this modern worldview, the distinction or separation between personal culture and collective culture, became possible and something one welcomed in science as a necessity to truth, "leaving nothing behind it but games" (Foucault, 1994, p. 51).

To Foucault (1966), the holistic and interconnected worldview of the renaissance ceased to exist at the beginning of the 17th century, when new meanings systems, such as rationalism, dualism, and empiricism, broke everything apart and separated the mind from the body, and the person from culture and environment. Left, we find a modern arbitrary and interconnected meaning system of separated categories, methods, and sciences, such as biology, philosophy, and mathematic:

> When natural history becomes biology, when the analysis of wealth becomes economics, when, above all, reflection upon language becomes philosophy, and Classical discourse, in which being and representation found their common locus, is eclipsed, then, in profound upheaval of such archaeological mutation, man appear in his ambiguous position as an object of knowledge and as a subject that knows; enslaved sovereign, observed spectator, he appears on the place belonging to the king, but from which his real presence has far so long been excluded. (Foucault, 1994, p. 312)

From the moment when it was no longer in continuity with a theory of representation, the renaissance worldview found itself, as it were, split in two: On the one hand, it invested itself in an empirical knowledge of grammatical forms; and, on the other, it became an analytic of finitude. However, the analytic of finitude has an exactly inverse role than the classical theory of sign (Foucault, 1994, p. 339). The theory of sign had to show how representations, which succeeded one another in a chain so narrow and tightly knit that distinction did not appear, with the result that they were all, in short, alike, could be spread out to form a permanent table of stable differences and limited identities. The analytic of finitude had an opposite role in showing that the human being was determined.

The analytic of finitude is, according to Foucault (1994), concerned with showing that the foundation of those determinations is the human beings in its radical limitations; it is concerned with showing that the contents of experience are already their own conditions. It shows how that origin of which the human is never the contemporary is at the same time withdrawn and given as an imminence. In short, the analytic of finitude is always concerned with showing how the other, the *distant*, is also the *near* and the *same*. Thus, we have moved from a reflection upon the order of *differences* to a thought of the *same*, which implies a dialectic, and that form of ontology which, since it has no need for continuity and must reflect upon being only in tis limited forms or in its distance, can and must do without metaphysics.

The modern episteme, established in the 17th century, is then related to the dissolution of discourse and the constitution of the person as subject and object of knowledge and power. The reappearance of language in modernity turns the "person" to lose its central position and to become the sunset of *homo dialectic*. The rise of the *homo dialecticus* made it possible to construct a semiotic field where the objects and persons could be observed and understood as a phenomenon on its own without any references to signs from the outer world. The loss of metaphysical interpretations of signs causes a naïve belief that there exists only one truth. That is, a scientific truth that one could bring forth through objective measurements and experiments. This deterministic and at the same time reductive beliefs falls together with a simultaneous rejection of the human experience and the autoethnographic narrative. Compared to the colorful semiotic garden of the renaissance, the one-dimensional semiotic garden of modernity becomes less colourful and less meaningful.

REFERENCES

Attlee, H. (2006). *Italian gardens: A cultural history*. Frances Lincoln.
Ballerini, I. L. (2011). *The Medici villas: Complete guide*. Giunti.
Butt, J., & Carter, T. (2005). *The Cambridge history of seventeenth-century music* (Vol. 1). Cambridge University Press.
Foucault, M. (1966). *Les mots et les choses une arch eologie des sciences humaines* [Words and things an archeology of the human sciences]. Gallimard.
Foucault, M. (1994). *The order of things: An archaeology of the human sciences*. Vintage Books.
Joranger, L. (2006). *Machiavellis medisinske metaforer: en abc for syke stater* [Machiavelli's medical metaphors: An abc for diseased states]. University of Oslo.
Joranger, L. (2007a). Machiavellis diagnosekunst—Machiavellis politiske teorier sett i lys av renessansens diagnose-, prognose- og behandlingspraksis [Machiavelli's art of diagnosis—Machiavelli's political theories seen in the light of Renaissance diagnostic, prognostic and treatment practices]. *Norsk statsvitenskapelig tidsskrift, 23*(02).
Joranger, L. (2007b). Renessansehumanisten Niccolò Machavelli: en moderne frihetsforkjemper [Renaissance humanist Niccolò Machavelli: A modern champion of freedom]. *1066 Dansk historisk tidsskrift, 37*(1), 3–12.
Joranger, L. (2011). Comedy and politics: Machiavelli's magical contemporary drama. *Journal of Language and Politics, 10*(2), 270–286.

Kemp, M. (2019). Leonardo's philosophical anatomies. *Lancet, 393*(10179), 1404–1408. https://doi.org/10.1016/S0140-6736(19)30584-7

Machiavelli, N. (1979). The discourses (P. Bondanella & M. Musa, Trans.). In P. Bondanella & M. Musa (Eds.), *The portable Machiavelli* (pp. 168–418). Penguin Books.

Machiavelli, N. (2000). *Discorsi sopra la prima deca di Tito Livio. Seguiti dalle Considerazioni intorno ai Discorsi del Machiavelli di Francesco Guicciardini* [Discourses on the first decade of Tito Livio: Followed by considerations around Machiavelli's discourses by Francesco Guicciardini]. (C. Vivanti Ed.). Einaudi.

Martin, J. J. (2003). *The renaissance: Italy and abroad.* Routledge.

Porter, R. (1999). *The greatest benefit to mankind: A medical history of humanity from antiquity to the present.* Fontana Press.

Siraisi, N. G. (1990). *Medieval & early Renaissance medicine: An introduction to knowledge and practice.* University of Chicago Press.

Siraisi, N. G. (2000). Alessandro Benedetti: *Historia corporis humani sive Anatomice* (Giovanna Ferrari, Ed.). (Biblioteca della Scienza Italiana, 21.) Florence: Giunti Gruppo, 1998. 365 pp. IL 55,000. https://doi.org/10.2307/2901542

Miho Zlazli (2018) *Yoron Island, one of the Ryukyu Islands in Japan.*

CHAPTER 8

CONSTANT FEAR OF OSTRACISM

Miho Zlazli
SOAS University of London

PROLOGUE

When I read Chihiro's evocative poetic autoethnography,[1] which was almost a declaration that elegantly portrayed her transformation from living and dying as a woman, wife, and mother to an autoethnographer who can express herself fully, I wondered what I have been through in my own turbulent life.

I was born Indigenous[2] and raised as a minority Christian girl in the Ryukyu Islands in the north-western Pacific of South Japan. Feeling alienated from the society where I lived in, I often dwelled in foreign folktales. When I was released from the cage, I started to chase after my imaginary *Bluebird of Happiness* (Maeterlinck, 1908)—a life with a sense of true belonging. However, I repetitively ended up pretending to be someone else.

I was fortunate that my path crossed with scholars who prompted me to explore my Indigenous identity. Relearning the traditional Indigenous knowledge system including my ancestral tongue has helped me rediscover

The Semiotic Field of the Garden, pages 167–193
Copyright © 2024 by Information Age Publishing
www.infoagepub.com
All rights of reproduction in any form reserved.

who I want to become. The traditional Indigenous knowledge system can be understood as a holistic system of knowledge that has developed over many generations through a complex fabric of practices and understandings based on physical and spiritual interdependence between individuals, their community, and Indigenous territories (Davis [1999] as cited in Howden, 2001; Howden, 2001).

This process deeply stirs my life and threatens close relationships that I have built over many years, but I have a hope that the Bluebird of Happiness will be within my reach soon when we find a new social equilibrium within which we can build a new relationship based on our true selves and mutual trust.

> Being trapped in a finite body
> A beautiful infinite soul
>
> Being blinded by dust and fumes
> A seagull's call from high up in the sky
>
> A key I found to depart today
> A beautiful infinite soul
>
> Opens the door to luminant realms
> A seagull's call from high up in the sky

SLEEPING BEAUTY

This section contains seven episodes from my childhood memory in a village where I was born and raised. They illustrate how my family and I lost access to our traditional knowledge system, what historical context we lived in, and what impacts they had on us. My diary entries contain composite motifs based on my real experience. People's names are pseudonyms to protect their privacy.

> (1) Saturday 20th September 1980—Reception
>
> Oh no! The neighbour's granny is sweeping the path.
> I can't go home (my grandmother's house)!

On Saturdays, I was supposed to go to my grandmother's house after school to wait for my mother to finish her work. Her house was at the end of a narrow path where I often found this lady over 100 years old. She was a monolingual Ryukyuan speaker who did not understand Japanese. I was scared to go near her. I did not know what to talk about with her nor even knew how to greet her in Ryukyuan.

(2) Sunday 28th November 1982—Year 2

I got a pair of red and white Karukan[3] buns. Yum! We had the 100th anniversary (of our primary school) today. Year 6 people wrote the anniversary song with their music teacher, and we sang it together in the gymnasium. So, my great *grandma also learned at this school, right? I wonder what it was like.*

I innocently imagined how the school was like a century ago, but it was the very beginning of the assimilation policy imposed by the Meiji government of Japan (Yoshimura, 2014) following the annexation of the Ryukyu Kingdom to Japan in 1879 (Mizuno, 2009). In the early years, the school attendance was low among children of commoner origin.[4] The lady in Episode 1 did not attend the school either. Except for a brief attempt of English language education under the post-war U.S. occupation (Masiko, 2014; Trafton, 1991, p. 25), the official language and knowledge system at school have always been Japanese since then.[5]

(3) Sunday 4th December 1983—Year 3

"**At 8 a.m.**, Mum woke me up and helped me prepare for Sunday school.

From 9 a.m., I played the organ for the children's service.

At 9:30 a.m., We received snacks and drinks from Sawa's mum and split into three age groups to learn today's Bible story.

At 10 a.m., I lit the first candle out of four for the first day of Advent for adult people's service.

At 10:10 a.m., I went to the rear of the prayer hall to make a cup of coffee with plenty of cream and sugar and waited for adult people to finish the service.

At noon, Dad took us to a nice restaurant.

At 1:30 p.m., we went to the Southeast Botanical Gardens.

In the evening, we got home, had dinner, watched TV, and fell asleep."

My teacher looked puzzled when she read my essay. The topic for writing was, "What did you do last weekend?" I thought I did well, but I was surprised to read other classmates' vivid stories about their joys and mishaps. I remembered that other kids were jumping up and down over cushions in the storage area next to the prayer hall, but I wondered what they were so excited about.

Our home atmosphere was slightly tense partially due to our implicit family language policy[6] introduced by my mother who was from a family of teachers who supported the assimilation policy (Ishihara & Ohara., 2019, p. 27). When we went to the restaurant, we ate in silence. My father and grandmother occasionally whispered to each other inaudibly in stigmatized Ryukyuan, which they felt most at home among themselves. Being unable to speak or behave freely under surveillance, I became emotionally detached.

Many years later, I once spent a week together with a family from Tokyo in the same house on a research trip. I had mixed feelings when I saw their children freely enjoy their mother tongue, which was *Kyōtsūgo* [the common language] in Japan (Sanada, 2019). They also had far more complex vocabulary than their Ryukyuan peers who had to correct their speech to adapt to Japanese society.

My worldview then was almost solely based on what I learned at Sunday school, which was significantly different from the traditional views in the Ryukyus. Feeling alienated from other children, I often immersed myself into TV anime series of folktales from Japan and Western countries.[7] I often spent time looking at the horizon at dawn or dusk as the colors of sky and ocean glided smoothly over the spectrum, which stretched out into my imaginary realms.[8] I also spent time alone in my own small universe at a corner of the churchyard while waiting for adults to finish their prayers.

(4) Date unknown

"Whoever strikes you on your right cheek, turn to him the other also. And if anyone would sue you to take away your coat, let him have your cloak also."

—Matthew 5:39–40

Am I an evil and wicked person?

I have a dark fantasy that I cannot reveal to anyone, never.

I get mesmerised by crucifying dainty fairies on the wall of the dining hall.

Am I insane? Would I rather not be alive?

I never said "No" to anyone. I constantly watched out for others. People loved me; I became empty. The more they took advantage of me, the more I felt that I was on a mission. I was eventually swallowed up in the *shadow* of myself (Jung, 1959).

(5) Monday 12th August 1985—Year 5

Grandma took me shopping today. Whenever I go out with her, I feel like we are wrapped in a translucent film. My hearing goes distant as we talk to people.

Many years later, I learned that my birth Christian community was ostracized by local society when it started as a group of 20 local Ryukyuan families in the beginning of the 20th century (Yomitan Church, UCCJ, 2016, pp. 26, 30). My grandmother might have inherited their psychological trauma and lived in an imaginary bubble which I experienced with her. I might have inherited it from her because I also felt detached from local society at every turn. I even thought that we might be aliens in disguise as villagers.

Constant Fear of Ostracism • **171**

(6.1) Monday 26th October 1987—Year 7

It's a hot day today. A mirage is hovering above the ground. The harness (of the marching bass drum) digs into my shoulders. The sun is baking my skin. Hm? There is a shadow of someone climbing above the score board of the stadium. Oh, the Hinomaru[9] is set alight![10]

In a few days, the protester's retail shop was burned down for revenge by Japanese right-wing extremists. That jet-black color and smell... I could not believe that it was the same place that I used to visit on the way home from piano lessons.

Black right-wing vans blasting military songs kept arriving from mainland Japan and flooded into our village. My poor grandmother was shaking. She screamed, "The war has begun again!" and hid under the dining table.

I knew by knowledge that our islands once turned into scorched earth during WWII. Many survivors repetitively shared their terrifying stories and emphasised, "No more wars," but it just did not feel real. I used to gaze blankly at American soldiers jumping off the helicopter in grey parachutes (Tanji, 2011) from a classroom window. It was part of my daily life. Seeing my gentle and calm grandmother panicking like that... For the first time, I realized that I was also part of the same history.

(6.2) Monday 9th November 1987—a few weeks later

The newspaper headline read, "Chibichiri Cave—The Statue of Peace Destroyed: Revenge Against Burning Hinomaru." The article said that a claim of responsibility by the extremists was found next to the statue: "The villagers who burn down the national flag do not deserve to have peace soon. We put down divine punishment!" (*Okinawa Times*, 1987)

The news struck me because the statue was very personal to me. It was just situated in April to commemorate civilians who lost their lives in compulsory group suicide at Chibichiri Cave under the influence of Japanese imperial ethos (Tanji, 2011; Yomitan Kanko Kyokai, n.d.). In the earlier months, we watched over the production site in the heart of our community. At the unveiling ceremony, I read aloud the community people's declaration of perpetual world peace...

(7) Sunday 2nd April 1989—Year 9

Mum: "Just put on anything, let's go! Hurry up!"

I reluctantly put my limbs through old baggy clothes for protection against Habu[11] snakes and mosquitoes. The clothes will get dirty and scratched up anyway.

> To prepare for "Shiimii" Festival,[12] we cut heavily overgrown grass and swept our family cemetery site (which was located just one step further from Chibichiri Cave).
>
> While having a quick lunch, a few tourists wandered towards us. They were looking for a path to go down to the cave (which became famous because of the incident). I quickly hid myself.

I was embarrassed, feeling that I was crude. They were dressed in fancy clothes and speaking Tokyoite-like Japanese. As I see the moon in double vision with my astigmatic eyes, I felt that our land had parallel worlds for locals who had flesh-and-blood memories there and mainlanders who pursued their imaginary paradise (Ina, 2010; Murray, 2017; Sudo, 2016).

ENCOUNTERS

The following nine episodes from my adolescence outside the village delineate ideological issues that I faced in gender, lifestyle, religion, and socio-politico-economic status.

> (8) Monday 16th April 1990—Year 10
>
> **Classmates:** "Wow, you know Hōgen! But you are a girl!"

Hōgen means "dialect" in Japanese. Ryukyuan people call their mother tongue a dialect (of Japanese) due to the historical context mentioned in Episodes 2 and 3 (Clarke, 2015). There is also a saying that a language is a dialect with an army and navy (Max Weinreich [1894–1969] as cited in Blackwood & Dunlevy, 2021, p. 238).

I went to a selective high school near the capital of Okinawa[13] to prepare for competitive university entrance exams in Japan, but later my parents only allowed me to apply for local universities because I was a girl (Hammine, 2020a, 2020b; Tsutsui et al., 2021). I was surprised to see that female students there spoke like Tokyoites despite the school being only one hour drive down south from my village where we spoke a contact language of our ancestral tongue and Japanese (Sugita, 2014). Romaine (2008, p. 103) argues that women tend to use more prestigious variants than men who are likely to have higher status and power.

> (9) Thursday 10th June 1993
>
> **Among classmates:** "Sorry, what did you just say? So many different dialects!"

I went to a local medical school. Nine out of ten were male students, and more than half of us were from all over Japan along with a few international students who passed the highest level of JLPT.[14] Female students became more masculine than male peers to survive patriarchal society in Japan (Froese et al., 2018). In group work, we often heard a variety of regional Japanese dialects and enjoyed the differences. If we were in Tokyo, they would simply adjust their speech to sound like Tokyoites (Ferguson, 1959; Sanada, 2019).

> (10) Friday 17th October 1997
>
> **Boyfriend:** "You think you must save me from the Path of Perdition. Don't you see how arrogant you are? You can't be better than my mother. She raised me alone by herself, working hard at a nightclub."

Pastoral care or counselling service was scarcely provided at that time. The only knowledge that I could rely on to survive my complicated adolescence was our Christian tradition that was only accumulated for a few generations (Trafton, 1991, pp. 29–31; Tomiyama, 2016). I took a leave of absence and dived into a professional night entertainment world to explore what my former boyfriend meant.

> (11.1) Friday 21st November 1997
>
> **Otōsan:**[15] "Oh, she's pretty. Welcome to our Okiya!"
> **Okāsan:** "Let's name her Aguri."[16]
>
> (11.2) Wednesday 25th February 1998
>
> **Onēsan:** "You've become much more feminine than before."
> **Okāsan**: "We'll miss you. I'll keep you registered at the Kenban. You can come back any time."

During the 3 months of work shadowing, I learned a lot indeed. While over-flattering superiors, ordinary people revealed *lust for violence* (Elbert et al., 2017) to inferiors or stigmatized night entertainers (Ashforth & Kreiner, 1999) when a moral system was not functioning. I was also impressed with their alternative underground safety network.

I understood that a rare gem was the one who was kind to people in vulnerable positions according to their inner moral value. An influential Japanese journalist Tsuneo Watanabe (1926) also reflects that what supported him during the student mobilization under the extreme war conditions was "the sky filled with stars above" and his "inner moral value" which were never spoiled by bullets flying towards him or absurd military codes (as cited in Yasui, 2020). I became more interested in embracing new worldviews.

> (12.1) July 1999—a field visit to Nepal
>
> Filled with nostalgic ambience everywhere…What makes me feel so?[17] But look at the disparity in the world…Shouldn't I have saved people's lives by do-

nating the cost for my field tour? I'm just watching how they give up their medical treatments after their long journey on foot. We are ugly extravagant savages.

(12.2) August 1999—at the IFMSA[18] General Assembly Meeting in Mexico

"That Yugoslavian boyfriend and Swedish girlfriend... He experienced the Kosovo War, and she is probably a migrant. They look so mature. I can't believe that they are of my age. And all those delegates from... more than 100 countries? Such a diverse world we live in. So much disparity here again."

I eagerly attended many field visits and student activities but got overwhelmed partially because I was too naïve to cope with brutal realities unfolding in front of my eye and because I lost spiritual connection to God. People were often nasty in the competitive environment. I was gradually worn out.

(13) Date unknown

Attempted suicide. When I woke up in the hospital, my former classmate was standing next to me as a medical intern.

I urgently needed spiritual guides. I envied people who managed to survive in the secular world on their own.

(14.1) February 2001

Me: "I'm tired of the worldly life. I cannot forget a sense of peace when I covered myself with a headscarf and gown as Saint Mary at a Nativity play as a child. Could you accept me as an apprentice at your covenant?"

Abbess: "Let's have weekly counseling first. When all doubts are gone, let's think about it again."

(14.2) April 2001

Me: "I've been thinking of my Muslim friends lately. They were always by my side whenever I was alone at the bottom. They also wear similar clothes and live a monastic life while living their family life. I wonder what it is like."

Abbess: "Go and examine their life. You will definitely come back."

(14.3) May 2001

Nor Huda (Malaysian classmate): "Salam alaikum, Miho. Is it true that you converted to Islam? Unbelievable!"

I took *Shahada*[19] to have a trial period in real-life settings. Since then, I have found one puzzle piece that perfectly fits my worldview—*Tawheed*.[20]

However, I still felt alone and isolated from society. I wondered how it is like to live in Muslim society as a family because I received extravagant support[21] from their society.

(15) Date unspecified

Supervisor (Prof of Neurosurgery): "So, family or career? Make up your mind. I also sacrifice my own family. I work from 7 a.m. to 11 p.m."

Me: "I think... family?"

After learning of the possibility of a transfer to Turkish medical school, I relocated to Turkey and married a local Turkish partner. However, as soon as my social status changed from an unaccompanied Japanese Muslim woman to someone's wife, I was embedded into their rigid social dynamics. I faced an intense patriarchy and traditional practices which were uncritically justified under the name of religion. I did not have a chance to transfer to medical school against my partner's will. Later, I remarried an Algerian British Muslim in England and fell into similar dynamics again.

(16) Date unknown

Why do I repetitively fall into a trap of patriarchy? A wife's destiny lies in her husband's hand just like children's destiny in their parents' hand.

Patriarchy, or a social system that prioritizes the rights of males and elders, may not be entirely blamed if the privilege holders take their proportionately increased responsibility for collective survival (Lakoff [1996], as cited in DeGagne, 2008, p. 22). For example, in Muslim society, I not only enjoyed unconditional financial maintenance (Gani & Khan, 2019) but also gender segregation (Sattari, 2020) as a person who was tired of sexual harassment in Japanese society (Tsunoda, 2003). I was content while I strategically managed to cope with a set of concrete constraints (Kandiyoti, 1988).

However, my suffering was greater than gratitude as a woman who wanted freedom in the public sphere in Turkey or as a convert Muslim woman in England who had poor access to Muslim women's networks which were typically reserved for women of the same ethnic origins.

AWAKENING

Accumulated encounters, including those mentioned in Section 3, eventually led me to important *turning points* (Elder et al., 2003, p. 8). I share four such turning-point moments or *epiphanies* (Denzin, 2013, p. xi) from my son's childhood and my postgraduate/research life.

(17) March 2014—Year 2 (my son)

I was told by Japanese Saturday School in London that my son had to leave because his Japanese language competence was not good enough.
My son: "Why am I excluded? Am I not Japanese?"

It was heartbreaking to witness my son's suffering. He had many friends there, and it was the only place where he could use his heritage Japanese language. He saw it as his first-order community where he would not be questioned about his membership. However, the main purpose of the Japanese supplementary school was to maintain the order of Japanese society among expats' children so that they would smoothly adapt themselves to Japanese society on their return (Doerr & Lee, 2009). The incident also rekindled my old wounds, but I could not identify the reason yet. To create a *Third Place* (Oldenburg, 1999) for heritage Japanese speakers, I started a master's degree in language pedagogy at SOAS University of London.

(18) November 2015—Postgraduate

Lecturer: "Which part of Japan are you from?"
Me: "Okinawa."
Lecturer: "Oh, so, do you speak Ryukyuan?"
Me: "Not really, why?"
Lecturer: "Do you know that your language is endangered? You should revitalize your own language, too."

Yes, older people do speak their mother tongue among themselves, but not even they use it to us. What was she so curious about our insignificant dialect?

My ancestral tongue never crossed my mind until she reminded me of it. I did not even know that Ryukyuan was a language group (Shimoji & Pellard, 2010), neither a single language nor a dialect of Japanese (Clarke, 2015). I also realized for the first time that there were thousands of Indigenous languages across the world according to Ethnologue (https://www.ethnologue.com) while there existed only a few hundred countries and territories.

(19) July 2016—Year 4 (my son)

After school, I took my son to a nearby park. Samira (an Algerian mother) was also sitting next to me. I called out to my son not to push his friend.

Samira: "Stop using Japanese to your son. Use Arabic. The language of paradise is Arabic.[22] You should help him perfect his Arabic first."

What she said connected the dots. The discourse was familiar to me as my mother also forbade me to mimic how my classmates spoke—mixing Ryukyuan into Japanese. By that time, I was aware that our people were oppressed for using their own mother tongue under a political campaign (Roche, 2021). Islamic and Christian hegemony also marginalized Indigenous knowledge systems as paganism (York, n.d., 2003) in varying degrees both in my partner's community and mine, respectively.

> (20) Monday 9th March 2020—returned from a research trip
>
> **Partner:** "Look what happens when you leave your home behind."
>
> **Me:** "I need your support. I know I cannot stay in the field too long. I understand it impacts our family life, but I still need to conduct brief field visits for my PhD research periodically for two years."
>
> **Partner:** "What's the point of your research?"
>
> **Me:** "It's about regenerating my community and exploring my own identity."
>
> **Partner:** "Converts are contaminating our religion."

As my research progressed, my partner's abhorrence grew stronger. It was partially due to his patriarchal gender view that women should not neglect her domestic responsibilities, but there was also something else, with which I still cannot pull a pierced thorn out of my chest. I thought that he would understand what I felt as Indigenous Ryukyuan because he was also Indigenous Kabyle Amazigh.[23] However, he was more concerned about the decolonization of Algeria from French influence. It was heavily influenced by an ethno-cultural unity centred around Islam and Arabic that actively suppressed Amazigh culture (Harris, 2020). Given the fact that the French colonial empire used the Kabyle identity to divide and conquer Algeria (Aïtel, 2014, p. 27), my partner projected his negative attitude towards the Kabyle people's political resistance onto my research activities.

After being constantly restrained within or bounced off ideological boundaries, I eventually broke a taboo of transgressing lingo-cultural (Turnbull, 2020) and religious (Ramadan, 2010) boundaries. My such actions have been threatening close relationships that I built over many years, but I am desperate to find another puzzle piece of my life—an intersection of my Muslim identity and the Ryukyuan knowledge system.[24]

INDIGENOUS EFFLORESCENCE

While my life is deeply stirred, the following episode has provided me with an insight on what to aim for in the future.

(21) Thursday 5th May 2020—Year 9 (my son)

I was attending an online meeting organized by English-speaking, mixed-roots Ryukyuan people mainly from Ryukyuan diasporas.[25]

My son overheard our discussions and asked, "Mum, am I also Ryukyuan? What's the difference between Ryukyuan and Japanese? Why do we have Japanese passports if we are Ryukyuan?"

My son's questions were inspiring. Even a teenager derives such straightforward questions. In fact, our ancestors were ruled under the Ryukyu Kingdom, which was annexed to Japan in 1879 (Mizuno, 2009) as mentioned earlier. More than a hundred people gathered there and shared their unique life stories, which my son found relevant to his own circumstances. He felt a personal connection to the Ryukyus for the first time. It never occurred to him during our family visits to Okinawa, where he was often singled out as a White *Hāfu*[26] who does not speak proper Japanese (Burke, 2016).

Since then, I have been interested in creating a *Thirdspace* (Soja, 1996) where self-identified Ryukyuans from varied backgrounds can negotiate their pluralistic identity and explore a new way of life (Ting-Toomey, 2015). Given that the memory and praxis of the Ryukyuan knowledge system are gradually disappearing due to the ongoing assimilation to Japan, such a space could be also beneficial for descendants of traditional Ryukyuan people to rediscover what it means to be Ryukyuan. Process- and future-oriented discussions may help the Ryukyuan people to build a new efflorescent[27] Ryukyuan society, which may also help them navigate through their turbulent geopolitical circumstances surrounded by great political powers (Iwama, 2021).

Since I identified two missing pieces (spiritual connection and intersectionality) and the future direction, I have often recalled the following Hadith:

The Prophet, peace and blessings be upon him, said:

God Almighty says, "Oh, Son of Adam, be unoccupied to submit to God. I will fill your chest with richness and alleviate your poverty. Otherwise, you will fill your hands with work, and I will not alleviate your poverty."

—At-Tirmidhī (9th century CE: No. 2466)

My troubled life was constantly haunted by fear of ostracism and unnamed void, which had been always filled with alternatives or readily available bounded ideologies. The void might have been created when my family and ancestors were suddenly stripped of their Indigenous knowledge system. They attempted to fill the gap with cut-and-pasted Christianity introduced by Western missionaries to fulfil their demands of everyday life. I also attempted to fill the void with whatever available around me.

EPILOGUE

Finally, I share four episodes related to the current pandemic of COVID-19 which has impacted me both negatively and positively. While feeling impatient to race against time to sustain the Indigenous knowledge system (FAO, ABI, & CIAT, 2021, p. ix), I also feel protected by physical boundaries created by lockdowns.

> (22) Tuesday 16th February 2021
>
> **Sister-in-law:** "Leila's father has passed away. Poor her, she can't even come back to attend his funeral."
> **Me:** "Innā lillāhi wa Innā ilayhi rāj'ūn..."[28]

Borders to Algeria were completely shut due to the pandemic. They did not even allow Algerian citizens to enter their own country. I felt sorry for Leila, a relative of mine who lived in England. I have many symbolic dreams these days. At times they alleviate my pain and other times make me fidgety with all sorts of other feelings.

> (23) March 2021—in my dream
>
> Walking on the seashore with Grandma at dusk...
> **Me:** "Grandma, that islet is glowing in turquoise. What is it?"
> **Grandma:** (explains in an inaudible voice)
>
> Suddenly, the tide went out, and we crossed to the islet together. When we arrived there, the scene switched to a churchyard in a historical site in Europe. We walked around together to enjoy sightseeing, then I was awake.

She is now over 100 years old and lives in a care home. She has never come to Europe, and her right leg is amputated. However, she used to pull me up a cliff[29] with a sac full of āsa[30] and urchins on her shoulders. In my dream, she was young and strong again as she used to be. I wondered what the dream was about. A few weeks later, my chest was tightened when I learned that islets were often used as cemeteries and that turquoise could be the color of the Hereafter in the Ryukyuan worldviews (Nakamatsu, 1975; Imaizumi, n.d.). It is also said that when the tide goes out coral reef lagoons $in\bar{o}$[31] surface to connect this life to the spiritual world (Hashio, 2017). Did my unconscious know the traditional knowledge without my conscious knowledge?

> (24) Summer 2019—at care home
>
> Grandma pointed out of her room window, saying "Kumā umi yagutu yo, ippē magasaru gai ga turari an. Yā ga tacchi, namā haman tōku natōn" in our ancestral tongue.

Translation:

"This area is sea, so large shells can be harvested. Now the seashore is far away because (so many) houses are built."

A peculiar history and unique atmosphere in her time, and my own childhood memories... Those vivid experiences are temporary and would eventually disappear along with our ancestral languages if we do not document them now, but travel restrictions due to the pandemic prevent me from visiting them. It is frustrating and heartbreaking, but the last words that I exchanged with my grandmother have been a relief to me.

(25) March 2020—the latest visit to my grandmother

I sang hymns in Ryukyuan to Grandma as she used to do in prayer meetings among our relatives (most of them have already passed away). Then, we said the Lord's Prayer in Ryukyuan together.

Me: "I'll be always praying for you, Grandma."

Grandma: "Nothing makes me happier than that, Nifee dō,[32] Miho."

Despite a negative impact of the pandemic, lockdowns have also protected me from direct exposure to ongoing cultural assimilation in the field. My PhD research is emotionally draining. The more you become self-aware, the more you get sensitive. It is also sad that there are not many people who I can share such feelings with. Many people turn away as if they are garden eels who stow away quickly as I move the water nearby.

UNRAVELING THE STORY

Brockmeier (2012) posited that narratives have four basic functions, which are communicative (intersubjective understanding), rhetorical (explaining), empathetic (being aware of the self and others), and cognitive (reflexive and imaginative).

I wrote my first-person narrative to share what it feels like to live as an Indigenous person whose community is under ongoing cultural assimilation, especially emotional insecurity and its coping mechanism—that is, to pretend to be someone else. I argue that it is difficult to fully embrace an *alterity* (Gillespie et al., 2012) to negotiate contingent self-identity (Ting-Toomey, 2015) when one's own knowledge system is undervalued.

As an Indigenous Ryukyuan researcher who supports new speakers[33] of Ryukyuan languages, I hope that this narrative will convince potential new speakers and stakeholders of language revitalization how important it is to maintain access to the Indigenous knowledge system and to facilitate a

Thirdspace (Soja, 1996) where new speakers can negotiate their pluralistic identities based on both Indigenous knowledge system and the current diversity observed among them.

In this section, I first examine *semiospheres* (Lotman [1982] as cited in Semenenko, 2016) in the narrative and discuss relations between individuals and groups, and then reflect on the implication of the Bluebird of Happiness in terms of semiospheres and relations.

Semiospheres and Relations

Zittoun (2012) argues that the mind of self who makes a meaning and develops through culture can be described as a semiotic system. Charles Sanders Peirce (1839–1914) triadically stratified the system's dimensions into *iconicity* (feeling or immediate consciousness) that is bound to time and space, *indexicality* (reaction or existential connection), and *symbolicity* (synthesis or habit-taking) that has a full degree of semiotic freedom and openness. However, he also regarded them as simultaneously present and constant ingredients of our knowledge (Atkin, 2010; Innis, 2012).

As an equivalent to the dimension of symbolicity, I use the term semiosphere which Semenenko summarized as a concrete collective mental sphere with an abstract character, including languages, where all communication and meaning generation take place (Lotman [1982], as cited in Semenenko, 2016; Semenenko, 2016). I listed major semiospheres, related relations (which can be categorized in the dimension of indexicality) and icons identified in the narratives in Table 8.1.

Among many motifs, I first touch upon a unique Ryukyuan spatial realm which also extends to a spiritual realm, in relation to Episodes 23 and 24, before exploring pivotal relations between individuals and groups which lead to the elucidation of the Bluebird of Happiness.

A Unique Ryukyuan Realm Inō

The Ryukyu Islands (Figure 8.1, left) are fed by the Kuroshio Current from the Western Pacific Warm Pool (WPWP), which makes the islands one of the richest centers of endemic species in the world's coral reefs (Kan, 2011). They are also located in the typical track of typhoons originating from WPWP (Kan, 2011), which also contributes to the unique spatial formation of the Ryukyuan communities (Figure 8.1, right).

As seen in Episode 23 and 24, the coral reef lagoon inō (Hashio, 2017) is both a pivotal element of the unique cosmological constructions (Abe, 2016) and a source of resource for their everyday life. However, inō, along with other ecosystems, has been destroyed by continuous land development (Imamura et al., 2020; Omiya, 2004).

TABLE 8.1 Semiospheres and Related Relations and Icons Identified in the Narrative (numbers in brackets indicate episode numbers)

Semiospheres (simbolicity)	Relations (Indexicality)	Icons (Iconicity)
The (un)conscious self i. inner moral value ii. the shadow (Jung, 1959)	iii. identity (identification with others) iv. physical and spiritual connections: a sense of peace (14); being suicidal due to self-doubt or feeling isolated and alone (4) (13)	i. the sky filled with stars above (11) ii. a dark fantasy (4); dreams (23) iii. all episodes iv. a finite body/an infinite soul (Prologue); Saint Mary's clothing (14.1)
Indigenous knowledge system (IKS) and ancestral tongue i. (un)conscious intergenerational transmission ii. intersectional IKS as Ryukyuan Christian	iii. historical context and its impact: Indigenous;[2] minority; marginalized; stigmatized; hogen (8); unable to speak or behave freely under surveillance (3); psychological trauma (emotional breakdown; shame) iv. *when unaware of IKS*: obedient to be taken advantage of/pretending to be someone else (4); silence (3); forgotten (18); feeling alienated/emotionally detached (4) (5) v. *when aware of IKS*: feeling at home (21); enabling to focus on who I want to become (21); enabling to embrace an alterity (Gillespie et al., 2012)	i. Indigenous territories and resources (23) (24); nostalgic ambience (12.1); ancestral cemetery (7) ii. Sunday school (3); prayers with my grandmother (25) iii. the moon in double vision with my astigmatic eyes/Indigenous territories being parallel worlds for locals and mainlanders (7) iv. *Sleeping Beauty* (Trites, 1997); becoming empty (4); wrapped in a translucent film/imaginary bubble (5); aliens in disguise v. self-identified Ruykyuan people's life stories (21)

(continued)

TABLE 8.1 Semiospheres and Related Relations and Icons Identified in the Narrative (numbers in brackets indicate episode numbers) *(continued)*

Semiospheres (simbolicity)	Relations (Indexicality)	Icons (Iconicity)
Ideology i. society ii/iii. nation state iv. religion	i. social order/moral system: patriarchy (8) (16); underground safety network; positionality; overflattering superiors/ economic disparity (12); lust for violence to inferiors (11); being nasty in competition (12) ii. *Japan*: assimilation policy; Kyōtsūgo as official language; family language policy (3); *diglossia* (Ferguson, 1959) (9); repercussions of imperialism/U.S. military occupation (6); singles out hāfu[26] people (21) iii. *Algeria*: decolonization movements under ethno-cultural unity/French colonialism using Indigenous Amazigh identities to divide and conquer the North Africa (20) iv. *Christianity/Islam*: hegemony against IKS (10) (20); prioritizing Arabic over other languages (19)	i. Geigi[15] community (11); lifestyle (15) (20); Third Place (Oldenburg, 1999) (18); physical boundaries by lockdowns due to the pandemic of COVID-19 (22) ii. monolingual Ryukyuan speaker (1); the 100th anniversary (2); the incident of burning Hinomaru[9] (6); fancy clothes/Tokyoite-like speech (7); Japanese Saturday School in London (17) iii. a pierced thorn in my chest (20) iv. extravagant support (14.3)
Imagination	i. imaginary paradise: mainlanders' image of Indigenous territories (7); my imaginary life as a nun / to live as a family in Muslim society (14); *Indigenous efflorescence* (Roch et al., 2018) (21) ii. associated emotions: healing, hope, a sense of true belonging iii. counter effects	i. Thirdspace (Soja, 1996) (21); Bluebird of Happiness ii. released from the cage/a seagull's call from high up in the sky/a key to open the door to luminant realms (Prologue); the horizon at dawn or dusk/a corner of the churchyard (3) iii. garden eels stow away quickly as I move the water nearby (Epilogue)

184 ▪ M. ZLAZLI

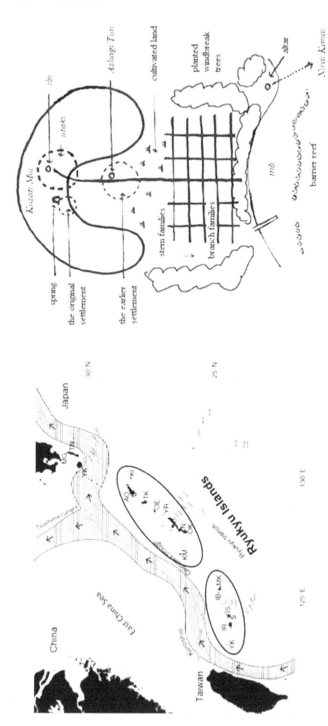

Figure 8.1 The Ryukyu Islands (left) (adapted from Kan, 2011) and a traditional community realm in the Ryukyus (right) (Adapted from Figure 1.4.3. in Nihon Kenchiku Gakkai, 1989). The community is surrounded by the mother forest "Kusati Mui" (腰当林: Cuddling Forest) which shields the community from typhoons and cold winds. It also has an ancestors' cemetery. The sacred grove "Utaki" has a sanctuary "Ibi" where their guardian deity descends, and only priestesses can enter there. The Worship House "Ashagi/Tun" is also situated near the forest. They believe that the Everlasting World "Nirai Kanai" exists far off the coast to the south-east. It is the origin of all life, and life is eternal there. The forest, coral reef lagoon "inō," and the cultivated land provide resources to the community.

Given that both my son and I experienced a pivotal turning point to rediscover our pluralistic identities for the first time when we felt reconnected to our Indigenous knowledge system, fading memories of blessing inō in Episode 24 is alarming because the destruction of Indigenous ecosystem may also lead to the destruction of our spiritual foundations.

Pivotal Relations

As identified in the narrative, individual life is simultaneously embedded in an array of semiospheres and entangled in a complex variety of relations with groups and other individuals (Table 8.1). Individuals congregate under *semipermeable symbolic boundaries* and associated feelings to form a group (Madureira, 2012), and different individuals have different constructs of semiospheres and group belongings.

Madureira (2012) posits that the meaning-making process occurs with differences and ambiguities and that belonging to a specific group creates an emotional tension between *Heimweh* (striving for the known and security) and *Fernweh* (curiosity for novelty and taking risks; Ernest Boesch [1916–2014], as cited in Madureira, 2012). She continues that needs for collective survival may promote Heimweh which reduces the permeability of group boundaries possibly to the degree of disqualifying others.

In fact, the Ryukyuan Indigenous knowledge system has been disqualified by Japan initially as part of their *Rich Nation, Strong Army* campaign in the early 20th century against the Western Powers (Samuels, 1994). My partner's abhorrence against my emergent Indigenous identity was also driven by his wish for decolonization of Algeria from repercussions of French colonialism (Episode 20).

In contrast, individuals also exert their imagination to *rupture* (Zittoun, 2012) their current entrapment to create a new dynamics of meaning-making (Episodes 7, 14, and 21). They are contingent upon the context where they emerge, and the process unfolds within the irreversible flow of time in their life course (Madsen, 2021).

Bluebird of Happiness

In Prologue, I described the Bluebird of Happiness as "a life with a sense of true belonging" and stated that it realizes when "a new social equilibrium within which we can build a new relationship based on our true selves and mutual trust" is achieved—in other words, when we create a new dynamics of meaning-making that is coherent with who we want to become (the true self) and what relations we want to have (identity). However, it could be "a real effort at an impossible task" (Valsiner [2007], as cited in Brockmeier, 2012) because we live in different developmental stages in our life course (that means we will not reach our true selves simultaneously at any time point) and our interests in relations do not necessarily coincide.

Nevertheless, I argue the importance of having an awareness in one's own roots or Indigenous knowledge system, recognizing the historical context or power relations that we are involved in, and negotiating one's pluralistic identity (Grossen et al., 2012; Zittoun, 2012). Having access to the holistic knowledge system which has been passed down for generations will contribute to the foundation of the self, from where one's inner moral value will develop and become a beacon to navigate through an uncertain future. Knowing power relations will reduce fear for unknown threats, and therefore Heimweh will be also reduced. Finally, updating one's pluralistic identity based on both traditional knowledge and one's acquired experiences will increase Fernweh to promote our reflexivity and empathy to others, which will facilitate the process of creating a new dynamic of meaning-making—that is, a step closer to the Bluebird of Happiness.

NOTES

1. It was part of our joint panel presentation at the International Conference of Autoethnography (ICAE) 2021 (Tsuchimoto et al., 2021; The presentation video is available from the reference). This article was also developed from my presentation within the panel.
2. When the word "Indigenous" is capitalized, it does not simply indicate that Indigenous peoples have unique history and relationship with their territories and resources, but also that they are marginalized in the mainstream of society (Merlan, 2009; UNDESA, 2008).
3. *Karukan* is a Japanese confection made from grated yam and rice flour. Red and white colors are often used for festive or auspicious occasions in Japan.
4. The late period of Ryukyu Kingdom had a rigid social class system (Akamine, 2016).
5. We had opportunities to sing Ryukyuan folk songs, cook traditional cuisines, and experience traditional performing arts as part of the curriculum. A few passionate teachers and students also delivered speeches or performed plays in Ryukyuan. I heard that such opportunities are increasing at school (Madoka Hammine, personal communication, 2020).
6. Family language policy means a policy on language use within the home and among family members (King & Fogle, 2017).
7. Kawauchi (1975) and Nippon Animation (1975).
8. Tsuchimoto also mentioned how a finite garden links to the infinity in our joint panel at ICAE 2021 (Tsuchimoto et al., 2021).
9. *Hinomaru* [the circle of the sun] means the flag of Japan.
10. For the full story, see Chibana (1988; English translation is available).
11. *Habu* is a venomous pit viper endemic to the Ryukyus.

12. The festival originates in China. During the third month of the Chinese lunar calendar, the whole clan gets together at the cemetery to honour their ancestors (NHK World, 2019).
13. Okinawa has been the political center of both the former Ryukyu Kingdom and the current Okinawa Prefecture of Japan.
14. Japanese Language Proficiency Test.
15. They were my *Otōsan* (father), *Okāsan* (mother), and *Onēsan* (sister) at *Okiya* (a lodging house for *Geigi* [Geisha]). *Kenban* means a *Geigi* association.
16. She named me after the heroine of a popular TV drama series called *Aguri* (NHK, 1997).
17. It could be because I projected what I had lost to their traditions.
18. International Federation of Medical Students' Associations.
19. *Shahada* is a testimony to become a Muslim.
20. *Tawheed* is a belief of the sole absolute Creator who surpasses the limit of our imagination.
21. For example, a free 3-months Islamic foundation course in Malaysia with provision of stipends RISEAP (https://riseap.org/), or an invitation to perform a mandatory pilgrimage *Hajj* for free of charge from Japan, to name a few.
22. There is a saying among Arab Muslim people that the Prophet, peace and blessings be upon him, said "Love the Arabs for three reasons: I am an Arab, the Qur'an is Arabic and the speech of the people of Paradise is Arabic" (Dūrī, 2012, p. 269), but it is said to be fabricated (As-Sakhawī, 1985, pp. 63–64). Meriem Sallemine (personal communication, 2019) identified that this belief had an impact on language use of the Zenata Amazigh people during her PhD fieldwork in Southern Algeria. Also, see Footnote 23.
23. Imazighen [plural of Amazigh] are Indigenous Peoples from North Africa (Harris, 2020). Also, see Footnote 22.
24. For example, I cannot worship ancestors nor spiritual beings but can recognize their existence and send greetings. The Ryukyuan people are exclusive in terms of their close-knit ties of kinship and community relations that are uniquely situated on their Indigenous land and sea, which extends to their relationships with ancestors and spiritual beings in their unique cosmological constructions (Abe, 2016) so as with other Indigenous peoples (e.g., Chilisa et al., 2016; Henry & Pene, 2001).
25. For details of migrations, see Kondo (2014) and Yomitan Village History Editing Room (2021).
26. Hāfu [half] means "mixed-race" in Japanese.
27. Roche et al. (2018, p. 225) proposed a new coined term *Indigenous efflorescence* to describe "political empowerment, economic success, and cultural flourishing" of Indigenous peoples.
28. It is a prayer and greeting of condolence in Arabic, meaning: "Surely we belong to God, and to Him shall we return."
29. That path was the only route to access the nearest seashore at that time.
30. āsa is an edible green alga *Monostroma nitidum* in my ancestral tongue.
31. For details, see Figure 8.1 (right).
32. *Nifee dō* means "thanks" in our ancestral tongue.

33. Here, "new speakers" means people who had little home or community exposure to the target endangered language but has acquired it through language revitalisation efforts (O'Rourke et al., 2015).

REFERENCES

Abe, T. (2016). *Seiji Jinruigaku no Riron to sono Gendai teki Igi* [The theories of political anthropology and its significance in the contemporary world] [Unpublished doctoral dissertation]. PMeiji University.

Aïtel, F. (2014). *We are imazighen: The development of Algerian Berber identity in twentieth-century literature and culture.* University Press of Florida.

Akamine, M. (2016). *The Ryukyu kingdom: Cornerstone of East Asia.* University of Hawaii Press.

Ashforth, B. E., & Kreiner, G. E. (1999). 'How can you do it?": Dirty work and the challenge of constructing a positive identity. *The Academy of Management Review, 24*(3), 413–434. https://doi.org/10.2307/259134

Al-Sakhawi, Muhammad bin Abdul Rahman bin Muhammad, Shams al-Din al-Sakhawi. (1985). *Al-Maqāsid al-Hasanah fī bayān kathīr min al-Ahadīth al-Mushtahirah 'alā al-Alsanah* [Good purposes in explaining many of the Hadiths well-known on the language]. Dar Al-Kitab Al-Arabi.

Atkin, A. (2010) Peirce's theory of signs. In E. N. Zalta (Ed.), *The Stanford encyclopedia of philosophy* (Rev.). Metaphysics Research Lab, Stanford University.

At-Tirmidhī, A. 'Isa M. ibn 'Isa. (824–892 AD). *Sunan at-Tirmidhī / Kitābu sifah al-qiyāmah wa ar-raqā'iq wa al-wara'i* [At-Tirmidhi's Hadith collections/A book of attribute of resurrection, subtleties, and piety].

Blackwood, R. J., & Dunlevy, D. A. (Eds.). (2021). *Multilingualism in public spaces: Empowering and transforming communities.* Bloomsbury Academic.

Brockmeier, J. (2012) Narrative scenarios: Toward a culturally thick notion of narrative. In J. Valsiner (Ed.), *The Oxford handbook of culture and psychology* (pp. 439–467). Oxford University Press.

Burke, R. S. (2016). Negotiating space and identity: The experiences of hafu children. *Japanese Early Childhood Education, 18*(2), 57–70.

Chibana, S. (1988). *Yakisuterareta Hinomaru: Kichi no shima Okinawa Yomitan kara* [Burning the rising sun from Yomitan Village, Okinawa: Islands of U.S. Bases]. Shinsensha.

Chilisa, B., Major, T. E., Gaotlhobogwe, M., & Mokgolodi, H. (2016). Decolonizing and Indigenizing evaluation practice in Africa: Toward African relational evaluation approaches. *Canadian Journal of Program Evaluation, 30*(3), 313–328. https://doi.org/10.3138/cjpe.30.3.05

Clarke, H. (2015). Language and identity in Okinawa and Amami: Past, present and future. In P. Heinrich, S. Miyara, & M. Shimoji (Eds.), *Handbook of the Ryukyuan languages: History, structure, and use* (pp. 631–647). De Gruyter Mouton.

DeGagne, A. (2008). *Constructing the patriarch in the Personal Responsibility Act* [Unpublished master's thesis]. University of Alberta.

Denzin, N. K. (2013). *Interpretive autoethnography* (2nd ed.). SAGE Publications.

Doerr, N. M., & Lee, K. (2009). Contesting heritage: Language, legitimacy, and schooling at a weekend Japanese-language school in the United States. *Language and Education, 23*(5), 425–441. https://doi.org/10.1080/09500780802651706

Dūrī, 'Abd al-'Azīz. (2012). *The historical formation of the Arab Nation: A study in identity and consciousness*. Routledge.

Elbert, T., Moran, J. K., & Schauer, M. (2017). Lust for violence: Appetitive aggression as a fundamental part of human nature. *e-Neuroforum, 23*(2), 77–84. https://doi.org/10.1515/nf-2016-A056

Elder, G. h. J., Kirkpatrick, J. M., & Crosnoe, R. (2003). The emergence and development of life course theory. In J. T. Mortimer & M. J. Shanahan (Eds.), *Handbook of the life course* (pp. 3–19). Kluwer Academic/Plenum Publishers.

FAO, ABI, & CIAT. (2021). *Indigenous peoples' food systems: Insights on sustainability and resilience from the front line of climate change*. Food & Agriculture Org.

Ferguson, C. A. (1959). Diglossia. *WORD, 15*(2), 325–340. https://doi.org/10.1080/00437956.1959.11659702

Froese, F. J., Sekiguchi, T., & Maharjan, M. P. (2018). Human resource management in Japan and South Korea. In F. L. Cooke & S. Kim (Eds.), *Routledge handbook of human resource management in Asia* (pp. 275–294). Taylor & Francis.

Gani, M. A. H., & Khan, M. N. (2019). Women rights of inheritance in Islam: Equity versus equality. *Journal of ELT and Education, 2*(3 & 4), 73–80.

Gillespie, A., Kadianaki, I., & O'Sullivan-Lago, R. (2012). Encountering alterity: Geographic and semantic movements. In J. Valsiner (Ed.), *The Oxford handbook of culture and psychology* (pp. 695–709). Oxford University Press.

Grossen, M., Zittoun, T., & Ros, J. (2012). Boundary crossing events and potential appropriation space in philosophy, literature and general knowledge. In E Hjörne, G. M. van der Aalsvoort, & G. de Abreu (Eds.), *Learning, social interaction, and diversity—Exploring identities in school practices* (pp. 15–33). Sense Publishers.

Hammine, M. (2020a). Educated not to speak our language: Language attitudes and newspeakerness in the Yaeyaman language. *Journal of Language, Identity & Education, 20*(6), 379–393. https://doi.org/10.1080/15348458.2020.1753200

Hammine, M. (2020b). Framing indigenous language acquisition from within: An experience in learning and teaching the Yaeyaman language. *The Language Learning Journal, 48*(3), 300–315. https://doi.org/10.1080/09571736.2020.1720786

Harris, J. (2020). Imazighen of France: articulations of an indigenous diaspora. *Journal of Ethnic and Migration Studies, 48*(9), 2115–2130. https://doi.org/10.1080/1369183X.2020.1788382

Hashio, N. (2017). An essay on the linguistic culture of spatial perception in the Ryukyu region: Thoughts on "Inō" and the world of "blue." *The bulletin of the University of Kochi. Faculty of Cultural Studies Issue, 66*, 33–50.

Henry, E., & Pene, H. (2001). Kaupapa Maori: Locating Indigenous ontology, epistemology and methodology in the academy. *Organization, 8*(2), 234–242. https://doi.org/10.1177/1350508401082009

Howden, K. (2001) Indigenous traditional knowledge and native title. *University of New South Wales Law Journal, 24*(1), 60–84.

Imaizumi, S. (n.d.). *Rensai 5: Okinawa & Kyubon no Eisa* [Series No. 5: Okinawa & Eisa in the Old Bon Festival]. Shinya Imaizumi Official Website. Retrieved April 11, 2021, from http://www.shinyaimaizumi.com/index.php?%E9%80%A3%E8%BC%89%EF%BC%95

Imamura, K., Takano, K. T., Kumagai, N. H., Yoshida, Y., Yamano, H., Fujii, M., Nakashizuka, T., & Managi, S. (2020). Valuation of coral reefs in Japan: Willingness to pay for conservation and the effect of information. *Ecosystem Services, 46*, 101166. https://doi.org/10.1016/j.ecoser.2020.101166

Ina, H. (2010) Constructing difference in Japan: Literary counter-images of the Okinawa boom. *Contemporary Japan, 22*(1–2), 179–204. https://doi.org/10.1515/cj-2010-011

Innis, R. E. (2012). Meaningful connections: Semiotics, cultural psychology, and the forms of sense. In J. Valsiner (Ed.), *The Oxford handbook of culture and psychology* (pp. 255–276). Oxford University Press.

Ishihara, M., & Ohara, Y. (2019). Ryukyuan sociolinguistics. In P. Heinrich & Y. Ohara (Eds.), *Routledge handbook of Japanese sociolinguistics* (pp. 25–42). Routledge. https://doi.org/10.4324/9781315213378

Iwama, D. A. (2021). Where does militarism go when bases close? *Boston Review*. Retrieved July 29, 2021 from http://bostonreview.net/war-security/daniel-akihiro-iwama-where-does-militarism-go-when-bases-close

Jung, C. G. (1959). The shadow. In *AION: Researches into the phenomenology of the self* (Collected Works of C. G. Jung, Vol. 9, Part II, pp. 8–10). Routledge & Kegan Paul.

Kan, H. (2011). Ryukyu Islands. In D. Hopley (Ed.), *Encyclopedia of modern coral reefs: Structure, form, and process* (pp. 940–945). Springer Netherlands. https://doi.org/10.1007/978-90-481-2639-2

Kandiyoti, D. (1988). Bargaining with Patriarchy. *Gender and Society, 2*(3), 274–290. http://www.jstor.org/stable/190357

Kawauchi, S. (1975). *Manga Nippon Mukashi Banashi* [Once upon a time in Japan]. Tokyo Broadcasting System (TBS). http://nihon.syoukoukai.com/

King, K. A., & Fogle, L. W. (2017). Family language policy. In T. L. McCarty & S. May (Eds.), *Language policy and political issues in education* (pp. 315–327). Springer International Publishing. https://doi.org/10.1007/978-3-319-02344-1_25

Kondo, K. (2014). Japanese language education in modern Okinawa until 1945. In M. Anderson & P. Heinrich (Eds.), Y. Ando (Trans.), *Language crisis in the Ryukyus* (pp. 54–81). Cambridge Scholars Publishing.

Madsen, T. (2021). Between frustration and education: Transitioning students' stress and coping through the lens of semiotic cultural psychology. *Theory & Psychology, 31*(1), 61–83. https://doi.org/10.1177/0959354320944496

Madureira, A. F. do A. (2012). Belonging to gender: Social identities, symbolic boundaries and images. In J. Valsiner (Ed.), *The Oxford handbook of culture and psychology* (pp. 582–601). Oxford University Press.

Maeterlinck, M. (1908). *L'Oiseau bleu* [The Bluebird] [Play].

Masiko, H. (2014). The politics of the movement to enforce standard Japanese under the U.S. occupation. In M. Anderson & P. Heinrich (Eds.), P. Heming (Tran.), *Language crisis in the Ryukyus* (pp. 82–102). Cambridge Scholars Publishing.

Merlan, F. (2009). Indigeneity: Global and local. *Current Anthropology, 50*(3), 303–333. https://doi.org/10.1086/597667
Mizuno, N. (2009). Early Meiji policies towards the Ryukyus and the Taiwanese Aboriginal territories. *Modern Asian Studies, 43*(3), 683–739. https://doi.org/10.1017/S0026749X07003034
Murray, A. E. (2017). Okinawa's tourism imperative. In *Footprints in paradise* (pp. 15–28). Berghahn Books.
Nakamatsu, Y. (1975). *Kami to mura* [Gods and villages]. Dento to Gendaisha.
NHK. (1997, April 7). *Renzoku Terebi Shosetsu: Aguri* [Serial TV Novel: Aguri]. Retrieved April 21, 2024, from https://www.nhk.jp/p/ts/MJR34N615Y/
NHK World. (2019, March 8). *Okinawa shiimii festival.* Retrieved August 3, 2021, from https://www3.nhk.or.jp/nhkworld/en/ondemand/video/6023015/
Nihon Kenchiku Gakkai [Architectural Institute of Japan]. (Eds.). (1989). *Zusetsu: Shuraku–Sono Kukan to Keikaku* (p. 42). [Illustration: Hamlets–The space and planning]. Toshi Bunkasha.
Nippon Animation. (1975). *Sekai Meisaku Gekijo* [World masterpiece theater]. Fuji Network System. Retrieved August 2, 2021, from https://www.nippon-animation.co.jp/work/meisaku/
Okinawa Times. (1987, November 9). *Chibichiri Gama Heiwa no zo Hakai sareru: Hinomaru yakisute heno Hofuku, Shisha no rei nimo Hokosaki, Yomitan* [Chibichiri Cave—The Statue of Peace destroyed: Revenge against burning Hinomaru, a spearhead even against spirits of the dead—Yomitan], p. 1.
Oldenburg, R. (1999). *The great good place: Cafés, coffee shops, bookstores, bars, hair salons, and other hangouts at the heart of a community.* Distributed by Publishers Group West.
Omiya, T. (2004). Terrestrial inflow of soils and nutrients. In M. Tsuchiya et al. (Eds.), *Coral reefs of Japan I* (pp. 64–68). Ministry of the Environment and Japanese Coral Reef Society.
O'Rourke, B., Pujolar, J., & Ramallo, F. (2015). New speakers of minority languages: The challenging opportunity–Foreword. *International Journal of the Sociology of Language, 231,* 1–20. https://doi.org/10.1515/ijsl-2014-0029
Ramadan, T. (2010) *The quest for meaning: Developing a philosophy of pluralism.* Penguin UK.
Roche, G. (2021). Lexical necropolitics: The raciolinguistics of language oppression on the Tibetan margins of Chineseness. *Language & Communication, 76,* 111–120. https://doi.org/10.1016/j.langcom.2020.10.002
Roche, G., Maruyama, H., & Virdi Kroik, Å. (Eds.). (2018). *Indigenous efflorescence: Beyond revitalisation in Sapmi and Ainu Mosir.* Australian National University Press. https://doi.org/10.22459/IE.2018
Romaine, S. (2008). Variation in language and gender. In J. Holmes & M. Meyerhoff (Eds.), *The Handbook of language and gender* (pp. 98–118). John Wiley & Sons.
Samuels, R. J. (1994). *'Rich nation, strong Army': National security and the technological transformation of Japan.* Cornell University Press.
Sanada, S. (2019). Japanese dialects. In Y. Ohara & P. Heinrich (Eds.), Y. Ohara (Trans.), *Routledge Handbook of Japanese sociolinguistics* (pp. 63–77). Routledge.

Sattari, N. (2020). Women driving women: Drivers of women-only taxis in the Islamic Republic of Iran. *Women's Studies International Forum, 78*, 102324. https://doi.org/10.1016/j.wsif.2019.102324

Semenenko, A. (2016). Homo polyglottus: Semiosphere as a model of human cognition. *Sign Systems Studies, 44*(4), 494–510. https://doi.org/10.12697/SSS.2016.44.4.02

Shimoji, M., & Pellard, T. (2010). *An introduction to Ryukyuan languages*. Research Institute for Languages and Cultures of Asia and Africa.

Soja, E. W. (1996). *Thirdspace: Journeys to Los Angeles and other real-and-imagined places*. Blackwell.

Sudo, N. (2016). Okinawa he Iju suru Wakamono tachi: Kirino Natsuo "Metabora" ni miru Ijusha Zo [Young people migrants to Okinawa: The image of migrants in "metabora" by Kirino Natsuo]. *Sociological Papers: Official Journal of the Waseda Graduate Students' Association for Sociological Research, 25*, 17–34.

Sugita, Y. (2014). The discovery of Okinawa-substrate Japanese as a "we-code": The language of Okinawan youth in the 1980s and its impact. In M. Anderson & P. Heinrich (Eds.), *Language crisis in the Ryukyus* (pp. 169–205). Cambridge Scholars Publishing.

Tanji, M. (2011). Human rights and community development in a U.S. Army village in Okinawa. *New Community Quarterly, 9*(33), 5–11.

Ting-Toomey, S. (2015). Identity negotiation theory. In C. R. Berger et al. (Eds.), *The international encyclopedia of interpersonal communication* (1st ed. pp. 1–10). Wiley.

Tomiyama, K. (2016). Ryukyu kingdom diplomacy with Japan and the Ming and Qing Dynasties. In M. Ishihara, E. Hoshino, & Y. Fujita (Eds.), *Self-determinable development of small islands* (pp. 55–65). Springer.

Trafton, T. (1991). *American influence on Okinawan Culture before 1972. Historical materials*. Education Resources Information Center (ERIC).

Trites, R. S. (1997). *Waking sleeping beauty: Feminist voices in children's novels*. University of Iowa Press.

Tsuchimoto, T. (2021, July 20). On the infinite border of the garden: A poetic inquiry. *The 8th International Conference of Autoethnography*. https://youtu.be/lxcpkBUCZSI

Tsuchimoto, T., Katsura, Y., Suzuki, C., Yokoyama, N., Takagi, Y., & Okawa, R. (2021, July 20). Spotlight Panel 1: Blurred borders touching territories with/without touching bodies. *The 8th International Conference of Autoethnography*. https://youtu.be/lxcpkBUCZSI

Tsunoda, Y. (2003). Sexual harassment in Japan. In C. A. MacKinnon & R. B. Siegel (Eds.), *Directions in sexual harassment law* (pp. 618–632). Yale University Press.

Tsutsui, M., Yokoyama, A., Hammine, M., & Zlazli, M. (2021, March 4). Effects of gender on language revitalisation & documentation in the Ryukyus. *The 7th International Conference on Language Documentation & Conservation (ICLDC)*. University of Hawai'i at Mānoa (Online), http://hdl.handle.net/10125/74474

Turnbull, B. (2020). Beyond bilingualism in Japan: Examining the translingual trends of a "monolingual" nation. *International Journal of Bilingualism, 24*(4), 634–650. https://doi.org/10.1177/1367006919873428

UNDESA. (2008). *Resource kit on indigenous people's issues.* United Nations Department of Economic and Social Affairs.

Yasui, K. (2020, August 9). *Tsuneo Watanabe: War and politics—Self-portrait of postwar Japan.* NHK Special. https://www2.nhk.or.jp/archives/movies/?id=D0009051179_00000

Yomitan Church, Unite Church of Christ in Japan. (2016). *Shu to ayumu Hyaku nen: Rekishi Siryoshu (1907–2007 nen)* [100 years with the Lord: Historical documents (1907–2007)].

Yomitan Kanko Kyokai. (n.d.). *Chibichiri Gama & Shimuku Gama* [Chibichiri Cave & Shimuku Cave]. https://www.yomitan-kankou.jp/tourist/watch/1611319972/

Yomitan Village History Editing Room. (2021). *Shashin de miru Yomitan son no imin & dekasegi: sekai no Yuntanzanchu* [Emigrant workers seen in the photos: Yomitan people in the world]. http://imin-visual.yomitan-sengoshi.jp/

York, M. (n.d.). *Defining paganism.* http://proteanrl.org/docs/general_info/defining_paganism.pdf

York, M. (2003). *Pagan theology: Paganism as a world religion.* New York University Press.

Yoshimura, S. (2014). Japanese language education in the Meiji period. In M. Anderson & P. Heinrich (Eds.), *Language crisis in the Ryukyus* (pp. 31–53). Cambridge Scholars Publishing.

Zittoun, T. (2012). Life-course: A socio-cultural perspective. In J. Valsiner (Ed.), *The Oxford Handbook of culture and psychology* (pp. 513–535). Oxford University Press.

Interaction with invisible entities (*Source:* Photo by the author).

CHAPTER 9

DJINNS AND RADIOACTIVE MATERIALS

An Abductive Autoethnography on a Garden of Invisible Entities

Yusuke Katsura
Japan Society for the Promotion of Science, Ritsumeikan University

ABDUCTIVE AUTOETHNOGRAPHY ON THE "INVISIBLE GARDEN"

A garden is "a small piece of landscape within which we negotiate our agency as cultivators with that of the growing nature" (Valsiner, 2014, p. 177). Within it, we see various flora and fauna and engage with the natural environment using our knowledge and skills.

Gardens are generally recalled with a sense of positivity. For example, Gomes discusses in Chapter 2 (this volume) that a garden "is a field-like sign as in 'place where I am fuller and happier'" (p. 41). However, as Hidaka and Kasuga discuss in Chapter 4, such a possibility can be undermined under some circumstances.

The Semiotic Field of the Garden, pages 195–210
Copyright © 2024 by Information Age Publishing
www.infoagepub.com
All rights of reproduction in any form reserved. **195**

As every other chapter shows, a garden is more than a physical place; it involves temporal, spatial, emotional, and semantic extensions. In this context, this chapter looks at the relationship between invisible entities and humans to further extend the garden concept. Such a relationship is constructed within a realm we all have in common, individually and collectively, where we make various decisions concerning invisible entities. Here, I use the term "invisible garden" to refer to a realm where nature and culture are negotiated concerning invisible entities.

The relationship with invisible beings varies greatly from place to place. To identify the similarities and differences between the original individual culture of the self and the collective culture of each place, I will use autoethnography to describe my own experiences and perceptions. Physically moving from one region to another can lead one to reevaluate one's personal and collective cultural assumptions and to learn about other cultures firsthand. Autoethnography can be very effective in depicting the process of such realization and the reasoning process that leads to the discovery of the overlap of collective cultures in multiple places. In other words, autoethnography is not only an evocative or analytical way of writing but is also suitable for writing the abductive process.

Following Brinkmann's (2014) discussion of "stumble data" (pp. 723–724), which surprises us, makes us unstable, and influences the way we see things, Mosleh (2020) called such events that occur in autoethnographic writing "abductive experiences" (pp. 417–418). Mosleh said it is important to "seek to highlight and make sense of surprising events that we, as autoethnographic researchers, stumble upon, and which have the potential to become data" (p. 418).

This chapter draws on my experiences in West Africa and Japan and highlights the nature of the "invisible garden" through descriptions of abductive experiences. First, I will explain how I came to understand the collective culture in West Africa, especially Mali and Senegal. Subsequently, I will focus on a practice concerning beings called "djinn" in Mali. Following this, I will present the characteristics of the Malian people's relationship with djinn and contrast them with the people's relationship with radioactive materials in Japan. This comparison will highlight the similarities between the characteristics of these two supposedly very different entities. Finally, I will focus on a discussion by natural scientists in Islamic society that regards djinns as an energy source.

I will argue how the boundaries of the various dichotomies that are generally considered self-evident can be ambiguous regarding the "invisible garden" and contribute to the debate about our relationship with the invisible entities, which is becoming increasingly important today.

COLLECTIVE CULTURE IN SENEGAL AND MALI

Meeting a singer from Senegal in Japan in 2007 sparked my interest in West Africa, and I traveled to Senegal in 2008. While I witnessed the so-called African culture where percussion and dance flourished as I had imagined, I became more interested in the fact that Islam has historically spread in Senegal to the extent that the Arabic greeting "As-salaam Alaykum (Peace be upon you)" is used by all generations at all hours of the day.

I wanted to live there for a considerable period. Thus, I applied to the JICA volunteer[1] program and was successfully accepted. In January 2011, I was assigned to the Republic of Mali, West Africa. Like Senegal, more than 90% of Mali's population is said to be Muslim. In Mali, the greeting "As-salaam Alaykum" was uncommon. However, I encountered the word "Allah" everywhere in daily life. For older people, for example, a greeting tends to be very long and becomes a prayer in the middle of a sentence: "Good morning. Did you have a good night? How are you? How is your family? How are the children? Any problems? May Allah makes it a good day for you. May Allah keeps you healthy. Thanks to Allah, your family will be well." These words go on and on. Finally, the greeted person would say, "Amin (Amen). May Allah bless you all."

No matter how small the village, unless it is a Christian village, it has a mosque. The "Azaan," the call to prayer, is played aloud over speakers five times a day. The earliest Azaan came before dawn when it was still dark, which often woke me up. It was common to meet in the village "after the noon prayer." Prayer is the foundation of a day's schedule and rhythm.

My occupation was vegetable farming. From my base village, I cycled to the villages to help plant vegetables in the community garden. Although staple foods, such as millet and sorghum, are Mali's most commonly cultivated crops, vegetable cultivation has recently become widespread. My role was to help plant them.

The vegetable garden and the way vegetables are grown differ entirely from Japan. The weather changes rapidly, with squalls during the rainy season and sandstorms during the dry season. The sunlight was so intense that just stepping outdoors made me dizzy. Vegetable fences were knocked down by strong winds, and seedlings were sometimes burned by sunlight and shriveled immediately after planting. The soil, which is low in organic matter, hardens into a crumbly mass during the dry season, and I even saw people plowing with pickaxes.

One time, I noticed the absence of a neighbor's kid for a few days. She used to annoy me by interfering with my vegetable cultivation. I heard that she was hospitalized with malaria, and then I received the news that she had passed away. She was eight years old.

Living in such an uncertain situation, I tweeted the following statement about 10 months after arrival.

> During the sun, storms, hard rains, sickness, and harsh environment, we do not even know what the future holds, so "the future is insha'Allah." (Twitter, 19 November 2011[2])

At this time, I realized that the extended, prayerful greeting I mentioned above was not just a string of words but an authentic feeling.

I began to feel more deeply the relationship between the transcendent beings and the local people in contrast to the situation in Japan. Then, exactly 1 year after March 11, I posted, "The words of a Muslim struck me, 'It proves that God is far above humans and science.'" (Twitter, March 11, 2012) One person said this to me after seeing the news of the Fukushima nuclear power plant accident following the Great East Japan Earthquake. Having lived without any connection to so-called "religion," the relationship between science and faith in the region was very stimulating.

At the same time, I was aware that another being in daily life was invisible as God, yet a little more familiar. In the local Bambara language, it is called "Giné." The existence and its relationship with people intrigued me.

GARDEN OF GINÉ

Giné Possession

In the rural area of Mali where I was staying, I would hear the sounds of percussion and singing from the central village every Thursday night or late at night. My neighbors told me it was the home of a person they called "Teacher (Kala moko)." As I had taken percussion lessons in Mali, I was curious, and one day I went there to participate.

Many people, especially women, gathered in the yard of the largest building in the village. A few percussionists were playing, and the songs were blaring through microphones from large speakers. Despite sounding like dance music, this dance was completely different from their usual joyful dance.

First, the gathered people danced gently, walking in a circle. It was just like the Japanese "bon" dance. Then, as the music started to pick up the pace, most of the people fell back, leaving only a few of them to dance in unison. Despite intense music, they did not move their lower bodies, but only their hands, upper bodies, and heads. Eventually, people were running around, moving, and even falling. This activity occurs in the so-called "trance" state. In Mali, it is regarded as the "giné" coming down.

An anthropologist Gibbal (1982), researched the culture of giné in Mali. In his ethnography, there is one phrase that particularly resonates with me:

> They read neither Artaud, nor Bataille, nor the others, but they live as if they had come out of their books. What have they become? (Gibbal, 1982, p. 51, my translation)

As Gibbal cited the names of the surrealist artist Artaud and the philosopher Bataille, it was an intense scene and an extraordinary experience for me.

After living under such circumstances for 1 year and 3 months, the security situation in northern Mali deteriorated, and a coup d'état occurred in the capital, forcing me to leave for Japan in a hurry.

Islam and Giné

A year later, in 2013, I revisited Mali to learn more about the situation after my sudden return. As preliminary research for enrolling in graduate school, I tried to conduct interviews and film[3] the giné during my stay.

It was late at night when I arrived at the village where I had stayed. A few people gathered at houses across the street. When I followed in, I realized that the woman of the house was obsessed with giné and moaning. Another woman tried to get rid of the giné by pouring smoke and whispering in her ear.

Later on, I found out through interviews with the "Teacher" and others that sometimes the giné comes down with music, and sometimes it is summoned by emotions like anger. When a giné is possessed, if you are an expert like the "Teacher," you can use the power of the giné to solve people's problems or treat their illnesses by listening to what giné speaks through the possessed person's mouth. It is a part of medical treatment and psychological consultation. On the other hand, if you do not have the knowledge or ability, the power of giné can drive you insane.

While interviewing and filming the "Teacher," I participated in dance performances as a percussionist and, once, even as a dancer. As a result, I became involved in situations where the existence of giné was shared as a collective culture. Gradually, I began to feel a different reality. I perceived something "surreal."

Ahmad, my boss, made one of the most unexpected comments when I was a volunteer. "Giné exists!" he said passionately. Ahmad's statement was surprising because, at this point, I considered giné to be an African animistic entity, which Ahmad, a devout Muslim, wholly affirmed.

One of my "stumbled" experiences changed my perception of giné as "djinn" in Islam, as described in the Qur'an.[4] However, while affirming the existence of djinn, Ahmad said that since Islam is a monotheistic religion, following the "Teacher" would put God and djinn on the same level. For this reason, he said it was forbidden for Muslims to visit someone like the "Teacher" to ask for advice.

On the other hand, the "Teacher" himself often uses phrases such as, "May Allah heal you" and "May Allah approve you" in his rituals and also on his website, and it seems that he does this as a part of his Islamic practice. His expressions provide glimpses of the complexity of the relationship between Islam and djinn.

Schulz also described such complexity of Islam and the practice regarding djinn in Mali: "There are Muslims who decry these practices and attendant belief as un-Islamic, they are also an essential characteristic of how certain Malian Muslims deal with different kinds of affiliation and misfortune" (Schulz, 2012, pp. 34–35).

The reasons for such a situation might be partly attributed to the syncretism of traditional Malian practices and Islam. However, the ambivalence about the practice involving djinns is widespread historically in the Islamic world, not just in West Africa.

El-Zein's discussion is a reference point. In her survey of historical texts on djinn and medical treatment in the Islamic world, she stated:

> Classical Islam stressed that Muslims should strive to find cures for diseases. Islamic physicians built up a huge and intricate medical corpus. This all-embracing literature was not confined to strict medical knowledge in the sense that modern medical literature is. Rather, it was blended with philosophy, natural science, mathematics, astrology, alchemy, biology, spirit healers, charms, and religion. In this sense, it was what we call today "interdisciplinary." (El-Zein, 2009, p. 87)

What El-Zein called "spirit healers" includes someone like the "Teacher" in Mali. Mali's complex situation may reflect a part of such an "interdisciplinary" attempt to deal with mental and physical problems.

Relationship Between Djinns and People

Through interviews, participation in rituals, and filming, I learned about various characteristics of djinns and their relationship with people. In combination with the descriptions in the literature, I identified the following items: (a) harmful, (b) beneficial, (c) types, (d) expertise, (e) demand, (f) gender, (g) segregation, and (h) norms.

Harmful

Djinns can cause physical and mental illnesses. While experts like the "Teacher" can use djinn possession to solve people's problems and cure their diseases, their power can also make them go crazy. In Arabic, the word "majnun" means a person who has gone mad and also a person who is possessed by a djinn (El-Zein, 2009, p. 74). This shows how djinns are connected to people's psychological symptoms.

Beneficial

Djinns are regarded as naturally existing but are extracted artificially and used for treatment. They use music and dance to invoke djinns and seek solutions to problems. This aspect was explained as "consultation with djinns." In doing so, people find a way to resolve not only mental and physical illnesses but also financial, occupational, and familial problems.

Types (Families)

Djinns are just like human beings. There are both male and female djinns. Some are kind, serious, or religious, but some are not. They consist of families and relatives. Gibbal described the names and personalities of various kinds of djinn (Gibbal, 1982, pp. 171–185), which partially overlaps with what I had heard.

Expertise

The "Teacher's" knowledge and words are essential. Learning about the names and characteristics of various djinns is necessary for treatment. Knowledge is also vital for understanding the language of djinns. So if you are willing to be a "Teacher," you need to accumulate knowledge by learning from different other Teachers.

Demand

Due to people's demand, practice concerning djinns creates employment and wealth. The "Teacher" was hiring many musicians and workers. The treatment sometimes involves the sacrifice of goats and sheep and is often very expensive. My initial impression of the "Teacher" was as follows.

> There is also a state-level official who lives in the village, but the sorcerer[5] looks richer than him. The sorcerer in my village is so famous that people from Senegal and Ivory Coast come to visit him. (Twitter, January 12, 2012)

Gender

Djinns are often tied to women and childbirth. Ahmad said, "More than 90 percent, more like almost 100 percent, of women believe in djinn." As far as I observed, there was a lot of female participation in the dance ceremony. The connection between djinn and childbirth is also often mentioned; Holten noted, "Having sex with *jinɛ* (djinn) was the only cause of congenital defects that my respondents named" during her research in Mali (Holten, 2013, p. 30).

Segregation

There are some places people should cautiously approach or are off limits. For example, djinns are often associated with bushes. One woman told me that a djinn came down for the first time when she passed by a bush. People played percussions at a ritual I attended and called out toward bushes. In an elementary school textbook, a boy was chased by a djinn who lived in a bush that his parents had told him not to approach. In addition to the bushes, I also heard stories of djinn living in certain places, such as under bridges, rivers, or seas.

In particular, the "third bridge (le troisième pont)" in the capital Bamako is often reported as where the djinns live.[6] There, rituals are performed to have the djinns grant wishes, while a series of suspicious deaths and suicides are sometimes attributed to the djinns. In addition, conflicts elsewhere in the country are sometimes attributed to the djinn's anger over the bridge's construction. Thus, the presence of the djinn is sometimes given social and political connotations.

Norms

The school textbook also tells a story about a man who promises to become wealthy but ends up breaking the promise and losing all his wealth. Holten also refers to the story in her research (Holten, 2013, p. 29). These stories teach moral behavior about the importance of following one's parents' advice and making promises. In addition to general morality, the relationship with the djinn is also related to the behavior of Muslims, as we have seen above. While the "existence" of the djinn itself is widely accepted, in other words, shared as part of the collective culture, relying on the djinn's ability is a matter of individual judgment.

Cultural and Context-Dependency: Difficulties in Translation

After returning to Japan, I had occasions for dialog while watching the videos I took. Some people found the practice positive and claimed they were reminded of "the value of spirituality."

Other people interpreted djinn in a functionalist way.

> I got the impression that he was using djinn as a symbol of the system. It may not be important whether or not the djinn exists, but it is a way to suggest that

by listening to the djinn's words, people will do the right thing, and as a result, their lives will improve. (Audience comment, December 5, 2015)

From this comment, which I assume is somewhat shared in Japan, the djinn is not considered real. I stumbled here again. Having spent time in Mali, I was already a part of the collective culture that regarded the djinns as not merely spiritual beings or symbols of a system but more as real entities that had a specific effect on people's lives.

RADIOACTIVE MATERIALS FALLING ON THE GARDEN

Radioactive Materials and Djinn

How did I see the djinn after returning from Mali, that is, what was my abductive experience? At that time, I conducted a self-interview for a part of the film and said the following:

> After living in a culture that entrusts the judgment of life and actions to such things, what I think now is... I guess it's like what we call science. However, this may be too much to call so. For example, radioactivity is invisible. You cannot see it, but if the experts tell you that this place is dangerous, you don't go there. You cannot see it, but you think it exists. If they say the food is contaminated, you don't eat it, and so on. (Self-interview, October 6, 2014)

At the time, around 2014, the psychological impact of the nuclear accident was still strong. Partly because of this, I felt that the reality of djinn in Mali was similar to that of radioactive materials in Japan.

People's Relationship With Radiation

Just after the nuclear accident in 2011, there were many uncertainties over issues such as contaminated water, the state of radiation exposure of the population, the effects on the ocean, mountains, fields, rice paddies, and other ecosystems, the cost of decommissioning the nuclear power plant, and the tremendous amount of time and place needed to manage radioactive materials. On TV, the phrase "no immediate impact" was repeated. Therefore, when, where, and what effects will there be? As the situation's uncertain aspects were clarified, citizens' movement to eliminate nuclear power was gaining momentum, while the government was going ahead with the restart of nuclear power plants. The "irrational" situation of losing part of the country's land and still being forced to rely on nuclear power plants shook my self-image of "modern Japanese society," which is based on scientific rationality.

When I compared the discourse on and behavior toward X-rays, radiotherapy, and nuclear power plants in Japan with people's attitudes toward djinn in Mali, I was surprised to find that there were many similarities between people's relationship with djinns and radioactive materials.

The items listed above as characteristics of djinn also apply to radioactive materials.

Harmful

Radioactivity brings physical illness. Therefore, people became very sensitive to radioactive materials after the earthquake, leading to a psychological burden. There was a widespread suspension of shipments and refraining from buying agricultural products produced around Fukushima due to fear of health hazards.

As discussed in Chapter 4, in the affected areas, private gardens of individuals became the "public garbage dump" for packages filled with radioactive waste. For the owners of those gardens, it is still a very emotionally taxing experience. This psychological burden was not limited to the disaster area but was also seen in places far away from there. As a result, a significant opposition movement emerged to remove debris from Fukushima prefecture as if the radiation pollution would spread to their houses and gardens.

Although it was common to be concerned about food and the environment, the term "radiation brain" was also used to describe excessive concern (Kimura, 2016). People sometimes spoke as if radioactive materials possessed them.

Beneficial

They naturally exist but are artificially extracted and used for treatment. For example, we know we are exposed to a certain amount of radiation by living in nature. However, it can be extracted using specific techniques and used in X-rays and radiation therapy.

Types (Families)

There are various types of radioactive materials, each with different half-lives and effects on living things. The conditions of radionuclides are often referred to as family-related terms.

For example:

> A nuclide resulting from the disintegration of a daughter nuclide (then from a parent nuclide) is sometimes called a granddaughter nuclide, and such daughter nuclide and granddaughter nuclide are collectively called progeny nuclides. (Ministry of the Environment Government of Japan, 2019, p. 10)

Expertise

The knowledge and words of specialists remain essential. Since there are many uncertainties, such as which level of radiation of food is safe to consume or go out, experts' explanations are crucial. On the other hand, there were times when the experts disagreed. Professional qualifications, such as X-ray technicians, are required for medical use.

Demand

Owing to the enormous energy demand, radioactivity creates employment and wealth. Therefore, many people in Japan's business, political, and academic communities have been promoting nuclear power generation under the phrase: "safe, cheap, and reliable" (Kingston, 2012, p. 1). This group is often known as "Japan's Nuclear Power Village or Nuclear Village."

These policies significantly impact the economic situation in rural areas. The municipalities where the nuclear power plants are located have received many grants and subsidies.

Gender

The "radioactive brain" mentioned above is often associated with "moms" and women. The lessons learned from the Chornobyl nuclear power plant accident led especially pregnant women and mothers with small children being active in taking radiation measurements because of their significant impact on their children's health (Kimura, 2016).

Segregation

Some places should not be approached due to radioactive contamination. Even now, more than a decade after the nuclear accident, it is difficult to return to some parts of Fukushima Prefecture. Evacuation-directed areas are still designated, and some are classified as "restricted areas" and off-limits. News reports about these areas also led to psychological segregation. As a result, even outside the affected areas, there were some overreactions, such as children of evacuees being bullied and crops from Fukushima or Miyagi prefectures being avoided, even though there was no confirmed radioactive contamination.

Norms

Nuclear energy is related to the fundamental level of our way of life, such as the economy, policy, and environmental issues. Therefore, the nuclear accident raised questions on the ethical and normative levels, such as where and how we should live.

Cultural and Context-Dependency: Difficulties in Translation

Although radioactivity has significantly impacted Japanese society, I found it challenging to explain it when I was in Mali. In the village where I was staying, after the earthquake and the nuclear accident, people who heard about it came to visit me out of concern. The tsunami was visually understandable to those who watched TV, and I could explain it, but the nuclear accident was difficult to explain.

I tweeted the following at that time.

> I can talk about radiation with Malians who understand French and watch and listen to French TV and radio. However, there is no such word as radiation in the local Bambara language, so I cannot explain it to ordinary villagers who do not understand French, no matter how hard I try. (Twitter, March 16, 2012)

As the Bambara language did not have the necessary vocabulary, I translated radiation or radioactive material as "bana kisé" (seed of disease). I realized that our daily lives in Japan depend on something that lacks a counterpart in some languages. When I looked at Japanese society from the outside, the abnormality of the situation stood out to me.

As described above, the situation in Japan since the nuclear accident has been very confusing. I began to think about the characteristics of radioactive materials and radiation. I realized that while radioactive materials themselves are natural entities, a sense of reality and fear of them is, in part, culturally constructed.

Even with technology and scientific knowledge, we can never fully know their existence and effects, so we have no choice but to "believe" certain discourses based on experts' opinions.

Through these experiences, I realized that the seemingly unscientific djinn and the scientifically proven radioactive materials have something in common concerning their existence, their effects on human beings, and how people regard them.

DJINN AND NUCLEAR ENERGY

For me, the connection between the two in the "invisible garden" became more apparent when I read the book *Islam and Science: Religious Orthodoxy and the Battle for Rationality*. In the book, the author, nuclear physicist Hoodbhoy, harshly criticized the so-called "Islamic science" advocated by the "highly placed members of the Pakistani scientific establishment" (Hoodbhoy, 1991, p. xiii).

Hoodbhoy stated:

> With breathtaking boldness, they laid claim to various bizarre discoveries that ranged from calculating the speed of heaven using Einstein's theory of relativity, finding the chemical composition of jinns, and even to the extraction of energy from these fiery divine creatures so that Pakistan's energy problems could be solved. (Hoodbhoy, 1991, p. xiii)

On this issue, the Wall Street Journal interviewed natural scientists who had led nuclear power technology and such Islamic science in 1988. This coverage attracted brief international attention, but their arguments were not generally accepted in Pakistan or Islamic society (Hoodbhoy, 1991, pp. 153–154) However, that such a debate arose is an interesting example of the "invisible garden," for the scientists leading Pakistan's nuclear power plants.

Of course, my intention is not to say that djinns and radioactive materials can be placed on the same level as some Muslim scientists suggest. However, this chapter has highlighted one aspect: The "invisible garden," where we interact with invisible entities, is a place where people negotiate between nature and culture or science and belief.

DOING FIELDWORK IN THE INVISIBLE GARDEN

So far, we have looked at the relationship between people and different invisible entities in different places, mainly Japan and Mali, based on my own experiences. To stay in plural places is to engage with others who live in more than one collective culture and learn about their differences and similarities.

Through living in multiple locations, I realized my perspective gradually changed. Mosleh (2020) said that an abductive process helped me "to move beyond the limitations we find ourselves constrained by, in initially trying to quickly impose a specific understanding onto the experiences we face" (p. 432).

When I began traveling to West Africa, I was surprised by how Islam spread there. It changed my image of "Africa." After spending some time, I understood how God, about whom I had never been seriously concerned, was close to daily life in an uncertain environment. However, I was interested more in djinns then, which were very particular and connected to everyday practice. At first, I regarded djinns as African cultural beings and then understood them as the Islamic existence written about in the Qur'an. When I returned to Japan and tried to explain the djinn, I realized how difficult it was to convey the reality I experienced in Mali. Rather than the typical Japanese "specific understanding" that is a "spiritual" being or a "symbol of the system," I found that it had properties and relationships with people, somehow like the radioactive materials. Thus, I came to be more conscious of, in other words, to start doing fieldwork at the "invisible garden."

Looking into the "invisible garden" leads us to find unexpected commonalities between beings usually considered entirely different. Djinns and radioactive materials are ontologically different, but they seem to have a similar "causal power" (Danermark et al., 2001, p. 198) that affects people in specific ways. Their power inspires people to use their imagination, brings hope to solve problems and bring about a better life, and gives severe physical and mental effects at times. Under such circumstances, especially in times of emergency, the invisible entities, which are usually grasped and represented in a limited way as point-like signs, become more multivalent and are perceived as field-like signs.[7] The "invisible garden," which contains contradictory elements, emerges as fields of hyper-generalized meanings, stirring people's emotions and overwhelming them with sensations that cannot be verbalized. As a hyper-generalized field, the "invisible garden" sometimes stirs up emotions that cannot be verbalized and can overwhelm people.

Autoethnography, a methodology that shows feelings and sensations and the process of abductive reasoning, brings this to light. In the process, various dichotomies I had taken for granted in my personal and collective culture were called into question. Djinn is a "cultural" entity from the Japanese perspective but a "natural" entity in a rural area of Mali. Radioactive material is a natural entity, but it has a "cultural" aspect to it. Both are invisible and have the ambivalent power to harm and benefit humans.

When we consider the "invisible garden" in this way, we can find ambiguous realms between several dichotomies, such as nature and culture, science and belief, Japan and West Africa, rationality and irrationality, materiality and spirituality, and the self and the other. They may overlap more than the extent to which it is generally assumed.

Today, COVID-19 can be an example of how the impact of an invisible presence on our lives can be felt worldwide. Some people worry so much that they have a mental illness, and the term "corona brain," just like "radiation brain," is being used to denote those who are obsessed with or panic-stricken about coronavirus. In a situation that limits our mobility globally, our relations to various kinds of gardens have been questioned. In particular, focusing on the "invisible garden" allows the possibility of learning how people negotiate with invisible entities or, to put it another way, what kind of causal power they have over human beings.

Whether djinns, radioactive materials, or viruses, the collective culture concerning invisible entities varies between periods, regions, and societies. Even among members of the same society, significant individual differences exist. While it is essential to focus on the visible differences, there are also areas common to human existence that cannot be captured by this alone.

As we have seen in this chapter, conceptualizing the "invisible garden" and studying its inner realities helps to capture the collective culture of regions and human beings and understand the commonalities therein. By looking at both regionally specific and universal contexts, the possibility of accessing a hyper-generalized meaning field is opened up. Consequently, we can draw a cross-cultural field of the relationship between invisible beings and "us," which differs from the geographical and historical divisions of West African, Islamic, and Japanese cultures. To develop this approach, we need further "interdisciplinary" study and practice for perceiving the situation more inclusively and thinking about our actions and behavior related to such invisible entities under uncertainty.

NOTES

1. According to the website of JICA (Japan International Cooperation Agency), "JICA's volunteer program is one of Japan's technical cooperation schemes operated as part of its Official Development Assistance (ODA). The program dispatches eager Japanese citizens who wish to participate in assisting developing countries and also have the calls for assistance from their governments (…) Since its first dispatch to Laos in 1965, more than 54,000 JICA volunteers have worked alongside local communities in 98 countries and regions." https://www.jica.go.jp/english/publications/brochures/c8h0vm0000a-vs7w2-att/jica_volunteer_en.pdf
2. Tweets and interviews in this chapter are my own English translations. Part of the film can be seen on my website. https://yusukekatsura.wordpress.com/film/
4. Djinns are mentioned repeatedly in the Qur'an as creatures of God, and Chapter 72 is named Al-Jinn (The Djinn).
5. At the time, I chose the word "sorcerer" to explain the Teacher, which is unsuitable from the current point of view. It also expresses one of the difficulties of the translation of djinn.
6. For example, Kontonron Seydou Diarra dit Simbo de Gomi: "La construction du 3ème pont à Sitadounou a provoqué le courroux du chef des djinns" (Maliactu, November 29, 2014). https://maliactu.net/mali-kontonron-seydou-diarra-dit-simbo-de-gomi-la-construction-du-3eme-pont-a-sitadounou-a-provoque-le-courroux-du-chef-des-djinns/; Sous le troisième pont de Bamako, vivent les djinns du fleuve Niger (Le 360 Afrique, July 28, 2021). https://afrique.le360.ma/autres-pays/culture/2021/07/28/35004-sous-le-troisieme-pont-de-bamako-vivent-les-djinns-du-fleuve-niger-35004/
7. See Introduction and Chapter 2 and Valsiner (2014) for more details on cultural psychological concepts such as point-like/field-like signs and hyper-generalization.

REFERENCES

Brinkmann, S. (2014). Doing without data. *Qualitative Inquiry, 20*(6), 720–725. https://doi.org/10.1177/1077800414530254

Danermark, B., Ekstrom, M., Jakobsen, L., & Karlsson, J. (2001). *Explaining society: An introduction to critical realism in the social sciences*. Routledge.

El-Zein, A. (2009). *Islam, Arabs, and intelligent world of the Jinn*. Syracuse University Press.

Gibbal, J. M. (1982). *Tambours d'eau: Journal et enquête sur un culte de possession au Mali Occidental* [Water drums: Journal and investigation into a possession cult in Western Mali]. Le Sycomore.

Holten, L. (2013). *Mothers, medicine and morality in Rural, Mali: An ethnographic study of therapy management of pregnancy and children's illness episodes*. Lit Verlag.

Hoodbhoy, P. (1991). *Islam and science: Religious orthodoxy and the battle for rationality*. Zed Books.

Kimura, H. A. (2016). *Radiation brain moms and citizen scientists: The gender politics of food contamination after Fukushima*. Duke University Press.

Kingston, J. (2012). Japan's nuclear village [日本の原子力ムラ]. *The Asia-Pacific Journal, 10*(37), 1–23. https://apjjf.org/2012/10/37/Jeff-Kingston/3822/article.html

Ministry of the Environment Government of Japan. (2019). *BOOKLET to provide basic information regarding health effects of radiation*. Ministry of the Environment, Government of Japan. https://www.env.go.jp/en/chemi/rhm/basic-info/1st/index.html

Mosleh, W. S. (2020). Autoethnographic data as abductive experiences. In A. F. Herrmann (Ed.), *The Routledge international handbook of organizational autoethnography* (pp. 415–434). Routledge.

Schulz, D. E. (2012). *Culture and customs of Mali*. ABC-CLIO.

Valsiner, J. (2014). *An invitation to cultural psychology*. SAGE Publications.

A garden in nursery school.

CHAPTER 10

THE TRANSITION OF A BEGINNING NURSERY TEACHER'S INTERACTION WITH CHILDREN FROM A "GARDEN" PERSPECTIVE

Kiyoshi Hamana
Mukoainosono Kindergarten

ISSUES AND CHAPTER OBJECTIVES

An Early Childhood Education and Care (ECEC) teacher's first year in a post is a period in which their identity as a childcare professional emerges and, through various ups and downs (Adachi & Shibasaki, 2010), changes occur in the different aspects of their consciousness of childcare (Tanigawa, 2013; Terami & Nishigaki, 2000; Ueda, 2014). In other words, it is probably true to say that, short as it is, a beginning nursery teacher's first year in a post is an important period in setting a firm foundation for their career in childcare.

The Semiotic Field of the Garden, pages 213–231
Copyright © 2024 by Information Age Publishing
www.infoagepub.com
All rights of reproduction in any form reserved.

Previous research investigating changes in the consciousness of beginning nursery teachers focused, for example, on the process by which they acquire a sense of having "cracked" the job (Ueda, 2014), the process of change in how problematic circumstances are understood and in attitude to practice (Tanigawa, 2013), and the process of change in consciousness relating to interaction with children with special needs (Terami & Nishigaki, 2000). Thus, through daily childcare practice, beginning nursery teachers need to learn how to understand and interact with children. The culture of the preschool where they work will influence the learning of beginning nursery teachers. In other words, it is thought that by entering the nursery school's garden, they are influenced by the collective culture to create their own personal culture of individual teaching styles (Tsuchimoto, "Editorial Introduction").

However, a limitation of the previous studies is that they collected data from beginning nursery teachers in a short span of time, about once a month; for example, monthly individual interviews (Tanigawa, 2013; Ueda, 2014) or interviews at childcare conferences (Terami & Nishigaki, 2000). However, it is assumed that beginning nursery teachers feel conflicts for the first time in their daily ECEC practice. Therefore, it is possible that the transitions of beginning nursery teachers cannot be fully captured in an interview survey conducted over the span of one month. This is because beginning nursery teachers are faced with the need to learn and adapt to new tasks immediately after starting work. Therefore, this study will use my diaries. Diaries help recall the daily events of that time (Alaszewski, 2006). Using my diaries is expected to capture the transition of beginning nursery teachers' consciousness on a daily rather than on a monthly basis. This research approach also allows us to show the actual state of consciousness transition from the beginning nursery teachers' perspective.

In this chapter, I analyzed my diary entries from when I was a beginning nursery teacher to determine how my awareness of interaction with children transitioned by autoethnography. To reflect the social environment of the team-teaching classroom in the analysis, my perceptions of advice from experienced colleagues, which may influence my attitudes toward working with children, were also included in the survey.

HOW I EXPLORED MY NURSERY SCHOOL'S GARDEN EXPERIENCE

My Profile as a Beginning Nursery Teacher

I was a beginning nursery teacher at Nursery School A, in charge of children for the first time. Four childcare professionals including the author

The Transition of a Beginning Nursery Teacher's Interaction With Children • 215

(see Table 10.1) were responsible for the 2-year-old class (eight boys and four girls). I was lucky enough during the period in question to be offered support by more experienced colleagues at difficult times and receive various advice in conversations during and after the working day. In particular, more experienced colleagues X and Y, with experience in formal responsibility for children, were kind enough to offer me advice, routinely and often, including about childcare procedures. In addition, although more experienced colleague Z, recently employed by Nursery School A in a special needs support role, rarely offered advice directly to me, we had many conversations about childcare. Thus, I had positive relationships with colleagues, and there were many occasions where I took note of scaffolding and other actions of more experienced colleagues within their everyday childcare practice, or reviewed my interaction with children after speaking with more experienced colleagues. Over the preceding 4 years while at graduate school, I took national exams for nursery teacher qualifications and had a part-time temporary job for 2 hours in the early evening once a week in a class of 3- to 5-year-old children at another nursery school. This job consisted mainly of supervising the children as they engaged in free play, and it required no experience in writing formal childcare records or teaching plans and no experience in supporting children's development or engaging in plan-based childcare in a way similar to a homeroom teacher. I neither received any guidance, nor any warnings from colleagues regarding my interaction with children. As a result, at that time, I had no consciousness of responsibility for helping children develop, and while he had experience with light-hearted interaction with children, his experience beyond that of an ordinary childcare student at a training institution on practical training was limited.

In this study, from the viewpoint of preservation of privacy, pseudonyms are used for specific individuals and the daycare centers, and so forth, and

TABLE 10.1 Profile of the 2-Year-Old Class

	Senior Nursery Teacher X	Senior Nursery Teacher Y	Senior Nursery Teacher Z	The Author
Role	Class teacher	Childcare assistant (Full-time non-regular employee)	Special needs support (Full-time non-regular employee)	Class teacher
Age	40s	30s	20s	20s
Gender	Female	Female	Female	Male
Years of Childcare Experience	10 or more years	3 years	1 year	0 years

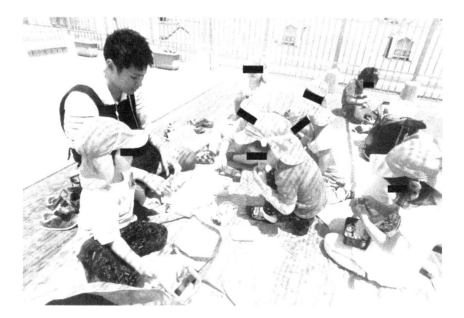

Figure 10.1 The garden in Nursery School A: Children and me playing.

the relevant date is expressed as 201X. Regarding the publication of research outcomes, I explained the content of the study to the principal of Nursery School A and to his colleagues in the 2-year-old class at the time, verbally and in writing, and obtained their consent (see Figure 10.1).

Autoethnography With My Diaries

In this study, auto-ethnography was conducted using a diary I kept when I was a beginning nursery teacher. In the diary, I recorded what I felt during childcare, advice from senior staff, and what I learned at study sessions. I had the habit of keeping a diary before I started working as a beginner nursery teacher to avoid forgetting impactful daily events and impressions. In this study, my diary entries recording her daily miscellaneous impressions, such as what she felt in the childcare setting and what she felt based on advice from seniors and talks at study groups, were the subject of analysis. The subject diaries cover 1 year (March 23, 201X–March 31, 201X+1), during which I was in charge of 2-year-old children as a beginner nursery teacher. The diaries were counted as one article if they recorded one day's events, and a total of 168 articles existed. The frequency of diary entries varied from month to month, but on average, one entry was recorded every 2–3 days. There are two reasons for using diaries in autoethnography. The first reason is that the diaries helped me to recall my thoughts about my interaction with the children at the time since I had written them in the diaries. The second reason was that to examine my transition of consciousness from the perspective of the social environment, I needed to know how I perceived the advice of the senior teachers. My diaries helped me to do that.

Exploring With Auto-TEM

In this study, I did autoethnographic trajectory equifinality modeling (Auto-TEM; Tsuchimoto & Sato, 2022). Auto-TEM is a methodology in which the researcher describes his or her own culture in terms of the interrelationship between personal and collective culture (Tsuchimoto & Sato, 2022). This methodology is a creative fusion between two methods, namely, autoethnography and TEM (Tsuchimoto & Sato, 2022). TEM is a research method that aims to understand the subject's experience with society by depicting the process of the subject's specific experience without discarding time (Sato, 2009; Yasuda & Sato, 2012).

There are two reasons for using auto-TEM. First, TEM allows me to examine my transitions with collective and personal culture. Second, I can understand the trajectories and influencing cultures regarding the transition of interaction with children (von Fircks & Campill, Chapter 3).

I did auto-TEM through stages ① to ③ and understood the transition of my interaction with children. ① Reading all 168 diary entries, I grasped the overview of my transition of interaction with children. ② Based on my diary, at the starting point of the scenes subject to analysis, I labeled my consciousness as [1. I am made aware that my interaction and use of words are harsh]. I labeled my consciousness as [EFP: I want to value the feelings of children more than the reason of nursery teachers] as the equifinality point (EFP). I created labels regarding the events leading up to EFP and placed them in chronological order from top to bottom. ③ I used TEM concepts (Table 10.2) and investigated turning points and influential factors in my transition of interaction with children. As TEM allows the introduction of new concepts in line with the purpose of the research (Yasuda et al., 2012), new concepts were used; namely, "guidance in spirit" (GIS), which refers to internal forces supporting the consciousness of the writer in nearing the EFP, and "direction in spirit" (DIS), which refers to internal forces impeding the consciousness of the writer from nearing the EFP as a result of internal factors.

TABLE 10.2 Basic TEM Concepts and Correspondence With Data

Basic Concept	Description	Data Correspondence
EFP (Equifinality Point)	The final point of the consciousness process within the scope of analysis set by the researcher	I want to value the feelings of children more than the reason of nursery teachers.
P-EFP (Polarized Equifinality Point)	The final point of a separate assumed process that complements the EFP	I want to value the reason of nursery teachers more than the feelings of children.
BFP (Bifurication Point)	A point in the process where there was scope for a consciousness that differs from the actual one	As a nursery teacher, I may be giving too many instructions to the children.
OPP (Obligatory Passage Point)	Passage point to almost all places within the process of moving toward the EFP	I don't understand the developmental characteristics of 2-year-old children.
SD (Social Direction)	For that person, an environmental factor functioning as a force that boosts the fact that consciousness is moving away from the EFP	Senior Nursery Teacher Y advises not to make the children wait because waiting is stressful for them.
SG (Social Guidance)	For that person, an environmental factor functioning as a force that boosts the fact that consciousness is moving away from the EFP	Senior Nursery Teacher X follows up with a crying child in response to my interaction.
DIS (Direction in the Spirit)	For that person, an internal factor functioning as a force that boosts the fact that consciousness is moving away from the EFP	I must ensure that the children's activities flow smoothly.
GIS (Guidance in the Spirit)	For that person, an internal factor functioning as a force that boosts the fact that consciousness is heading toward the EFP	I want to make sure there is no stress for the children.

RESULTS AND DISCUSSION

Overview of Results

I analyzed the process of transition in the consciousness of interaction with children on the author's part. As a result, I clarified phases of transition in the content of my consciousness of problems in each period. There were five such periods, each with a name that shows its characteristics. The consciousness labeled on the TEM diagram (Figures 10.2 & 10.3) can be

The Transition of a Beginning Nursery Teacher's Interaction With Children • 219

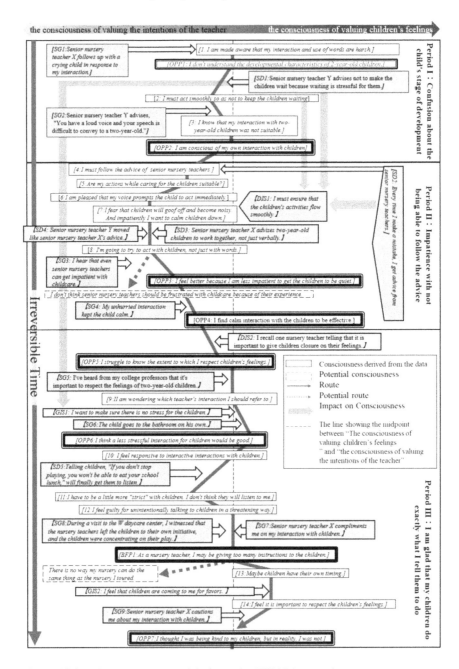

Figure 10.2 The consciousness labels on the TEM Diagram 1.

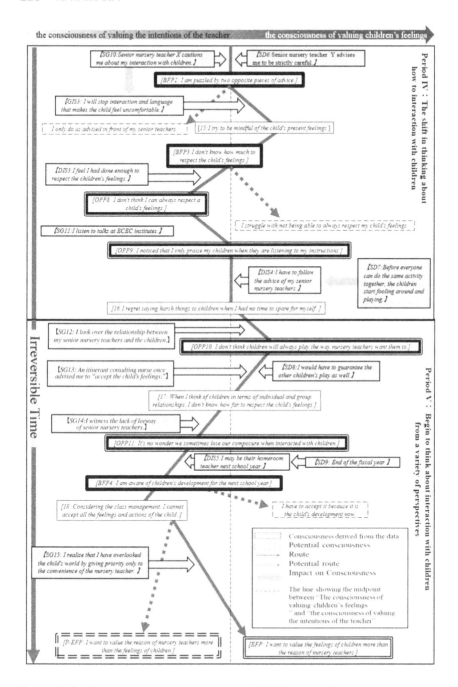

Figure 10.3 The consciousness labels on the TEM Diagram 2.

broadly classified as either "the consciousness of valuing the intentions of the teacher" or "the consciousness of valuing children's feelings." These two consciousness categories were set as the vertical axis, providing an easy way to understand what the author valued at any given time within interaction with children. Below is an overview of the change in the author's consciousness while he was a beginning nursery teacher, supported by the TEM diagram (Figure 10.2 & Figure 10.3), which gives visual form to the author's consciousness at that time. In autoethnography, one's own experiences are usually recorded in the first person (Ellis & Bochner, 2000), and so in the following sections, the author is denoted by "I."

Phases of the Transitions of My Consciousness in Each Period

Period I: Confusion About the Child's Stage of Development
From March 23 201X to the End of March of the Same Year)

I was not responsible for a specific class throughout March 201X, and I went into the "1-year-old class" during playtime in the role of childcare assistant. I became keenly aware of the difference between the stages of development of babies and toddlers.

DIARY ENTRY 1 (MAR 24 201X)

Today, I went into the 1-year-old class... Child J, who was playing, suddenly hit Child E. I was shocked and immediately said, "It hurts when you hit someone" and Child J cried. Seeing this, my more experienced colleague X said to Child J, "He was surprised because you did it suddenly," and I noticed that my interaction with children and my manner of talking to them was harsh... I was probably too harsh for the 1-year-old class. I mused that, perhaps, it is OK to behave like that when you are a toddler and so it could have been too harsh. In various situations, words do not convey the desired meaning, and it is difficult...

As in Diary Entry 1, I saw senior nursery teacher X calming a child who cried in response to my interaction (SG1). I realized how difficult it is to interact with children (1). I also felt that the 2-year-old was not verbal and that I did not understand the developmental characteristics of the 2-year-old (OPP1). Thus, I felt the difficulty of interacting with children. However, relying on the words of senior nursery teachers I gradually became aware of my interaction with children.

DIARY ENTRY 2 (MAR 30, 201X)

When asking children in the 1-year-old class to put their shoes on, I hesitated, not knowing how well they could put them on themselves, and not knowing how to help or how far it was OK to help them. When I did this, my more experienced colleague Y, who was watching nearby, advised me that "Waiting is stressful for the children, so please can you try to avoid it." I realized that I must act rather than wonder about the right thing to do. I will be careful to act in a way that avoids making the children wait.

As in Diary Entry 2, because I did not know whether 2-year-old children (in the 1-year-old class) could put on their shoes, I stood wondering how much help I should give them and did not act. However, senior nursery teacher Y advised not to make the children wait because waiting is stressful for them. I came to think that I must act smoothly so as not to keep the children waiting (2).

On another day, I was confused about how I should interact with children, and during the lunch hour, senior nursery teacher Y advised me: "You have a loud voice and your speech is difficult to convey to a 2-year-old" (SG2). I know that my interaction with 2-year-old children was not suitable (3). Through such events, I became aware that there were problems with my interaction with children (OPP2).

Period II: Impatience With Not Being Able to Follow the Advice
(Early April 201X to the End of April the Same Year)

In Period II, there were still many occasions when I did not understand how I should act. I received many concrete pieces of advice regarding my actions from the senior nursery teachers. Every time I made mistakes, I got advice from senior nursery teachers (SD2). I had to follow the advice of senior nursery teachers (4). And I came to worry whether my actions while caring for the children were suitable (5). An experience (SD1) made me come to feel that I must ensure that the children's activities flow smoothly (DIS1). So, I was pleased that my voice prompted the child to act immediately (6). On the other hand, I feared that children would waste time and become noisy (7). I had been impatient while caring for the children. But, having received advice (SD3) from senior nursery teacher X after work and seeing senior nursery teacher Y behave in line with the advice I received (8), I transitioned my interaction with the children. Also, at the monthly plan meeting, I heard that more experienced colleagues also sometimes become impatient while interacting with children (SG3). it made me alleviate my impatience and feel a little better (OPP3). Based on all this advice, I transitioned my interaction with children. My unhurried interaction kept the child calm (SG4), and I found calm interaction with the children to be effective (OPP4). Refer to Diary Entry 3.

DIARY ENTRY 3 (APR 25, 201X)

(Having taken on board recent advice), I tried striving to assist at mealtimes in as calm a way as possible. Instead of saying, "Just wait!!" impatiently, I looked Child C properly in the eye and gently said, "Please wait, I'll come once I've given Child J and Child E second helpings,"... Child C did not bang his spoon against his bowl as he usually did. I had the thought that the children were indeed calm and settled merely because I did not become impatient.

Period III: I Am Glad That My Children Do Exactly What I Tell Them to Do (End of April 201X to Mid-September of the Same Year)

The experience of how the children reacted to my interaction (OPP4) made me aware of how children reacted to my interaction. During this period, I was gradually focusing more on the children's feelings, but my attention turned to the methodological aspect of how to interact with children. On the other hand, as I respected the child's feelings, various conflicts arose. For example, I recalled something a senior nursery teacher told me that it is important for caregivers to give closure (DIS2). However, when I saw a child crying in front of me, I wondered to what extent I should respect the child's feelings (OPP5). On another day, I heard advice from a study group that it was important to accept feelings (SG5) when interacting with 2-year-olds.

As I listened to various pieces of advice and observed the interaction of various teachers, I became unsure of the correct answer (9).

One day, I remembered the advice not to stress children (GIS1). Then, I tried to give the child words that would make him go to the bathroom on his own. He was convinced and went there on his own (SG6). When I saw him, I realized that a less stressful interaction with the child would be better. From that event, I could later understand the meaning of SD1's advice (OPP6). The events of those days are described in Diary Entry 4.

DIARY ENTRY 4 (MAY 11, 201X)

In the early evening, I was taking Child C to the toilet. Even when I said "Let's go to the toilet" in a determined manner, without even looking at me, he said, "I don't want to." Seeing this, I approached the matter by talking about the train that he was playing with... I said, "Hey, the station is over there (the toilets) so let's go together" and Child C (looked at my face and listened).

Child C then immediately put down the train and walked towards the toilets. I did not expect that. Was it good that I had not forcefully communicated only my agenda?

Through several such experiences, I have come to feel that it is important to interact with children in a way that values their feelings (10). Nevertheless, I interacted with the children without stress, with the goal of "how to make them do what I say." Therefore, when the children could not stop playing, I felt that I had to be a little stern with them to get them to move (SD5, 11). However, I began to feel guilty because I realized that I had unknowingly used harsh words (12). This led me to reevaluate my interaction with children. In addition, praise from senior nursery teacher X (SG7) and visits to other preschools (SG8) made me rethink my interaction with children (BFP1). And as I continued to interact with the child in a way that respected his/her timing (13), I began to sense a change in his/her response to me (GIS2). These events made me realize the importance of talking to and interacting with children in a way that respects their feelings (14). However, one day, when I received a warning from senior nursery teacher X about how to interact with children (SG9), I realized that although I thought I was respecting their feelings, I was not doing so (OPP7).

Period IV: The Shift in Thinking About How to Interaction With Children (End of September 201X to Mid-November 201X)
After ECEC, I received two pieces of advice at different times: from senior nursery teacher Y, "Scold your children" (SD6) and from senior nursery teacher X, "Don't just scold them, but talk to them casually" (SG10). Rereading the diary at the time, I saw that the advice from senior nursery teacher X and teacher Y was in different contexts. However, at the time, I was focusing on the aspects of ECEC behavior that each piece of advice indicated. Therefore, the two pieces of advice seemed contradictory and I was confused as to their meaning (BFP2). After that, I was unsure, but after seeing the interaction of senior nursery teachers, I decided to stop the interaction that made the children anxious (GIS3). I then shifted my thinking to be more in tune with the child's present feelings (15). In reality, however, there were several situations in which it was difficult to interact with children in a way that respected their feelings. As a result, I was struggling to know to what extent I should respect their feelings (BFP3). One day I kept waiting for the children to finish playing. However, their play was not over. I thought I must have waited long enough and respected their feelings (DIS3). I came to think that although I might not be able to attend

to the children's feelings, it was inevitable (OPP8). This event was described in Diary Entry 5.

DIARY ENTRY 5 (OCT 5, 201X)

Child F and Child D, saying that they did not want to stop their game, stayed out in the sandpit in the nursery school's yard. Even when I told them, " It's home time" in a way that remained aware of the need not to be harsh, they continued to run around and play ... For about 20 minutes, I came and went, speaking to them and keeping an eye on them and ... I jokingly wondered where the switch was on the children to change their mode. There was no other way than to pick them up and carry them in. After all, it is surely necessary for a childcare professional to call a halt to matters to a certain extent.

As a beginning nursery teacher, I had been following the advice of senior nursery teachers regarding interaction with children. However, through accumulating trial and error experiences in ECEC activities in various contexts (e.g., Diary Entry 5), I have formed my standards of judgment regarding how to interact with children. In reality, I remained aware of the behavioral aspect of the act of working with children, and whether or not I could follow their advice. However, after listening to the talk at a training session (SG11), I realized that I had been praising children only when it suited me (OPP9). This event was described in Diary Entry 6. In other words, the only time I would gently interact with children was when I had time on my schedule and when they did as I told them to do. Based on my impressions of these two events, I thought I was well involved with the children. After this realization, my awareness of the issue shifted: how to respect children's feelings even when I am pressed for time and have little time to spare.

DIARY ENTRY 6 (OCTOBER 18 201X)

At Training Session E, there was talk of avoiding addressing children in a way that evaluates them from the viewpoint of the staff's agenda, and of praising them for their effort instead. This would allow such a child to, for the first time, form a relationship of trust with a childcare professional in a world without judgment... Indeed, I have intended to speak to children nicely, but my effort in this regard is perhaps superficial and I may only speak to them like that when it doesn't interfere with the timetable and it fits in with my agenda.

Although I was aware of the issue, I felt difficulty changing my behavior immediately. For example, when I saw a child start to joke around before the next activity (SD7), I knew I had to follow my senior nursery teachers' advice (DIS4). This made me lose my cool, and I would say harsh things to the children, which sometimes made me feel depressed (16). At that time, I thought I had to follow the advice of the senior nursery teachers, even though they had not told me anything in particular. Because of this, I was not able to interact with children as I thought. In other words, I was aware of my self-assignment but struggled with my inability to do so.

Period V: Begin to Think About Interaction With Children From a Variety of Perspectives (Early November 201X–End of March 201X+1)

One day, looking over the relationship between my senior nursery teachers and the children (SG12), I realized that even they do not always get the children to behave as directed. I came to accept the reality that children did not always play the way nursery teachers wanted them to (OPP10). On the other hand, I also began to think that it is difficult to respect children's feelings when considering their development in terms of the relationship between the individual and the group. For example, an itinerant consulting nurse once advised me to "accept the child's feelings" (SG13). However, I was concerned that by accepting the child's feelings and guaranteeing play, other children would not be able to play because I had to consider how to guarantee other children's play as well (SD8), and I was not sure how much to accept children's feelings in terms of the relationship between the individual and the group (17). When observing this concern, I was suffering an internal battle between "consciousness of valuing the children's feelings" and "consciousness of valuing the intentions of staff." But unlike before, the intentions of staff did not refer to their agenda in terms of "smoothly progressing the tasks of childcare." From the perspective of dialogical self-theory (Hermans, 2001), the I-positions of each, "I as valuing the intentions of the teacher" and "I as valuing children's feelings," were considered to be in conflict.

Instead, the child has become the actor in terms of "so that the other children can play." Thus, my consciousness relating to interaction with the children differed from mine. In addition, witnessing the lack of leeway of senior nursery teachers (SG14), I had come to believe that it is inevitable that the nursery teacher sometimes lacks leeway when dealing with children (OPP11). I used to think that I was the only one in a hurry to interact with the children, but now I realized that other nursery teachers were the same way.

As the year began, I began to think about taking over the class as a homeroom teacher (SD9, DIS5) and became more aware of the children's development for the next school year (BFP4). Moreover, given my classroom management, I sometimes felt that I could not take in all of the children's feelings and actions (18). However, I noticed that there were worlds of children that are overlooked only for the convenience of the nursery teacher (SG15). I realized the importance of valuing the child's feelings, not just the convenience of the nursery teacher (EFP). With that in mind, my year as a beginning nursery teacher was over. This event was described in Diary Entry 7.

DIARY ENTRY 7 (MAR 17 201X+1)

Child C continued playing after being told it was "time to tidy up to go home..." (On that day I had played with Child C) and, as I had observed him devising various ways to pretend to cook, I thought that he might like to play the same game again the next day, so, speaking to him, I said, "So that we can pretend to cook again, let's put the cooking things behind the tree." When I said that, Child C agreed, put the cooking things down and started to tidy up. I do not always think about what kind of games Child C enjoyed each day, instead, I address him with my agenda and neglect his feelings about what he enjoyed on that day. I feel bad about that.

In light of the above, by the end of Period V, I had come to think of my relationship with children as follows. Not in terms of how to relate to the child in front of me at that moment, but in terms of my relationship with the children around me and their development into the next grade level.

HOW DID I DEVELOP IN THE NURSERY SCHOOL'S GARDEN?

This autoethnography examined my transitions of interaction with children as a beginning nursery teacher over 1 year. Below, based on the results of the study, there is a general discussion regarding the transition in my consciousness of a beginning nursery teacher.

The Impact of the Garden of a Team-Teaching Classroom on Transition in the Consciousness of a Beginning Nursery Teacher

Examination of the TEM diagram (Figures 10.2 and 10.3) reveals that on occasions when the author, as a beginning nursery teacher, was at a loss or conflicted, the deviation between "the consciousness of valuing the intentions of the teacher" and "the consciousness of valuing children's feelings" was positioned at the midpoint of the diagram. In other words, hesitation and conflict were the catalysts for the return to equilibrium of the misalignment of consciousness regarding the interaction with children. The advice from senior nursery teachers was the catalyst for such anxiety and nervousness. This is because their advice seems to have the function of showing beginning nursery teachers how they should interact with children. For example, I was inspired by what my senior nursery teachers taught me about how to interact with children (SG2), which led me to rethink my current way of involving myself with children (OPP2). In other words, not only does the beginning nursery teacher lack knowledge of childcare (Adachi & Shibasaki, 2010), but he is also unsure whether his interaction is correct (Tanigawa, 2013). Therefore, receiving warnings (negative evaluations) in the form of advice from senior nursery teachers seems to function to help him recognize that his interactions with children are not good and to modify their attitudes regarding his interaction with children. It was also confirmed that advice from senior nursery teachers has a self-regulatory function (DIS1) for novice teachers, who feel that they should follow the advice and that such advice can cause impatience (7).

On the other hand, the children's reactions and praise from senior nursery teachers may have worked to strengthen the beginning nursery teacher's awareness of their interaction with children. For example, I perceived my interaction as good when I received positive reactions and evaluations, such as praise from senior nursery teacher X for my recent interaction with the children (SG7) or when the children favored me (GIS2). It means that the personal culture of the beginning nursery teacher's interaction with the children is formed by the senior nursery teachers of the nursery school's collective culture. This is because the beginning nursery teacher does not know whether their interaction with children is correct and can only judge from the reactions of their senior nursery teachers and children. In other words, taking the senior nursery teacher's reaction as a cue means incorporating the collective culture into the personal culture.

This study shows that there are many opportunities for beginning nursery teachers' interaction with children to be observed by senior nursery teachers. Because in a team-teaching classroom, the novice and senior nursery teachers must care for children together. It is, therefore, easy to receive advice about interaction with the children for beginning nursery teachers from ECEC senior teachers during and after work each day. Accordingly, a transition in the consciousness of a beginning nursery teacher in a team-teaching classroom regarding interaction with children occurs in the context of relationships that include those with senior nursery teachers as well as those with the children.

Findings Obtained From the First-Person Viewpoint of the Beginning Nursery Teacher

This auto-ethnography showed two possibilities that differ from previous studies about the development of beginning nursery teachers. First, past interviews indicate that for such beginning teachers, the first 3 months of employment are a time of confusion and bewilderment (Tanigawa, 2013). This study did autoethnography by using my diaries daily. In addition, the author as a beginning nursery teacher also felt bewilderment and confusion during that period. However, in the few short weeks from Period I to Period II, the content of those sentiments changed from "confusion because of not understanding the stage of child development" to "impatience with the inability to follow the advice." In other words, when a beginning nursery teacher first starts work, he experiences various things for the first time. Therefore, this period can be seen as one in which change in consciousness can occur week by week.

Second, previous research showed the experience of success has been suggested as a major point in transition in the consciousness of a beginning nursery teacher (Ueda, 2014). However, in the case of the author as a beginning nursery teacher, experiences when "inability" was felt were positioned on the TEM diagram (Figures 10.2 and 10.3). Such experiences included "the realization that all nursery teachers are impatient at times (SG3, 14, OPP11)" and "that it was normal for children to fail to behave as staff members hope (OPP10)." In other words, it is not only the experience of success that is important in the transition in the consciousness of a beginning nursery teacher. Acceptance of "inability" within childcare allows demarcation to be achieved between matters attributable to "one's lack of ability" and matters where "ability is not an issue, it is just that, in childcare, sometimes things do not go as you hoped." I think that this kind of experience is also important in the growth of a beginning nursery teacher.

THE DEVELOPMENT OF BEGINNING NURSERY TEACHER'S INTERACTION WITH CHILDREN FROM A "GARDEN" PERSPECTIVE

This study showed the personal culture of the beginning nursery teacher's interaction with the children is formed by the senior nursery teachers of the nursery school's collective culture. The process of constructing a garden makes nature the object, in which various liminal, aesthetic, and symbolic activities take place directly (Tsuchimoto, "Editorial Introduction"). In other words, the interaction of beginning nursery teachers with children can be described as "nature" because it is rough. Additionally, the senior nursery teachers as "gardeners" tend to the new caregivers' interactions with the children as "nature" by giving them advice. Beginning nursery teachers do not yet have the sense of "art" that professionals in childcare have. The beginning nursery teacher's interaction with the children is still "nature"; although, it is considered an individual culture. It becomes a garden through the influence of the collective culture of the senior nursery teachers as "gardeners." In other words, the development of a new caregiver can be described as the creation of a garden. The perspective of the "garden" reminds us once again that the development of nursery teachers is a socio-cultural development.

LIMITATIONS OF THIS STUDY

First, to depict the presence of the beginning nursery teacher at the center of events, it was decided to use first-hand data from his diary from that time. However, because the analysis and paper were written 2 years after his time as a beginning nursery teacher, it was potentially impossible to properly grasp changes in the consciousness of the author as a beginning nursery teacher with the feelings of that time.

Second, although analysis of the diary in question allowed depiction of the presence of the author at the center of events (in terms of what the author felt as a beginning nursery teacher), the comments in the diary were related to things to which the author paid attention at the time, and he is likely to have failed to write about consciousness relating to events which were of little interest to him. In this regard, there are, doubtless, aspects that the author was unable to investigate, for the very reason that he was the person concerned.

Third, the author, who is the subject of the research, has experience in a part-time job as a childcare assistant, and it is conceivable that that experience had some kind of impact on his consciousness regarding interaction with children. An attempt was made in the analysis results of this study to retrieve the consciousness at the time in question that came from experience in the part-time job and include it in the discussion. However, such consciousness was subconscious, as the author is the person in question, and it was hard to incorporate it into the results and discussion in this study. There is a need, in the future, to carry out analysis incorporating research methods that retrieve past values.

Fourth, the writer had responsibility for children for the first time and was trying out different ways of interacting with children with the support of more experienced colleagues. To this extent, he fits the earlier definition of a beginning nursery teacher. However, if you add in his existing experience, he likely differs in some way from an ordinary beginning nursery teacher who has just graduated from training college. To clarify that difference, there is a need, in the future, to conduct research that takes as its subject ordinary beginning nursery teachers who have just graduated from training college, making a comparative investigation.

REFERENCES

Adachi, S., & Shibazaki, M. (2010). Analysis of "swaying" and structure of reformation in the process of obtaining a nursery and kindergarten teacher identity: With a focus on classroom teachers. *Research on Early Childhood Care and Education in Japan, 48*(2), 213–224.

Alaszewski, A. (2006). *Using diaries for social research.* SAGE Publications.

Ellis, C., & Bochner, A. P. (2000). Autoethnography, personal narrative, reflexivity: Research as subject. In N. K. Denzin & Y. S. Lincoln (Eds.), *Handbook of qualitative research* (2nd ed.). SAGE Publications.

Hermans, H. (2001). The dialogical self: Toward a theory of personal and cultural positioning. *Culture & Psychology, 7*(3), 243–281.

Sato, T. (Ed.). (2009). *Qualitative research with TEM: Toward a study of time and process.* Seishin Shobo.

Tanigawa, N. (2013). Professional development of novice teachers through their crisis in nursery schools and kindergartens: Focusing on their reflective learning process. *Research on Early Childhood Care and Education in Japan, 51*(1), 105–116.

Terami, Y., & Nishigaki, Y. (2000). A nursery school teacher's growth through the practices of child care and education in the process of developing a newly appointed nursery school teacher's relation with a child and of changing herself. *Studies in Childhood Education, 19*, 17–48.

Tsuchimoto, T., & Sato,T. (2022). Career decision-making as dynamic semiosis: Autoethnographic trajectory equifinality modeling. *Culture & Psychology 2022*, 1–22.

Ueda, H. (2014). How does novice teacher Satomi acquire the "I got it" belief in the nursery school? Focus on teacher's beliefs and teaching styles. *Research on Early Childhood Care and Education in Japan, 52*(2), 232–242.

Yasuda,Y., & Sato, T. (Eds.). (2012). *Pathways of life as understood by TEM: New developments in qualitative research.* Seishin Shobo.

Foto personal archieve: Aalborg–Denmarc (2016).

COMMENTARY PART IIA

GARDEN AS AN EXPRESSION OF HUMAN LIFE

Ramon Cerqueira Gomes
Federal Institute Bahian of Education, Science, and Technology

First of all, it is important to conceive the perspective included in our minds about gardens in human life. What does a garden mean for you who are reading this text? If it is not easy to describe that, questions are: "What do you feel when you are in a garden?" or "What have you heard about gardens from other people in your life history?" In several personal an collective cultures it is possible to find so many kinds of answers, however they can have some aspects in common. In the chapters of this session, it will be seen an overview of the relationship between garden and culture, including its metaphorical way. For this, it will take the distinctions between collective and personal culture and the aspects investigated in these chapters in order to find semiotic interpretations of the garden in human life in different contexts. Welcome to cultures' garden.

Through the use of signs, human beings can transcend any here-and-now situated activity through the subjectively constructed personal meanings

The Semiotic Field of the Garden, pages 233–239
Copyright © 2024 by Information Age Publishing
www.infoagepub.com
All rights of reproduction in any form reserved.

(or "personal culture"). The personal culture is interdependent with (but not determined by) the realm of interpersonal signs-mediated communicative processes, which are goal-oriented by the active efforts of persons-in-their-assumed social roles. The multiplicity of such communicative messages (or "collective culture" in the present terminology) constitutes the heterogeneous "input" into the self-construction by individual human beings (Valsiner, 2007).

It is interesting to figure out the different possibilities of thinking about gardens during history like in Chapter 6, where Hakoköngäs discusses tensions in the way to manage and to plan graves and gardens in the Tervola churchyard in Finland. In this text, there are some important historical events that impact the collective culture of treating the deceased. The civil war in Finland political orientation (*Whites<>Reds*) and in 1923 the Act of Religious Freedom (*believers<>non-believers*) transformed the churchyard in a more patriotic and honorable place and with more restrictive areas for soldiers and determined religious people.

Elements of collective culture as economic and political factors developed a new way of conceiving graves in Tervola churchyard. After interventions of the Church in post-war in the 1950, the conception of God's garden transformed the churchyard in a similar place among every deceased in order to avoid too much differentiation based on social position. This was reinforced especially in a democratic welfare society.

Nevertheless, it occurred within the arena of appositive forces facing personal culture of several people. According to this last point, even so the stones were defined to be similar to each other in churchyards, people started to "push the limits of collective culture by first adding personal symbols to the uniformly shaped stones." People wanted more and more personalized stones for their deceased. Then "the pursuit of individuals to emphasize their uniqueness became a collective culture." It is very meaningful to realize as the collective culture can be step by step changed by personal cultures in coalition.

Cemetery garden is an example of how human beings can create new meanings in their experience in environments even if it is a place of the deceased. Garden is a powerful kind of cultural human production in several civilizations for different purposes. But many times it brings an intention within the collective culture of creating feelings, memories, sensations in a comfortable and more beautiful way, especially in churchyards since the 19th century.

Garden emerges as a human artifact, a cultural production related to new meanings about the treatment of people's death in collective cultures.

To Valsiner (2007, p. 48),

> The PERSON constructs MEANING COMPLEX X
> ↓
> ...OBJECTIFIES it by FIXING ITS FORM..,
> (e.g. internal—internalized social norm, or
> external—monument, picture of deity, figurine)
> ↓
> ...and starts to act <u>AS IF</u> the objectified
> meaning complex X is an external agent that
> controls the PERSON

That is, people use gardens as monuments to express their personal cultures about the deceased. Garden appears as a very powerful artifact that evokes people's position supported by hypergeneralized affective-semiotic field-like signs highly invested of affect. For example, people cultivate gardens in churchyards to create places for the deceased to be more beautiful and contemplative. This experience changes the way the person deals with the dead who can be honored and to be in a pretty environment.

Gardens are signs involved by important values in different collective cultures. Therefore, personal cultures are instigated to create the synthesis of these shared meanings. It would be thought-provoking to study the perceptions of people in churchyards as garden and churchyard without gardening. This psychological phenomenon is relevant to express what happens within the mind and body when people are there. It could be surprising to analyze a churchyard being experienced by people as a garden and on the other hand being experienced as a place unrelated to gardening.

The objective of Chapter 10—"The Transition of a Beginning Nursery Teacher's Interaction With Children From a 'Garden' Perspective"—is to show a different vision of transition of beginning nursery teachers' consciousness. In studies presented before, there is not a focus on the teacher's perspective nor a methodological approach considering the teacher's daily life. It is a very promising method by autoethnography. The diaries used have a power of recording subjective impressions of the interactions of person versus environment. This instrument demarcates sensitive moments of self in transition in times of relevant tensions as a beginning nursery teacher.

Experiences in the beginning were uncomfortable and voices from senior teachers brought new meanings to the perspective of the author. A vision of problems with interactions with children emerged. Hearing colleagues saying that sometimes they are impatient with children made the author feel better in a vision of shared humanity. Different positions argue within the self about whether he is a good or bad beginning nursery teacher. The author is called to define his own emergence of signs—voices in himself.

The perspective of an education for early childhood called "garden," implies a relevant conception in social point of view. As it was told before, garden is a sign with potent values from distinct contexts, such as religion, art, aesthetic, literature, as well as many people consider garden as a sign related to leisure. Anyway, collective culture brings several signs to enrich the symbolic use of gardens in social life, for example as an education for little children.

This conception affects the way professionals deal with this kind of environment, especially in their theoretical principles and their practical also. The author of this research lived through a lot of tensional moments in your beginning work as a teacher of these children. The diaries reveal the experience in a garden as a significant exploratory context on becoming a nursery teacher. Voices provided from older teachers were very relevant cultural resources that can severely change the experience of the researcher in this place. The construction of a self-position of beginning teachers is crossed by other social voices—"gardeners."

As it was told, human beings create signs to regulate themselves. Each gardener (co-workers teacher) is an element of the garden giving different signs/voices to the researcher's self. Although there is a general garden as an education for early childhood, the author was mobilized to create an own vision of the I-position in this context, personal culture. The dynamic of bothering voices in the work environment pressed the construction of new meanings of self-experience in this place. Garden here is a disturbing context where self has to synthesize new positions to survive as a competent professional.

Chapter 8—"Constant Fear of Ostracism"—consists of the author's autoethnographic narrative, including her diary entries, which delineates what she felt like to live as an Indigenous person whose community is under ongoing cultural assimilation, followed by its analysis.

Her main issues identified in the narrative were emotional insecurity and its coping mechanism—to pretend to be someone else. It brought to her many problematic and suffering moments since her childhood.

Voices provided from other peers and adults—mainly in the new school—were very mobilizing to herself. Her signs constructed in the indigenous culture were many times confronted by other dominant signs in Japan. Her learned inner signs were constantly belittled and many times left herself especially confused. It is interesting to realize that when the author felt "alienated from other children" she looked at the "horizon at dawn or dusk as the colours of sky and ocean glided smoothly over the spectrum, which stretched out into my imaginary realms." She associated this happening to Tsuchimoto that mentioned how a finite garden links to the infinity.

Although her life was empty and confusing since she was bombed hard by dominant collective culture in Japan, this aesthetic experience of seeing beautiful elements of nature as a wide garden could take her to other imaginary worlds. Her *via crucis* to find peace and comfort founded in her horizon of nature (as a garden) one of her salvation practices in childhood.

In this research, it is possible to conceive of the inner signs established from Indigenous culture when she reports about her dream with her grandmother, who is now 100 years old. The author discovered the location she was in the dream was a place where deceased were left several years ago in her traditional culture. Nevertheless the author never was told by anyone about it before. More interesting is that collective culture can have very powerful effects in daily life even in an unconscious way. So, how could it be possible to investigate unconscious psychological phenomena in semiotic cultural psychology?

In Chapter 7—"The Colorful Garden of the Renaissance"—discusses "the Italian renaissance garden, like renaissance art, philosophy, and architecture, emerged from the rediscovery by renaissance scholars of classical Roman models" (p. 150). According to this text, these gardens were "inspired by classical ideals of order and beauty, and intended for the pleasure of the view of the garden and the landscape beyond, for contemplation, and for the enjoyment of the sights, sounds, and smells of the garden itself and giardino segreto (secret garden) and fields for games and amusements" (p. 151). About that, "Medici, the ruling dynasty of Florence, used gardens to demonstrate their own power and magnificence" (p. 151). On the one hand, gardens in Renaissance in Italy are changed by classical models (collective culture), on the other hand the powerful family used the gardens to show opulence and high social level.

Human meaning-making is itself filled with ambiguities—of the boundary of time, social classes, and "we" <> "they" distinctions. The signs that are utilized on that boundary are themselves representative of such ambiguities of the opposite sides of everyday reality internally differentiating (Valsiner, 2007). This openness allowed by semioses is the principal aspect to analyse the use of garden as a multifaceted sign during the history. People with more power in certain moments of history could modify some garden meanings against traditional collective culture.

In a dialogical perspective it is what happens within the mind evolved by so many I positions. As minissociety the dominant I position can orientate rules, silence other I positions, and seek voices or other signs to support self-maintenance in the psychological system (Marsico et al., 2019). In this tension the personal culture and collective cultures clash their perspectives in a semiotic game of forces in which whoever has greater power in their position of the self wins. This is why Medici challenged the gardens in

Renaissance in Italy when created a garden mainly to make a spectacle of their richness to the society.

Chapter 9—"An Abductive Autoethnography on a Garden of Invisible Entities"—looked at the "relationship between people and different invisible entities in different places, mainly Japan and Mali, based on my own experiences" (p. 207). Despite Djinns and radioactive materials being different, they have an impact in imagination in people in their collective cultures. It reveals especially "in times of emergency, the invisible entities, which are usually grasped and represented in a limited way as point-like signs, become more multivalent and are perceived as field-like signs" (p. 208).

"Djinn is a 'cultural' entity from the Japanese perspective but a 'natural' entity in a rural area of Mali. Radioactive material is a natural entity, but it has a 'cultural' aspect to it. Both are invisible and have the ambivalent power to harm and benefit humans" (p. 208). Even though they do not have a "visible garden" to step on earth, they can bring some invisible elements such as Djinn and radioactive material as crucial elements of their lives.

On the other hand, what someone believes can become visible in his/her personal and collective culture. Even if a person can not see radioactive material, if he/she believes so much that, he/she can come to see this in his/her life. If, for example, a man gets sick suddenly, he can say he was affected by radioactive material and it can be reinforced by several social voices in his context. In this situation, the invisible becomes visible—illness. It is what he believes, it is the relationship between signs he created to explain his health.

In this aspect, it would be relevant to focus on this process of when an "invisible garden" is going to become a "visible garden" in people's daily life.

Gardens are human concrete or imaginary constructions that affect people's daily life. As it was seen in the churchyard at Tervola in Finland, in which garden was becoming an important part of planning a worthy place for the deceased. It was identified that the construction of a fragile self-position of beginning teacher is crossed by others challenging social voices—gardeners (other teachers). Here, the garden is a mobilizing experience to modify the mind's person. It was found how a wide garden could make believe other imaginary worlds as horizon of salvation in confusing childhood. Also, it was seen how Renaissance gardens were very inspired by classical ideals of order and beauty, and intended for human pleasure and even so were used to show off wealth. Finally, gardens can be invisible but affect so many people everywhere.

Considering such a rich scenario of uses of the garden sign, it would be very important to investigate the unconscious dimension of gardens in our minds. How can the garden sign be so powerful? What do we keep in our minds that can perhaps be related to the collective unconscious that we have about gardens? This can be an interesting way to illuminate the fascination that humanity gives to their gardens.

REFERENCES

Marsico, G., Tateo, L., Gomes, R. C., & Dazzani, V. (2019). Educational processes and dialogical construction of Self. In N. Mercer, R. Wegerif, & L. Major (Eds.), *The Routledge international handbook of research on dialogic education* (pp. 50–61). Routledge.

Valsiner, J. (2007). *Culture in minds and societies: Foundations of cultural psychology.* SAGE Publications. https://doi.org/10.4135/9788132108504

Culture meets psychology.

COMMENTARY PART IIB

ENRICHING THE SEMIOTIC FIELD OF THE GARDEN THROUGH METAPHORS

Enno von Fircks
Sigmund Freud University, Vienna

CULTURAL PSYCHOLOGY AND SOME CORE PREMISES

There is no doubt that the garden operates at the intersection of personal and collective culture (Valsiner, 2014). Yet, there is more to the scientific complexity of a garden than the inner and outer world of culture. In essence, culture provides us with an objective meaning making system (norms, scripts, narratives)—or in semiotic terms texts (Y. Lotman, 1990). However, these semiotic texts are not only out there but they are appropriated by concrete individuals within their concrete social environments (Jantzen, 2008, 2012; Leont'ev, 1978). Human beings appropriate these objective meanings making systems with personal sense, and the to-be-appropriated texts become personologically important (von Fircks, 2022a). Individuality and personality do emerge from these personal sense-making processes on the basis of objective meaning making systems which accounts for the diversity in human culture despite prevailing narratives or norms

(Bruner, 1990, 1996, 1997). Cultural psychology is thus a science that is able to overcome monistic worldviews by focusing on objective cultural patterns that become transformed personally and bear specific valences and connotations (Boesch, 1991, 1998, 2002). The personological relatedness towards a cultural object at stake is thus unimaginably rich and diverse, and as a consequence different people—with different experience—do interpret the same object in a different way, for example, family provides security vs. family is a place of authority (von Fircks, 2022b). Hence, culture operates in a liminal state uniting many different forms of relatedness towards an object at stake. These different interpretations might bear potential for conflict or rupture, yet this potential for conflict makes development possible and even necessary (J. N. Lotman, 2010; von Fircks, 2022c). Positions, counter-positions do combine to a fertile synthesis of a new personal sense-making process of a cultural object (Valsiner, 2014, 2017, 2019). Without conflict, without contradiction synthesis—or the development of culture—would not be possible. The liminality of culture is thus responsible for its very own development or self-actualization. However, the personal transformation of culture requires dialogue (Bachtin, 2011, 2021; Hermans, 1999, 2001; Valsiner, 2019). The development of cultural (life) patterns only comes into being if there is dialogue in the first place. Yet, this dialogue needs to be genuine (Lichtenberg, 2012). Positions and counter-positions do need their very own reason to exist in order for a synthesis to take place. If people do not reveal their true needs and goals, genuine dialogue is hidden behind a masquerade that inhibits organic growth for both communicative partners (Perls et al., 1994; Rogers, 1961). Genuine dialogue is the driving force of cultural and personal transformation (Rogers & Lewis, 2021). Yet, in order to know what one needs (including quasi-needs [goals]) people need to face themselves as well as their feelings (Jung, 2010; Peterson, 2002); a deep personological exploration of one's psyche is necessary in order to know how I do want to appropriate my culture and construct my existence (Pfeiffer, 1952). However, this appropriation is not eternally fixed but depends upon the environmental demands of a specific situation or the alteration of an objective cultural object (or life pattern).

So far, we can subsume four different milestones of cultural psychology. The first is centered around the notion of objective cultural objects (norms, scripts, narratives) that get appropriated personally and bear significant personal meaning. The second principle demonstrates the liminality of being, thus many different—often opposing personal—interpretations concerning a specific cultural object. Yet, as a third principle, these opposing forces do allow a synthesis to take place and to combine previously antagonistic positions into a qualitative, new whole. However, this synthesis or the development of personal as well as collective culture is only possible through genuine dialogue. This dialogue requires one to know his/

her needs as well as the ones of the social other. The deep exploration of one's own psyche as well as of the communicative partner is thus necessary in order to transparently lay out our personal appropriations of cultural objects. Only then transformation of personal and collective culture comes into being and organic growth possible (von Fircks, 2022d).

UNDERSTANDING GARDENS BETWEEN THE LIVING AND THE DEAD

The present chapters are not only an illustrative mirror of these cultural psychological principles, but they do expand them in significant ways. Hagoköngäs chapter, "From Gods' Garden to Gardens of Memories," is an important contribution in this regard. She analyzes how cemeteries are transformed—over multiple centuries—based upon specific semiotic guidance by particular authorities (church, political class, elites) and life-changing events (wars, political changes, etc.). For example, the Finish author explains that the cemetery became democratized during the Second World War in order to emphasize the mutual involvement of all citizens in the war, praising each and every individual in an equal manner for their service. This was shown for example in the reorganization of the cemetery's price categories (length of possession vs. location in the cemetery) as well as in the construction of burials (the size of stones was synchronized resembling suitcases). The semiotic guidance was clear: Equality was favored even in death. "Yet, this semiotic guidance unfolded specific consequences for the parts<>whole relationship of the cemetery" because the cemetery as a whole lost its diversity and became a mirror for uniformity and conformity. This conformity was negatively perceived by the local Finish society because it made people and their lives a-personal, left in a state of having had no personal history. As a consequence, people started to negotiate the liminal state of conformity<>non-conformity and began to ornament the uniform tombstones by adding personal symbols.

Hagoköngäs' contribution is especially dense in this regard as the Finish author can show the personal cleavage people are confronted with nowadays. Religious and political belief systems have lost their binding character for people (Kvale, 2003; May, 1981, 1991, 2007; Peterson, 2002), and it is within the personal construction of a meaningful and decent life for oneself and one's fellow man, that man in general tries to overcome an existential void (Pfeiffer, 1952). This is well shown in Hagoköngäs's chapter while people tried to negotiate the semiotic guidance of uniformity and conformity by personally meaningful symbols. What becomes evident in her chapter is man's drive for the appropriation of objective cultural patterns. Yet, this appropriation is negotiated between multiple actors implied.

Without the drive for the personal appropriation of culture man cannot live including mourning over his/her losses. Death in particular appears to trigger that personal appropriation of culture, illustratively.

Yet, I am highly interested in how Hagoköngäs would analyze the moderately new tradition of burial woods (wooden cemeteries). I am aware that some readers might not know that kind of German tradition. A burial wood is a natural cemetery in a particular forest district. People are allowed to purchase a tree within that district and place an urn next to the tree. Personal symbols are not allowed within that place as it would disturb the ecological balance of the forest. Yet, people try to negotiate the a-personal<>personal state of the cemetery while buying highly colorful flowers for their lost ones. Here, we see easily the transfer of Hagoköngäs' perspective onto different kinds of cemeteries. Yet, what would be interesting is doing a go-along ethnography (Kusenbach, 2003) and study the differences of perception, feelings (the mourning), contemplation between those different cemeteries while singling out the particularities of the semiotic guidance in both cases.

UNDERSTANDING HUMAN CULTIVATION ON THE BASIS OF THE RENAISSANCE EPOCH

Joranger's chapter—"The Colorful Garden of the Renaissance"—complements the above-mentioned in significant ways. The Norwegian author tries to restore the actual—highly diverse—meaning of the Renaissance epoch. She does so by outlining the general principles of the Renaissance, in particular man's physical and psychic connection to the larger order of things such as the state (Roeck, 2017). People during the Renaissance era were driven by the question of how to achieve or restore inner harmony within themselves including bodily and mental balance (Roeck, 2017). This body was interpreted as the microcosm that was ultimately embedded in the macrocosm—such as the state or nature in general. Man was thus perceived as the single cell of the world, and diseases, conflicts, issues in man or the state were undoubtedly intertwined with each other (Joranger, 2016). Man was thus not yet separated from the state, nature, his fellow human being but he was perceived as a unit or a whole. During the Renaissance Joranger points out that man was driven to discover and structure (including to restructure) signs. As man was concerned with the general notion of the state, equally he needed to look into himself and explore his psyche in order to get an idea of the state's circumstances. Man was thus driven by structuring himself in accordance with the wider world, and this drive was only to be accomplished if the signs were rightly interpreted.

Joranger argues in this regard that a specific semiology was invented that was complemented by hermeneutics, the way how to interpret the diverse sign-making processes between the ecological unit of man<>world or microcosm<>macrocosm. What Joranger so illustratively captures is the fact that personal<>and collective culture was not yet separated within the Renaissance epoch; the personal appropriation of culture was a cultural/poetic act in itself transforming culture in peculiar ways (Bachtin, 2011, 2021). Every personal sense-making process was inherently cultural because it could not be separated or singled out; culture and persons were thus ongoingly developing themselves forwards by their symbiotic intertwinement. In my opinion, this is the actual essence of a garden; man and nature are not separated. It is culture that bridges the gap between those two entities. Man tries to cultivate nature by means of his needs and goals, nature is thus transformed by concrete agents. Yet, this transformation by means of autocommunication or I-He communication is equally changing the structure of the personality (Lotman, 1990).

This is what cultural psychology—especially Lang (1988, 1992, 1993) or Valsiner (2021)—tried to teach us: Do not separate man from nature but look at their ecological interconnectedness in time. However, this interconnectedness is embedded in a feedback-like network constantly catalyzing a new whole by changing the nature of its parts (Valsiner, 2014). Cultural psychology in particular tries to break with our prevailing scientific narrative of empiricism, dualism, and rationalism and is thus loyal to the Renaissance worldview (Toomela, 2021).

It is in this regard that I'd like to argue that we are facing a second Renaissance era. Joranger rightfully argued that the Renaissance epoch was catalyzed by the beginning decline of Christianity. Christianity per se started to lose its general ties—its over-reaching semiotic guidance—with the people. And as people became more and more estranged from Christianity, Christianity was not able to develop further. The symbiotic interconnectedness between man and Christianity started to crumble and people turned to other narratives such as past ones to be found in antiquity.

The parallels to our modern days are striking. Churches are losing their last members, closing their doors in a lot of communities, and desecrating their buildings (Mumelter, 2021). But man is still on the search for meaning (Frankl, 2015, 2019; von Fircks, 2021a) which is visible in his voluntary turn to old philosophers such as Laozi, Confucius, Buddha, or the I Ging. Taoism, Zen-Buddhism, fasting cures are appreciated by a large part, monastery retreats became an own business branch, meditation is penetrating our everyday occurrence including mindfulness-based therapeutic offers/coaching as well as mindfulness-based practice at the workplace (Dyer, 2016; Fischer, 2010, 2015; Griffith et al., 2008; Khoury et al., 2013). I'd like to hear Joranger's perspective about that Renaissance light—which I call it. And it shows illustratively that man is not only driven to appropriate culture, but that man is essentially driven for the natural appropriation of culture based upon nature with the goal of reaching inner harmony (von Fircks, 2022e) that can create harmony within the world, in general.

REACHING INNER HARMONY THROUGH PERSONAL APPROPRIATION OF CULTURE

Reaching inner harmony within a specific culture was the ultimate goal of Zlazli's chapter, "Constant Fear of Ostracism." Imagine that you decorate or ornament a garden with cultural material that you learn to dislike after a while. You start to transform the garden based upon other people's needs and goals; you do justice to their wants and their particular taste, and you want to convince yourself that these foreign needs and goals might be yours too. But after a while you realize that something is wrong with your garden. You become aware that this garden is not yours but that it is a chamber of other people's voices. However, you start to appreciate this particular garden because the other people—whose taste you respect by means of transforming the garden based on their needs and goals—feel comfortable. They consider this garden relaxing, meditative, or even exciting because it is a mirror for themselves. And you start to appreciate that other people like the garden and you ask yourself whether you do like the garden yourself or whether you just like the feeling of other people appreciating your garden. This existential dilemma between personal sense<>culture is well-illustrated by Zlazli's poetic autoethnography. The Japanese author is on the search of her own personal compass in the width of encountering many different cultures. She shows illuminatively that this search for one's own personal compass is constrained by many cultural demands and comes with a lot of obstacles one needs to do justice to. What Zlazli accomplishes is to show that the cleavage of personal sense<>culture is never completed but needs to be negotiated lifelong depending on one's own social environment and cultural demands coming from one's own parents, school, peers, and so forth (see also von Fircks, 2021a). It is here that Zlazli's tries to show us pathways how to reach inner harmony, for example, by means of constantly negotiating our personal sense within particular cultural constraints—even if those constraints appear to be hurtful in the very beginning. Yet, the non-negotiation of cultural material and the gradual disappearance of any personological traces, of any personal signs of life leads into a deterioration of the human psyche (see also Toomela, 2021). This is well-documented by Zlazli.

However, there is one minor critique that I'd like to mention in regards to her chapter. Ruptures and conflicts based on cultural constraints are mainly interpreted in a negatively connotated way leading into alienation and estrangement causing eventually despair or even depression. While there is no doubt that those ruptures and challenges do have a severe impact on the individual's psyche unfolding negative consequences in the short term—ruptures and conflicts are from a semiotic perspective necessary for development as mentioned in the introductory paragraphs—especially in a long-term perspective (J. N. Lotman, 2010; Y. Lotman, 1990; Valsiner, 2014, 2021). Zlazli was only able to develop herself, to become an emancipated and free woman—choosing her very own destiny in the width of many different cultures—because there were cultural constraints in the first place. Without having contact with many different people and their experience—at the border of the semiosphere—she could not have become the person she is now. The painful experience at the border of the semiosphere, the constant negotiation of personal sense within cultural constraints were a necessary step for her to discover her own personality, dynamically. Breakdowns and setbacks might be perceived as negative in the short term, yet for Zlazli they were required in order to get to know what she really needs in her life and how she wants to lead an anthropologically sustainable life.

I am convinced that we do need a more positively connotated perspective in regards to ruptures and conflicts as advocated by various semioticians or psychologists and eventually a framework that incorporates the cleavage of short-term<>long-term consequences of the liminal imperative of personal sense<>culture (see, e.g., von Fircks, 2020 for leadership). Zlazli's work could then be perceived as inherently holistic—a key feature of cultural psychology.

INVISIBLE ENTITIES AT THE BORDER OF THE SEMIOSPHERE

Holism is an important term for Katsura too. In his chapter—"Djinns and Radioactive Materials"—the Japanese author tries to analyze invisible entities while comparing their cultural-psychological impact upon people. Katsura's autoethnography shows illustratively how personal meaning making is enriched by immersing into a relatively different (or new) culture from the ones a person was confronted with during childhood and adolescence. While living in Mali, the Japanese author was getting acquainted with a new religious belief system incorporating the notion of Giné, an invisible spiritual force that can be made fertile for medicine and spiritual guidance. Yet, the Giné also features negative spiritual forces, and an individual can be possessed by negative energies (sadness, mourning, anger). Moreover, the Giné is embedded in a complex—objective—cultural meaning making system coming with different types of Ginés, a teacher–pupil relationship, gender differences, employment opportunities, as well as specific norms that guide conduct within the everyday occurrence of people. Again, if we meet people at the border of the semiosphere, we do perceive some potential for ruptures within our daily meaning making (J. N. Lotman, 2010; Y. Lotman, 1990). As Katsura was trying to explain the complexity of the Giné to his Japanese colleagues or friends, they clearly showed some issues in understanding the Giné as a real thing structuring the daily lives of people, psychically and physically which goes beyond a symbolic function of the Giné. This is exactly what Toomela (2021) tries to argue when he states that culture enables us to perceive, interpret, and digest specific information but that it also limits our understanding of specific cultural givens that are foreign to us and that are not part and parcel of our daily cultural meaning making system.

Culture is for the Estonian psychologist born at the intersection of familiar<>foreign embedded in a constant stream of negotiation—at the border of the semiosphere. However, Katsura does not stop here. He tries to compare the Giné with the radioactive crisis in Japan following Fukushima 2011. Importantly, the Japanese author illuminates that the discourse about radioactivity was embedded in a similar objective cultural system in comparison with the Giné. Radioactivity also proves to be beneficial and harmful, creates employment, is context-dependent (nuclear energy = cheap = good for our industry vs. nuclear catastrophe = expensive = bad for our industry), is guided by specific underlying norms advocated by various experts and unfolds equally different effects on different genders. The comparison between the Giné and radioactivity—even if that looks quite brave from the outset—is highly illustrative and significant for cultural psychology as it shows how culture organizes and penetrates the daily life of concrete human beings (see also Valsiner, 2007, 2014). The radioactivity—as well as the COVID-19 crisis—all had advantages for specific industries. Newspapers were regaining their popularity; expert roles assigned; commissions were founded, and norms initiated how to deal with contaminated regions in the country. However, the concept of radioactivity and especially the crisis was also foreign for people in Mali—those who did not speak French and did not come into contact with European cultures—and there was literally no concept of how to transmit the crisis to those people living in Mali. As they had never experienced—nor did their forefathers—the cultural importance of nuclear energy—they could not understand the concept beyond it and neither could the crisis that emerged from that. Culture enables us to understand things, events, and peoples, or in short to make sense of various objects (Bruner, 1990, 1997). Yet, if we have not learnt how to look at an object from various viewpoints (nuclear energy), we can only look at it from our very own perspective that is embedded in the objective cultural system we grew up in (Toomela, 2021). And if this cultural system does not provide us with the objective meaning of a specific event or object, personally we cannot make sense of that event or object either. As a consequence, we even lack words for these kinds of situations. This is exactly what Katsura tries to show us, and he accomplishes that quite well: Cultures always come with peculiar meaning making opportunities as well as with specific meaning making limitations. Yet, those opportunities and limitations are not to be understood in a rigid way but essentially, they are negotiated and can become re-structured by meeting at the border of the semiosphere (Y. Lotman, 1990). What I'd like to see from Katsura in the future is to make the Mali and Japanese people (maybe some Giné teacher with a professor for nuclear energy) meet and to openly discuss their invisible entities and track down the cultural-psychological consequences of their significant discourse. Such a perspective would not only be fruitful for cultural psychology as a science but can catalyze important pathways on how to bridge the cleavage of personal<>foreign cultures.

STUDYING THE CULTIVATION OF CONSCIOUSNESS: THE IMPERATIVE OF NEGOTIATION WITHIN CULTURAL PSYCHOLOGY

Lastly, we need to discuss Hamana's chapter—"The Process of Change in Consciousness of Involvement With Children on the Part of a Novice Teacher in a Team-Teaching Classroom." The autoethnographic study took place in a kindergarten drawing on the author's experience (thoughts and feelings are poetically portrayed in the chapter) working in such an institution. Using the trajectory equifinality model (see Sato & Tanimura, 2016; Sato et al., 2009), the author modeled alterations of his meta-perspective (he calls that consciousness) concerning his ongoing and processual interactions with the children. He does so by showing us that a cultivation of a specific role (teacher) requires necessary time and importantly some detours. Appropriating and internalizing that role is a task in irreversible time that is never fully terminated but is permanently negotiated (Bruner, 1997). Yet, this negotiation can only succeed (or the growing out process of the teacher role) if there is sufficient semiotic guidance, thus if the novice is accompanied by peers that are likely to talk about their experiences as well as the experiences of their clients (here children; see also von Fircks, 2021b). Hamana shows us that genuine dialogue is key for the personal<>cultural negotiation of a specific role. Yet, Hamana has given us some insights what genuine actually means. This is a significant result as far as I am concerned. Drawing on Hamana's experience, genuine dialogue does not hide itself in euphemisms when two people come together to discuss their experience with children. On the contrary, genuine dialogue is necessarily straight (honest), for example, "If I see you having disturbed child XY, we need to talk about that." It was striking that these sharp comments from more experienced colleagues were a crucial learning experience for Hamana but more importantly Hamana did not interpret those comments in a destructive (personal offending) way. As far as I am concerned, the reason hides itself in an open learning culture where mistakes and detours are necessary for the personal appropriation of a particular role (e.g., teacher role). Even in a limited amount of time and in a stressful situation (to supervise several children at the same time), genuine dialogue is possible if it does focus on the objective interactions between the child<>teacher including the child's feelings that are at the foreground of the teacher's guidance. This is a stark but important contrast to person-centered (humanistic) approaches in psychology and psychotherapy where leading figures advocate that person-centered guidance does require a lot of time and energy (e.g., Rogers, 1961; Rogers & Lewis, 2021). On the contrary, Hamana has shown us that person-centered—humanistic—semiotic guidance is possible in a limited amount of time and in a systemic setting. However, for future works I'd like to appeal to Hamana to not only focus on the teacher's thoughts and feelings but to incorporate pupil's experiences too in order to assure that this small-scope humanistic attitude leads into the hypothesized benefits.

The analogy to the garden setting is striking. Cultivating a garden does not happen in a linear way: The more time I invest in my garden, the more likely it is going to flourish. On the contrary, it depends upon the symbiotic intertwinement (systemic perspective) of multiple organisms that if stimulated at the right time can be pushed towards growth. Trying to care about one part of the garden and helping this part to flourish will change the parts<>whole relationship of the garden. Hamana's personal sense making process of the teacher<>pupil cleavage (how do I feel into the pupils<> how do I do justice to structuring the day of my pupils) shows that illustratively. When the Japanese author started to make sense of the ambivalence while developing a specific circumvention strategy (there is time for showing empathy and there is time for structure), the appropriated semiotic text altered the whole teacher<>classroom (kindergarten) setting. The organic growth of a specific role—while allowing symbiotic intertwinement to take place—is the key to sustainable growth in the long term that does not only benefit oneself but multiple organisms that do form an ecological network (von Fircks, 2022d). This makes up for the beauty of life for gardens and human beings.

ENRICHING CULTURAL PSYCHOLOGY BY MEANS OF STUDYING THE CLEAVAGE OF PERSONAL<>COLLECTIVE CULTURE: THE ESSENCE OF THE FIVE CHAPTERS

It is now time for a short resumé and to evaluate how the discussed chapters have enriched the semiotic garden of cultural psychology.

1. Hagoköngäs' chapter has well illustrated the personal appropriation of cultural (life) patterns for the sake of a meaningful and decent life that becomes accentuated even in death. It is especially death that might trigger the personal appropriation of culture in peculiar ways, eventually triggering circumvention strategies on how to deal with one's loss. This personological appropriation appears to be even more significant for people as religious (and also political) belief systems have lost their binding and guiding character in the everyday occurrence of people's lives, nowadays.
2. It is in this regard that I read Joranger's chapter as an answer to Hagoköngäs's chapter. Because old belief systems have lost their mediating power, people do turn to alternative cultural life-patterns that might guide them through their various developmental stages (tasks) and emotional upheavals. The Renaissance epoch was especially illustrative in this regard as people tried to reach inner harmony that could be mapped onto the structure of the larger cosmos. Reaching this unity of life is expressed in a new Renaissance light that shows itself in the great popularity of mindfulness and old-Chinese teachers such as Laozi or Confucius.
3. Zlazli has shown us poetically that the personal appropriation of culture can be quite painful because of various cultural constraints and includes importantly misunderstandings, conflicts, and setbacks. Despite her drawing a rather negative picture of conflicts and ruptures, these conflicts and ruptures were necessary for her to develop and negotiate her personal appropriation of culture including her coming to terms with her very own history. For her, freedom was only discovered and achieved when facing its opposite, non-freedom (or suppression).
4. Katsura demonstrated that culture enables us with particular meaning making opportunities as well as with meaning making limitations. Becoming aware of those opportunities and constraints is only possible if willfully going to the border of our semiosphere. At the border of the semiosphere we will become aware of our cultural life-patterns and how they structure our everyday occurrence as well as of alternative cultural life-patterns that we might adopt in the near future. Dialogue only comes into being at the border of

the semiosphere (Y. Lotman, 1990). Yet, we need to throw ourselves constantly at the border of the semiosphere in order to grow.
5. Hamana illustrated that this dialogue can be genuine in a short period of time as well as in a systemic setting including various pupils. The personal appropriation of a specific cultural given (e.g., teacher role) does not happen in an empty space but is guided by our ecological network we find ourselves in. If focusing on objective interactional (processual) patterns between child and pupil (focus is here on the child's feelings), semiotic guidance can come into being that is not enforced or authoritarian but an offer to interpret specific events through an additional lens.

I am convinced that these five milestones enrich the semiotic garden of cultural psychology in a significant way.

REFERENCES

Bachtin, M. (2011). *Zur philosophie der handlung* [Towards a philosophy of the act]. Matthes & Seitz Berlin.
Bachtin, M. (2021). *Chronotopos* (5th ed.). Suhrkamp Taschenbuch Wissenschaft.
Boesch, E. E. (1991). *Symbolic action theory and cultural psychology*. Springer New York.
Boesch, E. E. (1998). *Sehnsucht: Von der Suche nach Glück und Sinn* [Longing: On the search of joy and meaning] (1st ed.). Huber.
Boesch, E. E. (2002). Genese der subjektiven Kultur [Genesis of subjective culture]. In M. Hildebrand-Nilshon, C.-H. Kim, & D. Papadopoulos (Eds.), *Kultur (in) der Psychologie: Über das Abenteuer des Kulturbegriffs in der psychologischen Theorienbildung* [Culture (in) psychology: About the adventure of the concept of culture in psychological theory formation] (pp. 67–95). Asanger.
Bruner, J. S. (1990). *Acts of meaning: Four lectures on mind and culture* (Vol. 3). Harvard University Press.
Bruner, J. (1996). *The culture of education*. Harvard University Press.
Bruner, J. S. (1997). *Sinn, Kultur und Ich-Identität: Zur Kulturpsychologie des Sinns* [Sense, culture and I-identity] (1st ed.). Carl Auer.
Dyer, W. W. (2016). *Ändere deine Gedanken-und dein Leben ändert sich: Die lebendige Weisheit des Tao* [Change your thoughts and your life will change: The vivid wisdom of the Tao]. Goldmann Verlag.
Fischer, T. (2010). *Tao heißt leben, was andere träumen* [Tao means living what others dream]. Rowohlt-Taschenbuch-Verl.
Fischer, T. (2015). *Wu wei: Die Lebenskunst des Tao* [Wu wie: The art of living with the Tao] (12th. ed.). Rowohlt-Taschenbuch-Verl.
Frankl, V. E. (2015). *Grundkonzepte der Logotherapie* (1. Auflage). Facultas. https://elibrary.utb.de/doi/book/10.24989/9783990305058
Frankl, V. E. (2019). *Man's search for meaning*. Random House USA.

Griffith, J. M., Hasley, J. P., Liu, H., Severn, D. G., Conner, L. H., & Adler, L. E. (2008). Qigong stress reduction in hospital staff. *The Journal of alternative and complementary medicine, 14*(8), 939–945.

Hermans, H. J. M. (1999). Dialogical thinking and self-innovation. *Culture & Psychology, 5*(1), 67–87. http://dx.doi.org/10.1177/1354067X9951004

Hermans, H. J. (2001). The construction of a personal position repertoire: Method and practice. *Culture & Psychology, 7*(3), 323–366. http://dx.doi.org/10.1177/1354067X0173005

Jantzen, W. (2008). *Kulturhistorische psychologie heute: Methodologische erkundungen zu L.S. Vygotskij* [Cultural-historical psychology today: Methodological explorations of L.S. Vygotsky]. Lehmanns Media.

Jantzen, W. (2012). *Am Anfang war der sinn: Zur naturgeschichte, psychologie und philosophie von tätigkeit, sinn und dialog* [In the beginning there was meaning: About natural history, psychology, philosophy of activity, sense and dialogue] (2nd ed.). Lehmanns.

Joranger, L. (2016). Psychology and the historical power–body conjunction: Foucault's different view of the history and philosophy of psychology. *Theory & Psychology, 26*(3), 304–323. https://doi.org/10.1177/0959354315623655

Jung, C. G. (2010). Analytical psychology. In R. B. Ewen (Ed.), *An introduction to theories of personality* (pp. 53–81). Psychology Press.

Khoury, B., Lecomte, T., Fortin, G., Masse, M., Therien, P., Bouchard, V., ... Hofmann, S. G. (2013). Mindfulness-based therapy: A comprehensive meta-analysis. *Clinical Psychology Review, 33*(6), 763–771. https://doi.org/10.1016/j.cpr.2013.05.005

Kusenbach, M. (2003). Street phenomenology: The go-along as ethnographic research tool. *Ethnograph, 4*(3), 455–485. https://doi.org/10.1177/146613810343007

Kvale, S. (2003). The church, the factory and the market. *Theory & Psychology, 13*(5), 579–603. https://doi.org/10.1177/09593543030135005

Lang, A. (1988). Die kopernikanische Wende steht in der Psychologie noch aus! Hinweis auf eine ökologische Entwicklungspsychologie [The Copernican revolution still lacks in psychology! Advices for an ecological psychology]. *Schweizerische Zeitschrift für Psychologie, 47*(2/3), 93–108.

Lang, A. (1992). On the knowledge in things and places. In M. von Cranach, W. Doise, & G. Mugny (Eds.), *Social representations and the social basis of knowledge* (pp. 76–83). Hans Huber.

Lang, A. (1993). Non-cartesian artefacts in dwelling activities: Step towards a semiotic ecology. *Schweizerische Zeitschrift Für Psychologie, 52*(2), 138–147. http://www.langpapers.org/pap2/1993-01noncartesartefact.htm

Leont'ev, A. N. (1978). *Activity, consciousness, and personality*. Prentice-Hall.

Lichtenberg, P. (2012). Culture change: Conversations concerning political/religious differences. In T. B.-Y. Levine (Ed.), *Gestalt therapy: Advances in theory and practice* (pp. 175–185). Routledge.

Lotman, J. N. (2010). *Kultur und explosion* [Culture and explosion]. Suhrkamp Taschenbuch Wissenschaft [Suhrkamp paperback science].

Lotman, Y. (1990). *Universe of the mind: A semiotic theory of culture*. Indiana University Press.

May, R. (1981). *Freedom and destiny*. W. W. Norton & Company.

May, R. (1991). *The cry for myth* (1st ed.). Norton.
May, R. (2007). *Love and will*. W. W. Norton. (Original work published 1969)
Mumelter, J. (2021, January 14). *Profanierung: Wenn aus Gotteshäusern eine Gastwirtschaft wird* [Profanation: When places of worship become inns]. BR24. Retrieved September 26, 2022, from https://www.br.de/nachrichten/kultur/profanierung-wenn-aus-gotteshaeusern-eine-gastwirtschaft-wird,SLoFuuw
Perls, F. S., Goodman, P., & Hefferline, R. F. (1994). *Gestalt therapy: Excitement and growth in the human personality*. Gestalt Journal Press.
Peterson, J. B. (2002). *Maps of meaning: The architecture of belief* (1st ed.). Taylor and Francis.
Pfeiffer, J. (1952). *Existenzphilosophie. Eine Einführung in Heidegger und Jaspers* [Existential philosophy: An introduction to Heidegger and Jaspers]. Meiner.
Roeck (2017). *Der morgen der welt: Geschichte der Renaissance* [The morning of the world: The history of the Renaissance] (3rd ed.). C. H. Beck.
Rogers, C. R. (1961). *On becoming a person: A therapist's view of psychotherapy*. Constable.
Rogers, C. R., & Lewis, M. K. (2021). *Therapeut und Klient. Grundlagen der Gesprächspsychotherapie* [Therapist and client: Basics of conversation psychotherapy] (25th ed.). Fischer Taschenbuch.
Sato, T., Hidaka, T., & Fukuda, M. (2009). Depicting the dynamics of living the life: The trajectory equifinality model. In J. Valsiner, N. Chaudhary, M. C. D. P. Lyra, & P. C. M. Molenaar (Eds.), *Dynamic process methodology in the social and developmental sciences* (pp. 217–240). Springer.
Sato, T., & Tanimura, H. (2016). The trajectory equifinality model (TEM) as a general tool for understanding human life course within irreversible time. In T. Sato, N. Mori, & J. Valsiner (Eds.), *Making of the future: The trajectory equifinality approach in cultural psychology* (pp. 21–43). Information Age Publishing.
Toomela, A. (2021). *Culture, speech and myself*. Porcos ante Margaritas.
Valsiner, J. (2007). *Culture in minds and societies: Foundations of cultural psychology*. SAGE Publications.
Valsiner, J. (2014). *An invitation to cultural psychology*. SAGE Publishing.
Valsiner, J. (2017). *From methodology to methods in human psychology*. Springer.
Valsiner, J. (2019). *Ornamented lives: Advances in cultural psychology*. Information Age Publishing.
Valsiner, J. (2021). *General human psychology: Theory and history in the human and social sciences*. Springer.
von Fircks, E. F. (2020). Existential humanistic leadership (EHL) as a dialogical process: Equality of the non-equality in organizations. *Integrative Psychological and Behavioral Science, 54*, 4, 719–741. https://doi.org/10.1007/s12124-020-09560-1
von Fircks, E. (2021a). Daseinssemiosis: A new look at the phenomenology of Theodor Lipps. *Human Arenas, 5*, 592–608. https://doi.org/10.1007/s42087-020-00159-x
von Fircks, E. (2021b). Culture and leadership: A Lewinian perspective of organizational problem solving. *Human Arenas, 7*, 1–14. https://doi.org/10.1007/s42087-021-00256-5

von Fircks, E. (2022a). Eine kurze kulturpsychologische Anleitung für zukünftige Freunde [A short cultural psychology guide for future friends]. *Cultura & Psyché, 4*, 277–291. https://doi.org/10.1007/s43638-022-00039-x

von Fircks, E. F. (2022b). Culture in the seminar room of poetry: Poetic insights for cultural psychology. *Culture & Psychology*. https://doi.org/10.1177/1354067X221097609

von Fircks, E. (2022c). Interdependence and cultural resources to mediate change: What was missing in Engeström's third generational activity theory. *Human Arenas*. https://doi.org/10.1007/s42087-022-00303-9

von Fircks, E. (2022d). Setting the seeds for a normative expansion of Lewinian Field theory for cultural-psychological practitioners. *Human Arenas*, 1–21. https://doi.org/10.1007/s42087-022-00307-5

von Fircks, E. (2022e). Cultural psychological implications of Hermann Hesse's Glasperlenspiel (glass bead game). *Culture and Psychology*. https://doi.org/10.1177/1354067X221132000

PART III

MOVING THROUGH GARDENS:
A JOURNEY TO SELF-CULTIVATION

A wild garden in B., made by the author

CHAPTER 11

CULTIVATION IN SELF AND ENVIRONMENT

When a Voice Echoes From One Garden to Another

Marc Antoine Campill
Free Researcher, Luxembourg

TARGET

The complexity of any phenomena is probably what inspires researchers over decades to challenge their generated meaning, improving the social and personal knowledge generation in such a manner that we as humankind can continue to grow and to overcome the limitations of the previous learned methods of meaning and knowledge generation. It is undeniable that our current knowledge generation is far from being at the peak of our possibilities. Challenging new ways are required to generate and to preserve knowledge, whereby this not only means to create new unknown procedures, but also means to cultivate what we already have from all the coexisting scientific fields.

We need to cultivate an alternative use of already generated knowledge, impressions by a double use of this generated meaning for possible identical running procedures/phenomena. For example, a process that is already well known in the scientific field is the concept of models/metaphors. It is essential to be aware that the use of models is essential in every scientific field, by providing specified links between theory and reality of scientific concepts. It is a tool that allows us to visualize knowledge in a more understandable manner. Deepening knowledge leads to knowledge condensation and redefinition of our already generated meaning. On one hand, models are restricted in their accuracy—a visualization does not allow a 100% matching rate toward a phenomenon, restriction of the model's dimensionality—on the other hand, models are still used to visualize complex constructions in a more understandable shape. Consequently, this simplified and interactive shape is able to retrace the relationships between the interacting forces and their positioning and role to each other (Chittleborough & Treagust, 2009). Leading to an improvement in our comprehension to the phenomena and its diversion of its Gestalt. It is important to underline the potential of model generations. One of the most famous forms of models is the symbol. A single sign obtains the ability to represent a more complex other, by creating a link or bond between non-related experiences, concepts, or relations. Nevertheless, such processes have to be further challenged not only by using simple two-dimensional or more dimensional mechanical constructions. By challenging the model's capacity and by integrating the biological or organic multi-dimensional field, we can reduce the restrictive "Gestalt" of the models and gain the possibility to preserve the multi-dimensional and multi-communicative whole of a phenomenon, that could otherwise disappear in a simply unseen, unmentioned, dimension. The reconstruction of symbols and their knowledge as elaborator of a less known field could otherwise also be called a homonym of symbol/meaning, that can simplify the interpretation of intern reactions of a phenomena by binding them into a construct that inhabits a similar inter-communicative construction and growth/development.

In other words, the process allows to connect dynamic and complex meta-level phenomena with other more elaborated observations of phenomena—with identical dialogical characteristics, from different fields. That allows a clearer insight into the unseen, while reducing the human information process by a resources reduced nexus of information.

In the chapters of the volume the focus is therefore directed to a specific example of such an interactive metaphor, the garden, in relation to dimension of self care, identity construction, and self-environment impact. In this occasion the garden overcomes the role of a simple analogy as "taking care of yourself as you have to take care of your garden." The goal is therefore to give the garden a multilayered meaning that helps to deepen and rechallenge our understanding of how the communication between environment and self in its multilayered self is processing as a whole.

HISTORICAL INSIDES OF GARDEN (SECOND PART OF BEGINNING)

> A garden is defined as a piece of land that is located near a house. It is a field, or often an area of grass, where flowers and other plants are growing.

At the first sight we can anticipate that gardening was probably first used in the ancient times, where families primarily wanted to simplify and to improve the conditions of food collection and security (Thacker, 1985). One of the decisions was probably to grow food close to where they lived so that the danger of wild animals and uncertainty of food collection could be reduced. The garden could therefore be defined instinctively as a tool of growing food, which explains that in several versions the caretaker eliminates everything that doesn't produce food. Nevertheless, the garden has not only connections to the "staying alive" goal, but it is also linked with the multitude of voices and interpretations of its meaning as we can find it in the self.

This means it is essential to remember that the origin of gardens was to produce food, so that moving from finding food in the environment to turning a part of the environment into a cultivation site has to be seen as a major cultural progress.

The meaning and relation between this specified piece of land and humankind is going far behind the previous definition. The experiences we made as human beings related to such an area differs from each other and with this diversity also the meaning behind it should be seen as slightly diverged, nevertheless in generality it has to be seen as the same core process of cultivation. Garden and gardening obtain a deep connection toward humanity and can be found in multiple forms and areas, around the world.

> This means that we can anticipate that the garden is an alternative version of a meadow. An open habitat, or field, vegetated by grass, herbs and other non-woody plants. Also, trees can be found in a meadow, as long as they maintain a more or less "open character" (Campill, 2021). If transitional meadows, perpetual meadows, or urban meadows, so if naturally occurring or artificially created (by human or animal invasion). The habitats describable as meadows, are a group characterized as "semi-natural" fields, meaning that they are composed of species native environmental influences, with only limited human intervention possibilities, whereby the intervention of other animals is not included but could also represent as an exterior influence.

Based on this perception we could assume that the garden can be seen as the representation of the more artificial aspect of the grassland's growth. It is crucial to underline here that it always is a "semi-natural field" and the artificial and natural dialogue is reducible or expandable but cannot be nullified.

Starting before 3,000 BCE in Mesopotamia, also known as the "land between the rivers" (Tigris and Euphrates), inhabits in the south area a flat and irrigated south. Sculptures and texts preserved from this time are evidence showing the garden of this time. In Western tradition, this location represents the Garden of Eden and the Hanging Gardens of Babylon (Figure 11.1; Dalley, 1993).

Focusing on the Hanging Gardens of Babylon known in Western society, listed by Hellenic culture, as one of the Seven Wonders of the Ancient World. The only one of the Seven Wonders where the location and the proof of existence has never been definitively established (Reade, 2000). Over the time these "gardens" were described as one of the most innovative and progressive constructed complexities of these times, probably even 5,000 years afterwards it could still be seen as progressive work. Describable as an ascending series of tiered gardens with a wide variety of flowers, trees, and vines, constructed on mud bricks. The word "hanging" was translated from the original Greek word, *kremastós* (translated as "overhanging"), whereby unfortunately its Greek form has a broader meaning than the modern English word "hanging," it refers less on the act of hanging and more on planted trees located on a raised structure such as a terrace (Dalley, 1993). A style that we can find as well in innovative works of today's

Figure 11.1 Hanging gardens of Babylon of, Maerten van Heemskerck in 1572.

Figure 11.2 Today's architecture, *Acros*.

architecture and gardening, as for example the Acros (Fukuoka, Japan; see Figure 11.2) or the *Waldspirale* (Darmstadt, Germany).

This green area called garden has not only a role in Western history, religion, and mythology. If in the Hindu texts as the Ramayana and Mahabharata, in the literature of Buddha, or the historical documents of the cultivation of food in the Maya civilization, the garden is an omnipresent construct that implies the human understanding of nature and underlines the beliefs that caring about a garden is somehow related to the care taking of the own meaning and existence/identity. This relation between garden and human can be found for example in the Kama Sutra. A work where the house or private gardens stand in relation with a good wife. A good housewife is supposed (based on the Kama Sutra) to plant vegetables, clumps of the fig trees, herbs, and flowers. Similar to the individual assumed wife duties, the expectations are directed toward an aesthetic appearance and her fertile abilities. Also, in the Italian Renaissance women and gardens were standing in relation. Water in the private garden for example was supposed to symbolize the women's fertility and abundance of nature (King, 2008).

In conclusion, the garden is a symbolic tool that is linked with the evolution of humanity. An organic field of voices, that is in a polysemic dialogue with each other and is in communication with its caretaker and environment (Bisgaard et al., 2024). Yet such dialogue is directly linked with the process of cultivation.

WHAT IT MEANS TO CULTIVATE NATURE

First of all, let us dive into the organic field itself, the garden, and into the process that we can easily connect with its cultivation, gardening. When speaking about a garden it is essential to reconsider that we are focusing on an organic field that has at the first instance a self-regulation and communication construction. Identical to the meadow, the plants are communicating and coexisting with each other. Nevertheless, the potential of the garden can be found in the fact that the field is not only determined by natural influences, but also by the gardener or caretaker. This means that in contrast to the more natural force we have a second influencing force that interacts with the organic field and can influence its Gestalt. In conclusion, we are confronted with a constant fight between garden (growth) and gardener (the cultivator).

In the position of natural growth, we could speak for example of a "junglification" of the field. The jungle represents an area overgrown with dense forest and tangled vegetation (typically in the tropics), which matches perfectly as an extreme example with the self-cultivative desire of the field that tries to generate an equilibrated self in which it can proceed by itself for the needed nutrition's and its generally conditions (see Figure 11.3). Adaptation and cultivation are therefore main poles used to generate these abilities.

Figure 11.3 *The Equatorial Jungle,* by Henri Rousseau (1909).

Cultivation in Self and Environment • **265**

In contrast to the natural growth, we can observe the gardener, as cultivator, in an alternative position trying to direct/lead the garden into a desired construction order. The gardener obtains in this occasion the role of an active voice that influences/impacts the field into a desired direction while cultivating, extracting, and adding plants in its close environment. The gardener is not a detached part of the garden. The gardener is part of the ecosystem of the garden, standing in constant dialogue with the plants in the garden. Nevertheless, the gardener is a strong influencer in this ecosystem, who tries to lead the field into a specified/desired form.

The role of the gardener is the role of an active voice that tries to react based on the other voices, flowers, in the garden and tries to support the resonating other voices, by nourishing the flowers or optimizing generally their "environmental" conditions. Nevertheless, there is no guarantee that the decisions made by the gardener can be realized easily. It is essential to be aware that gardening is not a one-time job but is a lifelong project that can result in individually defined achievements and failures. For example, not every flower looks good from the beginning onwards, not every flower can grow by absorbing the same nutrition, not every flower can coexist with each other, and not every step made by the gardener will result in a desired goal. Gardening is a process that inhabits the constant fight between the gardener's individual desires for the flowers, the natural demands of the ecosystem, the environmental conditions (weather), the capacities, and the changing meaning of the own goals of the gardener. In conclusion the gardener is in a lifelong dialogue with his own garden and has always to battle the junglification of his own field by the act of gardening (visualized by Figure 11.4, by a Japanese Gardener walking into a pond to reach wildly rampant greenery. That has been initialized in the position as cultivator for the purpose to extract the undesired wild growing weed).

In this conclusion I do not want to describe the junglification and gardening as counterparts. Both dimensions should be seen more like a diversion of more or less extreme directed examples of a cultivation way for their own field. In both ways we have a multiple construction of factors that can be elaborated by opposing different cultivation styles. In the garden we are aware of this multi dimensionality, but also the jungle is not an exception for this multi-connected environment. Even in the wildest jungles we can find animals, with the desire to create a nest, that interact as caretakers for the organic field.

GARDEN—A PUBLIC PLACE

Whereby we will now focus on a specific metaphor implying the dialogue between the individual multi voice (identity) with the social multi-voice (society).

Figure 11.4 A gardener in Japan, made by photographer Joshua Marx (reproduced by permission)

In this occasion we need to look into the conceptuality of a construct related toward the historical and literary definition of gardens. Speaking about the existence of the garden as an individual and a social construction. In the previous sub-chapter, we have seen the definition of a garden in general but if we look closer in the construct itself, we become aware that we have to differ between two constructs of gardens. Which are the private and the public garden. In this occasion we will use those two dimensions instantly as models of the dialogue between individual culture and social defined culture.

Cultivation in Self and Environment • 267

Figure 11.5 A public garden in Luxembourg, picture by Joshua Marx (reproduced by permission)

It is essential to underline here first how a dialogue in biological terms is described before we can elaborate the phenomenon that we want to elaborate. In basic biological terms we can say that plants in an ecosystem share water and nutrients through the networks, and also use them to "communicate." They send distress signals about changes and dangers, for example, insect attacks, to other trees so that they can alter their behavior when they receive these messages. These are called in biological terms the mycorrhizal network (Bonfante & Anca, 2009). These connections work through mainly two dimensions, the roots and the leaves. In this networking environment every plant is connected with each other in a more or less active and direct/indirect manner. This coexistence can be seen identical to a neural network, the brain of a human being, and allows to metaphorically describe the function and the potential of seeing the self as a multivoiced self, in an alternative form that can highlight other, less seen or less elaborated, phenomena and reactions.

I-POSITION IN SELF AND ENVIRONMENT

In the commune sense communication is an omnipresent construct, that defines the principal laws of living as a human, or for every other known living species, existence. Nevertheless, behind this well-known construct there is more knowledge hidden as we would first anticipate. Communication is probably the modification tool number one to improve individual or social distress in any form. As an example we could say that communication is related to the interpretation of the constructs of mental health or education.

Mental Health

To communicate how we feel, for example, stands strongly in relation with our mental health. Mental distress can affect our everyday life communication, describable by recalling how we feel when we tell someone something that's really important to us, whereby the listener does not react as expected. Such a factor can be the active listening in a relationship, so that not listening would become the unexpected behavior. Whereby this means that by trying to understand the own and other attitudes and behaviors we can make a difference in our mental health conditions (Elgar et al., 2013).

Education

Communication and education are bonded to each other. To educate is bonded to the ground roles of communication and vice versa. Which relates to the essential knowledge that what we can teach has to come from somewhere so that it is based on what has been learned before. Personalized meaning is shared by the act of communication. This means also that all kinds of educational outcomes result out of each other. This means that education requires meaning that the knowledge shared is reinterpretable by the proper experiences made by the listener and speaker (Salomon, 1981).

By using the semiotic potential of self-reflectivity in nature (Maran, 2020), we will be able to use knowledge derived from the study of human semiosis and sign systems to deepen our current understanding of the principles of communication and meaning making. The use of the perspectives of semiotics in the psychological fields is not only suitable for describing the semiosis and structures in our human culture. It inhabits the potential for critical analysis of diverged methods and premises in research by allowing an alternative way of looking into the field of phenomena. In the context of this chapter the meaning making process will not only be connected with psychological meaning it will also dive into the organic and natural principles of "Naturwissenschaften" by connecting with a phenomenon and construct called "Gardening and Garden." Describing the nature/culture relation in the garden from a semiotic and a psychological perspective appears to be challenging, whereby the potential of redefining and reconnecting the already accessible knowledge inhabits the potential to visualize the potential meaning behind "communication" in a completely new way.

It is crucial to dive first into the understanding that lies behind the construct of the Self and the environment before we can connect with the phenomena lying behind the multi-dimensional construct of "communication." Based on James's (1890) idea of an extended self, in which the self is considered as a mini society of multiple I-positions, defined by Hermans; voices or I-positions, are linked to the experiences made and created, based on the meaning generation which are rooting in past and in the current situation, by an individual in its environment. I-positions (as for example, I as enjoyer of life) are referring to hyper generalized meaning that inhabits a plurality of sub-voices and can be representing the individual's current Self or can be completely in dissonance (standing in contradiction) with other voices/I-positions (Hermans, 2014). In general, I-positions have to be seen as autonomic, directed toward each other's existence, and simultaneously functioning parts of the larger society of voices, definable as the individual culture: identity (Campill, 2021). It is essential to underline here the importance that the Self is only a fluid construct that changes through the time by elaborating new knowledge and re-elaborating or redefining already inhabited meaning. Whereby the change is linked to actual change and change in the positioning of the Self in its identity, the so-called what I can see by myself of my Identity (Campill & Valsiner, 2021).

The space in which one the current self is moving is restricted by *how* the self-sees its environment, whereby at the same time this also works vice versa. The different and opposite sides of voices have to be understood first before we can find out the valuable elements that are connectable in a coherent tension-filled, called the whole. In this occasion the alternative form of the meadow theory from (Campill, 2021) will be used, definable as previously mentioned as *the garden*.

In short, the "self," of the environment-self interplay that influences the individual's cultivation of a culture, is resulting out of an intense multi-dimensional inner dispute processing in between multiple-selves of the individual. That means to understand the *environment-self interplay*, we need first to explore the inner constellation of the *interactor self*.

GARDEN AS A METAPHOR

Let me first elaborate a small observation I made once while looking and following several times a natural procedure, describable as how a flower in a private garden changes our mindset of what we expect of a public garden/park.

Scene 1

While standing as a child in my garden I was observing one of my favorite flowers growing. It was a sunflower, we had not many of them actually, mainly only one or two. These flowers were impressively huge for me (at that time) and I always was impressed how these flowers were standing there, able to move their head in such a manner that the head always followed the sun. It fascinated me also to see them on sunless days to look at each other instead of searching for the non-existing sun. I was often standing quite close to the flower, so that sometimes in the summer some seeds were finding their way into my clothes. So, it came that I started spreading the seeds in the most random places, for example, in the shopping malls, in the car, or in the park while playing.

Let us now convert this scene into a model describing a dialogue between the Self and its environment. The garden will take in this situation the role of the identity and the public garden/park the role of a social myth (May, 1991). The self is always in dialogue with its environment, which is not simply describable as one myth or one culture, it is a polysemic multiverse of connections and socially hyper generalized "communities." In the case of our garden and private garden this can be described as not only the existence of one public green field, but by an extremely high number of diverged green areas, restricted in subareas and so on. This could be seen as representatives for communities as, for example, our sport clubs, online communities, and political parties.

The private garden on the other hand can be seen as the identity of an individual, in this occasion of my proper identity. The flowers in this private garden are still connected with the gardens of the others, one garden besides another one. In this field we as caretakers are moving in between the meaning we made, while redefining meaning based on an anticipated future (Campill, 2021). While moving we are restricted and unable to see all of our environment, wherefore the hierarchical order of what flower is personally seen the most important one can change easily as soon as one flower disappears and another one appears (Campill & von Fircks, 2022).

In the case of Scene 1, we now have the situation that we are spreading one of the sunflower seeds in another "environment." This is equivalent to a simple discussion between one individual with other members of a community, so all of them are for example members of the same sport clubs, for example, "The Red Lions." Now while discussing we shared some of our own opinions related to the meaning we made of our lifetime. We shared for example an I-position that was unknown from the other club members as for example the "I as an environmentalist."

Scene 2

A year later I was running again into the park, to play as usual on the swing or with my friends, while running through the whole playground area. And what a surprise behind one of my favorite hiding spots I found one of my favorite flowers growing silently and beautifully in its corner. Of course, I had to show it to all my friends, whereby some of them wanted to break the flower for fun, which made me quite sad.

While sharing for example of the seeds of the I-position as "environmentalist" some other players started to react toward the rupture created by the new meaning. In this moment the individuals that are together defining the socially constructed are challenged by a changeset that happens in relation toward their together compromised and elaborated role as community. Other similar and diverged perspectives, voices/flowers, started to spread and resulted in the process of redefining the shared myth in such a manner that it overlaps/resonances with the meanings/beliefs best matching with the communities' history and with its current members.

This example shows clearly that the influence of an individual into any social construct is happening and is even part of our everyday life. The evaluation and the redefinition of meaning is therefore not only an individual tool to influence the own identity but is also a tool that influences the social layers, definable in everyday language as culture.

Scene 3

Over the following years the flower was always appearing and disappearing again. Whereby more and more children started to admire the strong and quite rarely seen flower. One day I returned to the playground and found a small area protected by something more or less like a fence. My once favorite hiding place (while not a good one, as it appears) became the area for these beautiful flowers. I was sad of course, because I had lost my favorite spot, but nevertheless this situation also made me proud, because I experienced somehow the possibility for this flower to be loved by more people than only by myself.

In this last situation, we can now observe that the unrelated seeds found their way into the park and even became a cultivated part of it. By converting into a phenomenon, we gain the ability to see that a seed or voice once shared has not to disappear impact less. A voice can slowly be cultivated and integrated into a social identity, as for example, The Red Lions' team, would start to use only recycled material for their club merchandise. This example is identical to the metaphor that was discussed, evaluated, and finally added in an adjusted manner into the shared identity. This leads of course as well to a dissonance in the single self, because the I-as an environmentalist in its constructed multitude of other voices has also to accept the socially generated meaning. "Do I want to share this identity?" "And does this meaning match with mine?" are still accruing and challenging now the self as the caretaker of the own garden.

Condensed into one sentence, this means that the dialogical self is always connected with a dialogical self, of an environmental construction, and that this results in everyday life ruptures that roots from the cultivation of ourselves—we as fragments of a caretaker in the public garden while being also only a current fragment of the caretakers of our own self.

GENERAL DISCUSSION

By recapitulating the interrelation between the multi-voiced self, by using the garden as metaphor, we gain the ability to not only follow the self into its multiple connectivity, but also to emphasize with essential influences of nature and current self-realization in the form of cultivation. In the orchestra of voices, we gained the ability to crystalize the junglification and cultivation acts as two essential roles. These diverged forces, interacting with each other, initialize the suggestion that the cultivation of the own identity has to be able to counteract, if necessary, against the natural conditions imbedded in biology, genetics, or already initialized reactions. That means that the act of cultivation (Figure 11.4) is able to overcome the potential junglification (Figure 11.3), if the accumulation of the own voices is amplifying each other, into a strong enough current self that can manipulate the running natural procedure (as biological or in the past strongly cultivated behavioral tendencies, that distress with the current understanding of "Who-I-want-to-be" and "Who-I-am"—allowing the self can influence the own development.

Based on the previous metaphorical elaborations, we can underline that cultivation is an essential process in a human being's everyday life. To cultivate means to generate and reconstruct meaning based on our experiences and our anticipated "maybe" future while challenging the current now. Furthermore, experiences we are making in the "right now" can trigger the environment, leading to a polysemic-multi-voice in which the members of the environment or community are confronting new meaning initialized by a single individual. By visualizing the previous scenes (see Figure 11.6) we can underline the impact that can be found in the act of cultivating one's own identity by the current self.

It is essential to underline that Figure 11.6 is illustrating a process in a specific development—direction. It inhabits the particular meaning of an individual in dialogue with the social environment, while generating an identification rupture that leads to a new adapted social self. Furthermore, it can be used to underline the importance of the awareness of human

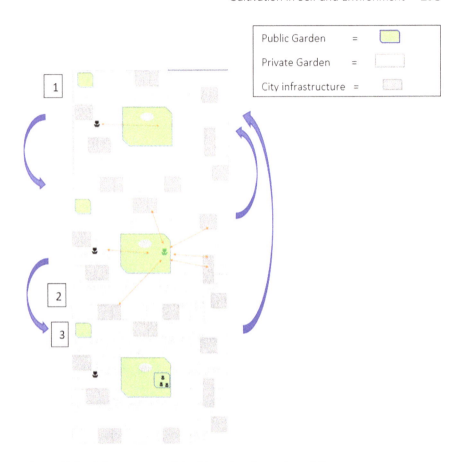

Figure 11.6 Infrastructure of the blooming flower in public.

complexity by growing and sharing. After sharing a belief of ours, those do not have to result in resonance, the potential of how the meaning, entered the social field, can grow, or disappear during the social meaning generation is infinite, leading us to the special use of Figure 11.6. On one side it allows us to follow a phenomenon of sharing into the generation of a social myth. An example of such an individual impact can be found in Scene 4.

Scene 4: *Kaze no denwa*
(風の電話: **The Telephone Booth of the Wind**)

It is a telephone box that a private citizen had placed in his backyard to make calls to his cousin, who was torn away from life. The line is visibly not connected. It was his individual way of fighting the pain in his heart.

The overwhelming force of a natural disaster, tsunami, on March 11, 2011, took thousands of lives, separated thousands of families forever. The tsunami brought pain, death, and grief to the cities of the *Iwatori* prefecture. After the disaster, the people had to reorganize their life while fighting the overwhelming grief and pain that the tsunami had brought. One of the resulting manners of challenging the pain in their hearts can be found in a garden of Ōtsuchi. Then the landlord and constructor of the telephone booth decided to share his garden with others, especially with those who try to fill the holes in their life, left by the natural disaster. Others beside him started to come to his garden with the wish to call those who were taken away by the force of nature or diseases. Even the local press started to be interested in this place and the people that were visiting it. The press reported on this, so the visit of the *Kaze no Denwa* developed slowly into a mass phenomenon. The private garden resulted into a symbol of hope, for those fighting the pain of losing their beloved (Figure 11.7).

Figure 11.7 *Kaze no denwa* (風の電話), Ōkinawa.

Secondly, we can experience through Figure 11.6 the awareness of how a shared I-position of beliefs and feelings grow separately to the initializing I-position. The shared position can be seen as the seed that generates a new flower, in a different new context.

In conclusion the current self's act of cultivation does not only result in changes of the own meaning-making process, but also in the initialization of a rupture in wider layers of society, communities. Cultivation of one's own identity is, therefore, related with the cultivation of the hyper generalized meaning in communities. This means that cultivation is always more than an individual directed act and can result in a social changeset of initialized meaning. Whereby it is elementary to understand that the reaction chain in Figure 11.6 has not resulted in the resonating social adaptation and integration of the flower/meaning. An initialized rupture provides only the possibility to change the environment, whereby it is not mandatory to result in such a change.

This allows us to see the concept of mainstream in different eyes. The mainstream-ghost is seen as an idea or activity that is shared by most people and is often linked with the hyper generalization of natural rules. We gain the awareness that the mainstream is in the social layers an equivalent of the current self. Leading to the belief that mainstream is of greater use as a fluid term that needs the ability to grow and change, by standing in dialogue with the multiple voices—inhabiting its myth. The mainstream that we are fighting in psychology is therefore not the existence of the mainstream, but the danger of conserving the already existing form of mainstream, generated by the older voices and voice constellations. Instead, it needs to be modified into a fluid term bonded to the always renewed voice-constellation and redefined meaning-making process, of the new experiences made by the current individuals living in its society.

In general, the garden and the meadow are tools that inhabit the potential to be more than only metaphors, they are able to become a new kind of symbols used to educate our self and change the world like we have seen it before. Nevertheless, as for every tool the garden as a symbol inhabits its own restrictions. The meadow and garden cannot simply be used without contributing a clear and well-constructed elaboration of the organic connections into the matching phenomenological context.

The construction elaboration of the metaphor is linked with the complex knowledge that we can visualize through such an organic field, meanwhile it can be linked with personal past experiences of individuals and their surroundings. It has to be underlined therefore, that the elaboration of such complexity is directly linked to the act of invading this same multidimensionality. Metaphors that inhabit the potential of generating a resonating field for complex knowledge, can also inhabit the potential to become allegories. Even when those two forms of defining the own meaning field are theoretically seen differently defined, the individual understanding is not bonded to a similar construct definition. Elaborating complex phenomena is therefore challenged in generating a manner of sharing knowledge that allows to trigger the symbolic interpretation of such concepts, as for example the garden, and those not interfere or invade the emotional relation that an individual could conserve in his allegorical and/or emotional understanding.

This means that the use of such a metaphor can challenge research to generate alternative holistic forms of complex knowledge, by using already generated and social manifested knowledge constructs as metaphors. Whereby this holistic view can result in a deeper understanding of the visualized phenomena, meanwhile the risk is reduced to neglect relevant and needed factors inhabiting the process.

REFERENCES

Bisgaard C. H., Campill M. A., von Fircks E., & Valsiner, J. (2024). Layered attunement: Internal dialogues of intersubjectivity. In O. Erstad, B. Hagtvet, & J. Wertsch (Eds.), *Education and dialogue in polarized societies: Dialogic perspectives in times of change*. Oxford University Press.

Bonfante, P., & Anca, I. A. (2009). Plants, mycorrhizal fungi, and bacteria: A network of interactions. *Annual review of microbiology, 63*(1), 363–383.

Campill, M. A. (2021). Towards a wholistic model of identity: Why not a meadow? *Integrative Psychological and Behavioral Science, 55*(1), 112–127.

Campill, M. A., & von Fircks, E. (2022). *The pluralistic-self* [manuscript in preparation].

Campill, M. A., & Valsiner, J. (2021). Spiral and helical models for psychology: Leaving linearity behind. *Human Arenas, 2021*, 1–21.

Chittleborough, G. D., & Treagust, D. F. (2009). Why models are advantageous to learning science. *Educación química, 20*(1), 12–17.

Dalley, S. (1993). Ancient Mesopotamian gardens and the identification of the hanging gardens of Babylon resolved. *Garden History, 21*(1), 1–13.

Elgar, F. J., Craig, W., & Trites, S. J. (2013). Family dinners, communication, and mental health in Canadian adolescents. *Journal of Adolescent Health, 52*(4), 433–438.

Hermans, H. J. (2014). Self as a society of I-positions: A dialogical approach to counseling. *The Journal of Humanistic Counseling, 53*(2), 134–159.

James, W. (1890). The perception of reality. *Principles of Psychology, 2*, 283–324.

King, M. L. (2008). *Women of the Renaissance*. University of Chicago Press.

Maran, T. (2019). Deep ecosemiotics: Forest as a semiotic model 1. *Recherches sémiotiques, 39*(1), 287–303.

May, R. (1991). *The cry for myth* (1st ed.). Norton.

Reade, J. (2000). Alexander the Great and the Hanging Gardens of Babylon. *Iraq, 62*, 195–217.

Salomon, G. (1981). Communication and education: Social and psychological interactions. *People & Communication, 13*, 9–271.

Thacker, C. (1985). *The history of gardens*. University of California Press.

To be *and* not to be: A matter of inclusive separation.
Source: Google Images.

CHAPTER 12

MOVING THROUGH RACIAL GARDENS

Personal and Collective Dimensions of Racial Becoming: A Transcultural Autoethnographic Account

Márcio de Abreu
Federal University of Bahia

As participants in this special issue on the relationships between the collective and personal dimensions of culture, we were challenged to use the garden metaphor as inspiration to discuss our individual research topics. Having accepted the challenge, I will begin this essay by sharing a story about plants and gardens that hopefully will lead us to reflect on some of the cultural-psychological aspects of racial identity-forming in transcultural contexts.

In 2013, an article from *The Sunday Times* entitled "Coca: Emerging Gardens of Evil" reported that residents from the Matara District (Sri Lanka) were under investigation by local authorities for cultivating illegal coca plants in their home gardens. The interesting thing about the story is that these homeowners claimed to have no idea they were growing the plant from which cocaine is derived. The blunder happened not because the gardeners were unaware of the connection between coca plants and the famous psychoactive intoxicant but because they thought they were cultivating sandalwood. Ironically, questions were being raised over whether the Forest Department was responsible for the confusion by distributing the coca plants some years back, under a project that was supposed to hand out sandalwood seedlings to the residents of Matara. Although sandalwood and coca plants can be visually distinguished from each other by some noticeable details (such as the tone of green of their leaves and how these are arranged on the twig of the shoot), it could be hard for the untrained eye to differentiate one from the other, especially during their seedling stages (*The Sunday Times*, 2013).

Gardens are one of those places full of hidden knowledge, accessible only to the initiated. As the above story shows, in a garden, not everything is what it seems to be. It takes some learning to detect certain nuances, such as the small details that indicate a relevant distinction between two plants that, at first glance, look the same. This also implies that gardens are an arena of negotiation between culture and nature. That's because as soon as we start categorizing and organizing the natural world around us, we inevitably resort to an underlying structure of culturally shared meanings and practices (see "Editorial Introduction: Expanding the Concept of the Garden: From Japanese Zen Gardens to Human Development"). Any plot of ground filled with plants becomes a "garden" once we attribute some culturally constructed meanings to its components, classifying and arranging them around according to such meanings (including which plants should stay in the garden and which ones should be ruled out).

If we think of the garden as a metaphor for a social order organized according to the parameters of a certain culture, we could also think of the members of that social order as the different plants that live in the garden. As in the case of plants in a garden, members of a particular social order are also restrained by the culturally produced categorization systems to which they are subjected. Different people occupy different places and play different social roles based on culturally constructed categories, such as race, class, and gender.

Nonetheless, there's nothing further from the truth than to think that plants in a garden and the people of a particular social order are passive beings, waiting to be categorized and put in their "proper" places. Plants can be deceiving and misleading, as in the case of the Matara gardeners, and so do people, as in situations when we are not completely sure of how to categorize someone in terms of their race, class, and even gender. Plants also have roots and branches that grow in different directions, regardless of the will of gardeners. In such cases, pruning becomes a form of domestication. The same happens to the people who refuse to be put in the "social boxes" created to keep them in "their place." There is always some form of negotiation that needs to occur so that a cultural system can be reproduced and a certain order maintained, no matter how violent, unequal, and unfair both the system and the negotiation processes may be. If the garden represents a particular social order and the plants represent its members, we can think of the gardeners as the cultural mechanisms behind the garden's organization.

Every culture has a dynamic repertoire of meanings and classificatory systems that provide a certain order. In a way, arriving in a new culture is like walking into someone else's garden. We have to become familiar with the repertoire of meanings from which things are individually categorized and collectively organized if we are to avoid overstepping boundaries and "disturbing the order." Much like the homeowners from the Matara district (who got in trouble for not knowing how to distinguish coca from sandalwood), it's a matter of time before we find ourselves in an awkward situation for engaging in some form of misinterpretation or misjudgment of actions, events, and even people, due to our lack of some specific cultural knowledge. One of the cultural domains where such misjudgments and misinterpretations often occur is the arena of racial identities, and this becomes particularly interesting in transcultural contexts.

Given the title that heads this chapter, it should be a little clearer now where these analogies are taking us. Like plants in a garden, we tend to perceive race as a feature of the natural landscape, fixed in the determining realities of biology. But despite some biological characteristics, arbitrarily chosen to create some form of coherent classification, a plant can be categorized differently and perform different functions in different cultural contexts, and so is the case with people when it comes to the ways they are racially labeled.

In this essay, I use an autoethnographic approach to address issues of racial identity-forming in transcultural contexts. As someone who describes how it feels to walk through someone else's garden, I draw on my personal journey as an expatriate in the United States to examine the relationships between the collective and personal dimensions of culture in my own experience of racial becoming (for more on autoethnography and immigration, see also Chapter 13, [this volume] Life in a Different Soil: My Existential Mobility as an Immigrant).

MOVING THROUGH RACIAL GARDENS

Social orders (much like gardens) are organized within the parameters of a certain culture. One definition of culture is that of a dynamic system of construction and exchange of meanings that produces more or less stable interpretations of reality, shared among members of a given social group. As meaning-making beings, our experiences in the world are mediated by the signs produced within and by the cultures we participate in (Valsiner, 2014). In semiotic terms, a sign can be briefly described as something that stands for an additional something, for someone, in some respect or capacity (Valsiner, 2007a). Thus, any element of reality can work as a sign for any person at any moment.

Human bodies are signs. First, because until it becomes the object of certain culturally channeled signifying practices, that which we call a human body is nothing more than an ordinary "something" existing in the physical world; a mere object of cognition. Second, because all human bodies always stand for an additional something other than just a human body. The same way a plant is not merely a plant but a coca plant, a sandalwood tree, a lady fern, and so on, human bodies are not merely human bodies but the body of a woman, of a man, of a child, of an elder, of an aborigine, of an Asian, and so on.

Being born and raised in Brazil, and having a certain combination of physical features, my human body had always been culturally interpreted as a sign that stood for "White male." At that time, one of the privileges of being White in Brazil (and probably in any other place where Whites are the dominant racial group) was to not have to worry or think about race. If, on the one hand, I was never socially harassed, insulted, or treated unfairly for being White, on the other, the social critique of Whiteness and White privilege had not yet become a hot topic outside the academic sphere. Accordingly, while I always knew I was White, I never looked at my Whiteness as a crucial dimension of my identity. To consider race an irrelevant category, with regards to the ways I understood myself as a human being, was part of my personal culture.

The idea that there is a personal culture, distinguishable from a collective culture, is a mere heuristic device to remind us that the person (in one's personal uniqueness) and the cultural world are always related to each other in a mutually constructive process of constant internalization, reconstruction and externalization of meanings and values (Valsiner, 2007b). Therefore, as a White person, to consider race an irrelevant aspect of my identity was to be part of a culture in which Whites were socially perceived as non-raced people. One of the structural properties of Whiteness is to be racially unmarked, that is, the ability to render itself "invisible" as a racial signifier (Green et al., 2007; Ibrahim, 2020). In most cases, Whites can navigate socially without having their race become a cause for concern regarding the preservation of their physical, social, and/or psychological integrity (e.g., Have you ever seen or heard of a White person being followed and harassed by store security merely for being White?). Nonetheless, the social perception of Whites as non-raced people is a culturally constructed "illusion"; a cognitive effect produced by White normativity (Abreu, 2020). And here is an interesting paradox: It is precisely because White bodies are socially perceived as White that, due to White normativity, they can enjoy the privilege of being racially "unnoticeable."

The countless minute decisions that organize social practices are constantly informed by judgments about people's capacities and worth, based on what they look like, where they come from, or how they speak, that is, racial judgments (Dyer, 2000). That goes to people of any race. However, Whiteness (as much as any other racial experience) is a culturally situated phenomenon. I had to learn this in practice well before I was able to put it in academic terms.

I lived in the United States for 4 years, during which I had the opportunity to experience how it feels to be socially perceived (and treated) as an ethnic minority. There is no shortage of examples in the history of that country in which race has been understood in terms of ethnicity, nationality, and even religion, whilst the very hegemonic notion of "Americanness" is marked by a historical conflation with Whiteness (see, e.g., Hitlin et al., 2007; Jacobson, 2001; Leiwei Li, 2004; Rana, 2016; Roediger, 2008). Therefore, many "White" Brazilians who move to the United States are generally doomed to experience the impossibility of fully integrating themselves into the dominant racial group. As pointed out by Fitts (2012), to a large degree, widespread tolerance and appreciation of ethnic and cultural otherness in the United States is a myth. This is all the more evident in the case of immigrants from so-called "Third World" countries despite their efforts to meet the enormous demands of assimilation.

However, it would be dishonest to say that we are not given any chance to enjoy certain racial privileges when we arrive in the land of Uncle Sam. When talking about the Jewish experience, Frantz Fanon (2008) said the following:

> All the same, the Jew can be unknown in his Jewishness. He is not wholly what he is. One hopes, one waits. His actions, his behavior are the final determinant. He is a white man, and, apart from some rather debatable characteristics, he can sometimes go unnoticed. (p. 87)

To a certain extent, that's the situation of many "White" Brazilians who venture into the United States. As in the case of the Jewish, it is the corporeal dimension of race that allows some of us to be able to, on certain occasions, go unnoticed among White Americans. However, in many of these cases, "passing" is nothing more than a circumstantial and ephemeral privilege. Although looking "White" and speaking English with a non-Spanish accent may enable some "White" Brazilians to pass for Europeans (or even for White Americans in some cases), Brazilian identity in the United States (as much as any other Latin American identity) is linked to a sociopolitical dynamic that ranks people from "Third World" countries (in general) and Latinos in the United States (in particular) as inferior, regardless of one's skin color (Beserra, 2005).

I was not "White like them," that was the new cultural reality with which I had to come to terms. For some "White" Brazilians, such a realization comes as a rude awakening. In my case, it came gradually, in the form of culturally specific experiences whose racial connotations I learned to detect as I became familiar with the new social dynamics in which I was immersed (see, e.g., Figure 12.1). It was rather destabilizing to witness my Whiteness slowly fall apart, denaturalized by a hierarchical structure in which I was not the point of reference from which non-Whiteness was measured and judged. For a "White" Brazilian, such an experience is lived as a transition from being the "signifying-subject" to become the "signified-Other." My personal culture was reshaped, and so was I. I had to adjust, and this meant that I had to resignify my own identity.

When exposed to new cultural contexts, the person constructs cultural novelty through the relationship between personal sense and personal conduct. Therefore, the notion of personal culture refers not only to the person-centered subjective experience of internalizing and reinterpreting collectively shared meanings but also to the immediate externalization of one's personal sense system through conduct (Valsiner, 2007b, 2014). Internalized collective-cultural meanings, such as the ethnic/racial categorization of Brazilians as Latinos, are transformed by the person into personal-cultural systems of sense: for example, I'm not "White like them." The person then contributes to the reconstruction of collective-cultural

Figure 12.1 The homogenization of Latino identity. On the right: me and my American brother on our way to a Halloween party (1995). At the time, I was living with a White American family in Lansing, Michigan. Having never heard of the comedy duo Cheech and Chong (picture on the left), I naively agreed to be Cheech. If, on the one hand, I was completely unaware of the racial/ethnic connotations of being chosen to impersonate a Mexican character, on the other, such a lack of racial awareness was also an expression of my Brazilian Whiteness. While the above episode may indicate that I was not "White like them," I was always regarded as part of the family and treated with the most love and respect by my American parents and siblings.

meanings by externalizing their personal-cultural systems of sense through concrete meaningful action. On most occasions, rather than hiding the ethnic markers that kept me from fully integrating into the dominant racial group, I highlighted them as a way of showing pride in my origins.

In *Immigration, Language, and Racial Becoming*, Awad Ibrahim (2020) quotes the following passage from the novel *Americanah* by Chimamanda N. Adichie:

> Dear Non-American Black, when you make the choice to come to America, you become black. Stop arguing. Stop saying I'm Jamaican or I'm Ghanaian. America doesn't care. So, what if you weren't "black" in your country? You're in America now. We all have our moments of initiation into the Society of Former Negroes. Mine was in a class in undergrad when I was asked to give the black perspective, only I have no idea what that was. (p. 168)

I believe my moment of initiation happened when, at the age of 16, I was asked to fill out a form at the public school where I studied during my first time in the United States. I had never had to racially or ethnically classify myself formally, and although I knew I was neither Black nor Asian, I had no idea what the word Caucasian meant. I sought the front desk lady for help. She looked at me and asked disinterestedly, "Where are you from, honey?" After hearing my answer, she told me to mark Hispanic. I thought about protesting (after all, we speak Portuguese in Brazil), but then I thought it would be pointless.

The passage from Adichie's novel is used by Ibrahim (2020) to introduce a discussion on how Black immigrants in the United States go through an intricate process of identity transformation where their identification is not with mainstream representations of "Americanness" but with North-American Blackness. In other words, for immigrants of African descent, to become American is to become Black. In our case, things seem to be a little more complicated. When we arrive in the United States, our primary identification is usually with Whiteness due to our own notions of racial identity as White Brazilians. We are then forced to enter an ethnographic process of observation and translation of what it means to be White in the United States. As a result, different forms of identity reconstruction begin to take shape, largely influenced by affective/subjective responses to our new personal experiences of being "seen" as members of an ethnic minority.

As pointed out by Marrow (2003), Brazilian immigrants tend to identify according to their pre-migration racial schemas. Nonetheless, the self-perception of White Brazilian immigrants as "White" often comes into real conflict with the way many U.S. natives view foreign-born Brazilians as Hispanics/Latinos. American and Brazilian notions of race and ethnicity are thus asserted, challenged, and reorganized in a dialectical convergence of identifications that are both internal (assertive and voluntary) and external (assigned and involuntary) to the person, thereby transforming both personal and collective notions of race and ethnicity in the United States. As White Brazilians are redefined (and redefine themselves) as Latinos, an extra layer of complexity is added to an already multiethnic, multiracial, and highly contested category, thus influencing the social construction of "Latinidad" itself.

One of the main features of culture is to provide social suggestions orienting feelings. What makes our personal experiences unique are the negotiations between social suggestions to culturally consistent meanings and the feelings that emerge during our personal trajectories (Tateo, 2018). As I was pulled into a social order structured around its own definition of Whiteness, I was forced to reconstruct my identity through an affective/subjective process of negotiations between new social suggestions regarding race and ethnicity (including quickly figuring out how I was racially and ethnically "seen" by Americans) and personal attachments to my previous racial identification as a White Brazilian (see, e.g., Figure 12.2). My personal-cultural process of sense-making required a resignification of the relationships between skin color, culture, and nationality that was highly influenced by the feelings produced by my personal experiences of being accepted/rejected into the dominant racial group. This process ultimately determined the extent to which I was personally inclined to reject/assimilate American Whiteness, strengthen/loosen the ties with Brazilian culture and community, or

Figure 12.2 Becoming an ethnic minority. English as a Second Language program. Class of 1995, led by Ms. Clark (on the far left of the photo). Classes were offered free of charge at Lansing Community College to foreign immigrants.

even adopt/reject a Latino identity. Looking back, there was no right path to be taken, just different possibilities of racial becoming.

RACIAL BECOMING AND THE LIMITS OF TRANSCULTURALITY

The father of Anglo-Ghanaian philosopher Kwame Anthony Appiah wrote a letter to his children shortly before his death. The letter reminded them of two basic things: their double ancestry (Ghanaian and English) and the fact that they were citizens of the world. According to him, to be a "citizen of the world" meant that wherever they chose to live (and, as citizens of the world, they could surely choose to live anywhere), they should make sure they left that place better than they found it (Appiah, 1997).

My father also constantly encouraged me and my brothers to become "citizens of the world." Nonetheless, whenever he expressed his idea of world citizenship, there was never any mention of the duties inherent in being a citizen. In a certain sense, for my father, seeing his sons become "citizens of the world" meant continuing the project initiated by my grandfather, a small-time farmer from the backlands of Bahia who managed to escape poverty and move to the state capital to provide better life opportunities for his nine children. However, my father's personal-cultural system of sense regarding world citizenship also reflected an aspect of Brazilian culture eloquently expressed in the words of Milton Santos (1996):

> The fact that the middle-classes enjoy privileges, not rights, keeps other Brazilians from having rights. That's why there are almost no citizens in Brazil. There are the ones who do not want to be citizens, that is, the middle-classes, and there are those who cannot be citizens, which are everyone else, starting with Blacks. (p. 134)

When I was born, we were already part of the first group. Today, whoever looks at me does not imagine that I am the grandson of a peasant. There are no visual clues that culturally suggest a link between my physical appearance and my family history of socioeconomic exclusion. Certainly, that is not the case for Black Brazilians.

Unlike Apphia, my brothers and I did not have dual citizenship. My father's insistence on the idea of world citizenship was driven by his dream of seeing us living in a "first world" country (preferably, the United States). That dream was accompanied by the conviction that we were free to move around most parts of the planet as we pleased and without suspicion (as is normally the case of those who enjoy the privilege of being born in certain countries). I tend to believe that such confidence originated, most likely, from a (personal-cultural) sense of entitlement produced by the internalization of the (collectively shared) social privileges of being White in Brazil. Back then, I was yet to discover the power of language and its sign systems.

Language is the vehicle through which collective-cultural meanings are produced and shared among members of a particular culture. Rather than just a passive means of describing or transmitting information about things, it is a constitutive feature of actions, events, and situations (Whitehead, 2017). When we attribute, through language, a certain label to a certain person (e.g., Latino), we are actively (culturally) selecting some characteristics of that person (while neglecting others) as the defining criteria of that particular label (e.g., having a certain origin, coming from a certain country or belonging to a certain culture). Once the label is applied, assumptions and expectations about that person are formed, which, by their turn, orient social practices and conducts, thus producing real practical effects in people's lives (Hall, 2016).

By looking at the relationship between the discursive aspects of language and the idea of racial becoming, one way we can think of the resignification of White Brazilians as Latinos is in terms of a process of racialization that happens under the rubrics of national origin and immigration. For instance, I've always felt that I was looked at with suspicion by American immigration officers as soon as they saw my Brazilian passport. Perhaps it was just a cultural thing, I thought. In any case, I had no reason to be worried, after all, according to my father, I was a "citizen of the world." But the feeling was always there. Was I misinterpreting their behavior? This question was answered the day I was denied entry in the United States despite having a valid tourist visa. It seems like one collective-cultural meaning shared by many Americans is that every Latin American trying to enter the United States is a potential illegal immigrant. While some nationalities seem to experience world citizenship as a birthright, others become the object of suspicion and rigorous border control. There are situations when the origin of a passport matters more than one's skin color.

Any adequate version of a personal life course has to be constructed along the lines specified by the cultural context in which we find ourselves (Valsiner, 2007a). From this perspective, it would be wise to reflect on what situations racial identities that were forged in specific cultural settings can operate as sufficiently stable cultural devices to allow a smooth transit across transcultural contexts. Eight years after being denied entry into the United States, I received a scholarship to attend a Master's program in Critical Theory and Cultural Studies at The University of Nottingham in England. After experiencing being "seen" as an ethnic minority during my time in the United States, I was well aware of the flimsiness of my Whiteness as a Latin American student on my way to the country that was the largest colonial empire of the 19th century. I learned that I could not afford to "be" White in cultural contexts where Whiteness was not likely to be fully granted to me. But I had also learned that there were some circumstantial advantages in being ethnically and racially marked, such as earning a scholarship specifically reserved for Latin American students.

Put in such terms, it may sound that racial identities can be joggled up based on direct contextual influence, as if the person could choose from two or more identities according to situations defined by outer contexts. Certainly, as much as I am aware of the social constraints that I am likely to experience due to the ways I am ethnically and racially marked in certain cultural settings, I also know that I will continue to enjoy the social privileges of being White in Brazil, regardless of my social experiences elsewhere. Nonetheless, such a pragmatic view of race seems to privilege its functional aspect as a social marker while concealing the affective/subjective processes involved in identity (re)construction in contexts of cultural novelty.

Experiences with cultural novelty inevitably make an imprint on the person. Any meeting with new cultural contexts is interpreted subjectively and becomes part of a cognitive and affective experience that orients choices and self-definition (Gamsakhurdia, 2018). Thus far, I have looked at my own transcultural journey to address some of the affective/subjective aspects of my own process of racial becoming. Nonetheless, one question remains: "How do I 'see' myself racially?"

Perhaps, there is no easy answer to this question unless I am willing to risk falling into social determinism, on the one hand, or to flirt with cultural relativism, on the other. Equally problematic is the idea that an awareness of the culturally constructed aspect of race can result in a mindset that completely transcends racial identification. However appealing, this might be just a naive idea, and a quite dangerous one if confused with an invitation to invest in the White liberal myth of "color-blindness." Besides, an awareness of the culturally constructed aspect of racial identities does not make us fully aware or in control of the affective dimension of our personal experiences, nor of its influence on our subjective processes as racialized and racializing beings. The truth is that even the very notion of racial becoming is invariably immersed in the politics of race and identity and the affects they inspire. Furthermore, to live a transcultural life does not mean dwelling above the relations of power that constitute us socially.

If racial identity is just an aspect of myself, perhaps I can resort to Jean-Paul Sartre's (1992) phenomenology to acknowledge that I am altogether in and out of this aspect at the same time. I am altogether within it because as I manifest myself in that aspect at a given moment in time and space, I am doomed to experience the objective/subjective effects of this manifestation. I am altogether outside, for this manifestation consists of a culturally cognoscible image of myself that will never be complete but only trusted to be so in a particular moment in time and space and, as such, it must always remain open for becoming.

BY WAY OF CONCLUSION

I began this essay by accepting the challenge to use the metaphor of the garden as inspiration to introduce a discussion about some cultural-psychological aspects of racial identity-forming. From there, I delved into an autoethnographic journey to explore the affective/subjective aspects of racial becoming by looking at the relationship between the personal and collective dimensions of my own transcultural experiences.

From a cultural-psychological perspective, the purpose of autoethnography is to offer an understanding of deep affective/subjective experiences from the vantage point of the researcher's personal trajectory (for more on autoethnography and cultural psychology see also Chapter 9, "Djinns and Radioactive Materials: An Abductive Autoethnography on a Garden of Invisible Entities"). This is done whilst simultaneously examining the dimensions of the self that develop with culture while being systemically connected to others (Tsuchimoto, 2021). Although this analysis is based on my personal journey, it also refers to the particularities of the cultural systems (or racial gardens, to stick to the challenge) through which I transit. As such, I hope to have been able to move beyond that which is purely personal so as to contribute to an understanding of the generic nature of my own transcultural experiences.

I should also say that my preference for the term transculturality points to the possibility of attributing to the prefix *trans*—a different meaning other than that of cultural diversity (as in the case of multiculturality) or cultural-crossing (as in the case of interculturality) to evoke the pervasive and persistent character of becoming, despite all historical attempts to convert any form of cultural identity into something fixed and stiffened by well-defined boundaries (Monceri, 2019). Multiple cultural connections are becoming ever more decisive in terms of identity formation. Whenever a person is cast into different cultural contexts, the linking of transcultural components becomes a specific task in identity-forming. Thus, to work on one's identity is becoming more and more to work on the integration/negotiation of components of different cultural origin (Welsch, 1999).

From this perspective, the awkward situations we are subjected to experience when arriving in a "foreign culture" can be seen as the very occasions from which cultural novelty is produced. Rather than mere moments of exposure to cultural diversity or cultural bridging, the transcultural experience reshapes both our identities and the cultural environment in which we find ourselves at a particular moment. This is also the case when it comes to racial identities. Racialized perceptions of ourselves and others shift over time, from one place to another, and for particular collective/personal cultural reasons. As such, no single dimension is a person's "true" or "correct" race, but each of these dimensions expresses something different about the way that people experience race in their daily lives (Roth, 2016). Thus, the concepts of transculturality and racial becoming come together in this chapter to remind ourselves that race does not reside on any predetermined fact of nature but in the contingencies of culture.

DECLARATION OF CONFLICT OF INTEREST

The author has no known conflict of interest to disclose.

FUNDING

The author is a scholarship holder from the Brazilian Federal Foundation for Support and Evaluation of Graduate Education (CAPES).

REFERENCES

Abreu, M. N. (2020). The cultural psychology of White normativity: A draft to the concept of *White psyche. Human Arenas*, 3, 297–309. https://doi.org/10.1007/s42087-019-00087-5

Appiah, K. A. (1997). Cosmopolitan patriots. *Critical Inquiry*, 23(3), 617–639.

Beserra, B. (2005). From Brazilians to Latinos? Racialization and Latinidad in the making of Brazilian carnival in Los Angeles. *Latino Studies*, 3, 53–75. https://doi.org/10.1057/palgrave.lst.8600131

Dyer, R. (2000). The matter of Whiteness. In L. Back & J. Solomos (Eds.), *Theories of race and racism: A reader* (pp. 539–548). Routledge.

Fanon, F. (2008). *Black skin, White masks*. Pluto Press.

Fitts, A. (2012). Coming of age and the transnational subject in the works of Judith Ortiz Cofer. *L'érudit Franco-Espagnol*, 1, 58–71.

Gamsakhurdia, V. (2018). Adaptation in a dialogical perspective: From acculturation to proculturation. *Culture & Psychology*, 24(4), 545–559. https://doi.org/10.1177/1354067X18791977

Green, M. J., Sonn, C. C., & Matsebula, J. (2007). Reviewing Whiteness: Theory, research, and possibilities. *South African Journal of Psychology*, 37(3), 389–419.

Hall, S. (2016). *Cultura e Representação*. Apicuri.

Hitlin, S., Brown, J., & Elder, J. (2007). Measuring Latinos: Racial vs. ethnic classification and self-understandings. *Social Forces*, 86(2), 587–611. https://doi.org/10.1093/sf/86.2.587

Ibrahim, A. (2020). Immigration, language, and racial becoming. In H. S. Alim, A. Reyes, & P. V. Kroskrity (Eds.), *The Oxford handbook of language and race* (pp. 167–185). https://doi.org/10.1093/oxfordhb/9780190845995.013.10

Jacobson, M. F. (2001). Becoming Caucasian: Vicissitudes of Whiteness in American politics and culture. *Identities: Global Studies in Culture and Power, 8*(1), 83–104. https://doi.org/10.1080/1070289X.2001.9962685

Leiwei Li, D. (2004). On ascriptive and acquisitional Americanness: The accidental Asian and the illogic of assimilation. *Contemporary Literature, 45*(1), 106–134.

Marrow, H. (2003). To be or not to be (Hispanic or Latino): Brazilian racial and ethnic identity in the United States. *Ethnicities, 3*(4), 427–464. https://doi.org/10.1177/1468796803003004001

Monceri, F. (2019). Beyond universality: Rethinking transculturality and the transcultural self. *Journal of Multicultural Discourses, 14*(1), 78–91. https://doi.org/10.1080/17447143.2019.1604715

Rana, J. (2016). The racial infrastructure of terror-industrial complex. *Social Text, 34*(4), 111–138. https://doi.org/10.1215/01642472-3680894

Roediger, D. R. (2008). *How race survived U.S. history: From settlement and slavery to the Obama phenomenon*. Verso.

Roth, W. D. (2016). The multiple dimensions of race. *Ethnic and Racial Studies, 39*(8), 1310–1338. https://doi.org/10.1080/01419870.2016.1140793

Santos, M. (1996). As cidadanias mutiladas. In J. Lerner (Ed.), *O preconceito* (pp. 133–144). Imprensa Oficial do Estado.

Sartre, J. (1992). *Being and nothingness: A phenomenological essay on ontology*. Washington Square Press.

Tateo, L. (2018). Affective semiosis and affective logic. *New Ideas in Psychology, 4*, 1–11. https://doi.org/10.1016/j.newideapsych.2017.08.002

The Sunday Times. (2013). Coca: Emerging gardens of evil. In *The Sunday Times*. http://www.sundaytimes.lk/130526/plus/coca-emerging-gardens-of-evil-46024.html

Tsuchimoto, T. (2021). Transfer of specific moment to general knowledge: Suggestions from cultural developmental autoethnography and autoethnographic trajectory equifinality modeling. *Human Arenas, 4*, 302–310. https://doi.org/10.1007/s42087-021-00220-3

Welsch, W. (1999). Transculturality: The puzzling form of culture today. In M. Featherstone & S. Lash (Eds.), *Spaces of culture: City, nation, world* (pp. 194–213). SAGE Publications.

Whitehead, K. A. (2017). Discursive approaches to race and racism. In H. Giles & A. Harwood (Eds.), *Oxford research encyclopedia of communication*. http://dx.doi.org/10.1093/acrefore/9780190228613.013.477

Valsiner, J. (2007a). Approaches to culture: Semiotic bases for cultural psychology. In J. Valsiner (Ed.), *Culture in minds and societies: Foundations of cultural psychology* (pp. 19–74). SAGE Publications. http://dx.doi.org/10.4135/9788132108504.n1

Valsiner, J. (2007b). Personal culture and conduct of value. *Journal of Social, Evolutionary, and Cultural Psychology, 1*(2), 59–65. http://dx.doi.org/10.1037/h0099358

Valsiner, J. (2014). *An invitation to cultural psychology*. SAGE Publications.

The author's grandmother's house. *Source:* Photo by the author.

CHAPTER 13

LIFE IN A DIFFERENT SOIL

My Existential Mobility as an Immigrant

Rennan Okawa
Otani University

PROLOGUE

The word "garden" constantly reminds me of the home I shared with my grandmother. Her house had a small garden. She enjoyed tinkering with the red soil, which was endemic to the region. Once, she asked me which flower was my favorite. When I responded, "sunflowers," she planted them for me in the garden. I enjoyed observing sunflowers. Her modest garden was neither opulent nor magnificent, but it has always been my favorite. I am writing this article 15,000 km away from the garden, on the opposite side of the globe. Next to my research lab is a large, well-kept, and aesthetically pleasing university garden. However, I have never attempted to visit the garden as the soil was not red (see Figure 13.1).

Figure 13.1 The author's grandmother's garden. *Source:* Photo by the author

INTRODUCTION

I live in Japan, 15,000 km from my grandmother's garden in Brazil. One word that can define me is "immigrant." I am a third-generation Japanese-Brazilian in my home country of Brazil and a second-generation Brazilian living in Japan, where I have emigrated. Thus, I am an immigrant in Brazil and Japan. As an immigrant—whether I want to admit it—"migration" has a significant meaning in my life. This chapter explores the subjective meaning of migration from an autoethnographic perspective, focusing on my experience as an immigrant.

I have undergone five international migrations and over 10 relocations within Japan. Each of these migrations has a distinct meaning, and none of them have been carried out with the same intent. I examine these migrations to gain an insider's perspective on the reality of migration.

Before discussing my migration in this article, let me examine the context in which children who have also experienced migration in Japan have been discussed in prior research. My family, along with many other Japanese Brazilians, immigrated to Japan around 1990 as *dekasegi* laborers (migrant workers) due to the economic recession in Brazil and the rising labor demand in Japan. These social movements resulted from a combination of the push–pull factors outlined by Castles and Miller (2009). My family became dekasegi for the mundane reason of "earning money in Japan to improve our lives in Brazil." After my grandfather, parents, and aunt immigrated to Japan, my grandmother and I followed a few years later. The increase in immigration to Japan following the 1990 revision of the Immigration Control and Refugee Recognition Act explains my migration history. Therefore, I am one of Japan's 2.8 million immigrants.

Since the 1990 revision of the Immigration Control and Refugee Recognition Act, newcomers to Japan—such as myself—have been referred to as "newcomers" and have become the subject of academic research in Japan—where a great deal of information has been accumulated regarding newcomers. In the field of sociology of education—upon which I rely—newcomer studies can be divided primarily into those conducted during the acceptance period and those conducted during the settlement period (Shimizu et al., 2014). The research in the acceptance phase primarily describes Japan's oppressive and assimilation-intensive school culture (Tsuneyoshi, 2011); whereas, the research in the settlement phase focuses on issues that arise while living in Japan, such as identity formation (Shimizu, 2006) and non-attendance at schools (Miyajima & Ota, 2005). An overview of research on Brazilians in Japan reveals that the majority of studies have focused on the transition of Brazilian youth in Japan (Kojima, 2013) and migration between countries (Yamamoto, 2014). Hatano (2006)—a researcher on Japanese Brazilians—noted that the image of Brazil demanded by Japanese schools does not necessarily correspond to the reality of Brazilian children and their parents living in Japan, and that Brazilian culture is consumed under the guise of "multicultural conviviality."

Previous research has primarily focused on the problems faced by foreign children and youth from a Japanese perspective and offered solutions to these issues. In other words, in previous migration studies in Japan, I was seen as an immigrant before being seen as an individual. I was swallowed up in the larger wave, and my problems—like those of many other immigrants—were focused on the difficulties of migration. Meanwhile, the study by the Brazilian Hatano raises the same issues but focuses on the problems facing Japanese society rather than those facing children. The primary distinction between them is the perspective from which they examine problems.

This chapter aims to capture reality from the perspective of Brazilians living in Japan. While Hatano's study focused on children within schools, this article extends this perspective to outside schools to clarify how the current situation of migration affects the lives of children and young people. Although children's migration has been addressed in previous migration studies (Shimizu et al., 2013), it has not been examined from the perspective of children and young people who have experienced migration. I use autoethnography to subjectively reflect on my own migration experience to clarify how migration meant to me as a child and how migration has impacted my life.

AUTOETHNOGRAPHY AND EXISTENTIAL MOBILITY TO EXPLORE THE MEANING OF MIGRATION

I employ the autoethnography research method to clarify my meaning making for my migration as an immigrant. *Autoethnography* is a research method that belongs to autobiographical description and research through it, disclosing the multilayered consciousness that links individuals and cultures and is subjective and emotional (Ellis & Bochner, 1999), whereas traditional ethnography aims to understand the subject (Liu, 2022). Given that the researcher's own experience becomes the object of investigation in autoethnography, research is also an act of introspection that evokes recurrent acts and feelings that reflect the position in which one is or was placed (Imoto, 2013). Thus, autoethnography research allows the researcher to study himself/herself subjectively, and it also enables confronting one's own inner self through research.

Autoethnography also has several strengths and weaknesses. Strengths include the ease of access to data—given that the researcher studies his or her own experiences—and the fact that the narrative uses essay-like rather than academic descriptions, which makes it easier to engage the reader, thus influencing the researcher and reader. It is also the ultimate research method in qualitative research, which is characterized by the interpretation of semantic worlds and the recapturing of phenomena from the subject (Okishio Harada, 2019). However, the data rely on memory and the descriptions are essay like, which makes them less scientific and artistic. Ellis argued that autoethnography is situated "between art and science" and that what is important in autoethnography is not the accurate portrayal of "facts" but rather the description of how the researcher made sense of his/her experience as a participant.

Moreover, the researcher cannot ensure validity and reliability by subjecting himself or herself to the subject and subjectively depicting his or her inner life. Contrastingly, Ellis argued that no standard exists for truth and that validity should be judged by how readers find the content convincing, plausible, and capable of improving their lives (Ellis & Bochner,

1999). The reason is because autoethnography is not merely about deepening our understanding of society and culture but about empathizing with readers (Imoto, 2013). Regarding the issue of reliability, Ellis stated that autoethnography cannot guarantee scientific reliability given that it is not produced in a specific place but is linked by the present, imagined future, and remembered past (Ellis & Bochner, 1999). In autoethnography, it is not fact-checking of a story that is important (Liu, 2022), but what can be thought about through that story.

To better understand the author's migration as narrated by autoethnography, this article employs Hage's (2005) existential mobility as a perspective for analysis. Hage claimed that—to understand human mobility—the subjective world of meaning—rather than objective, physical mobility—must be understood. In the life of an immigrant, migration is a one- or two-time event, and only 1 or 2 days in the life course. Those migrations are vital but the events themselves are not, and what meaning they attach to the migrations and what "traces" they leave on their lives must be traced. Thus, to capture the mobility of migrants, focusing on the relationship between physical and existential mobility is necessary. In using existential mobility, how the migration generated by the oscillation of the self stands in subsequent daily life must be clarified (Shibano, 2016).

To clarify how migration affected my life and how I made sense of each migration in my life, I analyzed my subjective migration narratives portrayed by autoethnography from the perspective of existential mobility. Among the many migrations in my life, I focus on three international and one domestic migrations, which I consider crucial.

MIGRATION FOR IMMIGRANTS

Moving From the Homeland: Brazil to Japan

Among the many migrations in my life, if there is one migration that I cannot avoid, it is certainly the one that brought me from Brazil to Japan. The reason is because migration marked the beginning of my status as an immigrant. Although this migration is symbolic, the extent to which it has affected my life is debatable. I cannot be certain of the extent of my ontological migration as opposed to my physical migration, so I am uncertain of the distance I have traveled. Thus, it is necessary to discuss my birth and family to explain why.

I was born in a town called Londrina in Paraná, Brazil. Londrina has a vast Japanese-Brazilian population. Although the city had a large population of Japanese descent, I hardly ever encountered any Japanese during my childhood. The reason was because my grandfather was the only Japanese member of my family. Therefore, I was raised as a normal Brazilian. Prior to my memory, however, my grandfather came to Japan with my parents as a dekasegi and passed away in Japan. Although I have few memories of my grandfather, I vividly recall loving him. Consequently, I occasionally ponder what my grandfather would think of me now that I reside in Japan and speak Japanese. I was never able to find an answer to this question.

My grandparents were the most important people in my life as they basically raised me. My parents were young when I was born, and I was left with my grandparents a few days later. As a result, I grew up without parental attachment. Instead, I regarded my grandparents and aunts as my parents. Therefore, I came to Japan not because my parents instructed me, but because my grandmother said, "Let's go and get to know your grandfather's country," and I came to Japan to see the homeland of my grandfather.

Cross-border migration is significant in migration research given that it changes the society in which a person lives, norms, and many external factors simultaneously. Despite the fact that these migration studies focused on the purpose and process of migration, they rarely considered who the migrants are moving with or what emotions they are experiencing. My first migration from Brazil to Japan was certainly remarkable, spanning tens of thousands of kilometers, but I did not attach much significance to it because I was "moving with my grandmother." As a young child, leaving my grandmother meant more to me than traveling to the unknown world of Japan. Therefore, this significant and symbolic first migration, "becoming an immigrant," was unimportant to me. The importance of subsequent migration was greater for me; it was a minor physical relocation, but a significant mental one for me.

Moving From an Important Person: Kanagawa to Aichi

Domestic migration in Japan was important to me, whereas international migration was not. The few hundred kilometers from Kanagawa prefecture to Aichi prefecture caused me more anxiety than I had ever experienced. This migration would leave an indelible mark on my life, as it involved separating from my grandmother.

I was 8 years old when I moved to Japan in 1997. My initial purpose in coming to Japan was to "get to know my grandfather's hometown," and I had no idea that I would remain there for so long. In retrospect, I did not need to drop out of the Brazilian school I was attending for a simple trip. It was impossible to determine my grandmother's initial beliefs. When I first arrived in Japan, I intended to reside with my grandmother in the same prefecture as my mother, Aichi. My mother was already living with a Japanese partner at the time and had a stable life. My mother's partner was a native

Japanese who had never left the country, but he welcomed my grandmother and me with open arms. However, life in Aichi was not easy. The issue was not with the Japanese partner, but rather with my mother. As a young child, I would cry at night due to severe knee pain caused by exacerbating pains. My grandmother was always there for me, but my mother could not comprehend my situation, possibly because she had never lived with a child. My grandmother observed that my relationship with my mother was deteriorating and consequently relocated me to the home of my aunt (my mother's sister) in Kanagawa prefecture. At the time, I did not believe it was essential for me to leave my mother. Subsequently, I lived in my aunt's house in Kanagawa for 6 years. So much had happened during those 6 years beyond the scope of this article. I experienced many successes and failures while attending a Japanese public school, and—despite being bullied—I also met friends who accepted me.

Bullying was one of the first difficulties I encountered in Japanese school. It all started with a small incident where I was ridiculed for not being able to say the name of the Pokémon I had hanging from my bag in Japanese and was teased for looking different and having a different name. However, this was not my first experience with bullying. I had also been bullied in the same way when I was in elementary school in Brazil, where I was bullied for looking Japanese. At the time, I could not understand why I was being bullied because I was born and raised in Brazil. But in Japan, I faced similar bullying, where I was called "*Gaijin*," whereas in Brazil, I was called "*Japa*." Looking back, I think that my problems with identity may have started in my early elementary school years, but at the time, I did not understand such things. I did not have any words to say back, and only the word "idiot" was floating around me.

Despite the bullying, I was able to continue attending school with the help of my friends. However, in the winter of my second year of junior high school, at the age of 14, I had to leave my grandmother and aunt's house, which was a huge move for me.

My grandmother also influenced my decision to relocate from the family side. I thought it was difficult for my grandmother, who lived in Japan and worked in a factory every day without being able to speak the language. My grandmother's casual words, "If you live with your mother, I will go back to Brazil." Simultaneously, my mother remarried a Japanese partner and she gave birth to my younger brother. At 14 years old, I was determined to live with my mother for the sake of my grandmother and younger brother. I was extremely anxious about leaving my grandmother. Compared to Brazil and Japan, the move from Kanagawa prefecture to Aichi prefecture was a small one, but for me, it was tremendously significant. It was more of an emotional burden than a physical one, but I knew I had to overcome it for the sake of my grandmother, who had done so much for me, and my infant brother.

In Aichi prefecture, I had my own positive intentions and knew precisely where and how I would live, in contrast to my first migration. However, this relocation was more difficult than the move from Brazil to Japan. Leaving my grandmother was difficult, and living with my mother was also challenging. Regarding this action, I found myself repeatedly pulling my hair back. If I could have stopped, I would have, but I would have also lost my desire to make my grandmother feel safe and at ease. In an act of near self-sacrifice, I handled all of the moving-related stress on my own. To be away from an important person was to be away from one's comfort zone, which was a significant mental burden for me.

Moving to the Homeland: Brazil Again

Living with my mother was simply a failure. It led to my grandmother's return to Brazil, but also worsened my relationship with my mother. The deterioration of that relationship led to my "return" to Brazil, which substantially influenced my identity.

The most challenging aspect of my life was my relationship with my mother, not my new school, my relationship with my stepfather, or my relationship with my brother. At my new school, there were no bullies, and my stepfather accepted me with the same graciousness as before. I attempted to get along with my sibling. However, a significant value gap existed between my mother and me. Importantly, I was supposed to have a stable life with my mother, but she divorced shortly after I moved out. I was supposed to have relocated to reassure my grandmother, but my life had become increasingly unstable. Despite my initial belief that I would be unable to attend high school, I was admitted to a public high school. Despite receiving poor grades in middle school, I was able to earn good grades in high school due to my own efforts. Although I had good grades in high school, I was the only student in my class who had not yet decided on a career path, whereas my less diligent and lower-achieving classmates had already chosen their higher education programs and careers. At the time, I believed that the phrase "hard work pays off" was reserved for those other than myself.

As I was feeling defeated in my life in Japan, my grandmother, who had returned to Brazil, advised me to attend college in Brazil, which gave me hope. This was a way out of Japan, where everything was going wrong, and a solution that would free me from being treated as a foreigner. However, as it turned out, everything went wrong in Brazil. In retrospect, the reason why things did not work out for me may have had something to do with the time I spent in Japan. First, having been educated in Japan from the age of 8 to 18, it was almost impossible for me to enter a highly competitive public university in Brazil. Having spent such a long period in Japan, I was already far from what Brazilians defined as Brazilian. My optimism that I would succeed in Brazil was short-lived. As soon as I arrived, I realized that things were not going well, and I spent many days contemplating what I should do in the future.

Migrating from Japan to Brazil was a significant mental shift for me, as it was an attempt to escape a failing situation in Japan, and by making the physical move, I also attempted to move ontologically. However, as evidenced by the results, I was able to move physically, whereas my existential mobility is debatable. Meanwhile, there was no ontological shift in the sense that I could not escape the difficulties I encountered in Japan, but I could see myself edging closer to the precipice. I believe that moving to Brazil will place me in a more difficult situation. My "Brazilian self" existed prior to the move, but I lost it as a result of the move. Ironically, the thing I sought most in Brazil was misplaced. Ultimately, I came to understand that the problem I had was not that I was a foreigner in Japan, but that I had my own problems. It was my inability to position myself in the world as either Brazilian or Japanese.

Moving From the Homeland: To Japan Again

I was only able to spend 1 year in Brazil. In Brazil, I had no place to call home, no friends, and no one who understood me; it felt as though everything had ended. I consequently returned to Japan. I had no hopes or expectations for my move to Japan, to be completely honest. This was merely a distraction from the fact that things were not going well in Brazil. Moving from Brazil to Japan was mentally simpler for me than moving within the same city. This was a peculiar sensation. Even though I was born in Brazil and could speak the language, I felt as though no one could understand me.

Despite my relocation to Brazil, Japan was the center of my life. I had no friends, and everything I enjoyed was in Japan, so I spent all of my time watching Japanese anime and television programs on my computer. Before I knew it, my life in Brazil had flipped from day to night. In this sense, I may have only relocated physically. First, the reason for my life's 180-degree turn was to maintain contact with my Japanese friends. However, this no longer served as a justification. My friends were moving on with their lives, attending college or finding jobs, while I appeared to be the only one left behind. My grandmother was concerned that I was depressed because I spent every night alone on the computer, so she arranged for me to see a psychiatrist. Although my grandmother was always kind to me, she had trouble understanding my situation in Brazil. With no money to spare and no prospects for further education or employment, I lost all my reasons to stay in Brazil and decided to return to Japan. It was a similar choice to the one I made when returning to Brazil from Japan. This time, however, I had no hopes or expectations for the new location. I simply desired to travel somewhere other than Brazil. I lacked the funds to purchase a plane ticket to Japan, so I followed the path of Brazilian migrant workers. In my entire life, I had never been able to connect with a Brazilian dekasegi; nevertheless, in Japan, I was able to do so for the first time.

I returned to Japan, where a new tale awaited me. No longer was I with my mother, nor was I on my grandmother's side. With a sense of defeat and frustration, I would try once more to attend college in Japan to "please my grandmother and aunt." After many turns and twists, I was able to reach my objective. Due to space constraints, I cannot elaborate on this story in this article, but I can say that it involves migration. Curiously, the first and second migrations from Brazil to Japan were mental migrations that were not proportional to physical distance. The first migration, nonetheless, was "with my grandmother" and was accompanied by relief, whereas the second migration resembled a "one-person escape." Neither migration observed any ontological migration. In this regard, the two migrations were comparable, but their underlying emotions were polar opposites.

MEANING OF "MIGRATION"

This article's account of my migration is not necessarily representative of that of immigrants. Therefore, it is challenging to generalize this study's findings. The results of this study were not intended to be generalized. However, I am an immigrant, and my story is one of many immigrant stories. My story may be unique, but it also has the potential to be representative of the experiences of other immigrants.

I have examined the meaning of mobility for migrants on the basis of my own subjective mobility experience. By employing the concept of existential mobility when contemplating the meaning of migration, it became possible to illustrate the mental movement that accompanies migration. Large physical movements were not correlated with large mental movements. In addition to where and why one moves, the significance of movement also includes with whom and how one moves, which has a significant impact on ontological movement.

In capturing mobility, it is necessary to examine the inner nature of that mobility. In Chapter 4, Miyamae discusses disaster survivors and describes how people faced with disasters talk differently before and after the disaster, even if they are in the same place. This is because people's inner selves have experienced movement, even if physical movement is not the same. Even if there is no physical movement, people can still experience mobility. Therefore, it is essential to focus on the meaning of mobility rather than just physical mobility.

My narrative describes four important migrations. One is domestic migration to Kanagawa and Aichi prefectures, which is small in comparison to other migrations. However, the significance of each migration was distinct, and I perceived the magnitude of each migration in terms other than the magnitude of migration. The first move from Brazil to Japan was certainly an important migration in my life, but because I was "moving with my grandmother," it was less mentally taxing than the physical distance. Family ties between my grandmother and I reduced the mental burden of the move, and even though we lived on the other side of the earth, I was able to live with my grandmother, which made the move less mentally taxing. Comparatively, the domestic move from Kanagawa to Aichi was minor in comparison to the international move, but the "move from my grandmother's side" imposed a significant burden on me and required me to leave my comfort zone by moving with a selfless mindset. Although the purpose of the move was to live with my mother—my closest blood relative—our lack of connection exacerbated the burden. The subsequent relocation from Japan to Brazil was also significant, as it was an international relocation. It was also a decision that left me feeling defeated that things had not gone well in Japan and filled me with optimism for a second chance in Brazil. Initially, it was a significant change in distance and significance for me, but when I saw that things were once again not going well in Brazil, I experienced a greater mental shift in a negative direction. However, it can be seen as a failed mental move due to the state of "turning day and night around and adjusting time to Japan. Finally, the move from Brazil to Japan again, as with the first move, was not proportional to the physical distance, as in the case of "mentally easier than going to the next town." Given that I failed to move ontologically during my previous move from Japan to Brazil, it is possible that I was still mentally connected to Japan.

As the trajectory of my migration has shown, the meaning and value attached to migration is not necessarily proportional to the distance traveled; rather, the factors that determine the meaning of migration are latent in the details of the migration. Previous studies on migration have focused on a single phenomenon and examined the events caused by migration. However, as discussed in this article, mobility does not necessarily have a single characteristic, and furthermore, the meaning of mobility itself varies depending on the environment and the subjective meaning of the world of the person concerned. The meaning of migration is diverse and multifaceted. However, this article does not merely aim to show that "each movement is diverse," but rather to argue that the nature of the social relations in which the parties involved are embedded must be further understood to elucidate the meaning of their movements. In my case, this was due to the fact that the family behind the migration significantly affected the meaning of migration.

CONCLUSION

I used autoethnography to provide a subjective account of my migration in this article. Autoethnography is a descriptive technique similar to ethnography, but it is superior because it enables access to emotional aspects that are difficult to approach if the author is not the subject. By analyzing the movement from the perspective of the individual's emotional state, it is possible to draw a distinction from previous research.

That is the question I have been having. I read multiples books that dealt with the issue of foreign children in Japan. Not all of them were wrong. Many researchers took the issue seriously, conducted research, and wrote articles on it. However, there was always something that stuck with me. There was a picture of us, but we were not talking. We talked during interviews, but our opinions about the problems we were facing were rarely portrayed. There was a description of what we should be, but nowhere was there a description of how we wanted to be. Then a question came to mind. I wondered if Japanese researchers could really understand how we felt and if they could see the same scenery as excellent Japanese researchers who graduated from top universities. I am not trying to criticize or deny the research they have done so far, but I feel that something is missing. I also noticed that there are few researchers from the same perspective as us, so-called children of migrants. Of course, we cannot see the same things because we are the people involved, but it is necessary for researchers not only to describe the reality as it is but also to be close to it. Autoethnography can work on such earnest feelings and discomfort of the parties concerned. And it can give power to the unvoiced words.

Moreover, autoethnography, nonetheless, had a healing effect on me. The reason is because the question—"What has migration meant to me in my life?"—is approachable. While the party in question becomes the researcher, it is advantageous to approach the set issues from various angles; however, it is necessary to conceal one's party status as a researcher. It refers to "a concerned party who is unable to speak." Autoethnography is one method for addressing this issue, and it has the potential to broaden the dichotomous relationship between the involved parties and the researcher.

EPILOGUE

My life has been filled with numerous relocations and gardens. However, regardless of how many beautiful court gardens I have seen, the garden at my grandmother's house is my favorite. My grandmother and her garden are no longer in the world. The garden of the house where I once spent my childhood is no longer there. This may have been the largest move of my

Figure 13.2 Sunflowers planted by my grandmother for the author. Source: Photo by the author

life. I did not physically relocate anything, but I consider my grandmother's passing and the loss of that house and garden to be my most significant mental relocation. While moving forward and focusing on the future, there are certain memories that one wishes to revisit. As I write this article, I am imagining a garden that used to be on the other side of the world, next to a beautiful garden that I have never seen before. And the story that began in that garden continues to this day. As an immigrant, I am a flower that must live in a different soil. The garden that remains inside of me will always be the garden in my grandmother's house (see Figure 13.2).

AUTHOR NOTE

This article is an English translation of the manuscript titled "'My Story' of Immigration: An Existential Mobility Captured by Autoethnography" which was originally published in *The Annual Review of Migration Studies*, *28*, 79–89, and has been revised and updated.

REFERENCES

Castles, S., & Miller, M. J. (2009). *Age of migration: International population movements in the modern world* (4th ed.). The Guilford Press.

Ellis, C., & Bochner, A. (1999). Heartful autoethnography. *Qualitative Health Research, 9*(5), 653–667.

Hage, G. (2005). A not so multi-sited ethnography of a not so imaginate community. *Anthropogical Theory, 5*(4), 463–475.

Hatano, T. L. (2006). Various issues of "multicultural conviviality" surrounding Brazilians in Japan. In K. Ueda & H. Yamashita (Eds.), *The inner reality of "Kyosei": Questions from critical sociolinguistics* [in Japanese] (pp. 55–80). Sangensya.

Imoto, Y. (2013). Autoethnography. In Y. Fujita & F. Kitamura(Eds.), *Contemporary ethnography new fieldwork theory and practice* [in Japanese] (pp. 104–111). Shinyousya.

Kojima, A. (2013). The possibility of transition support from the perspective of newcomer youth: The search for "independence" of Brazilian youth in Japan [in Japanese]. *Intercultural Education, 37,* 32–46.

Liu, H. (2022). Growing up Chinese in Japan: An autoethnography. *Social Theory and Dynamics, 3,* 142–157.

Miyajima, T., & Ota, H. (Eds.). (2005). *Foreign children and education in Japan—The problem of non-school attendance and the challenges of multicultural conviviality* [in Japanese]. Tokyo Daigaku Syuppan.

Okishio (Harada), M. (2019). Self-ethnography. In T. Sato, H. Kasuga, & M. Kanzaki (Eds.), *Mapping of qualitative research methods—To capture and utilize characteristics* [in Japanese] (pp. 151–158). Shinyousya.

Shibano, J. (2016). Career choice as a transnational mobility practice: Focusing on the ontological mobility of Japanese high school students in Guam [in Japanese]. *Intercultural Education, 43,* 104–118.

Shimizu, M. (2006). *Newcomer children: The everyday world between school and family* [in Japanese]. Keisou Syobou.

Shimizu, K., Takada, K., Horike, Y., & Yamamoto, K. (2014). Minority and education [in Japanese]. *Journal of Educational Sociology, 95,* 133–170.

Shimizu, K., Yamamoto, B., Kaji, I., & Hayashi, K. (Eds.). (2013). *Strategies for educating "people who go back and forth": Families in a global society and the challenges of public education* [in Japanese]. Asahi syoten.

Tsuneyoshi, R. (2011). The "newcomers" and Japanese society. In T. Tsuneyoshi, H. O. Kaori, & S. B. Sarena (Eds.), *Minorities and education in multicultural Japan* (pp. 129–148). Routledge.

Yamamoto, K. (2014). Career choices of youth Nikkei Brazilians who returned to Brazil: With a focus on the "story of movement" [in Japanese]. *Journal of Educational Sociology, 94,* 281–301.

My garden (Campus).

CHAPTER 14

CHINESE-BORN KOREAN PEOPLE'S EXPERIENCE AND PRESENT-DAY JAPAN

Using TEA

Akiko Ichikawa
Hitotsubashi University, Kunitachi, Tokyo, Japan

When I think of a garden, I think of the Hitotsubashi University campus itself and its gardens. Why is the campus itself a garden? For me, the campus is a place where I can feel safe, calm, and open, whether alone or with others. Sometimes it is the so-called garden, sometimes it is the university campus or the national city itself.

This time, I would like to present an unpublished paper I wrote as a graduate student in the Graduate School of Language and Society, not on Hitotsubashi University research. After entering the Graduate School of Language and Society, I began to engage fully in research activities in Korea and research on the Korean people living in China. When I was a graduate student, whenever I felt tired or depressed, I would often take a walk

---

The Semiotic Field of the Garden, pages 311–332
Copyright © 2024 by Information Age Publishing
www.infoagepub.com
All rights of reproduction in any form reserved.

around the university campus before the problem became more serious. Now, as I write this manuscript, I am engaged in research activities as a so-called postdoctoral fellow. Every day, I do my best in research, education, and support, but sometimes I feel a great deal of anxiety about the future. At such times, what calms me down is the garden, trees, and space itself on the university campus. When I look at the garden and the seasonal flowers, my depressed feelings disappear before I know it.

We who live in Japan sometimes use the following expression to describe a "garden" in reference to a place or town we are familiar with.

Kunitachi is my garden.	(国立は 私 の庭です)
Hitotsubashi University is my garden.	(一橋大学は 私 の庭です)
Kokubunji is my garden.	(国分寺は 私 の庭です)
Tachikawa is my garden.	(立川は 私 の庭です)

Thus, the noun "garden" may have the meaning of "garden"—"A term of endearment for a familiar place or city."

In graduate school, I studied people who came to Japan from East Asia after the late 1980s. These people are the so-called "minorities" in Japan. In this chapter, I would like to develop the story by defining "garden" as "a place or space where people live" instead of limiting it to so-called gardens with plants and fountains (see Figures 14.1 and 14.2).

Figure 14.1 Garden in the university.

Figure 14.2 The campus itself.

INTRODUCTION

This chapter, which studies the cases of two Chinese-born Korean people, visualizes the individuals' experience, their language use, and the effects that they receive when making a life decision through the use of TEA. In the final section, the author delineates whether it is possible to explain things by hypothesizing garden in cultural psychology as a social linguistic space.

According to the latest statistics by the Japanese Ministry of Justice, the total number of foreign residents in Japan is about 2.95 million; Chinese people make up the largest number of foreign residents at about 800,000, followed by South Koreans who number at about 430,000, then Vietnamese people at about 420,000, and then Brazilians at about 210,000. Based on this data, foreign citizens from Asian regions make up the majority percentage of foreign citizens in Japan (Japanese Ministry of Justice, 2020). Korean-Chinese people are not clearly shown in Japanese immigration statistics, and socially, they appear to have Chinese names with Chinese sounds. Unless they introduce themselves, there are few chances for Korean-Chinese people to be recognized in Japanese society (Kwon, 2013). Korean-Chinese people began to move to Japan after 1986 (Kwon, 2011), and many of them came to Japan as students.

Korean-Chinese people in Japan have many life choices, and their life plans vary; they must decide whether to settle in Japan, return to China, or move to another country. Regarding their nationality, Korean-Chinese people in Japan sometimes make the decision to live as a native Chinese person or switch to the Japanese nationality (Jin, 2015). In Japanese society, people tend to lump Korean-Chinese people all together as "Chinese," and they are often recognized as individuals who can speak both Chinese and Korean in their local communities and educational institutions. This situation occurs because these individuals do not have to speak any other languages on the daily aside from Japanese. In addition, Japanese society has discriminations and biases for individuals whose ancestors are descended from the Korean Peninsula. In these circumstances, some people choose to live inconspicuously by hiding their home country, nationalities, and ethnicity (Ichikawa, 2020). The Korean language has been influenced by several other languages, including Chinese, Mongolian, and Japanese. Of these influences, Chinese is said to have had the strongest impact on Korean (Umeda, 1989).

In China, the Open Door Policy dramatically changed society. According to Han and Xu (2012), after the Open Door Policy and other such reforms, Chinese people's international migration for labor became more active, and remittances from outside of China affected the economic development in local Chinese cities. This period is said to be a time when the Korean-Chinese began forming foreign language education, cultural, and educational movements for minorities (Cui, 2013). The researcher Kato, who studies classical Chinese opera, insists that recent young Chinese people try to learn foreign cultures—particularly the cultures of English-speaking nations rather than the culture of China—in order to put additional value on themselves (Kato, 2002).

In such a situation, research is necessary in order to clarify how Korean-Chinese people see Japanese society. Through the use of the Trajectory Equifinality Approach (TEA), which is an approach that focuses on and analyzes the human experience, this study aims to clarify the circumstances that affect Chinese-born Korean people as they choose how to deal with their environment. The two participants in this research have two features in common: (a) In childhood, just before coming to Japan, they both had Japanese-learning experiences at a school for Chinese-Korean students and (b) they both live in Japan.

METHODOLOGY: USING TEA

Research Outline

The author asked Chinese-born Korean people who have studied in Japan as international students and who are currently living in Japan to participate in this research. As a result of this request, two people agreed to participate in this study.

The first interview was conducted from October 2015 to December 2015. The second interview, which was a semi-structured interview, was held from December of 2016 to July of 2017. The locations for these interviews were selected by the participants and were locations such as cafés and universities. Before starting the interview, the author obtained permission from the participants to record their conversations using an IC recorder. This study was fully devoted to ethical research, and the researcher did her best to protect the participants' privacy. After the recorded data was transferred into script data, categories were created via labeling, which was done based on the meaning in the interview data. Then, focusing on changes within the flow of time in the participants' lives, the author created a TEM diagram.

A's Profile

> A Chinese woman whose maternal grandmother is from North Korea. She is in her late 20s. From kindergarten through high school, she was educated at a Korean school in her hometown in the Korean Autonomous Region. Currently, her parents live in Korea. She has one older sister who lives in Shandong Province in China, and during the summer and New Year holidays, they gather in China or South Korea as according to the convenience of her family. After arriving in Japan, she studied at a Japanese language school and then went to a graduate school. During graduate school, she received a scholarship thanks to her excellent grades. While studying at graduate school, she had a part-time job at a Japanese company to cover her living expenses and tuition fees. After graduating from the graduate school, she got a job at a Japanese company. She was the first Chinese worker in her company. She has reportedly reached her mental limit due to stress from her enthusiastic boss's strict education. She came to Japan in October of 2010.

C's Profile

> Born in the Korean Autonomous Region (at that time) in Jilin Province. He is in his late 20s. From kindergarten through high school, he studied at a school in the (former) Korean Autonomous Region in China. His mother is a teacher at a Korean school, and his father is a civil servant. He has one older sister. His family live in China. When he was young, his dream was to unify the Korean Peninsula and win the Nobel Peace Prize. In China, he can speak Chinese dignifiedly, but since he came to Japan, he has been living a life where he cannot use Korean or Chinese. His future dream is to work across Korea, Japan, and China. He came to Japan in July of 2012.

Research Methods

In Japan, TEA is widely adopted in fields such as developmental psychology, social education, and nursing, and TEA is considered a methodology for "supporting the enrichment of life" (Yasuda & Sato, 2017). In this study, after conducting semi-structured interviews with A and C, the author and participants checked the interview contents and TEM diagram mainly via email, three times for A and twice for C.

Yasuda (2012b) explained the significance of drawing a dotted line, stating that by actively drawing a route which is thought to be meaningful, it will be possible to visualize one's thoughtful proposals for life styles and supportive interventions. With this idea in mind, this study employed the concepts of TEA: equifinality point (EFP), polarized equifinality point (P-EFP), bifurcation point (BFP), lossy time (Irreversible Time), social direction (SD), social guidance (SG), and value transformation moment (VTM).

The meaning of the concepts in this study are shown in Table 14.1 with reference to Yasuda and Sato (2017).

TEA, as adopted in this study, is a methodology derived from cultural psychology which was advocated for and designed by Jaan Valsiner. Table 14.2 shows the profiles of the participants.

Next, their transition of language use at the educational stage and after employment will be shown in Table 14.3.

TABLE 14.1 The Meaning of the Concepts in This Study

Concepts	The Meaning in This Study
Equifinality Point: EFP	The point (Yasuda, 2012a) where the path of human behavior and choice reaches a certain steady state equally (Equi) due to historical, cultural, and socially embedded time constraints.
	Researcher's interest (Sato, 2012a)
Polarized Equifinality Point: P-EFP	Points opposite to the solstice
Bifurcation Point: BFP	Point where the route appears (Yasuda, 2012a)
Irreversible Time	The time that can never come back (Yasuda, 2012a)
Social Direction: SD	The power to prevent people from moving forward (Yasuda, 2012b)
Social Guidance: SG	The power that assists people to move forward, such as recognition supporting one's behavior and getting support from people, social support, and other systems (Yasuda, 2012b)
Value Transformation Moment: VTM	Points where value changes

TABLE 14.2 The Profiles of the Participants

	Gender/Age	Occupation	Nationality	Permanent Residency	Educational Background in Japan	Future Desire	Reasons for Coming to Japan	First Language	Area Where Parents Live
A	Female Late 20s	Office worker	Chinese	Aspiring to obtain	Japanese language school Graduate school (master's course)	To study in English-speaking countries, and then go back to China	Study	Korean	Korea
C	Male Late 20s	Graduate student	China	No desire to obtain	Japanese language school Graduate school (master's course)	To live in China or Japan	Study	Korean	Korea

TABLE 14.3 The Participants' Transition of Language Use (listed in order of frequency of use)

	Before Coming to Japan				After Coming to Japan		
National language	Birth-elementary school	Junior high school	High school	University	Japanese language school	Graduate school	Company
	Chinese					Japanese	
A	Korean	Korean Chinese Japanese	Korean Chinese Japanese	Chinese	Japanese	Japanese Chinese	Japanese Chinese
C	Korean Chinese Japanese	Korean Chinese Japanese	Korean Chinese Japanese	Chinese Korean Japanese	Japanese Chinese	Chinese Korean Japanese	NA

RESULT

Based on the story of A and C, the period of conflict in the participants' language use was divided, and the process leading to EFP was drawn in the TEM diagram. In order to analyze data and draw the diagrams, the author followed explanations from Hirose (2012) and Yasuda (2017).

Drawing the TEM diagram

The TEM diagram was created based on the stories of the two participants. The created figures are shown in Figures 14.3 through 14.5. The route described in the story was shown with →. The theoretically assumed route is depicted with ⇢, and the participants' words were written with "". The names of categories named by the author were written with < >, and the contents written in ( ) were additional explanations made by the author. With "..." the omitted parts were indicated.

A's Result

A, whose maternal grandmother is from North Korea, was <born in her hometown in the Korean Autonomous Region in China>. When she was young, <her father decided to go to Korea for work>. She was educated at a school for Korean people from the preschool level. She entered junior high school and <started learning Japanese>. Although she had the choice to quit at a school in China, go to Korea and <study at a school in Korea>, after discussion with her family, she decided to <study at a junior high school and high school for Korean people in China.> She came to think "<I want to study in Japan> in order to make use of the Japanese I learned."

She took a university-entrance examination, and <entered university> where the Han Chinese made up the majority of students. Since classes were conducted in Korean at the previous schools where she studied, she experienced <language shock (because she couldn't understand Chinese)> for the first time.

After entering a university, she <started learning English in earnest.>

After that, she <graduated from university>, and she made her dream come true, which was <coming to Japan>. Immediately after arriving in Japan, she completed the <Japanese language school admission> procedure and studied at a Japanese language school, and then she entered a <graduate school>.

At the graduate school, she went to Korea for the research in her master's thesis. However, <she could not do the research she wanted in Korea>,

320 ■ A. ICHIKAWA

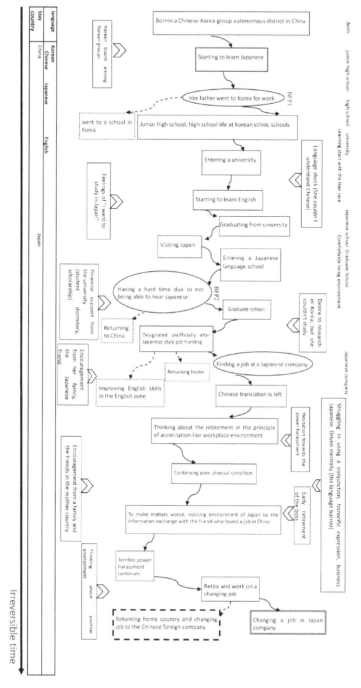

Figure 14.3 A's TEM.

Chinese-Born Korean People's Experience and Present-Day Japan ▪ 321

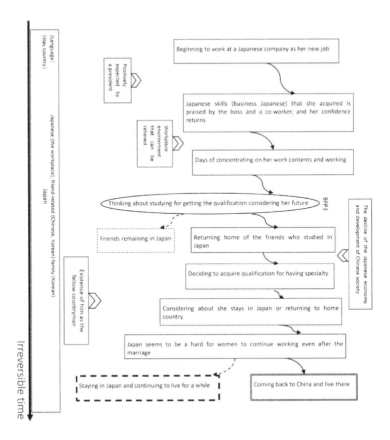

Figure 14.4 A's TEM.

so she had to change her research theme. Then, she wrote her master's thesis without problems and <got employed at a Japanese company>.

The working environment at the Japanese company was more severe than she had expected. Although she was supported by <encouragement from her family and friends>, she struggled with < (contents not written in the textbook) such as conjunctions, honorific expressions, and business Japanese>. She started to become mentally tired.

She experienced a 【language barrier】. "I am not supposed to say "nan-ka"... Also, I am not supposed to mention "demo," and I have to write "sumimasen" and "douzo yorosiku onegaisimasu" in emails I send... If I do not write emails without those phrases... I am recognized as a person who is not responsible... I was seen as a person who was not responsible because I just did not write "sumimasen"... I wondered whether her boss was such a respectful person... I may not continue to work at a Japanese company after I return to China... I am planning to study English... I have to adjust to Japanese circumstances and senior workers...Some people say that if I want to work in Japan, I have to adjust to Japanese people."

Some people evaluated A's language ability as great, and <she had the chance to be asked to do Chinese-Japanese translation>. However, she was not treated as equal with Japanese employees, and she became unable to work calmly. In a company whose employees are mostly Japanese, she had not been able to adjust to <the assimilation-oriented work environment>. Also, <she did not feel good physically for a long time>, and this made it difficult for her to get up in the morning.

A said, "Chinese is the easiest to speak. Korean is the same as Japanese because they have many polite expressions...I didn't expect to work (in such a work environment). If I had known that, I would have gone back to China without getting a job in Japan. (My friends) are preparing to go back to their home countries next year...When I asked the reason why they wanted to go back to their home countries, they said it was because of a language problem; they did not want to be singled out in their language use, and this problem caused them mental pain. It doesn't matter where I work, even at night...I don't want small matters to be pointed out."

With <the encouragement by her family and friends in China>, <she realized that she had other options>. While feeling <hesitant about early retirement>, <she moved to a different Japanese company>. <After she moved to a different Japanese company>, her Japanese ability came to be recognized as great, and she spent <days when she concentrated on her work>. After considering <her friends' return to China> and while being influenced by <the decline of the Japanese economy and the development of Chinese society>, she has chosen to <return to China and live there>.

She has a desire to apply for permanent residence in Japan, and this was the goal she set when she started to work in Japan. She stated that after obtaining permanent residence, she wants to go to Shanghai where she wants to work for a foreign-affiliated company rather than a Japanese company. She has a fondness for Japan, where Japanese, which has been a familiar language since her childhood, is spoken, and she is completing her daily work with the hope that one day she may be able to visit Japan without a visa whenever she wants.

C's Result

C was <born in the Korean Autonomous Region of Jilin Province in China>. The elementary school he attended did not have Japanese classes, but he asked his neighbor's older male friend to teach him Japanese, and he <proceeded to learn Japanese>. Around this time, C often had <quarrels with Han Chinese children (as he was insulted by them)>. A piano teacher

Chinese-Born Korean People's Experience and Present-Day Japan ▪ 323

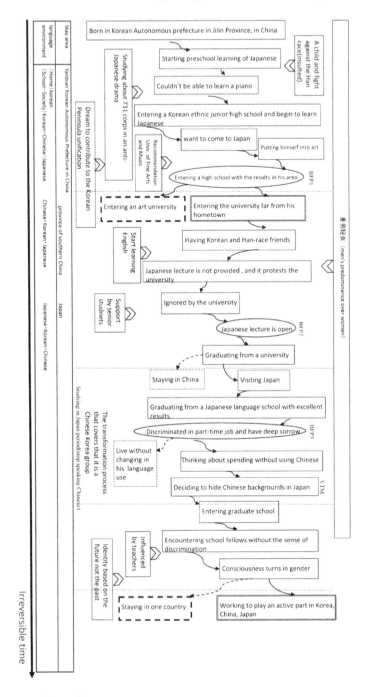

Figure 14.5 C's TEM.

told C that the length of his fingers was not suitable for a pianist, and <he could not take piano lessons, which made him frustrated>.

At that time, he had many chances to watch cruel videos showing Unit 731, which made him familiar with war, and this has made him think about peace since he was a child. <His dream at that time was to unify the Korean Peninsula.>

He gave up playing the piano and spent his new free time <dedicated to art>, and <sometimes he was recommended to enter art universities>. He very seriously considered entering an art university, but ultimately <he entered a high school with the highest grade in his area> and he was admitted to <a university far from his hometown> instead of <going on to an art university>. The university he was admitted to was a famous university in China. At university, he <started learning English>. He spent a fulfilling student life <making Korean and Han-Chinese friends>. However, due to a national policy, Japanese language lectures were not offered even once. <Since he could not study Japanese, he argued with the university>, claiming that "It is strange that the Japanese language, he has studied so far, will not be offered only this year." Despite this, <he was ignored by university>.

Thanks to <the supports from senior students> who sympathized with C, <Japanese lectures started to be held>. After that, he decided to study in Japan, thinking that he wanted to make use of the Japanese he had learned over the years. For C, studying in Japan was natural and many of his Korean Chinese school friends often choose to study in Japan.

After <coming to Japan>, he was chosen as a model student at a Japanese language school. One day, an elder man talked with him and his friend on the train.

"I told him that I was a Chinese-born Korean man and he said, "What? Korean?"... He said phrases like "Korean?"; "Do you understand what Korean means?"; and "inferior race" ... I wanted to hide everything about me, like the fact I was Chinese and a Chinese-born Korean.

<Being told he was an "inferior race" made C very sad>, and this made him <decide not to speak Chinese anymore>. He also decided to hide his Chinese nationality. After that, <affected by his teacher>, <C came to focus on gender>.

"I am Korean and Chinese. If I go back...they are actually not past things. I mean exploring the past through past problems. Now, I think that I can find my identity by not only exploring the past but also thinking about the future. Trying to find the option where the future I will live comfortably somehow connects to the feeling of belonging and my identity...Seeing the future as one type of identity...I will try to find a way to live as myself rather than focusing too much on Korean, Chinese, and this moment."

C seemed to be supporting himself with an idea that <his identity was created by the future, not the past.> As for his future, <getting a job that he can actively work in Korea, China, and Japan> was recognized.

DISCUSSION

This study visualized the path of life of Chinese-born Korean people, A and C. First, the author discussed the results obtained from the TEA analysis, focusing on turning points, social assistance, and social guides. Tables 14.4 and 14.5 show the concepts and analyzed results of A and C. At the turning point, A's father's moving to South Korea for work and her Japanese language education were shown. In terms of social assistance, differences in society, differences in customs, and peculiar Chinese values were shown. At the social guide, points such as financial support and contributions to the unification of the Korean Peninsula were seen.

TABLE 14.4 Analyzed Results of A

	Concepts	Analyzed Data
A	Turning point	BFP1 Her father's moving to South Korea for work
		BFP2 The difficulties in listening to Japanese
		BFP3 Thinking about studying to obtain qualifications for her future
	Social assistance	SD1 Language shock (she can't understand Chinese)
		SD2 She can't do the research she wants to do in Korea
		SD3 Conjunctions, polite expressions, and business Japanese (the contents not written in the textbook); being mentally drained [language barrier]
		SD4 Decline of Japanese economy and development of Chinese society
	Social guide	SG1 Korean boom among Koreans in China
		SG2 Desire to study in Japan
		SG3 Financial support from universities (student dormitories/scholarships)
		SG4 Encouragement from her family and friends in Japan
		SG5 Encouragement from family and friends in home country
		SG6 Considering another environment
		SG7 Expectations of the president
		SG8 Work environment where she can feel relaxed
		SG9 Boyfriend from same country

TABLE 14.5 Analyzed Results of C

	Concepts	Analyzed Data
C	Turning point	BFP1 Entering a high school with the highest grade in his area
		BFP2 Japanese lectures started to be held
		BFP3 Being called an "inferior race" made C very sad
	Social assistance	SD1 Men's predominance over women (value)
	Social guide	SG1 Learning about 731 Unit progress Anti-Japanese dramas/movies
		SG2 His dream at that time was the unification of the Korean Peninsula.
		SG3 Sometimes he was recommended to enter art universities
		SG4 Started learning English
		SG5 The supports from senior students
		SG6 Effects from his teacher
		SG7 His identity was created by the future, not the past.

What the two participants had in common was that their elementary, junior, and high schools were Korean schools. After coming to Japan, both A and C studied at a Japanese language school, then studied at a graduate school, and then chose to work in Japan. On the other hand, there are differences in their parents' migrant work experience. A's father and mother have experience in migrating to South Korea, but C's parents have no experience in migrating. According to an interview by Kojima (2016), most people from rural villages in Yanji have migrant work experience in South Korea. The reason why C's family did not go working was because of his parents' occupation and their area of residence.

Chinese-Born Korean People's Experience and Language Use

In the cases of A and C, the differences in the use and meaning of the Korean language was shown. After coming to Japan, A has been living almost entirely without using Korean. Sometimes she speaks Chinese or Korean to communicate with her friends to keep in touch. Thanks to <SG/encouragement from A's family and friends in her home country>, she was able to move on to her next job while she was thinking of retiring due to her difficulties in getting used to the assimilationist work environment. After coming to Japan, C spends his time without using Korean due to his experienced discrimination. He has been trying to speak Korean since he was in China. After coming to Japan and maintaining Korean fluency, he has been trying to speak Japanese rather than Chinese. SG <influence of teachers> worked as a big motivator in his trying to live by only using Korean and Japanese while also hiding himself as a Chinese Korean speaker. In A's SD, the fact that her Japanese proficiency, which is of a graduate level, could not be fully utilized at her place of work was noted, and in C's case, it was shown that the Chinese-specific value of male-dominated women (SD1) had a huge impact as well.

The Japanese government ratified the Convention on the Elimination of Racial Discrimination in 1995, but domestic laws that ban racial discrimination have not been created yet. Local governments with a large number of foreign residents should consider enacting an ethnic discrimination prohibition ordinance without waiting for the enactment of a law (Yamawaki, 2004, p. 240).

In the process of research cooperation, A and C both (a) had teachers and friends at their universities who accepted people of different cultural backgrounds and (b) experienced discrimination within Japanese society outside of their universities. Regardless of the enactment of laws prohibiting ethnic discrimination at the national level and the number of foreign residents currently in Japan, it will be a task for Japanese society to create a law prohibiting ethnic discrimination.

When looking at studies on foreigners living in Japan, Okawa (see Chapter 13, "A Life in a Different Soil: Subjective Perspective of Foreigners in Japan") notes that most of them are conducted by Japanese researchers. Noting that these studies are conducted solely from the Japanese perspective, he compared Okawa's experience with studies of foreign children, comparing the world as seen by the people involved with the world as seen by the researchers.

> "The garden of the house where I once spent my childhood is no longer there."
>
> "As I write this article, I am imagining a garden that used to be on the other side of the world, next to a beautiful garden that I have never seen before. And the story that began in that garden continues to this day. As an immigrant, I am a flower that has to live in a different soil" (Chapter 13, "A Life in a Different Soil: Subjective Perspective of Foreigners in Japan").

From Okawa's perspective, the gardens of A and C, the subjects of this study, are in the Korean Autonomous Region, and as long as both remain in Japan, they can be considered as flowers that must live in soil different from that of their homeland.

In this study, the life stories of A and C were analyzed by TEA. The sociolinguistic space was then represented in terms of language and country of residence in A's diagram, and in terms of region of residence and language environment in C's diagram. Looking at each figure in detail, A is mentally trapped in a work environment where Japanese is the main language at a Japanese company after studying in Japan.

If a garden is a "safe" place, as I first defined it, then for A, the space of the Japanese company was not a garden. However, the connection and encouragement he received from his family and friends in his home country helped him to regain his spirit and move on to a Japanese company. He said, "I was connected and encouraged by my family and friends in my home country, and this connection was reassuring, even though we mainly communicated in a language other than Japanese."

C stopped using Chinese during his studies in Japan. It can be said that for C, the post-graduate world became his "garden," a place where he felt safe.

Valsiner (2007) points out the relationship between the environment (action within the collective cultural world: creation of one's own ring world) and the individual (psychological—internal personal cultural world) in terms of internalization and externalization as interdependent construction processes.

Figure 14.6 Flowers blooming on the university campus.

Culture

When crossing cultures, people are exposed to differences, their world is distorted, and they are forced to interact with the self, but depending on how they tackle difficulties, new possibilities can also open up (Tezuka, 2007, p. 8). Lee (2007) states that when people encounter behavior or value judgments that they could not have predicted from their previous experiences or that they did not expect, they often assume the existence of a "different culture" there, and the item "culture" is brought up to explain the behavior and beliefs of others that are different from their own.

Cultural psychology operates on the idea of culture as an "inherently systemic subject," and culture operates on how individuals relate to their environment, whether in the form of symbols, cultural practices, models shared by peoples, or other forms. In other words, culture is not an external "causal force," but a resource that people use for their own adaptation (Valsiner, 2007).

From these definitions of culture, it follows that culture is within people and operates through the interaction of the environment and the individual.

Whether It Is Possible to Explain Things by Hypothesizing Garden in Cultural Psychology as a Social Linguistic Space

The functioning process of a sign means semiotic mediation. The purpose of cultural psychology is to depict the moments and processes of individual transformation as a function of the sign (Sato, 2012b, pp. 216–217). In cultural psychology, culture works with the idea of a systematic culture of the Lord. Culture works in any form, such as symbols and cultural practices and models shared by ethnic groups, and this affects how individuals relate to the environment. Culture is an external cause and a resource that people use for their adaptation, not a "power to become causes" (Sato, 2012b, pp. 193–195). Based on this idea, Figure 14.7 was created, referring to Sato (2012b, p. 194).

In cultural psychology, humans, who generate meaning, work in a symbolic sphere full of diverse complexity and historical expansion (Valsiner, 2013, pp. 487–488). Culture can be illustrated through psychological processes, which differ based on the number of relationships people use to relate to their world (Sato, 2012b, p. 192). Considering the case of A and C, it would be possible to consider that interacting with people creates a sociolinguistic space, and in the process of living, people play and encounter in a number of gardens where the symbols surrounding them function invisibly.

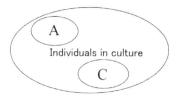 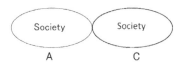

It is considered that the boundary line of "the culture" is strict and clear.

It is considered that the social boundary line is unstable, and it changes.

Figure 14.7 Comparison of the positioning of culture.

CONCLUSION

This study visualized the experiences among two Chinese-born Koreans and the circumstances that they encountered using TEA. It is emphasized that all meaning generation at the personal cultural level occurs by putting oneself in social life (Valsiner, 2013, p. 488). The Chinese-born Koreans studied in this research selected their own language use; this is the result of their putting themselves in the sea of symbols, which certainly work invisibly, and this creates the interactions between personal culture and societies.

Although A and C's choice of language changed with their jobs, family connections, and interactions with friends, they did not come to the conclusion that sociolinguistic space = garden. A separate chapter needs to be written. One thing we do know is that from the TEM diagram, we can infer that they learned language to enhance themselves, to find their roles, and made language choices according to their roles.

These can be considered part of human development. What should the garden look like then? It would be a safe place to be and a place where we can turn to ourselves.

One cannot carry a garden with one in the process of moving through boundaries and borders from the time one enjoys life in this world. However, we may take our garden (our cherished memories, our safe space, our beautiful flowers and trees, our personal experiences and actions) into our personal lives.

REFERENCES

Cui, X. (2013). *Led by Korea group society after the nation unification in China and the foreign language culture founding of a country*. Sotsuchisha. (Original in Japanese)

Han, M., & Xu, Y. (2012). An analysis of international labor migration and the sending home of income: The case of Jilin Province, China. *The Journal of Economics of Kwansei Gakuin University, 65*(4), 121–144.

Hirose, M. (2012). 1–2 the meeting of the parent is stable as a mutual self-help group. In Y. Yasuda & S. Tastuya (Ed.), *Understanding of life path by using TEM: New development of the qualitative study* (pp. 71–87). Seishinshobo. (Original in Japanese)

Ichikawa, A. (2020). A Chinese-born Korean woman's process of selecting to live in Japan: From the case of returning to her home country in the last stage of her language acquisition. *Journal of Science for Human Services, 9,* 67–80.

Jin, H. (2015). Educational strategies of Korean immigrants in Japan : focusing on school selection and the language used at home. *Studies in Humanities and Social Sciences, 10,* 49–70. (in Japanese)

Kato, T. (2002). Beijing opera—Actor group of "Country of politics" and the language used at home. *Studies in Humanities and Social Sciences, 10,* 49–70. (Original in Japanese)

Kojima, Y. (2016). Mobility of Chaoxianzu and land transfer in rural Yanji. Region and environment. *Society for "Region and environment" Graduate School of Human and Environmental Studies, Kyoto University, 14,* 25–35. (Original in Japanese)

Kwon, H. (2011). *Migration Koreans in China: Self government of ethnic minority.* Sairyusha. (Original in Japanese)

Kwon, H. (2013). A newspaper report of horizon Japan of the invisible Korea group and ethnicity theory to a clue. In M. Motoji (Ed.), *The close area/community zone 4 Korean Diaspora and East Asia society which transform* (pp. 77–97) Kyoto University Press. (Original in Japanese)

Lee, Y.-S. (2007). Special feature: Identity beyond culture; challenges and possibilities when one confronts 'culture.' *Kokoro to Bunka, 6*(1), 11–19. (Original in Japanese)

Sato, T. (2012a). Session 2: I become me who do a qualitative study. In Y. Yasuda & T. Sato (Ed.), *Understanding of life path by using TEM: New development of the qualitative study* (pp. 4–11). Seishinshobo. (Original in Japanese)

Sato, T. (2012b). TEA as methodology or the culture psychology not to abstract theory—time. In Y. Yasuda & T. Sato (Ed.), *Understanding of life path by using TEM: New development of the qualitative study* (pp. 209–242). Seishin Shobou. (Original in Japanese)

Tezuka, C. (2007). "Special issue on identity beyond culture: Challenges and possibilities," Kokoro to Bunka. *The Multicultural Psychiatric Association, 6*(1), 8–10.

Valsiner, J. (2007). *Culture in minds and societies: Foundation of cultural pshychology.* SAGE Publishing.

Valsiner, J. (2013). *Construction of the new culture psychology and culture in society* (T. Sato, Trans). Shinyosha. (Original in Japanese)

Yamawaki, K. (2004). Foreign policy of the local government in contemporary Japan: Human right, globalization, multicultural. In A. Utumi & K. Yamawaki (Eds.), *Across a wall of the history: A settlement and commensal irenology* (pp. 219–248). Horitsubunkasya. (Original in Japanese)

Yasuda, Y. (2012a). Section1: Understanding VSI basic concept. In Y. Yasuda & T. Sato (Eds.), *Understanding of life path by using TEM: New development of the qualitative study* (pp. 2–3). Seishinshobo. (Original in Japanese)

Yasuda, Y. (2012b). Session 5 9±2. How to determine EFP from studies on human subjects and typology of Pathway. In Y. Yasuda & T. Sato (Ed.), *Understanding of life path by using TEM: New development of the qualitative study* (pp. 32–47). Seishinshobo. (Original in Japanese)

Yasuda, Y. (2017). The process of finding meaning in a woman's experience of infertility while receiving in-vitro fertilization: Trajectory equifinality modeling (TEM). *Society of Health and Medical Sociology Essays, 28*(1), 12–22. The Japanese Society of Health and Medical Sociology.

Yasuda, Y., & Sato, T. (Ed.). (2017). *Society implementation using TEM: Supporting fullness life*. Seishinshobou. (Original in Japanese)

Dictionaries

Umeda, H. (1989). "Korean." In T. Kamei, R. Kono, & E. Chino (Eds.), *Linguistics unabridged dictionary* (Vol. 2). Sanseido.

Official Documents

Japanese Ministry of Justice 2020 2 of Table 1, Nationality, local distinction, Residence status (the residence purpose) distinction, total resident alien. Retrieved June 25, 2021, from https://www.e-stat.go.jp/stat-search/files?page=1&layout=datalist&toukei=00250012&tstat=000001018034&cycle=1&year=20200&month=12040606&tclass1=000001060399

Komyo-in (Mirei Shigemori)

This garden embodies Mirei's belief of a "living garden," incorporating the passage of time, wind, rain, and all nature activities.

CHAPTER 15

"QUALIA" OF TRANSGENDER EXPERIENCES

What Visual Images Tells Us

Naoto Machida
Nara Women's University, Nara

PROLOGUE

"I can't write this essay."

A voice echoes in my head.

"It is too personal, not appropriate for an academic book."

The voice makes me fear exposing such private thoughts. Frankly speaking, even as I write the manuscript, I remain torn between a sense of resistance toward publishing it as part of a book and a kind of obligation to present it to the world as documentation of the living experience of a transgender person. What I am trying to write about might be too personal and perhaps would better stay within my diary. In any case, let us take up a pen and see what it writes.

The Semiotic Field of the Garden, pages 335–341
Copyright © 2024 by Information Age Publishing
www.infoagepub.com
All rights of reproduction in any form reserved.

INTRODUCTION

During the period of social distancing measures taken to curb the spread of COVID-19, I often walked around my neighborhood to counter my lack of exercise, as I could not travel freely to and from distant places. Even though I have lived in this neighborhood for many years, I have found many unexpected things. My biggest discovery was the gardens. Although the houses here are similar in design, their gardens reveal the individuality of each home. There are gardens with colorful hydrangeas, ornaments of mating animals, clay sculptures on the wall that seem to be children's work, and so on. The gardens symbolize the daily lives of the people in each house.

Hayao Kawai, a pioneer of psychotherapy in Japan, adopted an approach called *Hakoniwa therapy* (Japanese sandplay therapy) to understand the mental reality of his clients. Just as a sandplay garden expresses its creator's inner world better than mere words, a garden also serves to express the atmosphere of its house.

Psychotherapy and qualitative research share common features in that they approach psychological reality. Qualitative research seeks to reveal aspects of people's lives and experiences that cannot be illuminated using quantitative methods. A person's "way of life" or "experience" cannot be captured by an x-ray, nor can it be taken out of the human body through an incision and presented in a visible and tangible form. Since people's way of life and experiences cannot be captured as they are, researchers try to approach them indirectly through narratives and other means.

As one such researcher, I have been trying to get closer to the world of experiences, especially those of transgender people, through narratives. Through my doctoral research, I have been able to describe the world of their experiences to a certain extent. However, I have now run an obstacle to sharing my findings internationally: a language barrier. I have attempted to translate interviews conducted in English into Japanese for analysis and to translate interviews conducted in Japanese into English for publication, but perhaps due to my limited language skills, I have not yet been able to develop and share cross-cultural knowledge.

To develop trans-cultural knowledge about the experience of living as a transgender person, I would like to use two things as clues.

The first is my personal experience. Paradoxically, in looking at the universal, we must first revert to the personal. Just as classical psychological clinicians such as Sigmund Freud and Carl Gustav Jung developed their theories based on their own personal experiences, it seems to me that thoroughly submerging myself in my own experiences can lead to the discovery of universal themes that are common to others' experiences as well.

The second clue is the use of visual images. I will analyze my non-verbal expressions, or "garden," in the broad sense of the word, with pictures, movies (anime), manga, and other representational works. The content of this chapter is an attempt to describe the way I live my life by describing my "garden," and through this, to elucidate the experience of living as a transgender person.

THE STORY OF MY LIFE AND ITS CONNECTIONS WITH VISUAL IMAGES

I identify as transgender. The sex assigned to me at birth was female, but I do not think of myself as a woman; this condition is diagnosed as *gender dysphoria*.[1] I introduce myself as non-binary, or as a transman.

My life history can be traced through its connections with visual images. When I was a child, I loved drawing. My primary subjects were men, and I rarely drew women. Every time I found myself with free time, I took up a pen to draw fictional characters. Drawing was a kind of ritual for me, similar to brushing my teeth before going to bed. In addition, I was attracted to movies and animation. While watching these, I was able to dive into their fantasy worlds and immerse myself in the characters.

However, after entering high school, I stopped drawing and watching animated programs. I was afraid of being labeled as a "geek" by my friends. At that time, I wanted to hide my subculture affinity. However, I occasionally felt a great urge to draw. At such moments, I would secretly draw on a scrap of paper, in a diary, or anything that would allow me to maintain my privacy. As shown in Figure 15.1, all of these were also drawings of men, and when I drew them, some part of me felt calmer. However, at the same time, the act left me with a feeling of emptiness.

After starting university, I rarely drew. Instead, when I had some time on my hands during vacations, I looked back at the manga and anime I had been addicted to in my childhood. At this point, I had just learned about the concept of *gender identity disorder* (formerly named gender dysphoria). I was particularly fascinated by the gender-bending characters in manga and anime series. For example, in "Ranma 1/2," the body of the male protagonist becomes "female" when he gets doused with water in water, and in "Sailor Moon" (anime version), there is a character whose biological sex is female, but who usually uses "Boku" (the first-person pronoun used mostly by men in Japanese), wears a male uniform, and has a female partner.[2] In addition to such gender-bending characters, I also looked to works such as "Detective Conan," (Aoyama, 1994) in which the appearance of the character as seen by others differs from the character's actual self. Watching it brought me a kind of catharsis.

So far, I have discussed the characteristics of the pictures I have drawn and the anime and manga works I have been absorbed by. What I would

Figure 15.1 Drawings from my diary.

like to examine here is why I drew these pictures (or was compelled to draw them impulsively) and why I was attracted to certain anime and manga.

The pictures I drew were of male characters, like those in girls' comics, which portray the image of men in the culture I was allowed to live in (i.e., the female gender). I saw in them the image of what I wanted to be, and, while I was drawing them, I felt as if I could be that person. However, after I finished drawing, I used to feel empty because I had to return to the reality of who I was and face the fact that I was still myself (i.e., "female").

Another significant feature of the drawings is that they have relatively thin and male gendered bodies. This may be because I created images as an extension of my current self and expressed what I wanted to be. In addition, the hair is drawn with particular emphasis; it is not depicted below the neck. Only one eye is drawn on the faces. I did not consciously plan these details, but perhaps I drew them because I felt that my own body was far from my ideal body shape. If we consider the object relations theory[3] of "partial object," we may conclude that I was still at the stage where I had not obtained a unified self-image. The fact that the images are one-eyed suggests that they are halved: By being one with myself, they will become a unified entity.

PROSPECTS OF *QUALIA*-TATIVE PSYCHOLOGY

There is a special issue regarding "qualia" in the 5th volume of the Forum of the Japanese Society for Qualitative Psychology. This provides a platform for theorists to contribute to their suggestions. Each discussant offers thought-provoking insights. For example, Arakawa (2013), referring to fans of idols, argued that "qualia" are expressed through modifiers and mimetic words, and can be approached through the use of poetic language. Morioka (2013) defines qualia as things that are perceived as one interacts and struggles with subjects and argues that "the individuality of the researcher" is exuded in it.

I believe that "qualia" are the unique feelings or physical sensations that accompany the experience of events. By merely reading a list of events, we cannot understand what others have experienced. Only when that physical sense is evoked in the reader can the reality of the experience be conveyed to them (and the reader can relive the event).

THE RELATIONSHIP BETWEEN "QUALIA" AND VISUALS, AND DRAWING AND REPRESENTATIONAL WORKS AS A "GARDEN"

Visual images can play a major role in expressing the "qualia" of experiences that the individual has not yet articulated. For me, experimenting with the self-image of who I wanted to be through drawings and diving into stories where I could repeat conflicts were acts of searching for my own identity. This is why, as I mentioned earlier, it led to "cathartic," or therapeutic, effect (Vygotsky, 1971). A painting or a work of art in which a person has been absorbed can be a clue to the qualia of their experience and to the resolution of their conflict.

At the time of my drawings, I had not yet been able to articulate my concerns about gender, nor was I aware of the term "transgender." However, I was unconsciously attracted to work linked to my personal themes. In other words, I felt there was a gap between the way I was seen by others and how I wished to be. I experienced the desire to live in a way that transcended my gender. I may have used my drawings as a "garden" which surrounded me, as an expression of my desire. Additionally, by drawing pictures, I was able to live the way I wanted in my imaginary world, albeit only for a short time.

However, it was also an act that brought me face-to-face with the disparity between the real world and my own, and that is why it also brought about a sense of emptiness.

According to Yamada (2010), visuals allow images to leap forward and facilitate the communication of feelings and emotions more easily than language, which is constrained by temporal structures and conceptual frameworks. By employing visual images, we can represent experiences in a way that can be understood internationally. Thus, I use this essay as a starting point for developing international knowledge of the experience of living life as a transgender person.

EPILOGUE

Qualia is closely related to the concept of "deep experience" in cultural psychology, which refers to an experience that cannot be expressed in words. A theoretically refined version of this concept based on semiotics is "hyper-generalized meaning" (see "Editorial Introduction"). Visual images are a medium to express such hyper-generalized meaning more directly and sensitively. Through a discussion of visual images, we will be able to get closer to the "qualia" of experience.

I am still afraid of what readers will think of this essay.

The voice still rumbled in my head as the deadline approached. I could not find an answer by sitting at my desk, so I decided to go out for a short walk. Suddenly, I felt like listening to Sakanaction's[4] "Moth"[5] as I walked.

> I'm still
> (I can't create)
>
> I want to keep searching
> (such words)
>
> You can't hold on to it
> Things that can't be realized.
>
> You can't compare
> I knew I'd lose
>
> Breaking the cocoon and becoming a moth, minority
> A heart in turmoil, all the way to the third eye
>
> Becoming a flying moth, minority
> Even though my wings are folded by the falling rain
> Even if the feathers fold in the rain

Sending out my writings and drawings makes me feel like a moth that has broken open its cocoon and crawled out to join the butterflies. My writing has likely become impressionistic prose. I would like to participate as a moth for the time being, and put my pen down.

NOTES

1. According to *Diagnostic and Statistical Manual of Mental Disorders DSM-5*, gender dysphoria is defined by the discomfort or distress that may accompany the incongruence between one's experienced or expressed gender and one's sex assigned at birth (APA, 2013).
2. The relationship between the two is not clearly described in the work.
3. A theory that assumes the existence of an individual's inner world and believes that the conditions of the inner world in which the self and the object interact affect the individual's interpersonal relationships in the external world.
4. A Japanese rock band with highly literate lyrics and nostalgic folk melodies.
5. Baku Idegami, known as an androgynous model, appears in the last scene of the promotional video.

REFERENCES

American Psychiatric Association. (2013). *Diagnostic and statistical manual of mental disorders: DSM-5.* American Psychiatric Pub.

Arakawa, A. (2013). 現場の質感とは何か, そしてその記述を妨げるものは何か [What is the sense of quality in field site? What is the obstacle to describe it?]. *Japanese Association of Qualitative Psychology, 5,* 5–12. https://doi.org/10.24525/shitsuforum.5.0_5

Aoyama, G. (1994). 名探偵コナン [Detective Conan]. Shogakukan.

Morioka, M. (2013). 言葉の臨界―質的なものの行方 [Clinical zone of speech: On the vicissitude of the quality in the human discourse]. *Japanese Association of Qualitative Psychology, 5,* 57–63. https://doi.org/10.24525/shitsuforum.5.0_57

Vygotsky, L. S. (1971). *The psychology of art.* Massachesetts Institute of Technology.

Yamada, Y. (Ed.). (2010). この世とあの世のイメージ―描画のフォーク心理学 [Images of this world and the other world: Folk psychology of drawing]. Shinyosha.

Eye in Eye by Edvard Munch, Norwegian 1899–1900.

COMMENTARY PART IIIA

SELF-CULTIVATION

The Process of Finding Space for Oneself and Others

Line Joranger
University of South-Eastern Norway

As human beings we are busy understanding other human beings to achieve wisdom, while the key to understanding another mind may be through our own mind. When Socrates was once asked what self-cultivation was and to sum up what all philosophical commandments could be reduced to, he replied: "Know yourself." The phrase, "Know thyself," is centuries old and connects to the art of self-cultivation. Self-cultivation is about knowing yourself in a broader context. It is about understanding your real (and true) needs, desires, goals, weaknesses, and everything else that makes your life good and liveable. It requires a deep understanding of your past and current self and how your life connects to family, culture, history, and current situation. Your personal theories (self-narratives) about who you are, influence how you behave, and how you understand others. An accurate sense of who you are in yourself and in connection to others makes self-improvement possible.

In this part of the book, you will get a deeper understanding of what self-cultivation may look like, for different people, in different societies.

In Chapter 11—"Cultivation in Self and Environment: When a Voice Echoes From One Garden to Another"—Campill, uses the cultivation of the garden as a metaphor of self-cultivation, that is, selfcare, identity construction and self-environment impact. The chapter shows that the process of self-cultivation is full of paradoxes and contrasts. At one side our identity is influenced by the environment, it grows by co-existing with the world, on the other hand, our need of self-cultivation makes us form and influence the same environment to get a broader space for our individual shapes and colors. The different dialog that goes on between the self and the world shows that cultivation is always more than an individual directed act. Like the cultivation of the garden, it cannot totally be controlled, suddenly something unforeseen happens that forces us to think otherwise and to see ourselves and the world with new eyes.

In Chapter 12—"Moving Through Racial Gardens: Personal and Collective Dimensions of Racial Becoming: A Transcultural Autoethnographic Account"—de Abreu, uses autoethnographic data to illustrate how self-cultivation and identity formation appears through multiple cultural connections. In the modern world, to work on one's identity falls together with integration and negotiation of different cultural origins. Like the plants in the garden, it is a never-ending negotiation and fight for recognition, social order, and space. Like the shape and colors of the plants, the human bodies are signs that tell a lot of who we are. Like plants in the garden, people can be deceiving and misleading in situations where we are not completely sure of how to categorize someone in terms of their race, class, and gender.

In Chapter 13—"A Life in a Different Soil: My Ontological Mobility as an Immigrant"—Okawa, elaborates the challenges connected to the negotiation and integration of culture and identity through her autoethnographic research on herself as an Japanese-Brazilian immigrant. Being a third generation Japanese-Brazilian in her home country of Brazil and a second-generation Brazilian living in Japan, Okawa is an immigrant in both countries. The chapter examines the meaning of mobility for migrants. Using the concept "ontological mobility," when contemplating the meaning of migration, the chapter illustrates the mental movement and self-development that accompanies migration. In this case the physical movements that connect to migration did not correlate with the mental movements. The chapter shows that where and why one moves, and with whom and how one moves, has a significant impact on ontological movement in an immigrant's life.

The concept of self-cultivation and cultural background is further discussed in Chapter 14—"Chinese-born Korean People's Experience and Present-Day Japan: Using TEA." By investigating individual experiences, language use, and effect of life decision, from the narratives of two Chinese-born Korean people, Ichikawa, elaborates a content rich TEM diagram that shows different and varied experiences connected to being a Chinese-born Korean. The narratives show how the informants, like plants in a garden, develop different coping strategies to survive in a more or less hostile society: "Being told he was an 'inferior race' made Mr. C very sad, deciding not to speak Chinese anymore. He also decides to hide his Chinese nationality." Mr. C seems to support himself with an idea that his identity was created by the future, not the past. As for his future, he would work hard to get a job that was recognized in both Korea, China, and Japan.

Last chapter in this section—"Qualia" of Transgender Experiences: What Visual Images Tells Us"—is written by Machida. In the absence of words that can describe his experience as a transgender he uses visual images. To develop a universal transcultural knowledge about being as a transgender person, he uses his personal experience or his inner garden of experiences. The visual images replace his non-verbal expressions of deep unique feelings and physical sensations that accompany the experience of events. The concept "Qualia" relates to deeper experiences that cannot be expressed in words.

All the chapters show examples of different journeys of self-cultivation and how these journeys depend on cultural and personal recognition. Like the plants in the garden, to grow up as a certain person with a certain identity, color, and shape, you must affect the environment that you live in as well as adapt to it. There seem to be different gardens in a person's life. If the self as an individual belongs to the psychological level of the garden, gathering, and regulating all its experiences and its biological needs, the self as a person belongs to the sociological garden on which it serves as an agent-in-society, so that all of one's social rules come into play. If we also think of the individual, as a physical plant or an organism, as having a certain kind of relationship with death and the cosmos, we may also think of the self as a social and spiritual organism knowing one's destiny as vulnerable and dependent on the environment and other human beings.

The self-cultivation extends from inner reflection (wisdom) to outer social action (praxis). The chapters show that the self is aware of the inevitable obstacles facing it, both in terms of its social roles, within various contexts of social interaction, and its biological needs and limitations. It absorbs the relevant knowledge based upon its own physical condition and social-historical-cultural background, and then transforms this knowledge into "insight wisdom" which it may act upon or project in the form of concrete social action or praxis. The different chapters show that one in certain extent can draw some universal models of self-cultivation on the one hand, and on the other hand, a model that can describe the operation of self-cultivation within the limits, and under the constraints, of various socio-cultural systems.

My husband Charles photographing the garden we cultivate in an urban public space.

COMMENTARY PART IIIB

THE GARDEN AS A METAPHOR FOR CULTIVATION OF THE SELF AND THE OTHER

Daniela Schmitz Wortmeyer
Independent Researcher

This is the story of the heavens and the earth when they were made, in the day the Lord God made the earth and the heavens. Now no bush of the field was yet on the earth. And no plant of the field had started to grow. For the Lord God had not sent rain upon the earth. And there was no man to work the ground. But a fog came from the earth and watered the whole top of the ground. Then the Lord God made man from the dust of the ground. And He breathed into his nose the breath of life. Man became a living being. The Lord God planted a garden to the east in Eden. He put the man there whom He had made. And the Lord God made to grow out of the ground every tree that is pleasing to the eyes and good for food. And He made the tree of life grow in the center of the garden, and the tree of learning of good and bad.

—Genesis 2:4–9

Since ancient times, the relationship with nature has been deeply linked to human existence, raising questions, stimulating imagination and the search for meaning. We grew out of Nature, with Nature, and sometimes against it, and we are always striving to adapt to natural conditions while trying to shape the environment to our will. Thus, it is not surprising that meaning making processes with different degrees of generalization and abstraction are nurtured by these seminal experiences, which acquired strong and profound affective meanings throughout individual and collective trajectories.

By observing how life perpetuates itself, how seeds interact and are nourished by countless environmental factors and can develop, continuously transforming themselves and also promoting changes in the elements that surround them, and revealing that, although they are autonomous systems, they are also part of a broader natural system, human beings sought knowledge for the cultivation of their own existences. Sometimes they identified with the seed that is growing and making exchanges, sometimes with the gardener trying to channel the seed's development, sometimes with a plant that is transplanted from its original environment and struggles to adapt to a foreign soil, among manifold semiotic constructions.

As first explored by Vygotsky (1988, 2001) and further elaborated by Valsiner (2012, 2014), the semiotic mediation entails a particular kind of psychological development in human beings, enabling the transcendence of the here-and-now by its imaginary projection through the use of signs. According to Charles S. Peirce's definition (1973/1986, as cited in Valsiner, 2012), a sign is an object that lies to the mind (or eyes) of someone rather than something else. It may be a word, an image, a sound, a gesture or a material object that evokes some idea, feeling, or object beyond itself. Thus, by making use of different types of signs, which are infinitely combined, overlapping, transformed, and interconnected in our minds, we may relate immediate body sensations to other experiences and meanings, reaching high levels of generalization and abstraction (Valsiner, 2012, 2014; Wortmeyer, 2022; Zittoun et al., 2013).

Therefore, the relationships with and within the natural environment can be analyzed from different perspectives and acquire meanings that go far beyond its materiality, for instance, being considered as metaphors for several phenomena. As argued by Campill (see Chapter 11—"Cultivation in Self and Environment: When a Voice Echoes From One Garden to Another"), the use of metaphors in science can help to deepen knowledge, leading to knowledge condensation and redefinition of our already generated meaning. The metaphorical thinking is an attempt to shed light on complex experiences and generate new knowledge, by creating a link between previously non-related objects and exploring their connections through symbolic lens.

In this context, the particular properties of the phenomenon that will be highlighted (and the ones that will remain overshadowed) will depend on the interpretation frame proposed by the analyst. So the psychological interpretation of metaphors, as pointed out by Christensen and Wagoner (2015), is not a mere descriptive logical issue, but a complex perceptive activity that resonates with the phenomenological experience of a particular person in a given context.

The five chapters that make up Part III of this volume illustrate well how a particular sign—"garden"—can evoke multiple and varied meaning making processes, catalyzing rich personal accounts related to different spheres of life, intertwined with original theoretical elaborations. The symbolic power of gardens and gardening as metaphors for human existence, which was expressed in many cultures across times, is actualized in these texts. The authors often start from experiences related to special gardens that punctuated their life trajectories, and move beyond these specific events to creatively explore various challenges of human development in connection with complex social and cultural environments.

In this brief commentary, I intend to recover some of the highlights of these chapters and try to establish a dialogue between them, taking as an axis the dynamics of cultivating the self and the other through semiotic mediation processes that were explored by each author. Some expansion possibilities with a view to future studies will also be discussed.

CULTIVATING THE SELF AND THE OTHER

As approached throughout this volume (e.g., see Tsuchimoto, "Editorial Introduction"), human development is a complex, co-constructive, and bidirectional process, in which person and environment, the self and the other, are constantly mutually affected and transformed (Branco & Valsiner, 2012; Valsiner, 2012, 2014; Zittoun & Gillespie, 2015; Zittoun et al., 2013).

However, this relationship of exchange and mutual transformation is generally not free of tensions and resistances from both parties. As I previously explored (Wortmeyer, 2022), human beings intentionally strive to change the world to meet their own expectations, values, and goals, while constantly being confronted with the resistances of that world to their actions. Trying to expand our limits and cross borders to the next moment in time, we experience otherness, the different or the unknown, feared or desired. Hence, despite our usual attempts to turn "others" into objects that fit our subjective agendas, they generally resist our agency—acting and reacting in favor of their own stability or intentional demands (Marsico & Varzi, 2015; Valsiner, 2014, 2016).

The authors of this part of the volume analyzed these dynamics of interaction between the self and the other in different areas and contexts, showing that, while we strive to cultivate our "gardens"—that is, to shape the social and material world according to our intentionality—the "natural environment"—which can mean the natural and physical world, but also other intentional beings, social institutions, and so on—resists our attempts at cultivation. And, particularly in relation to the social world, others often make us objects of their own agency, and somehow we need to negotiate and adapt our initial goals to others' agendas in order to be able to live together in community. As argued by Glăveanu (2015), an individual's agency is always "co-agency," as it requires interaction and coordination with the material and social world.

Campill (see Chapter 11—"Cultivation in Self and Environment: When a Voice Echoes From One Garden to Another") analyzes this dynamic based on the garden metaphor, in which he identifies a constant "fight" between the "gardener" and the "garden": While the self is constantly trying to mold the environment, the natural environment is oriented to its "junglification," which means to develop without human influence. The author considers that the gardener needs to establish a dialogue between his own goals and, for example, the natural demands of the ecosystem, the characteristics of the cultivated species, the weather, and other external factors, in ways that "cultivation" and "adaptation" constitute dialogic poles that need to be balanced for a garden to succeed.

Applying these principles to a more general developmental perspective, Campill analyzes that, in a person's dialogical interactions with the environment, on the one hand, his or her identity is guiding this dialogue, but, on the other hand, it is constantly changing as a result of communication with otherness. In such interactions, there is a cultivation of hypergeneralized meanings that are continuously reconstructed both by "the individual multi-voice (identity)" as well as "the social multi-voice (society)." Therefore, when an individual promotes the evaluation and redefinition of meanings in his dialogue with otherness, he can also promote transformations in the collective culture.

Campill concludes that "cultivation is an essential process in a human being's everyday life," which encompasses changing one's own internalized meanings and personal culture, as well as externalizing new meanings and promoting ruptures and changes in wider layers of society. How challenging these processes can actually be is clearly evidenced in intercultural experiences, as we will see below.

MOVING THROUGH DIFFERENT GARDENS

The foregoing reflections converge with Abreu's autoethnographic analysis (see Chapter 12, "Moving Through Racial Gardens: Personal and Collective Dimensions of Racial Becoming: A Transcultural Autoethnographic Account") of his experiences as a Brazilian expatriate in the United States. This author points out that, as an arena for negotiation between culture and nature, gardens are objects of human-made categorization systems, linked to culturally shared meanings and practices. Thus, considering the garden "as a metaphor for a social order organized according to the parameters of a certain culture," he analyzes that "as in the case of plants in a garden, members of a particular social order are also restrained by the culturally produced categorization systems to which they are subjected." However, he stresses that plants—and people—are not passive beings in these processes, and there is always some form of negotiation implicit in such relationships.

In the mentioned chapter, Abreu focuses on the strangeness that he, as a foreigner, felt in relation to the categories of "race" in the United States. To interact in this new "garden," he had to become familiar with the repertoire of meanings that underpinned the collective culture and redefine his own self-image and identity. As the author reflects:

> Like plants in a garden, we tend to perceive race as a feature of the natural landscape, fixed in the determining realities of biology. But despite some biological characteristics, arbitrarily chosen to create some form of coherent classification, a plant can be categorized differently and perform different functions in different cultural contexts, and so is the case with people when it comes to the ways they are racially labeled.

In his previous life trajectory in Brazil, Abreu didn't consider skin color as a relevant aspect of his identity—as he was perceived as "White" in this cultural categorization, he had the privilege of being "socially perceived as non-raced" (since the references were based on "White normativity"). Things changed when he migrated to the United States, and began to be classified in an "ethnic minority," as he points out: "Brazilian identity in the United States (as much as any other Latin American identity) is linked to a sociopolitical dynamic that ranks people from 'third world' countries (in general) and Latinos in the United States (in particular) as inferior." Thus, according to the racial classification system of this collective culture, Abreu was suddenly no longer a "White," but a "Latino," and even a "Hispanic"—despite not speaking Spanish at the time—experiencing the concrete impacts of the cultural meanings associated with these identities.

Similar challenges to adaptation in a "foreign garden" were faced by Okawa (see Chapter 13, "A Life in a Different Soil"), who migrated as a child from Brazil to Japan. Despite being of Japanese descent, Okawa reports that he was raised as a "normal Brazilian" until elementary school, so when he moved to Japan, he faced difficulties in mastering the language and other cultural references. The way this echoed in the social environment provoked negative reflections on his self-image and relationships, as described by the author:

> When I was in elementary school in Brazil, I was also bullied in the same way. I was also bullied in Brazil because I looked Japanese. At the time, I could not

understand the bullying. I could not understand the bullying because I was born and raised in Brazil. But in Japan, I faced the same kind of bullying. In Brazil, I was called "Japa," but in Japan, I was called "Gaijin." In retrospect, I think that my problems with identity may have started in my early elementary school years.

Thereby, Okawa expands the discussion of problems related to immigration to a broader framework that encompasses the subjects' entire life trajectory, considering the challenges of building an individual identity in different socio-cultural contexts. He adopts a critical position in relation to the mainstream trend of research on the topic: "In migration studies, I am seen as an immigrant before I am an individual. I am swallowed up in the larger wave, and I, like many other immigrants, focus on the difficulties of migration."

The author proposes to look at the complexity of migrants' experiences and challenges, which include not only their relationships with a supposedly homogeneous dominant society, but also with other foreigners, with their own family members and with other migrants of the same nationality. In all these relationships, the subjects are not passive beings. Okawa observes that the studies on the topic commonly adopt a cultural assimilative approach, which does not consider the migrants' perspective and their intentionality oriented to the future: "I wondered if Japanese researchers could really understand how we felt...it is necessary for researchers not only to describe the reality as it is, but also to be close to it."

It can be analyzed that an individual's identity is a dynamic synthesis from various semiotic positions (Leiman, 2002) occupied in different spheres of experiences and sociocultural contexts. This internalization does not correspond to a mere importation of the external, but to a complex process of reconstruction of lived experiences in cultural structures, which allows the emergence of new possibilities and the enrichment of the social environment (Shotter, 1993a, 1993b; Valsiner, 2012, 2014; Wortmeyer, 2017, 2022; Wortmeyer & Branco, 2019; Zittoun & Gillespie, 2015). Abreu and Okawa's autoethnographic studies shed light on the processes of identity reconstruction of the authors throughout these interactions, as well as their attempts to promote changes in the external environment through their active participation in social practices.

Furthermore, the aforementioned chapters show that, despite being mediated by signs, psychological experiences go far beyond strict attempts at description and classification by means of cognitive tools. Generalizations and anticipations based on linguistic labels (e.g., foreigner, immigrant, White, Latino, Gaijin, etc.) cannot fully translate the complexity and richness of unique active beings, nor can they predict never-before-lived experiences. Moreover, verbal language is never enough to adequately express the dense affective-semiotic fields that are at the core of collective and individual cultures, as will be discussed in more detail next.

WHEN VERBAL LANGUAGE IS NOT ENOUGH

The role of language in intercultural relationships is focused by Ichikawa (see Chapter 14, "Chinese-Born Korean People's Experience and Present-Day Japan: Using TEA") in her research about the experiences of Chinese-born Korean people immersed in Japanese society. In her analysis of the life trajectories of two research participants through the trajectory equifinality model (TEM), it is possible to observe how the definition of the language predominantly used by the subjects in each phase of life—Chinese, Korean or Japanese—is not only guided by practical aspects, but also by identification with values and ideals related to the worldview of a given collective culture, which resonate with their identities and life projects in the making.

In the mentioned research, both participants had prior knowledge of the Japanese language when they emigrated to Japan to study and then work, and felt the desire to integrate into the new collective culture. However, as they experienced concretely, to be socialized in a specific culture, the formal learning of verbal language only reaches the tip of the iceberg. Worldviews, meanings and values that are hypergeneralized and internalized at a post-verbal level underpin communication in a given sociocultural context—and it takes a long coexistence to really capture these nuances that are implicit in everyday interactions (Shweder & Much, 1991; Valsiner, 2012, 2014; Wortmeyer, 2017, 2022).

Adichie (2014) beautifully expresses this phenomenon when referring to the adaptation challenges of her character Ifemelu, a Nigerian student who migrated to the United States:

> Ifemelu laughed, too, although she did not fully understand the joke. And she had the sudden sensation of fogginess, of a milky web through which she tried to claw. Her autumn of half blindness had begun, the autumn of puzzlements, of experiences she had knowing there were slippery layers of meaning that eluded her. (p. 143)

The "slippery layers of meaning" indicate message contents that cannot be fully captured by the pure domain of verbal language. The difficulty in making sense of and managing this lack of control can result in great stress and frustration, in the feeling of not being able to fully integrate into the host society. In the case of Ichikawa's research, one participant chose, in the end, to return to China, where she had "family and friends" and perhaps would feel truly belonging.

Even so, the affective connection with Japan and the Japanese language continued to be part of the subject's identity, and the participant projected to find a more satisfactory solution in the future: for example, returning to work in Japan at a foreign company—we can infer that perhaps the participant expects to be better integrated into a "globalized organizational culture," where her idiosyncrasies, ideally, could be positively valued. In turn, Ichikawa's second research participant struggled to detach himself from previous identifications (Korean, Chinese) that were devalued in his current cultural context in Japan, and dreamed of finding a new identity in the future—"getting a job that he can actively work in Korea, China, and Japan"—which perhaps would allow him to integrate the different dimensions of the self and be positively recognized for the cultural mosaic that makes up his identity.

Ichikawa's work brings to light the ongoing tension between the self and the other, which are far from being monolithic entities—as discussed in the chapters by Campill and Okawa. The self is a bricolage of multiple experiences, values, and meanings and, at the same time that it aims to preserve its own autonomy and agency, it paradoxically desires the encounter with the other, to be valued, accepted, and integrated into a community—which means, in to some extent be subjected to the agency of others. Of course, there are different possible solutions in between these two poles from a collective and individual point of view. In any case, meaning-making processes play a key role in these negotiations—and the way particular experiences are canalized in a collective culture can sometimes leave narrow room for variability in individual expressions.

The previous reflections can be extended to other dimensions of human experiences such as gender. In this regard, Machida (see Chapter 15, "'Qualia' of Transgender Experiences: What Visual Images Tells Us") addresses the difficulties of building cross-cultural knowledge about the experience of people labeled "transgender" due to language barriers. To deal with this, the author proposes to go beyond the limits of verbal language, analyzing her own personal experiences and non-verbal expressions related to the theme.

Machida analyzes the images that helped her to deal with gender identity questions: By drawing and watching gender-bending characters in manga and anime series, she found a channel for expression, catharsis, and subjective elaboration. She considers that visual images can express the unique feelings ("qualia") related to experiences that have not yet been articulated by the individual: "A painting or a work of art that a person has been absorbed in can be a clue to the qualia of their experience and to the resolution of their conflict." In this context, she compares the visual images that surrounded her (drawings and animations) as a "garden" that was being cultivated, as an expression of her subjective world:

I experienced a desire to live in a way that transcended my gender. I may have used my drawings as a "garden" which surrounded me, as an expression of my desire. Additionally, by drawing pictures, I was able to live the way I wanted to in my imaginary world, albeit only for a short time. However, it was also an act that brought me face to face with the disparity between the real world and my own, and that is why it also brought about a sense of emptiness.

Through imagination and visual languages, the subject built an alternative space for the construction of meanings that, on the one hand, created new possibilities for self-expression and exploration. Although, on the other hand, it seems to have increased the distance between these experiences and her actual life, leading to a feeling of "emptiness."

Machida's work also uncovers how personal culture and individual identity are nourished by the meanings available in the collective culture, specifically with regard to gender meaning making. She points out how artistic expression can be a channel to overcome the limitations of verbal language and social discourse, paving the way to accessing hypergeneralized affective meanings and envisaging alternatives for internal and external dialogues between the self and the other.

CONCLUDING REMARKS

When I sit in my living room, I look at the several objects of decoration that are on the shelves and hanging on the walls: Ceramics bought on an unforgettable trip to Peru in my 20s; old pieces "saved" from a laboratory that was deconstructed in a school I worked on, which caused me a lot of pain; embroideries on nature motifs made by me, and also by my mother and mother-in-law; a reproduction of a poppy from *Flora Danica*, from the time we have been in Denmark; a blessing in German engraved on wood, which came from my grandmother's house when she passed away—later found out it was a gift to her from my father; and, among many other objects with special stories and meanings related to various places and people, a painting with a significant landscape of Brasília by Otoniel Fernandes, which we acquired when visiting the first in-person exhibition of this collection and is reproduced at the opening of Chapter 1 ("The Garden as a Symbolic Space: Trajectories of Affective-Semiotic Cultivation"). Is this my garden of memories? Although apparently very diverse, such as plants of different species and origins, these objects reflect experiences lived in multiple relationships and sociocultural contexts throughout my life trajectory, and are linked by affective meanings that make up my innermost self.

As my living room reflects, we develop as human beings through bonds and experiences lived in different sociocultural spheres—gardens—and we end up creating our own internal gardens, composed by our unique and constructive synthesis of the affective meanings internalized throughout this trajectory (Valsiner, 2019). These processes were analyzed in different ways in the chapters covered in this commentary, which creatively explored images related to the garden and gardening as metaphors for the relationships between the self and the other, involving processes of mutual cultivation and transformation.

In a sense, we are always migrating through gardens, encountering and establishing different kinds of interchanges with unique individuals and social groups, in ways that our personal cultures acquire traces of these interactions, just as we leave marks of our individual agency in other personal and collective cultures. With a view to future studies, it would be fruitful to explore more closely the processes through which these border transactions actually occur: How do certain collective cultural experiences—signs, places, artifacts, ideas, and so forth—become personal? How can what initially was "other" become "mine"? And through what processes do individuals actually promote transformations in collective cultures over time?

Furthermore, it would be interesting to deepen how uniqueness is built from multicultural experiences, especially considering the scenario of intense migration and globalization in which we live. In addition, how do individuals build bonds and a sense of belonging in this reality? How can respect for autonomy and diversity be balanced with the integration into a collective culture that enables communication and cooperation around a common project? The themes explored in the chapters mentioned here certainly have a vast area of cultivation ahead.

REFERENCES

Adichie, C. N. (2014). *Americanah*. Companhia das Letras.
Branco, A. U., & Valsiner, J. (2012). Editor´s introduction: Values as culture in self and society. In A. U. Branco & J. Valsiner (Eds.), *Cultural psychology of human values* (pp. vii–xviii). Information Age Publishing.
Christensen, T. S., & Wagoner, B. (2015). Towards a cultural psychology of metaphor: A holistic-development study of metaphor use in an institutional context. *Culture & Psychology 21*(4), 515–531.
Glăveanu, V. P. (2015). From individual agency to co-agency. In C. W. Gruber, M. G. Clark, S. H. Klempe, & J. Valsiner (Eds.), *Constraints of agency: Explorations of theory in everyday life* (pp. 245–265). Springer.
Leiman, M. (2002). Toward semiotic dialogism: The role of sign mediation in the dialogical self. *Theory and Psychology, 12*(2), 221–235.
Marsico, G., & Varzi, A. C. (2015). Psychological and social borders: Regulating relationships. In J. Valsiner, G. Marsico, N. Chaudhary, T. Sato, & V. Dazzani (Eds.), *Psychology as the science of human being: The Yokohama Manifesto* (pp. 327–336). Springer.

Shotter, J. (1993a). Vygotsky: The social negotiation of semiotic mediation. *New Ideas in Psychology, 11*(1), 61–75.

Shotter, J. (1993b). Bakhtin and Vygotsky: Internalization as a boundary phenomenon. *New Ideas in Psychology, 11*(3), 379–390.

Shweder, R., & Much, N. (1991). Determinations of meaning: Discourse and moral socialization. In R. A. Shweder, *Thinking through cultures: Expeditions in cultural psychology* (pp. 186–240). Harvard University Press.

Valsiner, J. (2012). *Fundamentos da psicologia cultural: Mundos da mente, mundos da vida* [Fundamentals of cultural psychology: Worlds of the mind, worlds of life]. Artmed.

Valsiner, J. (2014). *An invitation to cultural psychology.* SAGE.

Valsiner, J. (2016, July 27). *The human psyche on the border of irreversible time: Forward-oriented semiosis* [Conference session]. 31st International Congress of Psychology, Yokohama, Japan.

Valsiner, J. (2019). *Ornamented lives.* Information Age Publishing.

Vygotsky, L. S. (1988). *Thought and language.* Cambridge University Press.

Vygotski, L. S. (2001). *A construção do pensamento e da linguagem* [The construction of thought and language]. Martins Fontes.

Wortmeyer, D. S. (2017). *O desenvolvimento de valores morais na socialização militar: Entre a liberdade subjetiva e o controle institucional* [The development of moral values in military socialization: Between subjective freedom and institutional control] [Unpublished doctoral dissertation]. Universidade de Brasília.

Wortmeyer, D. S. (2022). *Deep loyalties: Values in military lives.* Information Age Publishing.

Wortmeyer, D. S., & Branco, A. U. (2019). The canalization of morality in institutional settings: Processes of values development within military socialization. *Culture & Psychology, 25*(4), 589–604.

Zittoun, T., & Gillespie, A. (2015). Internalization: How culture becomes mind. *Culture & Psychology, 21*(4), 477–491.

Zittoun, T., Valsiner, J., Vedeler, D., Salgado, J., Gonçalves, M., & Ferring, D. (2013). *Human development in the life course: Melodies of living.* Cambridge University Press.

PART IV
THE "GARDEN PROJECT"

Ritsumeikan University Osaka Ibaraki Campus
(the boundary between the park and the university is blurred)

CHAPTER 16

THE "GARDEN PROJECT"

Initiating International Cultural Exchange Through Gardens

Teppei Tsuchimoto
Chukyo University

Yuki Saito
Ritsumeikan University

Misato Furuse
Ritsumeikan University

Tatsuya Sato
Ritsumeikan University

Gardens exist worldwide and hold emotional value for humankind. They are both visual and narrative and embody personal culture. Based on the work of Jaan Valsiner, we engaged in an international exchange workshop called the "garden project" to understand both Japanese and Danish culture. This chapter, however, does not cover Danish culture. Here, we

The Semiotic Field of the Garden, pages 363–375
Copyright © 2024 by Information Age Publishing
www.infoagepub.com
All rights of reproduction in any form reserved.

consider an exchange program through the concept of a garden, with specific focus on Japanese culture.

This workshop was arranged as an exchange program between Aalborg University (Denmark) and Ritsumeikan University (Japan). As we could not physically stay with and meet each other because of the COVID-19 pandemic, we decided to arrange an online international exchange program on March 18–19, 2021. Twelve students participated in the program. Among them, nine were Japanese and three were Danish. The Japanese participants included a professor (Tatsuya Sato), a postdoctoral fellow (Teppei Tsuchimoto), and a doctoral student. Three Danish professors participated in the program. The students attended lectures on cultural psychology provided by the Japanese and Danish universities on-demand and did some prior coursework. Finally, they participated in live classes for 2 days (4.5 hours per day).

One of the lectures provided by the Japanese side was on "the garden as an object of cultural psychology." The lecturer (Teppei Tsuchimoto) explained how gardens represent "signs," and highlighted the elements that make them interesting as objects of cultural psychology (based on Introduction). The garden project was a part of the live class, wherein students presented their "favorite garden" to each other based on the lecture. Teppei provided the following instructions (Figure 16.1) for the live class (presentation of the students' favorite garden).

The garden project was conducted not only as a part of this international exchange program, but also during Jaan Valsiner's intensive lectures at Ritsumeikan University (2019, 2020). Previous garden projects have included childhood memories of gardens, gardens for spending time with family, ideal gardens, and Japanese and Chinese gardens. Some of these themes have evolved into spin-off chapters (Chapter 17, 18, 19, 20).

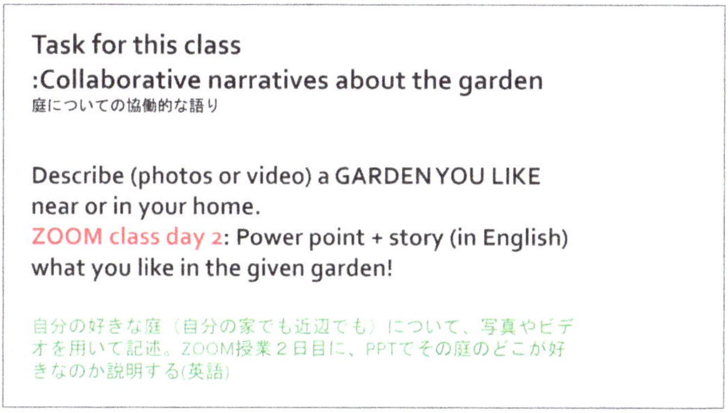

Task for this class
:Collaborative narratives about the garden
庭についての協働的な語り

Describe (photos or video) a GARDEN YOU LIKE near or in your home.
ZOOM class day 2: Power point + story (in English) what you like in the given garden!

自分の好きな庭（自分の家でも近辺でも）について、写真やビデオを用いて記述。ZOOM授業2日目に、PPTでその庭のどこが好きなのか説明する(英語)

Figure 16.1 Instructions for the presentation about "My Favorite Garden."

Consequently, the international exchange of participants' favorite gardens was more interesting and easier to communicate than the introduction of their respective countries. This chapter discusses the meanings and possibilities of garden-based international exchange programs, including the presentations and reflections of Yuki (the second author) and Misato (the third author), participants in the international exchange program.

AN EXAMPLE OF THE "MY FAVORITE GARDEN" PRESENTATIONS

In this section, Yuki and Misato each present their favorite garden.

Yuki's Presentation

My house has a small garden (Figure 16.2). It is bordered by a large living room window and is easily visible. Most of it is paved with concrete, and approximately a quarter of it comprises soil for planting. The garden is home to an olive tree planted by the real estate agent (Figure 16.3), blueberries bought by my father, and flowers and other plants bought by my mother. There is no sense of coherence, and it looks somewhat awkward.

Figure 16.2 My small garden and my dog "Kojiro."

Figure 16.3 My olive tree.

I started living in my current house when I was in my second year of high school. My old house had a balcony, but not a garden, so this garden was a unique experience at the time.

This garden reminds me of "Yoshio." *Yoshio* is the larva of a moth, an olive leaf-eating pest (Figure 16.4). Two years ago, at the end of summer, I found a large quantity of feces under the olive tree; when I carefully examined the leaves, I found moth larvae. I wanted to get rid of them, but I knew that a typhoon was imminent; I left them alone, presuming that they would die. However, after the typhoon had passed, the fat moth larvae were still devouring the leaves. I could not bear the thought of exterminating them, and I decided that the olive tree would survive at least one larva. Before I knew it,

Figure 16.4 Where is Yoshio?

the larva had a name: Yoshio; in my spare time, I would look at it and feel relaxed. Incidentally, Yoshio is a name that is given to boys in Japan. I do not know Yoshio's actual gender because I am not familiar with insects.

However, Yoshio died. It was gone before I knew it. There were no pupae, so the birds had probably eaten them. A larger bird that must have acquired its taste visited the olive tree the day after Yoshio's disappearance. I felt a little sad because it had become my routine to look at Yoshio when I came home from university. Two years have passed since then, and every year, Yoshio's friends appear on our olive tree, and birds come to peck at the olives. I find it surprising that so many creatures come to an olive tree that just happens to be in our garden.

This event reaffirmed how I deal with my own garden; I pay careful attention to insects, birds, and other living things there. The beauty of flowers and the pretty decorations are not important. I remember how I used to play in the garage of my previous house, picking up sowbugs, and I feel that I have an important connection with the garden and living things. Incidentally, while I am soothed by the creatures in the garden, my mother tries to grow beautiful flowers in it, and my father plants trees on a whim. My sister plays with her dog. Yoshio taught me that each person has a different way of interacting with the same garden, and that it is a living thing occupying a large part of my life.

Misato's Presentation: Relationship With the Garden

The Garden at Jin-ai Girls' High School

This is the rooftop garden of the high school I attended (Figure 16.5 & Figure 16.6).

Figure 16.5 The garden of Jin-ai Girls' High School.

Figure 16.6 A panoramic view from the garden.

I took pictures for my graduation albums and other commemorative photos in this garden. Consequently, when I look back on my high school days, this garden comes to mind. As it was an all-girls school, we put everything into our friendships, and I made many precious memories that are irreplaceable. Even today, when my friends and I get together, we always talk about the trivial things that happened in high school. This school was built in 1898 by Ryokyo Toku and his eldest daughter, Sumi, embodying the founding spirit of benevolence and love. Every morning, the students at the school chant a lesson called "Today's Modesty":

> Let us not forget the four-link (with ancestors, people, nature, and Buddha), and feel contented today.
> Let us not get angry today.
> Let us not tell lies nor do anything unreasonable today.
> Let us not speak ill of others nor well of ourselves today.
> Let us rejoice in our lives and do our duties today.

Today, Sumi's daughters continue to nurture her principles to be a light for tomorrow. When I was in high school, I did not understand its deeper meaning; it was only after graduating that I came to understand the importance of this lesson.

The garden is off-limits, but students are allowed to enter for commemorative photos. Although it is not a place that students can casually enter, it comes to mind whenever I think of my high school. While it is not a strong impression, the very fact that it comes to mind is an interesting feature of this garden.

This garden was created by the school management who visited high schools in Tokyo and elsewhere prior to the construction of a new school building and were impressed by school buildings with rooftop gardens. The garden was designed in the Japanese style to match the atmosphere of the Japanese classroom used for classes such as etiquette.

The Garden at My Grandmother's House

This garden is a part of my grandmother's house. My grandfather enjoyed the garden and kept it clean and tidy. He planted seasonal flowers, which he said would make visitors happy. After my grandfather passed away, my grandmother took care of the garden. When relatives visited, they gathered in the garden for commemorative photos. The garden is beautiful in any season—spring, summer, fall, or winter.

There are three gardens (Figures 13.7, 13.8, & 13.9), each with a different expression. Whenever I look at any of the gardens, I can picture my grandfather's face and hear his voice. Although there are no traces of him

Figure 16.7 Favorite part of my grandmother's garden.

Figure 16.8 Grandmother's plum tree.

Figure 16.9 My grandmother's garden from the entrance (tended for many years)

left and things have changed from when he was alive, I remember him vividly, even after all these years.

This garden was based on the idea that a garden and a house together make a home. Like the house, the garden was also designed in the Japanese style. My grandparents planted a plum tree in one of the gardens when they got married.

My Relationship With Gardens

These gardens have been the places where I take commemorative photos. Every time I look at them, I am reminded of the Buddhist teachings that have greatly influenced my outlook on life. The high school I attended places emphasis on Buddhism, especially the teachings of Jodo Shinshu. My grandparents were also Jodo Shinshu believers. The learning imbibed from my grandparents and at the high school overlapped with the Buddhist teachings I could feel from the garden. One of them was that of the three dharma seals. Koike (2009) found the following:

> The fundamental principle underlying the three dharma seals is the law of luck. Because all things are causal entities, they are always changing (*shogyou*

mujou), and there is no entity that remains unchanged forever (*shohou muga*). The state of being that realizes these things is peaceful (*nehan jakujou*).

I believe that the concepts of the three dharma seals and Wabi-sabi, which are intrinsic to Japanese culture such as gardens, are similar. Wabi-sabi is a uniquely Japanese aesthetic that has been greatly developed as the beauty of naturally feeling something profound and rich amid quietness. If we trace the roots of this esthetic sense, it is more Taoist than Buddhist. However, what Wabi-sabi states is similar to the essence of enlightenment in Buddhism. Even the most beautiful things change and are not eternal, which is probably why we are fascinated by them. The appearance of a garden transforms over the years, even during the same season. It seems that the pleasure of discovering the charm of the four seasons has been passed down from ancient times to the present. This project has provided me with a deeper understanding of why my grandparents always cherished their gardens.

DISCUSSION

In this section, we will discuss the meanings and possibilities of international exchange programs through gardens, based on Yuki and Misato's presentations and reflections. Through ZOOM online meetings (three times, about 3 hours in total), they developed a mutual understanding of each other's presentations and then wrote their reflections. Although there are some "online" characteristics, we will focus our discussion on the garden as a catalyst for international exchange owing to space limitations.

"Garden" as a Field-Like Sign

First, we introduce Misato's reflections:

I think of my grandmother's garden as a place that reminds me of my late grandfather. For my grandmother, however, the garden is a place where she planted a plum tree to commemorate her marriage to her husband (my grandfather). For me, the high school garden is a place where I remember special memories, such as photographs. On the other hand, when I asked my friends about it, they had forgotten that the garden even existed. They were aware that it was just a part of the school. The Japanese garden reminds me of Buddhism but may evoke different memories in others.

This is what Yuki and I have in common when it comes to gardens: We feel and remember different things even when we see the same garden. This can also be true for other online study abroad participants.

Here, Misato mentioned that the similarity with Yuki's presentation is that they "feel and remember different things even when [they] see the same garden." In other words, the *plurisignificance* (Werner & Kaplan, 1963) of the favorite garden as a field-like sign emerges. Plurisignificance is the phenomenon wherein one symbolic vehicle represents many referents (see Werner & Kaplan, 1963 for details and an experimental demonstration of this concept). From a different perspective, Yuki reflected the following:

> I believe that the common denominator between these two cases is "memories." Similarly, when each student in the online study abroad program gave a presentation on a garden that was important to them, many of them introduced the gardens with familiar episodes. If you are an expert in gardens, you may have a favorite garden among the famous ones, but most people fondly remember gardens that are familiar to them or that they have memories of. I also found it interesting to observe the elements that people focused their attention on within gardens. For example, I mentioned living things, and Misato mentioned Buddhist teachings. What we notice in a garden, which is a space with a high degree of freedom, can also lead us to reflect on ourselves.

This reflection includes many levels of perspective, but interestingly, Yuki pointed out that the similarity between the two presentations is "memories"; many of the participants described personally memorable gardens.

From the cultural psychology perspective, presentations based on "memories" are related to the *pre-construc*tion (Valsiner et al., 2023) of the memory—humans create affective sign fields from their experiences, even while reconstructing memories, toward an unfolding future. In the case of the garden project, participants reconstructed their own memories, which were not necessarily the same as past experiences. In this project, the memories of the plum tree in my grandmother's garden, the high school garden, the small garden at home, and the olive tree were constructed in order to communicate with others in the near future.

As Yuki reflected, it is noteworthy that although the garden project was conducted as an international exchange, most of the participants mentioned familiar gardens (e.g., home garden) rather than traditionally famous ones (e.g., the Japanese garden). The garden project, which tells the story of "My Favorite Garden," can evoke personally significant memories and provide unique perspectives and interpretations of that garden. This feature is rooted in a mutual understanding that each individual constructs a representation of personal culture and its uniqueness, rather than the external dimensions of the different countries of origin.

CONCLUSION: THE MEANING OF INTERNATIONAL EXCHANGE THROUGH GARDENS

In general, international exchange can lead to an abstract introduction of the features of one's own country (customs, food, sightseeing areas, etc.). This assumes that international exchange occurs as an inter-country event, such as that between Japan and Denmark. The implicit expectation is that the participants' first-person narrative will draw out their country's culture (in the sense of comparative cultural psychology), rather than their personal attributes. The revelation of one's personal lifestyle to strangers is often met with resistance—such communication tends to be public, conventional, and superficial. In contrast, an international exchange where people are introduced to each other's favorite gardens is fresh, personal, and makes for comfortable conversation compared with directly introducing one's own country.

This international exchange through gardens is interesting as it promotes the process of proculturation (Gamsakhurdia, 2019). Proculturation implies the creative synthesis of all available ideas by making sense of realized and possible developments with respect to the web of familiar (native or not) and unfamiliar (foreign or native) signs (Gamsakhurdia, 2019). Gamsakhurdia (2019) refers to this concept in the context of emigration, but students in international exchange programs also have some preliminary knowledge about the host country and their own country and have expectations from the program, albeit vague. The proculturation that synthesizes the initial semiotic opposition (nativeness <> foreignness) and creates new meanings from it can also be found by learning through international exchange.

Proculturation takes place at the boundary between "native" and "foreign." The garden is an essential sign field for the participants to integrate this opposition and develop awareness of their own culture. This is because the garden is a place where nativeness and foreignness are dynamically evolving. For instance, the garden of one's parents' house, which always felt like home, may appear to be a distant foreign place when returning after 20 years. In the example of the garden project, the participants were surprised to see the diverse gardens of other participants, who were similar people from the same country. Additionally, it was easy for participants from different backgrounds to find similarities in their memories. The garden project promotes deep learning of the participants' culture by relativizing the pre-assumptions of nativeness and foreignness and facilitating participants' encounters with other "foreign" (irrespective of nationality) cultures.

REFERENCES

Koike, H. (2009). *Introduction to Buddhism for high school students: From Shakuson to Shinran-shonin.* Honganji Press. (in Japanese)

Gamsakhurdia, V. L. (2019). Proculturation: Self-reconstruction by making "fusion cocktails" of alien and familiar meanings. *Culture & Psychology, 25*(2), 161–177. https://doi.org/10.1177/1354067X19829020

Valsiner, J., Tsuchimoto, T., Ozawa, I., Chen, X., & Horie, K. (2023). The intermodal pre-construction method (IMPreC): Exploring hyper-generalization. *Human Arenas—An Interdisciplinary Jouranl of Psychology, Culture, and Meaning, 6*(3), 580–598. https://doi.org/10.1007/s42087-021-00237-8

Werner, H., & Kaplan, B. (1963). *Symbol formation.* Psychology Press. (Digital printing, 2009)

Nishi Hongwan-ji Temple
(head temple of Jodo Shinshu Hongwan-ji school)

CHAPTER 17

THE INNER SANCTUM AS A "GARDEN OF BUDDHA" AND THE PEOPLE WHO "TAKE CARE" OF IT

How the Priest's Eldest Son Discovered the "Garden"

Gishin Tsukuba
Child Psychotherapeutic Facility Hibiki, Shimamoto, Osaka

The concept for this chapter was born while the author was taking the "Advanced Human Sciences" course offered by the Graduate School of Human Science, Ritsumeikan University in January 2021. In this course, I and the other students were asked to "narrate freely about your own garden." In the process of approaching this assignment, I likened the inner sanctum of a Buddhism temple to a "garden of Buddha." This chapter discusses the concept in more detail from the perspective of Buddhism scripture, cultural psychology, and my own experience as the eldest son of a Buddhism temple priest.[1] The purpose of this chapter is to explore new ways of narrating religious autoethnography by reflecting on the place of religious experience in my life using the metaphor of garden.

"THREE MAJOR SUTRAS OF PURE LAND BUDDHISM" AND THE PURE LAND

Three major sutras of Pure Land Buddhism is a general term for three scriptures: "the larger sutra on Amitāyus," "the sutra on contemplation of Amitāyus," and "the smaller sutra on Amitāyus." These three sutras are the fundamental scriptures of Jodo Shinshu Hongwan-ji school. The temple where my father is the priest belongs to Jodo Shinshu Hongwan-ji school, and we sometimes recite these sutras.

Not only these sutras, but all Buddhist sutras are the written form of the teaching orally transmitted by the Buddha (Godama Siddhartha). However, from a historical point of view, it is difficult to assume that the sutras that have been handed down today are direct reflection of what the Buddha taught (Shigaraki, 2011). There is no original sanskrit version of the sutra on contemplation of Amitāyus on three major sutras of Pure Land Buddhism. In addition, the content of these sutras, including other sutras that remain in their original form, varies from translation to another. The main reason for the difference in translations is that the ideological currents of the era and regions in which the monk who is the translator lived have influenced the translation.

So, how does the three major sutras of Pure Land Buddhism describe the Pure Land? The landscape of the Pure Land is described in detail, especially in the smaller sutra on Amitāyus. The smaller sutra on Amitāyus is in the form of the Buddha explaining to his disciples what the Pure Land is like. The Pure Land is a country, and its name comes from the fact that "the people in that country do not suffer in any way, but only receive various pleasures" (Jodo Shinshu Hongwanji-ha Research Institute, 2013). The country is filled with treasures of gold, silver, lapis lazuli and crystal, and lotus flowers that emit light of diverse colors. There is a building that is decorated with gold, silver, lapis lazuli, crystal, white coral, red pearl, and agate. In addition, there are various birds (including species that do not exist in this world) that preach Buddhism with graceful voices. In the smaller sutra on Amitāyus, after showing these scenes of the Pure Land, and it is said that Amida Buddha (Figure 17.1), the Lord of the Pure Land, is praised by many Buddhas.[2]

There are attempts to recreate scenes like these, even if only a little, in the inner sanctum of temples. For example, the candlesticks are decorated

The Inner Sanctum as a "Garden of Buddha" ▪ 379

Figure 17.1 Amida Buddha.

with bird designs, and the Buddhist objects, which are suspended from the ceiling for light, reproduce flowers (Figure 17.2). The altar, which houses the statue of Amida Buddha is richly decorated with gold leaf, making it look even more gorgeous than the great monks[3] on either side. The inner sanctum is also a space for rituals, so it cannot simply be a reproduction of the Pure Land. It is thought that an attempt was made to recreate the paradise in the inner sanctum to increase the solemnity of the rituals and to express the longing for and belief in the Pure Land without compromising the convenience of conducting the rituals.

Figure 17.2 The inner sanctum viewed from the outer sanctum.

EXPERIENCES—TENDING THE GARDEN OF BUDDHA

In my experience, the care of the inner sanctum can be generally classified into two types. It was "cleaning" and "decorating." Cleaning means cleaning the inner sanctum and other parts of the temple. I have been helping with some of this work since I was a child. However, nowadays, the author's father and the author's younger brother share the work. The first step in the process is to vacuum the tatami mats and flooring in the outer and inner sanctum, hallways, and meeting areas. Until the author was in elementary school, there was also the task of wiping tatami mats with a rag. At that time, there were many more children than now at the temple's "Kids Sanga" meetings for children, so all the children worked hard to clean the tatami mats with rags. Now, there is no more work to do with Kids Sanga, but the cleaning has been simplified. The dusting in Kids Sanga is only possible if a certain number of children can be expected to gather. The region where I was born is one of the areas in Japan where the birth rate is declining. Considering that the absolute number of children is decreasing, it may be inevitable that Kids Sanga will be smaller than it was 15 years ago when I was in elementary school. However, the loss of the physical experience of contact with the local Buddhist temple through the act of dusting seems to have a significant impact on the phenomenon of faith succession, which I am interested in.

The second step of the work is to wipe the urushi-coated threshold of the inner sanctum. Urushi lacquer has a unique luster that gives a sense of luxury by being applied to the surface. However, even that gloss has its weaknesses. Urushi loses its luster in the presence of moisture and humidity. Therefore, when my family and I clean the Urushi threshold, we use a dry rag to lightly wipe over it. This avoids deterioration of urushi due to moisture but makes it difficult to remove adhered wax and other dirt. There were several times when I was tempted to wipe hard or use some special detergent to remove the stains that have soaked through while wiping dry. However, urushi is a material that can retain its beauty for several decades if it is used with reasonable care. It is better to take care of urushi in such a way that it will last for a long time, even if the beauty of the new one fades a little, than to treat it badly and make a mess of it and spend a considerable amount of money in repairs.

After these cleaning procedures are completed, the "decoration" is done according to the type of ceremony. For example, if a funeral is to be held, all the doors of the inner sanctum must be closed, and the funeral altar must be set up. In the case of important memorial services unique to the sect, such as Hoonko (a ceremony held in gratitude for Shinran, the founder of Jodo Shinshu Hongwan-ji school, before and after the anniversary of his death), luxurious cloths called *uchishiki* are set in various parts of the inner sanctum to make it more vivid. In the inner sanctum are enshrined the seven high priests (seven Buddhist priests from India, China, and Japan who developed the doctrine of Nembutsu and who met the criteria set by Shinran), Rennyo (the eighth leader of Hongwan-ji; he expanded the Hongwan-ji school), Amida Buddha, Shinran, and Prince Shotoku (imperial family members who established Buddhism in Japan; Figure 17.3) are enshrined in the temple. Each of them has an altar, and when uchishiki is hung on these altars, I feel a very slight glow of the world where they (especially Amida Buddha) exist, the Pure Land.

"Decoration" is not just about putting on a cloth. Offering food such as sweets, rice, fruits, and flowers are also an important work. Lighting candles and burning incense[4] are also an important part of *oshogon* (decorating the Buddhist altar and inner sanctum). When I was a child, the most questionable part of this was the offering of food, especially rice. Even as a child, I understood that the wooden Buddhas and the people in the pictures did not eat rice offered to them. So why do we offer rice to be the Buddha before we eat it ourselves? I remember that it was no later than the 4th grade of elementary school that I understood that these offerings were an expression of gratitude.

Figure 17.3 Prince Shotoku.

At the temple, my family also clean the Buddhist objects that they usually use. Some of the Buddhist objects used in the inner sanctum are made of brass (Figure 17.4). Brass Buddhist objects turn yellow with soot and dirt after a year of neglect. Therefore, at the temple where I grew up, my family polish the brass Buddhist objects just before Hoonko. This process is called *omigaki* by me and my family. The first step in omigaki process is to remove the Buddhist objects from the inner sanctum and carry them to the work area. Even though the Buddhist objects are made of brass, there is still a possibility that it could be deformed by being dropped. Therefore, the person who carries them must be careful, for example, when carrying hanging Buddhist objects. The next step is to disassemble the carried Buddhist objects. Many Buddhist objects have a combination of two objects as a set. However, if the parts of the other Buddhist object are used when assembling, the parts may not fit together, and the assembly may fail. Therefore, when disassembling the device, it is necessary to place the disassembled parts in the right way so that the combination of parts is not mistaken. The disassembled parts are soaked in a cleaning solution diluted with water. At this time, the parts may be scrubbed with a brush while dipped in a cleaning solution to remove dirt from the fine decorative parts of the Buddhist objects. Next to the cleaning solution, soak the parts in hot water to wash off the cleaning solution on the parts. After dipping the parts in hot water, carefully wipe off any moisture on the parts on the parts with a towel to avoid causing rust. Then wipe off the adhering dirt with a special cloth using powerful force. By the time the water is wiped off, the yellowish color of the Buddhist objects has been restored to its former glory, but it can be further cleaned by polishing it with a special cloth. When I was in elementary school and junior high school, my father asked me to do this strong

Figure 17.4 Brass lamp in the shape of chrysanthemum.

polishing work, and he took it very seriously. My hands and fingers ached from polishing so hard, so I took a break to work on it. I did not want my hands to get sore, but I liked the work itself. After these tasks are completed, the Buddhist objects are reassembled and put back in their original places, and omigaki process is complete. The more I polish Buddhist objects, the more it shines, and the more I feel a sense of "nothingness," where no thoughts other than the desire to see its shine arise. In this section, there are many examples of temple "care" work, is the most impressive and my favorite.

Reflecting on these "tending" tasks, I thought that cleaning and decorating the inner sanctum was as laborious as caring for a real garden. The Pure Land does not require human care. However, if someone tries to recreate the Pure Land in this world, it will not be able to maintain its brightness and beauty without someone's hands. Campill (see Chapter 11) discusses that the gardener fights against *jungleification*. In this chapter, "garden" is treated as a metaphorical concept, but jungleification as a metaphor exists in the inner sanctum as well. It means the dust on the floor, the flowers left to wither, the brass Buddhist altar covered in soot and losing its shine, and so on. I find the impermanence of all things in such a reproduction of the Pure Land—the inner sanctum itself.

DISCUSSION—THE GARDEN OF BUDDHA AND SYMBOLS: SUMMARY AND ISSUES

As a summary of this chapter, this section will discuss the phenomenon of my finding the garden of Buddha in the inner sanctum, with a cultural psychology perspective. First, the impetus for writing this chapter came from a challenge to me to "narrate freely about your garden." If it were not for this assignment, I would not have written this chapter, nor would I have not found garden in the inner sanctum of the temple.

The basis of cultural psychology is the concept of "symbol," and a symbol, in the sense of cultural psychology is "something that points to something else by it" (Sato, 2019). The assignment that triggered the writing of this chapter was also a symbol as an aspect of "submission for the grading of the class," but for me, it also acted as a symbol for an opportunity to review my own life history and upbringing environment. This chapter is an autoethnography based on the context of the garden of Buddha and focuses on its care. However, I have a variety of religious experiences that were not narrated in this chapter. There is a possibility of developing the autoethnography into a study of my own more comprehensive religious development by extending the narrative to my other experiences. This means that the writing of this chapter becomes a new promoter sign.

It is my opinion that the inner sanctum of a Buddhist temple can be seen as a garden, which allows us to examine religious activities and daily life in a more familiar way. To maintain a garden, it needs to be "tended." The Pure Land, which normally does not require any maintenance by humans, becomes an existence that requires care when it is reproduced in the inner sanctum. This fact can be "shogyo-mujo"[5] proposition, but throughout this chapter, it brings to light the people (the family of the priest) who have been involved in the care. The work of caring for the temple, which is done at every annual event, is an extraordinary activity in the ordinary life. In this chapter, a small part of what I felt in the accumulating of "the extraordinary in the ordinary" was presented. As the eldest son of a priest, I have had other religious experiences such as participating in ceremonies, and there are many episodes that can be told about them. However, based on the theme of this chapter, I have shown many episodes related to the care of the inner sanctum and the tools therein. The context of "garden" and "care" allowed me to recall and describe the specific steps in detail. This allowed me to remember my emotions at the time I was working on it. On the other hand, there are also experiences that are detached from this work. The conversations I had while working on the project, and how I returned to his daily life after the care. What did I receive as a reward? How did I feel about such an experience? Although the work of grooming is "the extraordinary within the ordinary," it is not disconnected from the ordinary, but has continuity. If I were to engage in autoethnographic research on religious development in the future, the first task would be to focus on those experiences as well, and to reconstruct and reexamine the experiences organized in this study.

NOTES

1. In modern Japan, it is legally and conventionally accepted as normal for Buddhist priests to marry and have children. In the past, in most Buddhist schools in Japan, it was forbidden for Buddhist priests to have wives due to the precepts of the order and government ordinances. In 1872, the new government issued a notice allowing meat-eating and marriage in all schools to be publicly recognized. However, as for Jodo Shinshu, marriage and having children by priests have been openly permitted since the founding of the school (Osawa, 2014).
2. The landscape of the "Pure Land" partially resembles the Eden of the Old Testament and the New Heaven and Earth of the New Testament, with artifacts decorated with precious metal and jewels, beautiful creatures, and the presence of those who praise the Lord. In both Buddhism and Christianity, each presents its own code of desirable and taboo ways of life. As Gomes (see Chapter 2) noted, the garden paradise image in each religion may have the power to orient people's behavior toward the norms of each religion.
3. In this chapter, the author has made a distinction by referring to Buddhist priests before the establishment of Jodo Shinshu as "monk" and modern Jodo Shinshu priests as "buddhism priest." A particularly important difference is that monks in primitive Buddhism are ordained and practice Buddhism in an environment away from the secular world, whereas Jodo Shinshu Buddhism priests live in an environment just like that of ordinary people, except that they are engaged in temple-related work.
4. The smell of incense is very special to me. Whenever I smell incense somewhere, I am reminded of the inner sanctum of my family temple. It is a kind of sensation described by Wortmeyer (see Chapter 2) that triggers memories.
5. It is one of the fundamental ideas of Buddhism that all phenomena change from moment to moment and that nothing is unchanging (Furuta, 2021).

REFERENCES

Furuta, K. (2021). What is Buddhism? In Nippon Buddhist Research Association (Eds.), *Encyclopedia of Buddhism* (pp. 2–5). Maruzen Publishing.

Jodo Shinshu Hongwanji-ha Research Institute. (2013). *The three pure land sutras: Original, modern translation and explanation.* Hongwanji Publishing.

Osawa, A. (2014). The establishment of Jodo Shin Buddhist practice on marriage: Edo period punishment of clerical marriage and biographical accounts. *Nihon Kenkyū, 49*, 27–56.

Sato, T. (2019). Time and sign: Sign and cultural psychology. In A. Kido & T. Sato (Eds.), *Cultural psychology: Theories, itemized discussion, and methodology* (pp. 41–51). Chitose Press.

Shigaraki, T. (2011). *Shinshu scripture studies Vol.1: The three Pure Land sutras.* Hozokan.

The garden of Fuyo-chi in winter
(Photos provided by Toji-in Temple)

CHAPTER 18

ANALYSIS OF PERSONAL CULTURE APPEARING IN THE JAPANESE GARDEN

Megumi Nishikawa
Ritsumeikan University, Ibaraki, Osaka, Japan

Culture emerged from human beings. However, humans still do not sufficiently understand culture. Research on human culture started long ago, and continues from various points of view (e.g., cultural anthropology, cultural sociology, cultural economics, and cultural psychology).

From the perspective of cultural psychology, Valsiner (2007) insists that there are three forms of relations between people and culture. First, a person belongs to culture. This means that individuals belong to specific groups that share the same culture; this theory is mainly used in cross-cultural psychology. Second, culture belongs to a person. Individuals absorb various cultural meanings and construct a personal culture. A personal culture leads a person and integrates an intra-psychological system. Third, culture belongs to the relating of a person and the environment. Culture is exemplified through the processes of "internalization" and "externalization" between individuals and their world. According to Valsiner (2007), *internalization* is the process of

The Semiotic Field of the Garden, pages 389–395
Copyright © 2024 by Information Age Publishing
www.infoagepub.com
All rights of reproduction in any form reserved.

analyzing externally existing semiotic materials or messages and synthesizing them in a new form in the intra-psychological domain. In contrast, *externalization* is the process of analyzing intra-psychologically existing personal–cultural materials while transposing from inside to outside and approaching the world as a form of new synthesis of these materials.

The culture of each person is generally thought to be invisible and unobservable. However, according to this theory, personal culture can be analyzed through internalization and externalization.

In this chapter, I investigated how personal culture appeared using the "garden task." The *garden task* involves a person describing a garden they like. The reason I chose this task is that culture is based on "cultivation," or the constructive modification of something and addition of values and meanings (Valsiner, 2007). Tsuchimoto also explains that gardening is a process by which humans transact with or cultivate nature while integrating the duality of personal and collective culture (see the "Introduction," "Personal and Collective Culture in the Garden," this volume). Gardening is the act of cultivating a place and giving it personal meaning. Hence, it is expected that personal culture can be observed in the process of selecting one's personal garden.

The investigation of the garden task in this chapter was conducted in the "garden project" (see "Introduction" and Chapter 16, this volume). I attended Jaan Valsiner's intensive lectures at Ritsumeikan University in 2019 and thought of the garden I liked. This chapter attempted to analyze my own personal culture from the perspective of cultural psychology. I wrote this analysis in the form of "purpose (introduction), method, results, and discussion."

METHOD—HOW WAS PERSONAL CULTURE INVESTIGATED?

Participant—Whose Personal Culture Was Analyzed?

The participant was the author (me). I am a Japanese woman, who was 23 years old and a graduate psychology student at Ritsumeikan University at the time of the task.

Materials and Procedure—How Was the Favorite Garden Investigated?

I described the garden I liked near or in my house and why I chose it. I also made PowerPoint slides about the garden using photos. I showed and explained the slides in Valsiner's lecture at Ritsumeikan University.

Instructions for the garden task were written and explained in both Japanese and English. The instructions in Figure 16.1 (Chapter 16, this volume) were shown through PowerPoint on a large monitor in the lecture (see "Introduction" and Chapter 16, this volume).

RESULTS—WHAT GARDEN WAS DESCRIBED?

The garden I showed and introduced is illustrated by Figures 18.1 and 18.2. I chose the garden in *Toji-in* Temple (等持院) in Kyoto.

Toji-in Temple is a Buddhist temple founded in 1341 by Takauji Ashikaga (Kawakatsu & Imatani, 2009). Takauji Ashikaga (足利尊氏, 1305–1358) was the founder of the Ashikaga shogunate. The Ashikaga shogunate family valued Toji-in Temple and buried the family's dead at this temple generation.

The gardens of Toji-in Temple were created by Soseki Muso (Kawakatsu & Imatani, 2009). Soseki Muso (夢窓疎石, 1275–1351) was a renowned Buddhist monk and garden designer. Gardens are divided into western and eastern areas.

The western area is called *Fuyo-chi* (芙蓉池, Figure 18.1). In Fuyo-chi, lotus flowers bloom in early summer; lotus flowers are called *Fuyo* (芙蓉) in Japan. Although Soseki Muso laid the foundation for the garden, Yoshimasa

Figure 18.1 The garden I chose. This picture is of the garden of Fuyo-chi in Toji-in Temple in Kyoto (Photos provided by Toji-in Temple).

Figure 18.2 The garden I chose. This picture is of the garden of Shinji-ike in Toji-in Temple (Photos provided by Toji-in Temple).

Ashikaga carried out a large-scale renovation of Fuyo-chi in 1457. Yoshimasa Ashikaga (足利義政, 1436–1490) was the eighth shogun of Ashikaga shogunate. Yoshimasa often enjoyed tea parties in the garden.

The eastern area is called *Shinji-ike* (心字池, Figure 18.2). In Shinji-ike, there is a pond shaped like *kanji* (Chinese characters used in Japan) that read *Shin* (心). Shin refers to heart, mind, and spirit. According to Tsuchimoto, there are many Shinji-ike all over Japan, and many Shinji-ike are included in Soseki Muso's gardens, which are deeply related to Zen philosophy (see the "Introduction," "Autoethnography and Gardens," this volume). In contrast to Fuyo-chi renovated by Yoshimasa Ashikaga, Shinji-ike at Toji-in Temple is said to retain Soseki Muso's gardening techniques and Zen philosophy.

Process of Selecting the Garden—Why Did Participants Choose the Japanese Garden?

When I was an undergraduate student, I lived near Toji-in Temple in Kyoto. As a graduate student I lived in Osaka, not Kyoto. The task was to describe my favorite garden in or near my home; therefore, I tried to choose a good garden in or near my current house in Osaka. However, I was unable to find my favorite garden in or near my current house. I lived in an apartment and had no garden with soil or plants. At the university, I frequently used a lounge. However, it was not outdoors, and there were only some desks and chairs. Near my house, there were a few outdoor gardens, but I did not like them and did not feel that they were attractive. Therefore, I chose the garden of Toji-in Temple, which I had liked since I was an undergraduate student.

I had found the Toji-in Temple gardens by chance. Although I had walked the road next to this temple every day to go to university, I was not interested in it. Furthermore, the garden was located inside the temple and could not be seen from outside, so I did not know of the garden. I had entered Toji-in Temple for the first time when my friend came to Kyoto for sightseeing and wanted to go there with me. I saw the garden and I was struck by its beauty. I was surprised that every day I passed by such a fantastic space. The garden was located near my apartment in Kyoto, but it was extraordinary to me. After that, I visited the garden when I wanted to escape my daily life.

I thought that the Toji-in Temple gardens were beautiful, compact, and quiet. I liked compact and small gardens. This was because I could enjoy viewing many beautiful components, such as ponds, plants, stones, or buildings from one angle, like Fuyo-chi (Figure 18.1). In addition, I thought that the garden was not too crowded or loud. Therefore, I could relax and stay there for long periods. I sometimes took a walk and saw the beautiful landscape full of red leaves in autumn, as shown in Figure 18.2.

DISCUSSION—WHAT DOES THIS GARDEN ANALYSIS REVEAL?

This chapter aimed to identify how personal culture emerged through an analysis of the garden I liked. From the results, I report six points important to the perspective of cultural psychology.

First, I chose traditional Japanese gardens with soil and plants, which indicates that I selected my garden while internalizing social meanings. The garden task asked me to think about the garden that I liked. In the Japanese dictionary, a garden is a piece of land around a house where people grow flowers or plants (Shuzui & Imaizumi, 1965). However, in the garden task, the word "garden" is vague and not defined in the instruction. Thus, I could select any place (e.g., my room or university, or the sea or town) as my personal garden. Nevertheless, I rejected my room and the university lounge because they were not outdoors and did not have soil or plants. I thought my garden must be a place that was traditional and outdoors that had soil and plants, which may be a result of internalizing social meanings.

Second, although I selected a traditional garden with soil and plants, I also described my personal garden as compact, extraordinary, and quiet. This clearly shows my personal meaning and culture. I stated that compact and small gardens are beautiful and allow me to enjoy seeing many components from one angle. I felt that the garden I selected was extraordinary and allowed me to escape my daily life. The garden was quiet and was not crowded, so I could relax and stay alone for a long period. These personal meanings were constructed through my own experiences with the gardens.

Third, I mentioned that the compactness and quietness of the garden were beautiful, which shows how my personal culture was constructed. These personal values are thought to be related to Japanese culture of *Chanoyu* (茶の湯) and *Wabi-sabi* (侘び寂び). Chanoyu is the culture developed by Sen no Rikyu (千利休, 1522–1591) and describes the manners and aesthetics of tea ceremony in gardens or tatami rooms (Akasegawa, 1990). Rikyu preferred "the beauty of compactness." Rikyu reduced a large space to smaller ones and he admired such spaces, stating that they were beautiful. According to Chapter 16, Wabi-sabi is a uniquely Japanese aesthetic that has developed as the beauty of naturally feeling something profound and rich amid quietness (see Chapter 16, "Misato's Presentation: Relationship With the Garden," this volume). My response to the garden task suggests I internalized these collective cultures.

Fourth, although collective Japanese cultures such as Chanoyu and Wabi-sabi are internalized in my world, my personal culture is unique. Tsuchimoto explains that gardens can be both collective and personal (see the "Introduction," "○△□ Garden: The Universe of Mind and Its Continuity," this volume). The compactness and quietness of the garden I chose are similar to the concepts of beauty in Chanoyu and Wabi-sabi. Furthermore, Wabi-sabi also admires beauty that changes with the season, which is represented in my thought that the changing autumn leaves were beautiful. With these similarities exist differences as well. Chanoyu revolves around the social elements of tea parties, but I liked staying alone in the garden. I stated that I enjoyed the garden by myself and felt it was beautiful.

Fifth, I mentioned that the garden was beautiful, compact, quiet, and extraordinary, which suggests that I internalized these feelings into my deepest intra-psychological system, and sometimes hyper-generalized them. Valsiner (2007) explains that three psychological domains involve internalization. The first domain focuses on external messages brought in. The second domain generalizes the messages abstractly. The third domain adds personal feeling tones to messages, and is the deepest in the intra-psychological world. I had a subjective preference for and enjoyment of beautiful, compact, and quiet gardens, so these values were integrated into my deepest system. Moreover, the garden was extraordinary to me. I was surprised that such a fantastic garden was located near my apartment, but I cannot explain the reason why I thought that it was extraordinary. Tsuchimoto explains that hyper-generalization is a process of affective synthesis of signs, where a vague meaning field that overwhelms the human psyche emerges (see the "Introduction," "Garden Border: A Poetic Autoethnography," this volume). It is thought to be hyper-generalization that I felt that the garden was extraordinary.

Finally, the personal garden I chose was guided by the "sign" of the garden, in this case the "field-like sign." According to Valsiner (2007), culture can also be semiotic (sign) mediation that is part of the system of organized psychological functions. The sign leads from the past state to something new in functions facing the future. Moreover, it generally assumes that complexity is reduced to signs called "point-like signs." By contrast, field-like signs allow us to consider the complexity of real-life experiences. The original complexities are transformed into complex field-like signs. I described my personal garden as traditional, outdoor, compact, extraordinary, and quiet, allowing me to enjoy viewing alone. I had complex feelings about the garden, which indicated that the garden was a field-like sign. In conclusion, based on Valsiner's (2007) theory, the result shows that I externalized my personal meanings and personal culture while being guided by the field-like sign of the garden.

In this chapter, I investigated an individual case of personal culture using the personal garden task. This research is contrary to mainstream psychology, which assumes human homogeneity and tries to eliminate individual differences. However, Valsiner (2007) claims that the science of human psychology can provide general knowledge because human psychological phenomena are unique. Valsiner (2007) insists that the ways in which psychological phenomena are organized are universal and that the analysis of the process is crucial. Going forward, mainstream psychologists should be more receptive to the subjective and qualitative nature of individual differences, as evidence indicates that there is more to science than objective, quantifiable data.

REFERENCES

Akasegawa, G. (1990). *Sen no Rikyu mugon no zenei* [Sen no Rikyu mute avant-garde]. Iwanamishoten.
Kawakatsu, J., & Imatani A. (2009). *Toji-in* [Toji-in Temple]. Tankosha.
Shuzui, K., & Imaizumi, T. (1965). *Kokugojiten* [Japanese dictionary]. Obunsha.
Valsiner, J. (2007). *Culture in minds and societies foundations of cultural psychology*. SAGE Publications.

Yu Garden (Photo by Jakub Hałun, CC BY-SA 4.0, Wikimedia Commons)

CHAPTER 19

PERSONAL FEELING TOWARD THREE GARDENS IN MY LIFE

Example of the Yu Garden

Xiaoxue Chen
Ritsumeikan University, Ibaraki, Osaka

THE LITTLE GARDEN NEAR TO MY HOME

My first memory of a "garden" is that of a rather small one behind the apartment building where I lived since I was born until I was in the third grade of primary school. At that time, low-rise buildings in the style of Soviet Khrushchevka were in vogue, and every building looked like a gray, square box. As a prank, I scratched the white wall of the staircase with my fingernails, and the thick plaster fell to pieces, revealing the red bricks. There was not much greenery in the area where I lived apart from the few bonsai trees that my grandfather and the other residents had planted in the corridor and a small garden behind the apartment.

It was a quiet, small garden; perhaps, it is more appropriate to call it an aisle connecting two apartments with plants, rather than a garden. A gray brick path encircled the thick bushes in the middle and went on. The garden always appeared wet to me, because I often went there after it had rained, to look for snails and gophers in the mud. I was young and short, mostly squatting in the green shade that would fall on the ground. Despite their viscous and unseemly mucus, I would tirelessly search for snails. I do not remember anyone else there besides me. Even if other kids were around, we did not talk to each other; we just tossed around the mud under our feet with small branches and concentrated on looking for gobies. I even looked for grasshoppers and dragonflies which are more difficult to catch than snails. When I did grab a dragonfly, I would observe its beautiful wings and eyes.

This experience of wandering and looking for snails and gophers in that small area shaped my first concept of a garden, even though I was too young to recognize it as a garden. All the memories, the view I saw (i.e., the green shade that was falling), and my activities (i.e., squatting and looking for gobies) were so personal that there were no other participants in the activities that I created in the garden.

Yet, one cannot avoid contact with the culturally-collective organized world (Valsiner, 2007). The area of clusters of low-rise buildings that I lived in lacked greenery. People who lived there were the employees of the Bureau of Electricity Supply, and comprised a huge number. Hence, there was no area designed for children to play with each other. We played in the square, which was stacked with giant electric coil higher than an adult, with various shapes of long steel on which my friends scratched their legs, and with pick-up trucks around which we jumped at the cargo. We also undertook some adventures at night in the dark office building and cafeteria, when everyone was getting off from work. There was no place for children to play, and we would make do with what was available, which was sometimes even dangerous. Wandering in the small garden was a safer option as opposed to playing in the square, office building, or cafeteria; perhaps it was a natural consequence of looking for a quiet and peaceful place.

THE IDEAL GARDEN IN THE BOOK

I realized that there were beautiful gardens in the world when I read the *Dreams of the Red Chamber* (Cao, 1997) in the fifth grade. Our Chinese teacher taught us this novel after school because it was useful for the junior high school entrance exams. Though none of the questions from *Dreams of the Red Chamber* were asked in the exams, I gradually realized that it was a valuable insight into literature and aesthetics. The teacher mainly taught the ancient poems in *Dreams of the Red Chamber*, some of which foretold the fate of the main characters, while others described the gorgeous, large, classical Chinese garden *Daguanyuan*, where the story takes place. As a fifth-grade student, it was quite difficult for me to understand the depth of this novel; however, the ancient poems that I had recited at that time were ingrained in my mind for a long time. When I was old enough to understand the story, I realized that all the poems were tragedies. In fact, the entire story is a huge tragedy. My heart fluttered with the pathetic fate of the characters, but the sadness was diluted by detailed observations of 18th century Chinese society and the depth of the psychological descriptions. I felt peace in "all the love, wealth, happiness will fade away, but come back sometimes."

> All Good Things Must End
>
> All men long to be immortals
> Yet to riches and rank each aspires;
> The great ones of old, where are they now?
> Their graves are a mass of briars.
>
> All men long to be immortals,
> Yet silver and gold they prize
> And grub for money all their lives
> Till death seals up their eyes.
>
> All men long to be immortals
> Yet dote on the wives they've wed,
> Who swear to love their husband evermore
> But remarry as soon as he's dead.
>
> All men long to be immortals
> Yet with getting sons won't have done.
> Although fond parents are legion,
> Who ever saw a really filial son?

Reading *Dreams of the Red Chamber* (Cao, 1997) shaped my concept of traditional Chinese gardens, and perhaps, the ideal garden. Though I have never ever visited one, and am unlikely to do so since Daguanyuan is fictional, my fascination with Daguanyuan is due to the touching story of *Dreams of the Red Chamber*, the feelings and emotions towards its characters, and not just the garden itself. However, even an imaginary experience of Daguanyuan impacts my impression of gardens, and in my mind, it will always be unique in the world because of its involvement in my imagination.

My mind often recalls the image of Daguanyuan and the poetry that I recited, sometimes without any association at all. It is hard to say what the poem *All Good Things Must End* (Cao, 1997) meant to me when I was young, although I understood certain aspects such as signs like grave, wife, gold, and son. However, gradually, I started to understand the poem in its totality, not just as separate sections. I finally understand the title, *All Good Things Must End*. In *Dreams of the Red Chamber* (Cao, 1997), the death of the characters and fading away of the prominent political family is also true for not just me and my life, but for everyone, as we all will eventually fade away in the universe someday. It becomes the field-like sign, shaping the hyper-generalized feeling, shaping my feelings toward the world, and shaping the concept of the world in my mind at the same time, like the intrapersonal infinity (see "Introduction," this volume).

THE IDEAL GARDEN IN THE REAL WORLD

The Yu Garden in Shanghai was the first typical Chinese classical garden I visited. But I have "visited" gardens like this so many times in novels and TV plays like "Dreams of the Red Chamber" (Cao, 1997) and "The Peony Pavilion" (Tang, 1963). The Daguanyuan in the drama was spectacular and faithful to the original story to some extent. While it may have intended to portray the original idea that "all love, wealth, and happiness will fade away," the latest video technology has been used to blur the background, making it look like a non-existent heavenly world. I do not really like it. In the book, Daguanyuan is of course full of gorgeous buildings, such as the mansions of the upper class, but even a single flower or a tree is depicted in great detail, so it is not an empty, heavenly world. Therefore, when I went to Yu Garden, observing various plants and buildings closely was just like viewing the Da Guan Garden that had been so fascinating to me all this while.

According to the process of coordinating, generalizing, and specifying processes in aesthetic discourse (Valsiner, 2020), the point-like signs (Level 2) are processed and become a combination with field-like signs (Level 3). They are then generalized into a hyper-generalized affective sign field (Level 4). This process, and every step can be reversed, (specification) but cannot be skipped. Perhaps that is why I felt uncomfortable with the misty Daguanyuan. It was inconsistent with the Daguanyuan that was built by point-like signs in my mind. The painting, the visible static signs, help express the mood of the scene, rather than the event or the story in it. However, the video is obviously different from the language of painting, and fails to express the dream-like atmosphere of this novel.

In Chinese culture, there is a saying, "The winding path leads to a secluded place" (曲径通幽). It means "to go through a winding road to reach a quiet, deep, and mysterious place." The word 幽 speaks of seclusion, secrets, and the curiosity to keep exploring. However, in a grand and empty garden, all the buildings, plants, mountains, and water are exposed to sunlight, and the pleasure of exploration is gone. In such a secluded place, one can free one's thoughts and feelings, feel safe, and meet their real self. Therefore, I believe that the ideal garden should have such a small, crooked, and deep place.

In classical Chinese gardens, such small, elaborate designs can be found in many places; on the carvings on the doors and windows, on the ancient poems and paintings on the walls, and decorations in the rooms; the gardens are filled with dazzling delicacies. There are far too many human creations in the gardens. A garden like Yu Garden seems to say, "I definitely want more than just plants, trees, mountains, and water." That is why I think it is difficult to appreciate Chinese traditional gardens. There are not many people who can understand those ancient poems, pictures, and calligraphies, possibly even during the time the gardens were being built. If they were so difficult to understand, why did they try so hard to read them?

HOW TO UNDERSTAND 曲径通幽
IN CHINESE TRADITIONAL GARDEN

I think this is also a kind of 曲径通幽. What is it that I am following on the winding path (the process of trying hard to read)? For me, the people who lived here, the people who wrote this title, what they were thinking, and what they wanted to do with the rest of their lives, are the very essence of 幽. To explore these, is the source of my curiosity, because even though the characters on the surface were hard to understand, I am sure that there lurks something beneath that surface that we can share as human beings, even across time.

The word 曲径通幽 was a hyper-generalized feeling, constructed in my mind when I read the word for the first time. Later, when I walked on the winding path which led to secluded places in some gardens, it always reminded me of this word, which is also the process of schematization (categorizing the complexity to the sign recognized before). When I am actually walking on the path in a garden (as a mundane experience in real life) and thinking about the 曲径通幽 (the hyper-generalized feeling), I can feel the conflict between them. The word 曲径通幽 dramatized these mundane moments and created a dynamic zone of the sublime.

I think the space of a garden is a subtle space. The trees, mountains, buildings, sculptures, all the things you can see in a garden, can also be found in other places, such as the streets. But what makes it a "garden" if it is surrounded by walls? A walled garden is an area independent of the main street where people come and go. In that quiet place, one can coexist with one's true feelings and imagination. Further, we have not even gotten to the small domestic space where clashes with other people's personal mental space often take place. I think this is one of the reasons why gardens have always been so popular.

I think there are three zones: street, garden, and the domestic place. The street is too wide to find ourselves, while our homes are too narrow to expand our mind and emotions. When we cross the border of the street and garden, which always has a wall, we enter a mysterious place that exists between the private and the public. Especially with those intense human creations (sculptures, paintings, poems, decoration), our mind wanders and floats, experiencing the conflict of the mundane and sublime, sometimes, reaching the aesthetic zone.

REFERENCES

Cao, X. (1997). *Dreams of the red chamber.* People's Literature Publishing House.

Tang, X. (1963). *The peony pavilion*. People's Literature Publishing House.
Valsiner, J. (2007). Personal culture and conduct of value. *Journal of Social, Evolutionary, and Cultural Psychology, 1*(2), 59–65.
Valsiner, J. (2020). *Sensuality in human living: The cultural psychology of affect*. SpringBriefs in Psychology.

A tiny garden in Kyoto.

CHAPTER 20

GARDEN AS INFINITY

Fumiyuki Taka
Ritsumeikan University

GARDEN AS PART OF DAILY LIFE

I was born in a Japanese family which consisted of grandparents, parents, and an elder sister. We lived in a house in Hokkaido, the northern island of Japan. The house had a front garden and a back one. My grandmother used to decorate the front garden with various flowers and trees, and the back one was filled with vegetables such as radishes, Japanese parsley, tomatoes, snow peas, and strawberries. We enjoyed eating them in different seasons. Hokkaido is covered with snow in winter for nearly half of the year, and every life form flourishes in June as if they were born to love sunlight. My grandmother's gardens were the places to see them grow as well. The front garden attracted people who were walking through the street in front of it and she often made friends with the people who talked to her about her flowers and trees. The front garden was a gate for social contact in a way.

In the center of the front garden there was a big tree and as a child every year I looked forward to watching cicada larvae climbing up the tree from the soil to turn into cicadas in the early morning. My grandmother told me that cicada larvae spend 7 years in the soil and die in just 1 week after they

---

The Semiotic Field of the Garden, pages 405–418
Copyright © 2024 by Information Age Publishing
www.infoagepub.com
All rights of reproduction in any form reserved.

emerge from the ground. I was surprised to know the story and I made it a rule to watch them every summer since then. I remember keeping a new cicada in the cage even though my grandmother told me not to do so as a cicada's life on the ground was only 7 days. One day I found it dead. My grandmother said nothing about it except her sad face. I regret what I did for the cicada. Since then, I did not keep one again. On the other hand, the garden was a place to bury my pets such as little birds, small turtles bought at open-air festivals, and tropical fish. The front garden was a place for me to breathe life, and the back garden was a place to experience blessings of nature. The back garden was also a private one as my grandmother did not show it to others except our family. For me both gardens were small in nature themselves.

GARDEN AS PLACE OF IDENTITY

Hokkaido island is the frontier of Japan as it was not inhabited much until 150 years ago except by our indigenous people, Ainu. Therefore, there were no old temples or shrines which you can see in a travel guidebook or a book on Japanese history. It was not until high school that I visited Kyoto and Nara on the school excursion in the second year. On a bus tour with some 400 students of the same age, I visited the shrines and the temples which I used to see only in the textbooks and guidebooks were standing in front of me as reality. I was fascinated by them so much and especially a temple with a dry landscape garden (Karesansui) left a strong impression on me as it produced water without real water. This school excursion gradually stimulated my awareness of my identity as Japanese, which became conscious for the first time, and this experience was not obtained in Hokkaido until this visit to Kyoto and Nara. A garden at this school excursion meant a heritage to witness my Japanese cultural background. I moved to Tokyo to study at university. At that time, I strongly believed that Tokyo had something exciting that I wanted. As a person who started living alone without knowing anyone, I had to do everything by myself to survive in my new life in Tokyo.

GARDEN FOR CHANGE

When I was a senior at university, I decided to have a year off from my law studies, and I flew to Denmark to study at an international folk school for cross-cultural experience. At that time, I believed it would be my first and last opportunity to live in a foreign country as it was common for a typical Japanese person (especially male) to work at one workplace until his retirement day without a break. At that time, life-time employment was the standard in Japanese society. My parents did not understand me as they thought that I was going to be derailed and I would not recover from the derailment. One of my seniors from the university, and who was a journalist, told me that Denmark was a country with no future, and it would be a waste of life to go there. Although nine out of ten pieces of advice discouraged me, I went to Denmark anyway. At the school I met students from more than 20 countries from all over the world. We lived in a dormitory and in a setting of multiculturalism 24 hours a day.

The school had a big garden in front of the dormitory. It simply consisted of a lawn and a pond. The garden was different from the Japanese gardens I saw. We played volleyball there, studied there, and sometimes brought chairs in for sunbathing without top clothes, which was a luxury as Denmark has shorter sunshine hours from autumn to spring. We could use the garden for various purposes, which was also different from the Japanese garden. The school was surrounded by trees which looked more open than a Japanese garden surrounded by walls. I felt that the school garden represented freedom rather than orders which I used to see in Japanese gardens. A garden became an archetype for me to represent a culture. There is a well-known expression to explain the difference of philosophy between Japanese culture and Western culture using a garden. A fountain in a Western garden is an embodiment of Western culture to conquer nature while a waterfall or a Shishi-odosi is one of Japanese culture to get along with nature. While I was in Denmark, I came to feel the opposite. Western culture encourages a person to be honest to himself/herself (individualistic) while Japanese culture encourages a person to be obedient to the majority (collective) or to be harmony oriented.

I was often asked, "How about Japan?" which gave me the opportunity to think about Japanese culture. Some of the questions were ones which I never questioned about myself. I came to know a common sense I obtained in Japan that was not one abroad. On the other hand, there were several Japanese students at the school. They were from different parts of Japan as well. There was no internet available as it was late 1980s at that time, so the Japanese students collaborated to answer the questions about Japan. Interestingly, we noticed the differences in ourselves even though we all came from such a small country. Some Japanese students were disciplined at home not to trump newspapers while others were not. The Japanese students who lived with their grandparent/s had this experience, and the students who did not live with grandparent/s did not have the experience. I guess that is the reason why the grandparents told us such a thing was that they regarded newspapers as the source of knowledge or wisdom, and some of their generation could not finish elementary school as Japan was poor when they were young. The days in Denmark brought me cultural awareness as a Japanese and self-awareness as an individual as well. I obtained different viewpoints to see things which I did not have before. When I arrived at the Danish school, I had nothing to prove my identity as Japanese except my passport. At the end of my stay in Denmark I was confident that I was Japanese because I was a successor of Japanese culture therefore, I was Japanese.

I believed that I had made the right decision in my life to study in Denmark.

I had another reason to go to Denmark. I wanted to make good memories of my life to prepare myself for the worst scenario. I was given a diagnosis of scleroderma when I started living in Tokyo. The doctor told me that I would have a possibility of dying if the disease would cover my entire body. I was not sure if I would survive the next 5 years. At that time the disease was not well-known. Now it is clear that a partial one would not be fatal, but even a doctor did not know the disease well at that time. In a way, I went to Denmark to have my best days for the possible limited days. At the end of my stay in Denmark I saw the disease had disappeared from my skin. I survived.

GARDEN IN JAPANESE LIFE TODAY

I am sorry, I am going off on a tangent now. It is often emphasized the connections between Japanese culture and nature to discuss Japanese culture and Japanese life, and Japanese style veranda (Engawa) is introduced as indispensable for a Japanese house as it is believed to connect Japanese life and garden which leads to nature. In Hokkaido many houses do not have Engawa as it snows so much in Hokkaido and cold climate in winter. Therefore, Japanese traditional style veranda does not match the life in Hokkaido. On the other hand, many of the houses in Tokyo today do not have a garden. It is not easy to own a house in Tokyo as prices of real estate property are high and the availability of land is limited due to its high population density in Tokyo's metropolitan area. As a result, people live in apartment buildings which do not have a Japanese traditional Engawa. This is a reality of today. I am not sure how many percent of Japanese people have experience sitting down on Engawa today, especially young Japanese. Maybe the story of the Japanese style veranda has become a part of history.

GARDEN FOR AWARENESS

In Francis and Hester (1990) Dean MacCannel states that a primal garden in the unconsciousness level for Western people is an immoral place and the place of instinct where moral rules do not reach. In Western culture, especially from a Christian point of view, a garden does not always have a positive meaning because of the story of Adam and Eve, while the word "home" in Japanese language consists of two kanji characters which are house and garden, which makes you feel warm. However, my 2-month trip around Europe during the break of my study in Denmark brought me a new awareness or a drastic change of viewpoint. It seemed to me that a Western garden was an embodiment of release of instinct while a Japanese garden was an embodiment of Japanese way of life to obey rules or discipline. I started feeling cramped for comfort about Japanese ways as is often the case with a person who has been abroad. Now I can see that I had to question my value as Japanese to build up again with my new value which I obtained in Denmark by communicating with the people from different parts of the world. On the other hand, my 2-month trip around Europe by rail gave me an awareness. When I crossed borders, I had no problem, but I sometimes saw people take time at passport control. I could cross the borders without problems because of my Japanese passport, which was the result of the effort done by Japanese predecessors. I was still struggling with my identity, but I realized it was immature to just hate Japanese culture in spite of the fact I was receiving the benefit of the efforts of unsung Japanese heroes.

In Denmark I was experiencing the notion of love based on the Christian way. I had already had the Japanese way under the influence of mercy based on Buddhism. Both of my grandfathers became Buddhist monks after their retirements from their jobs and some of my relatives were Buddhist monks who started training from their childhood and already had their own temples. I commuted to a Buddhist kindergarten by bus due to this family background even though there was a Christian kindergarten just 100 m away from my house and many of my childhood friends commuted to the Christian one. Buddhism was a part of my life without being aware even though I did not practice it enthusiastically.

STARTING CHANGE

My days in Denmark changed my attitude toward my life. I came to give more importance to intuition or instinct rather than the rules or insurance for my future financial stability. In other words, I chose what I wanted to do rather than what I should do or benefit I would receive in the future. Ultimately, I realized that I had never done something with believing in myself. When I passed the entrance exam for a prestigious high school in Hokkaido, I was not happy to find my name at the announcement of the entrance examination results. My family, friends, teachers, and relatives congratulated me, but I felt empty. I did not understand why I felt that way at that time. I realized that it had not been what I had wanted to do. I did not want to have the same experience again. I was interested in psychology before, but I chose law studies as I could not expect myself to obtain good job opportunities if

I studied psychology. I decided to study psychology after my completion of law studies. I worked at a telephone company as a telegram operator during the daytime and studied psychology at an evening university which I could study with a reasonable tuition fee. The tuition of the evening university was very reasonable. I could also obtain a scholarship. Even though it was not a huge amount of money it helped me a lot. Nothing was more exciting for me than believing in myself for my future career as a psychologist even though it was common sense that one cannot make a living as a psychologist in Japan. I came to think of studying counseling psychology in the United States for my career as a psychologist. One day the professor in law studies at my first university took me to his colleague who was a professor in clinical psychology at a national university. She told me that Japan did not need a psychologist who was trained abroad and did not let them in Japan so that an overseas trained psychologist could not obtain a job as a psychologist. She was not favorable to me at the very least. I passed a graduate exchange program to study at an U.S. graduate school in exchange for teaching Japanese language to university students. I did not have to pay the tuition. However, the program I was accepted by was a school counselor program which was different from my future career as a clinician in psychology. I had to decline the offer. I did not know what to do next. My parents helped me financially. So I could start my study in counseling psychology next year. At that time the Internet was not available and it was common to utilize agents to obtain the information to study abroad. I did not have money to utilize their service. From a library I borrowed old guidebooks on study abroad and chose several universities and sent letters to them to obtain information on their programs. I chose less expensive programs. The graduate school program I was accepted by was not a prestigious one, but I was happy with it as I did my best under my circumstances. Moreover, I was happy with myself as I accomplished something by believing in myself. While I was studying for my first master's degree in the United States after Denmark, I crossed over the American continent twice by my second hand, tough, one-thousand-dollar Plymouth Horizon. It took me 7 days in total to go from San Francisco to Boston. When it comes to Japan, it would take only 5 or 6 hours to drive across Japan from the Pacific Ocean to the Sea of Japan. From a geographical point of view America was big enough to feel the earth whereas Japan was small enough to feel compact like a garden.

THINKING A NATION AS A GARDEN AND ITS BORDERS AS FRAMEWORK

While I was in Denmark I enjoyed listening to Eurobeat and American music. Every weekend students danced in the common room until late or even until morning. I discovered that music was also a communication tool other than a language. However, when I was in the United States, no Americans around me knew about Eurobeat. Denmark is such a small country with less than 6 million people while the United States was such a big country with a population of 330 million. To my surprise, small Japan, which the majority of the people do not speak English and surrounded by seas and far away from both Europe and America was the place where you could listen to both Eurobeat and American music as well as domestic Japanese music. Sometimes Japan can be explained by insularism, but from the viewpoint of openness toward music this insular country is more open than other bigger countries in size. This reality gave me an idea to apply for the notion of a garden. It does not depend on size but on openness or an adherence-free mind.

AMISH WAY OF LIFE

While I was studying in the United States, I had a summer break for 2 months to live with an Amish family in a Midwest state. It is because I wanted to experience something I could have only in the United States. I was also interested in the line of thinking of Christians and I believed that the Amish way of life which is loyal to the Bible would give me a new perspective of new thoughts based on Christianity. There was a problem, however. I knew no Amish person. No friend and nobody at university had contact with the Amish. What I did was to drive my Plymouth Horizon to the Amish village and ask a police officer where I could meet an Amish person. The Caucasian police officer looked at me wonderingly at first, and he gave me the address of the Amish village headman. I visited the headman right away. The headman was a cabinetmaker. I told him that I wanted to live with Amish people. He seemed to be somewhat confused with this Asian stranger. The headman told me that I was the first Japanese person he talked with in his life. He gave me an address of an Amish person and advised me to visit him a couple of weeks later. I visited him and his family every other week to build the sense of trust and finally started living with the family. Three months passed since I asked the police officer where I could meet an Amish person.

The Amish family was a farmer's family. The family consisted of parents and three children of early teenagers. They had dairy cows. My typical day started at 3:45 a.m. to wake up for the morning milking. The evening milking finished around 5 p.m. My typical day ended with the sunset which was around 8:00 p.m. The Amish do not use electricity basically. They usually use gas lamps, but my room did not have one. I was given an oil lamp. One oil lamp was not bright enough to allow me to read a book, so I had no choice but to go to bed after the sunset. The family had a big garden and they raised vegetables. Every morning we ate the vegetables which were harvested from the garden in the morning. The Amish mother often said, "Fresh from the garden." She said that the onion harvested in the morning was sweet but the one harvested after midday was sharp. I felt I was connected to nature. I remembered having eaten the fresh from the garden vegetables from my grandmother's garden when I was a child. I enjoyed eating vegetables from the Amish garden.

The family had a big field and their cows walked around the field to graze grasses. One day a cow gave birth in the field which does not happen often. Until that time, I thought that nature and a garden were on opposite sides. As a disaster shows, nature is sometimes hard on us while the garden is not. However, this birth in the field gave me an opportunity to think that nature and a garden are in one continuum. For a cow there is no distinction between a garden and nature. It does not matter at all for her whether or not it is a garden or nature as long as she can give birth safely.

GARDEN AND NATURE

Today we can witness the same phenomena in our daily life. The gardens on tops of some buildings in Tokyo are utilized as breeding places with wooden birds and prepared nests which make birds feel comfortable to breed. Needless to say, they are artificial, but they are helping conservation of species which have been done in nature. A garden has gone beyond the conventional roles. It is not for human-beings only. Even in Kyoto I can see birds of prey attack small birds in the middle of the city. At this point it does not matter where the place is. It matters whether or not one can survive, and nature and cultural artifacts are now the continuum rather than opposite.

It is as if land and sea are opposite, and we human beings forget that these two are intertwined. Water circulates from land to sea through river. The fact lies not in the fact but in our cognition. We created the notion and I obeyed it without question. I am the one who tied myself up by not questioning the past or common sense. The days with the Amish family also gave me an insight that empathy had something to do with mercy which is based on Buddhism. The Christian way of thinking and the Buddhist way of thinking seemed to have a common point in deeper thoughts.

During the days with the Amish family, I had a car accident. I lost consciousness and I was taken to a hospital by an ambulance, and my beloved Plymouth Horizon was scrapped. I had a fracture, but I returned to the Amish village 2 weeks later as I thought I would never have such a precious experience again. Now I can definitely say that my choice was right.

PRACTICING ZEN BUDDHISM

In the Summer of 2001, I practiced Zen-Buddhism at a Zen temple in Kyoto for 2 weeks. My first 2 years as a psychologist in Australia in a rural area was hard for me to adjust myself to Australian regional culture as well as Australian English language which was different from European English I was originally used to, and American English I was used to for more than 3.5 years. (However, I enjoyed watching Australian gardens used for various purposes such as car washing and Christmas decoration.) I succeeded in obtaining my permanent residency in Australia, so I decided to give a present to myself. I wanted to dip myself into the Japanese culture where I came from. My stay in Denmark changed my life so much and 12 years have already passed since I visited Denmark. Much of my experience was done in Western culture and I wanted to focus on Asian cultures this time. So, I started with the Japanese culture which I came from. The most impressive thing at the Zen temple more than Zen practice I remember is breakfast. I cleaned my plate and my bowl with pickled radish using a pair of chopsticks. The breakfast finished with eating the pickled radish after cleaning table wares. I never used dishwasher liquid and water to wash them during the days I was there, and I never had a stomachache due to bacteria or food poisoning. The Zen master had two senior disciples. Both came from Western culture. They did not get along with each other. They had quarrels during my 2 week stay. I realized that religion and personality do not necessarily coincide, and we cannot get rid of kleshas.

EXPERIENCING CHRISTIANITY AS A VOLUNTEER AT MOTHER TERESA'S

After Zen practice I flew to India. The break had another purpose. The main purpose for this break was to do some volunteer work at Mother Teresa's House to touch the heart of Mother Teresa who devoted her own life to the poorest of the poor, and I believed that I could have a life-change experience to understand Christianity through volunteer work. At that time, I never did volunteer work so I had no experience doing something for others without expecting returns. One day I joined the outreach team to pick up senior people who were dumped by their families. Kolkata Station was one of the places where senior people were taken from their hometown by their children to be dumped. We could pick up quite a limited number of senior people who appeared to be sick. Japan had the same story before, but it was several hundred years ago. My typical day at Mother Teresa's started with cleaning rooms. Usually, rooms had excrements on the floor as some of the residents had health problems. They did not speak English. When they wanted some water, they called me "brother" and showed me an empty PET bottle in their hands. I saw some of them dead the next morning. On the street I saw an Indian woman trying to find food in a garbage. One dog was doing the same next to her. She was happy to find an egg. On the other hand, one day a young Indian woman dressed in a beautiful sari got out of a German car with a driver and came into a cake shop where I was and talked to me in English. She appeared to be rich. The gap between these Indian people struck me. I repeatedly thought about what the dignity of human being was and what a family was. What I could obtain was not a conclusion but a confusion. In a travel guidebook about India, it is often stated that a 1 week stay in India would be enough to change one's life. I think 3 days are enough.

One of the locations of Mother Teresa's House I was assigned to had a garden cared for by nuns. The garden was planted with vegetables, but it was different from my grandmother's one even though they appeared to have the same purpose: to grow blessings of nature. The vegetables in Mother Teresa's were more vital for survival whereas my grandmother's was for more psychological satisfaction rather than survival for life. These gardens were totally different in the perspective of purpose.

After India, I started to plant radishes in my grandma's garden when I visited Japan in spring. I do not know how I came to do that. It might be because I wanted to keep the memories of the Amish and Mother Teresa, to communicate with my grandma, to feel nature, or to reconstruct my line of thinking. My garden ended the next year as the garden was filled with radishes and my parents did not know what to do with them.

ENHANCING THE FRAMEWORK OF GARDEN TO BORDERS

During the years I was living in different countries for 15 years I flew so many times. On the map I can see the names of countries. However, no country has its name in nature. A border is the one we placed for our convenience. Now I can see that each of Japan, Denmark, the United States, Australia, India, and other countries I visited was also a garden themselves. Through each surrounded circumstance I could dip myself into each country and unify myself with new awareness from a spatial recognitional point of view.

TYPES OF GARDENS

The garden with life forms such as vegetables and insects gave me a temporal perspective to feel the transition of time by sharing the same time axis. Or the types of architecture in gardens such as the Kinkakuji Temple and Ginkakuji Temple give you the sense of history. Most impressively, the Karesansui Garden, which may be easier to be called as the Zen Garden, has gone beyond the concept of time by being lifeless or being dry. By not having any lifeforms in it or being dry, Karesansui is free from time and therefore appears to us beyond the concept of time.

GARDEN AS A TOOL FOR INTEGRATION

A garden was a gate for me to integrate myself in different points of view and experiences. When I integrated my identity, I thought about religion as well. In the United States I was given a subtle question by an American woman. It was an opportunity to seriously think about the meaning and the influence of a religion on us in our daily life. As a child I was disciplined to pray to Buddha and for my ancestors at our household altar every day before morning and evening meals. It was already my ritual even though I did not do this since I moved to Tokyo. I never questioned myself about religion. I took time to make sure of my religion. The most significant factor was the enlightenment in Buddhism. Everyone who obtains enlightenment could be a Buddha. On the other hand, a Christian asks God for forgiveness as God owes sin. An enlightenment seems to require self-discipline which fits my attitude toward life. Therefore, I chose Buddhism. However, I recently came to know that there seems to be a similarity between Buddhism and Christianity. For example, Sange, during a series of Buddhist events of Omizutori of Shunie at Todaiji Temple in Nara in March, a Buddhist monk asks Buddha's forgiveness of his sin, which is the same conduct as a Christian asks God's forgiveness for his/her sin. This series of events has a history of some 1,200 years. As the main reason why I chose Buddhism was the enlightenment, this was shocking to me, but later felt relieved to know that Buddhism and Christianity have a common aspect and flexible rather than strict frameworks. I remember visiting a 3,000-year-old tree in Yakushima Island in the past. The tree was alive and as it was a life form the tree was supposed to have its limited life. However, I felt the life of the tree was also beyond the notion of time due to its uncountable length of life until today. Compared to the length of my life and the tree's life, I felt my problems were trivial things. I felt lighter in my mind.

I sought the way to integrate my experiences and thoughts inductively or deductively, but both were not essential. Kawakita (1986) was the best answer for me. I did not have to integrate them. I just needed to let chaos talk and let it be.

GARDEN AS ARTWORK—SUBJECTIVE POINT OF VIEW

In Francis and Hester (1990) Francis states that a garden is an embodiment of an individual, one can express his/her value, emotions by creating a garden. If so, a garden is an expression of a subjective view of one's world which has nothing to do with the real nature. I realized that what I disagreed with in the past was not nature but the worldview of someone who created the garden. As a young person I mistook a garden for nature. What I shall do next is not to evaluate a garden but to create my own garden as someone's garden is a completed value by someone else even though I do not agree with his/her value at all.

Hasegawa (1983) strongly recommends not to understand a garden through a photobook. As an amateur photographer, I definitely agree with him. It is because the photographs are the artworks which represent the photographer's views, and it is impossible for a photograph to get rid of a photographer's subjectivity which is not yours. He also states that a real artistic Japanese garden has voice and soul without fail and it is alive. He also states the attitude to listen to what the garden says and to catch the mind of your partner which communicates with your mind without being bothered by the beauty which attracts your five senses.

Therefore, this chapter does not adopt someone's theory. I introduced only some thoughts I agree with. Because someone's theory could play the role of a photobook above. I decided to listen to myself and write this chapter by accepting myself.

GARDEN AS INFINITY

I introduced different types of gardens in different locations so far. A garden can transcend culture, place and time, and it is not only for human beings. A garden has a framework but paradoxically the framework brings infinite possibilities. The point is not what you can see but also what thoughts are behind.

Hasegawa (1983) states that the basic notion of a Japanese garden is that it is a place which is an enclosed space only, there are no absolute rules. What I was believing as a young Japanese person was that a garden, especially a Japanese one, represented the strict rules. Moreover, a Japanese garden is an artwork which embodies the designer's or owner's own interpretations/reproductions of nature. It is not a perfect copy of nature. If I do not like a Japanese garden, it is not a matter of right or wrong but a matter of what I receive and feel from it. It is pointless to make a judgment on someone's garden as it is someone's interpretation or artwork which has nothing to do with right or wrong. The best way to respond to someone's garden is to create my own garden which represents my own view or my own interpretation about nature or life. In this respect, do I have to have my own garden? I do not think so. I live in an apartment which does not have a garden. How can I embody my own thoughts about the garden? My answer is to establish my own style of psychotherapy as a psychologist.

LIVING IN KYOTO FOR INTEGRATION

Currently I am enrolled in a PhD program in clinical psychology. During my stay in Australia for more than a decade I flew from and flew back to Kansai International Airport, and always spent some days in Kyoto. I visited Buddhist temples and sometimes I had opportunities to be talked to by Buddhist monks. I do not know why. I had chances to ask about Buddhism. Because of this experience I wanted to learn from Buddhism to establish my own style of psychotherapy. For me Kyoto is a special place to obtain inspiration. I chose to settle down in Kyoto. Since I started living in Kyoto I often wondered if there are many garden-like places in Kyoto that Kyoto could be called a garden city even though those gardens are not surrounded by walls which are the essential for the definition of a garden in a traditional interpretation. I walked around Kyoto. I made it a rule to not utilize transportation much as I believe that walking would give me more chances to experience and know Japanese culture better by feeling the atmosphere of the places I visit.

CONCLUSION

Under the influence of COVID-19 I spent much more time home, which gave me opportunities to think about my experiences up until today and thoughts as a clinician of psychology. Finally, I integrated my attitude toward psychotherapy. My therapeutic style is based on a tea ceremony. The host is the therapist, and the guest is the client. Tea itself is the client's problem to explore, (and the bowl to put tea in is a type of psychotherapy to fit to the tea). They could be PCA, CBT, CPT, mindfulness, and so on with the notion of treasuring every meeting (*Ichigo-ichie*), for it will never recur. Some psychologists may say that a psychologist should provide psychotherapy or counseling in a counseling room only. As a psychologist who has experience in outreach service, I disagree with it. As a matter of fact, there are situations in which you cannot have a session in a counseling room. Do you give up having a session? As a helping professional, of course not. With my new attitude toward psychotherapy, I am looking forward to visiting Karesansui at Ryuanji Temple again.

REFERENCES

Francis, M., & Hester, R. T. (1990). *The meaning of gardens, idea, place, and action.* The MIT Press.

Hasegawa, M. (1983). *Nihon Teien Zakkou—Niwa to Sisou* [Miscellaneous thoughts for Japanese garden—Garden and thought]. Toyobunkasha.

Kawakita, J. (1986). *KJ Hou—Konton wo site Katarashimeru* [KJ method—Let chaos talk]. Chuokouronsha.

A garden can be seen over hot tofu lunch (湯豆腐) at Ryoanji Temple (竜安寺) photo by Teppei Tsuchimoto

COMMENTARY PART IV

REFLECTING ON ONESELF AND GARDEN

Projecting Happy Memories Into the Future

Tatsuya Sato
Ritsumeikan University

Due to the COVID-19 pandemic, Jaan Valsiner, who was a visiting professor in the College of Comprehensive Psychology at Ritsumeikan University, conducted online classes for the 2020–2022 academic year. Unfortunately, the circumstances prevented his physical presence in Japan.

Despite the unfortunate inability of Jaan Valsiner to come to Japan, online classes offer their own advantages. Moreover, I believe the "Garden Project" yielded particularly positive outcomes.

The online class provided an opportunity to kickstart the project and prepare the manuscript remotely. Thankfully, as the COVID-19 situation improved in FY2022, Jaan could come to Japan for in-person classes and discuss the Garden Project.

The book's editor, Teppei Tsuchimoto, provided dedicated support throughout these processes.

Furthermore, students from Aalborg University in Denmark participated in the online class, highlighting one of the advantages of online learning. During a discussion about gardens, a Danish participant remarked, "In Japan, you put on shoes when you go out of the house into the garden!" This comment left a lasting impression on me, and I remember it vividly. The difference in customs regarding wearing shoes inside houses is well-known between Western culture and Japan. It has become quite common to explain to non-Japanese individuals that in Japan, it is customary to take off your shoes when entering a house, and they should do the same. However, it is rarely mentioned that in Japan, it is customary to put on shoes when stepping out from inside the house into the garden.

Notably, many Japanese wear shoes in the garden, even without explicit instructions. The surprise of the Danish participants might have been due to their assumption that if the Japanese remove their shoes when entering the house, they would neither wear shoes in the garden. However, cultural practices and customs can vary, and the Japanese tradition of wearing shoes in the garden is an interesting example of such variation.

I now understand that the discomfort I felt at that time stemmed from whether the garden was considered outside or inside in Japan.

The Japanese word for "home" is "家庭" (*katei*). As explained in this volume, Chapter 20 by Taka, the word home comprises the words "house" and "garden." This implies that the garden is considered a part of the Japanese home. If that is the case, it is not incorrect to assume that one should take off their shoes in the garden. Conversely, the common practice of wearing shoes in the garden suggests that it is considered outside the home.

In many Japanese households, a garden surrounds the residence, whereas in the Western world, gardens are often in courtyards. Western gardens are safe spaces without exposure to the outside world. The differences between Japanese and other countries' gardens may have been inherited from differences in medieval castles. Since the 1970s, the common people's dream has been to own cars and homes. Those who could afford a home would metaphorically say, "I have finally become the lord of a castle." Specifically, Japanese homes are modeled after medieval Japanese castles, and their residences are surrounded by gardens. Japan has an intermediary space called an *engawa* (縁側) or boundary area when going from the room to the garden. Usually, one takes off their shoes and sits down, but it is possible to sit on an engawa with shoes on while extending their feet outwards. The garden is considered *soto* (外) or outside concerning its relationship with the residence. Nonetheless, it is also a part of the home, making it *uchi* (内) or inside. From the perspective of putting on and taking off shoes, the garden is considered soto. Thus, the garden becomes a boundary area between home and outside

Figure P4.1   Photo showing a hedge posted on the Kodaira City website. *Source:* https://www.city.kodaira.tokyo.jp/kurashi/006/006081.html

concerning its relationship with home. Furthermore, Japanese residences often have a wall between the garden and outside. A hedge is sometimes used as a wall type. A hedge is a wall where trees of uniform height are planted, wherein bamboo or logs are used as posts (see Figure P4.1).

Figure P4.1 shows a photo of a hedge posted on the Kodaira City website. This is a photo of the house from the outside, with the public street in the foreground and the garden in the background. The garden is not completely shielded from the street when a hedge is used. Individuals in the gardens can talk to those outside. From this perspective, we can observe that the garden in Japanese residences does not possess a distinct boundary that separates the house from the outside world. Instead, it functions as an area that shares boundaries with the house and the external environment. This concept aligns with the liminal model (Valsiner, 2014). Without delving into the extensive discussion, let us briefly overview the content covered in each chapter.

COMMENTARY

Let us briefly examine the contents of each chapter.

Chapter 16 discusses an online international exchange program held between March 18–19, 2021. The program aimed to foster mutual understanding between Japan and Denmark and was implemented through participant presentations on their "favorite gardens." This section introduces the two participants' presentations. Yuki (the second author of the chapter) described the garden in her home. There was a caterpillar on an olive tree in the garden. She gave a presentation about the time she had named the caterpillar Yoshio. Misato (the third author of the chapter) mentioned her grandparents' and high school gardens. Both of these gardens were related to *Jodo Shinshu* (浄土真宗). Jodo Shinshu is a Japanese Pure Land Buddhist school that emphasizes the path of faith, grace, and compassion. She reflected that the images of these gardens evoked thoughts of the Buddhist teachings that have profoundly shaped her perspective on life. In Chapter 16, The authors argue that the Garden Project, where they share their memories and discuss "my favorite garden," serves as a means of exchanging their experiences and fostering a process of proculturation (Gamsakhurdia, 2019) for everyone involved.

The author of Chapter 17 was born the eldest son of the head priest of a Jodo Shinshu Temple (Japanese Pure Land Buddhist school). He used the metaphor of a garden to reflect on the place of religious experience in his life. He argued that this was a new way of narrating religious autoethnography. He regarded the inner sanctum of a Buddhist temple as a "garden of Buddha" and reflected on the process of "tending" to maintain the inner sanctum as a garden of Buddha. However, when viewed through cultural psychology, he could make sense of tending the "garden of Buddha" as distinct from mere household cleaning. This implies that if we strive to recreate "Pure Land" in this world, we cannot sustain its radiance and beauty without the assistance of others.

In Chapter 18, the author reveals how unique culture manifests itself by analyzing her favorite garden. Having spent her college years in Kyoto, her favorite garden was the Toji-in Temple, which she passed on her way to and from college while walking to school. Toji-in was a temple founded by Ashikaga Takauji (1305–1358), founder of the Ashikaga shogunate. The garden was an extraordinary place for her, representing the Japanese collective culture of *wabi-sabi* (a Japanese aesthetic philosophy emphasizing beauty in imperfection, impermanence, and simplicity). It encompassed her culture, which she experienced by spending time there alone. The "extraordinary feeling" she experienced when she first stepped into the garden may be explained by the concept of hyper-generalization.

The author of Chapter 19 is an exchange student in Japan who describes the time spent in China. She took three important gardens to her and talked about her own relationship with them as an autoethnography based on a cultural-psychological approach. She refers to the small gardens she encountered in her life, the imaginary garden in one of her favorite books, *Dreams of the Red Chamber* (Cao, 1997), and the Yu Garden in Shanghai, which she regarded as the epitome of an ideal garden in the world. She introduced a Chinese saying, "The winding path leads to a secluded place" (曲径通幽). This proverb signifies a meandering path to a tranquil, profound, and enigmatic destination. She recalled that she experienced a hyper-generalized feeling when she first encountered the word "曲径通幽." For her, the garden is a place to walk and feel hyper-generalized.

The author of Chapter 20 is native to Hokkaido, Japan's northernmost island. Sapporo, the prefectural capital of Hokkaido, is at a latitude of 43°N, equivalent to the latitudes of Toronto and Monaco in Canada and Marseille in Spain. According to him, Hokkaido represents the "frontier" of Japan, which was sparsely inhabited until approximately 150 years ago, except by the Ainu people, an indigenous community. Furthermore, the region lacks traditional temples and shrines, typically highlighted in travel guidebooks and Japanese historical literature. Notably, The author cherished his childhood experiences in the natural splendor of Hokkaido. During a high school trip to Kyoto, he gained exposure to historic structures and gardens, prompting him to contemplate their cultural significance. Later, while still in college, he studied abroad in Denmark, which led him to travel through various cities worldwide. He noted, "The garden at the Danish international school provided me with an alternative perspective, encouraging me to trust my own instinct rather than unthinkingly adhering to rules. Similarly, observing a dairy cow in an Amish ranch in the United States helped me challenge my preconceived notion that gardens and nature were contrasting concepts. The gardens at Mother Teresa's in India played a more vital role in life than kitchen gardens."

The author of Chapter 20's exposure to gardens across different countries was vital in shaping his worldview. Subsequently, he concluded that establishing his own psychotherapeutic approach was essential to expressing his personal beliefs about garden design. Since then, he devoted himself to developing a novel form of psychotherapy rooted in the principles of Japanese tea ceremonies.

CONCLUDING REMARKS

Gardens are universal. Obviously, the style of the garden itself varies from culture to culture, but the relationship between the garden and people is universal. Thus, we can see that the garden is a suitable subject for cultural psychology. Recalling the various gardens that an individual has experienced in his/her life is not limited to reminding the individual of the gardens themselves. It helps people to re-experience their lives in the present based on memories of the past and to integrate future life trajectories.

Taking this one step further, recalling one's favorite garden triggers imagination (Zittoun & Gillespie, 2016). In many cases, this is a happy image of the past. Therefore, garden projects have an exciting future.

REFERENCES

Cao, X. (1997). *Dreams of the red chamber.* People's Literature Publishing House.

Gamsakhurdia, V. L. (2019). Proculturation: Self-reconstruction by making "fusion cocktails" of alien and familiar meanings. *Culture & Psychology, 25*(2), 161–177. https://doi.org/10.1177/1354067X19829020

Valsiner, J. (2014). *An invitation to cultural psychology.* SAGE Publishing.

Zittoun, T., & Gillespie, A. (2015). *Imagination in human and cultural development.* Routledge/Taylor & Francis Group.

A little garden on my desk.

EPILOGUE

LIVING WITH GARDENING, LIVING AS GARDENING

Teppei Tsuchimoto
Chukyo University

Why do we need "gardens"? Some answers to this question may be found in this book's 20 chapters and seven commentaries, which, while diverse, create a *Gestalt*. A garden is a place where everyone can freely spend time; along these lines, the garden serves as a boundary between the home and the public. Some gardens are also art forms, while others are fundamental symbols of the human "universe of the mind" (see the "Introduction" and Chapter 20, this volume). In the process of creating a garden, we cultivate plants, anticipating their future. Sometimes we make mistakes in watering and fertilizing and, at other times, a particular plant unexpectedly blooms into a beautiful flower. In the negotiation process between "nature and culture" that occurs when cultivating a garden, we can find many similarities with human development. This epilogue presents a multi-voiced conclusion based on the "voices" in this book. Mr. Endo's narrative (Chapter 1) provides a good starting point for understanding how gardens relate to our lives.

> When you see a healthy plant, right, bearing fruit, flowering, you feel, feel good, let's put it that way. Not only to enjoy, you know, but you feel good

because you helped to take care of that plant... When the opposite happens, a termite spoils, right, you don't feel good... It doesn't feel good, because you... *it is part of you, of your feeling with Nature.* (Chapter 1, p. 14)

As we cultivate the garden, "we become the garden." Certain kinds of nature, such as carefully tended flowers or a memorable cherry tree in a childhood garden, are part of our lifeworld and deeply meaningful to us. We will continuously work to maintain these parts of nature so that we can live with them. Therefore, for gardeners, living involves an ongoing negotiation with "*junglification*" (Chapter 11), the act of gardening. Here, we can observe the metaphorical connection between the cultivation of our subjective world and the real act of gardening. Such an idea of tending carefully to one's inner garden is clearly linked to the "cleaning" and "decoration" of the inner sanctum, the recreation of the Pure Land (see Chapter 17). Of course, "gardens" are sometimes hybrids, including not only natural objects, but also artifacts valued by the community. For instance, the flag of a favorite soccer team in a garden can serve a central life function by representing and cultivating deep communication among fans (see Chapter 3). Such symbolic objects are not just decorations, but also ornaments that allow us to experience our lives more deeply (Lehmann & Valsiner, 2017; Valsiner, 2014; Valsiner, 2018). Therefore, as Hidaka and Kasuga (Chapter 4) suggest, the transformation of such a meaningful place into a public dump (i.e., the loss of the garden) can lead to dissatisfaction, injustice, and psychological distress about one's existence. From an autoethnographic point of view, I would like to reflect on an experience that occurred while I was editing this book to further *pleromatize* the feeling of garden loss.

Figure E.1 shows the view from my room. This photo may seem ordinary, especially for Japanese people. However, when I look at this photo, I cannot help but imagine what is missing from it. There are large trees in my area. One of these trees once served as a boundary, blocking the view of the house in front of my own. On warm days, birds used to gather to eat the fruit from this tree; their presence added color and sound to my daily task of writing at home. However, a few months before I took this picture, the tree was suddenly cut down. I felt restless in this now completely clear landscape.

In this example, we can observe how the garden can function as a boundary between the self and the world (i.e., the environment). The removal of the tree in front of my window and the consequent new view of the blue house (and its windows) evoked a feeling that my room was now exposed to the public world. The boundary created by the distance between my room and the large tree was a buffer zone—a "garden"—that prevented the inner world from being directly exposed to the outer world. Thus, the loss of such a garden may evoke affective reflections on the environment (the fear of "being watched") or promote the construction of new kinds of interactions

Living With Gardening, Living as Gardening ▪ 431

Figure E.1 The view from my room.

between the self and the environment (e.g., I "began to close the curtains so as not to be watched"). Several chapters of this book speak to these functions of the garden.

We interact with certain natural objects and perceive them as parts of our lives. Accordingly, gardens are socio-culturally constructed environments—*milieus*—inseparable from ourselves. Berque and Kawakatsu (2019) described the term *milieu* as a relationship constructed by human beings that conditions human existence. The term relates the human being in the "center" and the "environment" outside not as independent entities but ambivalent and "trajecting." As a milieu, the garden is proximal in our minds, so it is difficult to recognize its existence unless it is destroyed by an external power or physically separated from us.

A meaningful garden can function as a milieu that facilitates well-being or that can help people communicate better with others. For example, the garden's communicative function is clearly demonstrated in Miyamae's chapter (Chapter 4). It is remarkable that even if we face a catastrophic incident, "simply spending time sitting on a bench in the garden, enjoying the warmth of the sunshine, and carrying on an aimless conversation can restore the human connection" (Chapter 4, pp. 85–86). Additionally, as Ramon argues, gardens are "important resources for creating new possibilities for life's sensational horizons"; accordingly, a garden can be considered a "sign of happiness" that allows people to live vibrantly with sensory pleasures (Chapter 2, p. 41). Gardens are an essential part of the environment in which we live. However, they are also worlds to which we are deeply related, as mentioned above. Thus, the gardens we construct and relate to are both at the peripheries and the centers of our daily lives, and it is precisely for this reason that we experience the garden as a crisis when ambiguity is eliminated.

The book takes the "garden project" (Chapter 16) as its starting point. Part 4 (Chapters 17, 18, 19, and 20) is written by the peers who participated in the project. The idea of considering the concept of the garden as a *semiotic field*—let alone trying to relate the garden to human development!—seemed strange at first, even to me. However, when the series editor, Jaan Valsiner, invited me to edit this book, I was reminded of how the garden is intimately connected with our daily lives, bodies, and feelings in many different ways. Such personal and collective interrelationships are woven throughout the book. Along these lines, this book considers how meaningful and colorful "gardens" related to human life contrast with the one-dimensional "garden of modernity" that Joranger (Chapter 7, p. 163) warns about. Understanding the garden as a field-like sign that includes opposition shows how it allows for an aesthetic dimension of *communion* (Valsiner, 2014) with oneself and others.

ACKNOWLEDGMENT

I am grateful to Koyama Tamiyo for her help in assisting the editing of this book and discussing ideas for the epilogue. Also, I would like to thank Editage (www.editage.com) for English language editing.

REFERENCES

ベルク, A. ・川勝平太 (2019) ベルク「風土学」とは何か：近代「知性」の超克. 藤原書店. [Berque, A., & Kawakatsu, H. (2019). *What is Berque's "Mesology"?: Trajecting beyond modern "dualism."* Fujiwara-Shoten.]
Lehmann, O. V., & Valsiner, J. (2017). *Deep experiencing: Dialogues within the self.* Springer.
Valsiner, J. (2014). *An invitation to cultural psychology.* SAGE Publishing.
Valsiner, J. (2018). *Ornamented lives.* Information Age Publishing.

Printed in the USA
CPSIA information can be obtained
at www.ICGtesting.com
CBHW071711050824
12520CB00015B/1